Routledge Library Editions

DJANGGAWUL

I0091980

ANTHROPOLOGY AND ETHNOGRAPHY

Routledge Library Editions
Anthropology and Ethnography

RELIGION, RITES & CEREMONIES
In 5 Volumes

I	Anthropological Approaches to the Study of Religion	
		Banton
II	Djanggawul	*Berndt*
III	The Rites of Passage	*van Gennep*
IV	Death and the Right Hand	*Hertz*
V	The Interpretation of Ritual	*La Fontaine*

DJANGGAWUL

An Aboriginal Religious Cult of North-Eastern Arnhem Land

RONALD M BERNDT

Routledge
Taylor & Francis Group

LONDON AND NEW YORK

First published in 1952

Published 2014 by Routledge

2 Park Square, Milton Park, Abingdon, Oxfordshire OX14 4RN

711 Third Avenue, New York, NY 10017

First issued in paperback 2014

Transferred to Digital Printing 2006

Routledge is an imprint of the Taylor & Francis Group, an informa business

Reprinted in the USA with the kind permission of Philosophical Library, New York

British Library Cataloguing in Publication Data
A CIP catalogue record for this book is available from the British Library

Djanggawul
ISBN 978-0-415-33022-0 (hbk)

ISBN 978-1-138-86198-5 (pbk)

Miniset: Religion, Rites & Ceremonies

Series: Routledge Library Editions – Anthropology and Ethnography

DJANGGAWUL

AN ABORIGINAL RELIGIOUS CULT

OF NORTH-EASTERN

ARNHEM LAND

by

RONALD M. BERNDT

Routledge
Taylor & Francis Group

LONDON AND NEW YORK

First published 1952
by Routledge & Kegan Paul Ltd.
68–74 Carter Lane
London, E.C.4

TO MAUWULAN AND WONDJUG

CONTENTS

FOREWORD   *page* xvii

I. SIGNIFICANCE OF THE DJANGGAWUL   I

II. THE DJANGGAWUL MYTH   24

III. THE CONTENT OF THE MYTH   49

IV. THE DJANGGAWUL SONGS   60

V. THE DJANGGAWUL SONG CYCLE: PART ONE   63
   *In which the Djanggawul cross the sea from Bralgu
   Island, and eventually reach the Arnhem Land main-
   land for the first time*
   Songs 1–27

VI. COMMENTS ON PART ONE OF THE SONGS   81

VII. THE DJANGGAWUL SONG CYCLE: PART TWO   93
   *In which the Djanggawul land at Port Bradshaw and
   walk around in its immediate vicinity*
   Songs 28–43

VIII. COMMENTS ON PART TWO OF THE SONGS   108

Contents

IX. THE DJANGGAWUL SONG CYCLE: PART THREE   119

In which the Djanggawul continue their journey through the Bush country behind Port Bradshaw in a north-westerly direction until they reach Banbaldji, at Arnhem Bay on the north coast

Songs 44–56

X. COMMENTS ON PART THREE OF THE SONGS   131

XI. THE DJANGGAWUL SONG CYCLE: PART FOUR   138

In which the Djanggawul confine their travelling and observations to the region of Arnhem Bay, particularly around Wagulwagul

Songs 57–70

XII. COMMENTS ON PART FOUR OF THE SONGS   151

XIII. THE DJANGGAWUL SONG CYCLE: PART FIVE   160

The Djanggawul continue their journey along the coast of the mainland, about Arnhem Bay

Songs 71–88

XIV. COMMENTS ON PART FIVE OF THE SONGS   174

XV. THE DJANGGAWUL SONG CYCLE: PART SIX   183

In which the Djanggawul reach Madi at Arnhem Bay, spend some time there, and continue down the Bay westwards

Songs 89–118

XVI. COMMENTS ON PART SIX OF THE SONGS   201

XVII. THE DJANGGAWUL SONG CYCLE: PART SEVEN   215

The Djanggawul continue along the Arnhem Bay coast until they reach Duwalgidjboi

Songs 119–128

XVIII. COMMENTS ON PART SEVEN OF THE SONGS   221

Contents

XIX. THE DJANGGAWUL SONG CYCLE: PART EIGHT   225

The Djanggawul reach Marabai, where the Two Sisters lose their sacred emblems, the men taking over their rituals. The long penis of the Djanggawul Brother and the clitorises of the Sisters are shortened. More people are born, and some are circumcised

Songs 129–144

XX. COMMENTS ON PART EIGHT OF THE SONGS   236

XXI. THE DJANGGAWUL SONG CYCLE: PART NINE   249

The Djanggawul reach Dulmulwondeinbi, where the clitoris of each Sister is again shortened. More children are born. The Brother has coitus with his young Sister, who has an armband within her; the breaking of this causes blood to flow. Dancing follows

Songs 145–174

XXII. COMMENTS ON PART NINE OF THE SONGS   264

XXIII. THE DJANGGAWUL SONG CYCLE: PART TEN   278

The Yirrkalla version of the Djanggawul epic is drawing to a close. More people, both male and female, are taken from the Sisters, and the sacred quality of woman is emphasized. Rangga and feathered strings are removed from the ngainmara and baskets; the nara ritual continues, and the fringe of the baskets is cut

Songs 175–188

XXIV. COMMENTS ON PART TEN OF THE SONGS   285

XXV. EPILOGUE   292

GLOSSARY   309

GENERAL INDEX   314

ILLUSTRATIONS

1   Two *nara* postulants emerge from the sacred shade on to the   16
dancing ground, carrying a *rangga* on their shoulders.

2   Embracing the *rangga* on the sacred ground: one postulant   16
lies between his companion's legs.

3   Left-hand panel: *djuda* and *mauwulan rangga*; the former are   17
arranged at each side, with three pairs of *mauwulan* in the centre.
These belong to the people who have issued from the
Djanggawul Sisters.

Right-hand panel: Bildjiwuraroiju and Miralaidj, in the
position taken for childbirth, with *rangga* folk streaming from
them. Their eyes are wide open, with tears flowing; they wear
waist-bands and head-bands, and on their arms are armlets
with feathered pendants.

Female children are under the round fringed *ngainmara* mats,
one at each side of both Sisters, while the male children are
unprotected. Each group of people belongs to a certain
region.

4   This whole drawing shows in detail various Djanggawul   17
nara ceremonies.

From left to right:

First panel, bottom: arm-band dance.
    above: the black *gagaga* bird perched on a rock at Walbinboi
just outside Jelangbara.

Illustrations

Second panel, above: the *weiga*, 'young' fresh-water snake dance, postulants each holding spear and womera.

below: *djirindidi* calling of the invocations (*bugali*) on the *gararag* pole. Three men are dancing around him, invoking.

Third panel, above: tide flowing in.

below: the Sea dance, flowing water, etc.

Fourth panel, above: Flying Fox dance—two men on *gararag* pole.

below: Water dancing.

Fifth panel, above: two men dance the male and female goanna.

below: the goanna *rangga*, which is danced by the two men shown above.

band: two *mauwulan rangga*.

Sixth panel, above: wild duck dancing.

below: red parakeet dancing.

5   The *rangga* emblems are displayed on the sacred ground,   32
while special songs relating to them are sung.

6   This is the central panel of a long drawing showing Jelang-   33
bara. In the lower right-hand panel, the Djanggawul Brother
is holding a *ngainmara* on his thighs (this symbolizes the
younger Sister, and his drawing it on to his thighs refers to the
conventional position taken in coitus). He then removed
rangga (*djuda* and *mauwulan*) emblems, shown beside and above
him.

The younger Sister is seen in the middle of the left-hand
panel, with *rangga* at each side.

The central band, with the two *djanda* goanna, represents the
sacred shade.

7   *From left to right:*   33

First panel (left), above: *djuda rangga*.

below: a black bird on Gagubam Island, near Port
Bradshaw. Flying foxes hanging from the sacred *djuda* tree.

Second panel (right): male and female goanna, frightened
by the approach of the Djanggawul, and about to dive
into the billabong at Gagubam Island.

above: two goanna *rangga* representing these two goanna,
and at the extreme right are two *djuda rangga*.

Illustrations

8 The showing of the Goanna Tail *rangga*, with its parakeet-   80
feathered pendants and decorations, by a ceremonial leader.

9 Postulants dancing the Incoming Tide, coming on to the   81
sacred ground; they imitate the *rangga* folk, who emerged from
the Sisters.

10 Invocations are called, while *jiritja* moiety postulants await   81
the emergence of the sacred emblems.

11 Left hand panel: a turtle, which has entered a *ngainmara*, after   96
being caught by two men in a canoe; it is surrounded by waves,
at Jelangbara.
    Second panel, above: Miralaidj, pregnant, showing the long
clitoris, on her arrival at Jelangbara. She holds a Goanna Tail
and a *mauwulan rangga*.
    below: arm-bands with feathered pendants, hanging from a
rail of the sacred shade.
    Third panel, above: Bildjiwuraroiju, also pregnant; she had
been carrying a Goanna Tail *rangga*, but it had slipped from her
grasp and fallen to the ground (below, same panel).
    Fourth (right-hand) panel, above: the Brother, holding
djuda rangga which have almost become trees; he is about to
plant them.
    below: the two *djuda rangga* 'copied' from those the Brother
is holding.

12 A ceremonial leader representing the Djanggawul Brother   96
after his landing at Port Bradshaw. He bends forward to taste
the fresh water which gushed up after he had inserted the
mauwulan rangga.

13 At Gumararanggu, Port Bradshaw (the Yirrkalla side of   97
Jelangbara). Beach and sandhills are shown, with male and
female goanna (*rangga*). The central panel shows an Aboriginal
camp, comprising people left by the Djanggawul.
    On the right-hand side, the upper panel shows the sun
rising, casting its rays.
    Below is Belabinja, where the Djanggawul first tasted fresh
water when they landed at Jelangbara (*vide* Song 28).

14 The sacred *djanda* goanna on the sandhill at the Place of the   97
Mauwulan (see, e.g., Song 35).
xiii

Illustrations

15   Calling the *bugali* invocations in front of the sacred *nara* 144
      shade, before the emergence of a totemic being.

16   The Goanna emblem emerges from the shade, which in this 144
      case is constructed from iron.

17   This design represents various sacred shades belonging to 145
      different linguistic groups.
      Left-hand panel, top: sacred goanna on *djuda rangga* tree:
      the Djanggawul Brother with his *djuda* and *mauwulan* and
      beating sticks.
      below: goanna on *djuda* tree; and sacred Goanna Tail
      rangga.
      The two panels are divided by goanna tracks.
      Right-hand panel, top: goanna on *djuda* tree; tracks, and
      sacred design.
      below: goanna on *djuda* tree: one Djanggawul Sister with
      beating sticks, beside Goanna Tail *rangga.*

18   *Nara* postulants representing male and female Goanna. The 145
      Goanna Tail *rangga* rests across the younger man's neck.

19   The Djanggawul Goanna emerges from the shade. 160

20   Postulants in stylized attitudes, with the Goanna Tail 160
      rangga; sacred shade, at the Place of the Mauwulan.

21   Two men singing, rhythmically clapping sticks, and blowing 161
      the long, sacred Julunggul Rainbow Snake or Rock Python
      drone pipe, above the posturing sacred goanna of the Place of
      the Mauwulan.

22   To the rhythmic beat of clapping sticks, the Julunggul 161
      Rock Python drone pipe emerges from the *dua* moiety *nara*
      shade. Postulants are lying on their backs, huddled together,
      with the *rangga* emblem resting upon them.

23   Left-hand panel: Bildjiwuraroiju, Miralaidj and the 208
      Djanggawul Brother (top). The Two Sisters have long
      clitorises, and the Brother a long penis, which drag on the
      ground, and resemble *djuda rangga.* They hold goanna tail and

Illustrations

mauwulan rangga, one in each hand. People (symbolized by dots) have come from the Two Sisters: a small circle of *rangga* folk is seen dancing, among them the Two Wauwalag Sisters.

Right-hand panel, above: the Djanggawul Brother is inserting his hand into Miralaidj's vagina, and removing *rangga* folk, shown flowing from her. *Rangga* emblems are ranged beside the Brother and Sister. This took place at Dulmulwondeinbi, near Marabai.

Right-hand panel, below: Bildjiwuraroiju, opposite Miralaidj. The Djanggawul Brother has lifted aside their clitorises, and put his hand into their vaginae. People flow out, male *rangga* folk on one side, and females on the other. This took place at Jalwuljalwul.

24 *From left to right:*   208

    First panel: Miralaidj as central figure; on each side of her is a woman, one (above) being her elder Sister and one (below) Bammarimarawi, her daughter and 'sister'.

    Afterbirth blood flows from Miralaidj into a hole, and she stands holding two poles; as soon as the hole is filled, it overflows and runs from each side. It is after this that the elder Sister, by hitting the young Sister's hips, stops the flow of blood. Four rangga folk then come out (two men and two women).

    Central panel of clapping-sticks (above), and two *mauwulan* with sacred dilly bags attached (below)—(penis and uterus symbols).

    Right-hand panel, top: the sun comes up, casting its rays.

    below: sunset on the mainland beyond Milingimbi, towards the west.

    At Jelangbara.

25 Postulants (both Goanna actors) using the Goanna Tail   209
rangga emblem; one supports it on his shoulder, while the other guides it.

26 *Jiritja* moiety *nara*: *rangga* are removed from the shade, and   209
postulants dance.

27 Dancing with the *jiritja* moiety *rangga*: dust rises, as dancing   224
feet pound the sacred ground.

Illustrations

28   Neophytes wait with heads bowed, before the showing of   224
the sacred Djanggawul emblems.

29   Meditation before the sacred Goanna Tail *rangga*. Postulants   225
caress the feathered pendants—symbolic of the sun's rays, the
clitorises, foreskins or umbilical cords.

Map   8–9

NOTE ON ILLUSTRATIONS

The crayon drawings illustrated here represent only a small selection of those available, and stored at the Department of Anthropology, Sydney University. They do not show to advantage in black and white and it is hoped that later on a wider selection will be presented in colour. Only brief descriptions of each drawing have been inserted here; each drawing contains a great deal of detail, which ideally requires considerable explanation, not possible in this volume.

All these drawings were collected between 29th January, 1947 and 15th June, 1947 at Yirrkalla, in north-eastern Arnhem Land. They were done on brown paper with coloured lumber crayon and black pencil, and were used by the writer as an adjunct to his field notes. They conform to traditional patterns and representations, which would normally be drawn on stringy bark boards in coloured ochres.

FOREWORD

T HE Djanggawul religious cult of north-eastern and north-central Arnhem Land has been selected for detailed study because it is more important to the Aborigines themselves than other religious cults in that region. It is older established than, for example, the well-known Wauwalak cycle[1] which sponsors the *djunggawon*, *kunapipi* and *ngurlmag* rituals. The Wauwalak themselves are really the daughters of the Djanggawul, while the *kunapipi* and *ngurlmag* have both been introduced into eastern Arnhem Land. The Djanggawul myth substantiates and gives traditional sanction to the performance of its relevant rituals, known as the *dua nara*. *Dua* is the name of the moiety primarily concerned with this myth and its rituals; the opposite moiety, the *jiritja*, has a counterpart in the *jiritja nara*, sanctioned by Laintjung, an Ancestral Being who is usually described in conjunction with his son, Banaitja. The Djanggawul, Laintjung, Banaitja and the Wauwalak are the principal ancestral characters who, in eastern Arnhem Land, serve as institutors of religious ritual, dogma and behaviour. However, the Djanggawul Brother and Sisters are by far the most important of these. The *dua nara* Djanggawul cult is also more conservative than, for example, that of Laintjung and Banaitja, for the latter has admitted alien elements, whereas the former has remained, as far as we can ascertain, more purely traditional.

During the course of field work in the Yirrkalla region of north-eastern Arnhem Land, the importance of Djanggawul ritual and songs was brought forcibly to my attention. The Aborigines

---

[1] W. L. Warner, *A Black Civilization*, New York, 1937, pp. 244–334. See also R. Berndt, *Kunapipi*, Cheshire, Melbourne, 1951, Chapter III.

Foreword

themselves considered the Djanggawul to be the dominant figures
in the Ancestral Times, and this attitude was borne out in the
reverence they gave and the attention they paid to all features
relating to the Djanggawul. Even those of the opposite moiety,
people who looked to Laintjung and Banaitja, admitted the primary
importance of the *dua* Djanggawul. I was fortunate, during this
period, in being able to examine and record a number of versions
of Djanggawul mythology from a relatively wide range of informants, the majority of whom were ceremonial headmen for
their particular linguistic groups, and in addition to record in detail
the greater part of the associated song cycle. I was able also to attend
most of the *dua nara* rituals that took place during my visit. My
knowledge of these rituals and songs was considerably enhanced
later after a further visit to the north-central region, Milingimbi,
where the Djanggawul song cycle was again obtained in detail,
and relevant rituals observed.

The social organization and the culture of eastern Arnhem Land
have already been treated partially in other works,[1] so that there is
no need here for repetition. The reader is warned, however, that
he will find it necessary to refer to these for information on various
points such as the *dua-jiritja* moiety system, the clan and linguistic
group organization, marriage rules, economic background and
natural resources of this region, and so on, which although relevant
to this study cannot here be treated in full. Arnhem Land is to-day
an Aboriginal Reserve in the north-eastern region of the Northern
Territory of Australia,[2] and a similar cultural pattern extends from
Blue Mud Bay in the south-east to Cape Stewart on the north-
central coast. That is to say, all the Aborigines within this area
(approximately 1,500 to 2,000) possess a common social organization and religious ideology, and speak varying dialects of one

---

[1] *Vide* L. Warner, *op. cit.*, 1937; also, by the same author, 'Morphology and Functions
of the Australian Murngin Type of Kinship', *American Anthropologist*, n.s., 33, 2,
184; T. T. Webb, 'Tribal Organization in Eastern Arnhem Land', *Oceania*, Vol. III,
No. 4; A. P. Elkin, 'Marriage and Descent in East Arnhem Land', *Oceania*, Vol. III,
No. 4, pp. 412–16, and his 'The Complexity of Social Organization in Arnhem Land',
Southwestern Journal of Anthropology, Vol. 6, No. 1, pp. 1–20; W. E. Lawrence and
G. P. Murdock, 'Murngin Social Organization', *American Anthropologist*, 1949, Vol. 51,
No. 1, pp. 58–65; A. P. Elkin, R. and C. Berndt, *Art in Arnhem Land*, Cheshire,
Melbourne, 1950, and *University of Chicago Press*, 1950, pp. 20–7; R. Berndt, *Kunapipi*,
Cheshire, Melbourne, 1951, Chapter I *b*.

[2] For its geographical position and natural resources, see A. P. Elkin, R. and C.
Berndt, *op. cit.*, 1950, pp. 20–1, R. Berndt, *Kunapipi*, Chapter I *a*, and R. and C. Berndt,
Arnhem Land—Its History and Its People, for publication, Cheshire, Melbourne. See also
accompanying map to this volume.

Foreword

language. Their society is constructed on the moiety principle, and descent is in all cases primarily patrilineal. There is no clearly defined tribe, but a series of linguistic groups associated with clans; all of these may be called, collectively, the Wulamba bloc of the Miwaitj language group (referring to the sum total of the different dialects). Yirrkalla is situated on the extreme north-east corner of Arnhem Land between Melville Bay and Cape Arnhem, and Aborigines gather there from places as far distant as Blue Mud and Caledon and Trial Bays, Rose River, and Woodah and Groote Islands in the south and south-east, and Arnhem and Buckingham Bays, Elcho, English Company and Wessel Islands in the north-west. Milingimbi is in the Crocodile Island group on the central-north coast; it is also a meeting place for members of many groups, particularly those from the mainland around the Blyth, Goyder and Woolen Rivers.

Virtually all the writer's field work has been carried out through the medium of the native language, both at Yirrkalla and Milingimbi. Knowledge of local dialects is essential in social anthropological work, and particularly in a study of Aboriginal religion. Field work at Yirrkalla was carried out in 1946–7 and at Milingimbi in 1950 (a total period of thirteen months actually working on the field in this particular region); the first period was made possible by grants from the Australian National Research Council, and was under the auspices of the Department of Anthropology, University of Sydney, while the latter period was financed by grants from the Research Committee of the University of Sydney and the Department of Anthropology of the same University. Writing up of this material was also made possible by grants from the Research Committee.

So many informants have helped in the process of collecting the data presented here that a list of their names would be tiresome and meaningless to the reader. Not only main *dua* moiety headmen, but also those of the *jiritja* moiety, contributed; and these were members of many linguistic groups. In addition, attitudes of local Aboriginal women towards this religious cult were discussed with them by my wife (Catherine Berndt), and this aided directly the analysis of certain sections. This study of the Djanggawul, then, does not express solely the information and attitudes of male natives, but takes into account both male and female elements in the culture. The practice in recording the interlinear phonetic renderings of the songs was for informants belonging to a particular area through which the Djanggawul passed to put forward those songs themselves, for it was their country and they were expected to have more complete knowledge of the songs. In this way, each

xix

Foreword

part was presented by the most capable leaders and song men available for the particular territory concerned. This was the case also in recording the myth, which unfortunately cannot here be presented in its phonetic rendering. All features of the myth and songs were collectively discussed, and interpretations made by the Aborigines themselves.

A considerable amount of thought has gone into the question of presenting the available data on the Djanggawul. It has finally been decided to present as much as possible of the 'raw' material without, apart from interpretation and partial analysis, engaging in theoretical discussion, for material of this type obviously lends itself to such treatment. It is our contention that the rôle of the anthropologist in the Australian Aboriginal field should be one of recording data, and of presenting these in an accessible form, so that the maximum amount of material may be available for the consideration of students interested primarily in theory. That is not to say that we disparage that particular branch of anthropological science, but that we ourselves are more intimately concerned with Australian Aboriginal problems as such and, although taking into account the wider implication of our material, we must of necessity restrict our outlook to some extent. This, to us, is an important point, for we in Australia are acutely aware of the limitations of available anthropological data. Considering the geographical extent of the Australian continent, and the apparent diversity of Aboriginal cultural groups within it, we must admit that our knowledge of these societies is sparse. It is our duty, as we see it, to compensate in some degree for this deficiency. We do of course realize that, although our problems seem to us momentous, they diminish somewhat with distance, and when viewed in relation to the sum total of human experience throughout the world they become of much less pressing significance.

During the last two decades Australian Anthropology has received an impetus, principally through the personal efforts of Professors A. P. Elkin and A. R. Radcliffe-Brown, and the Australian National Research Council has sent on to the field a series of anthropologists: this activity, and its results, have helped to counteract in some degree the errors of the past. Nevertheless, we in Australia are aware that although much has been done, there still remains more to do.

To say 'errors of the past' is not to disparage the monumental works of Sir Baldwin Spencer and F. J. Gillen, Carl Strehlow and others. What they lacked in anthropological method they made up in energy, and in their power to stimulate interest among anthropologists and others; they inspired, for instance, Émile Durkheim and Sir James Frazer, and their individual importance may not be underestimated.

It is our plan to present in one volume the substance of the Djanggawul cult; this includes the significance of the myth and ritual, the myth itself, the song cycle, and a partial analysis. A great deal rests on the cycle itself, which is essentially the core of the work; so we have deliberately chosen to give poetic renderings of the songs in English. The second volume is devoted entirely to the interlinear phonetic renderings,[1] with detailed notes attached; the reader is advised to read the English translations in conjunction with these, which of necessity include many additional references. This arrangement still leaves untreated a great deal of material relating to the Djanggawul. It is planned, therefore, to present at an early date the complete Milingimbi version of the song cycle, with analysis, for this differs in several major points from the Yirrkalla version presented here. The Yirrkalla song cycle as set out here contains 188 separate songs, and the Milingimbi cycle 264 songs.[2] There is also a mass of material relating to the rituals themselves, and to dreams. Here we are able to give only a brief sketch of the sequence of *dua nara* ritual, without treating it in detail. The dreams of various informants at Yirrkalla about

[1] In this volume native words are recorded (for publication purposes) in an anglicized version of our usual phonetic rendering, without using special symbols—whereas usually we follow the system recommended by the International Phonetic Association, with modifications and additions by Dr. A. Capell (*vide* 'Methods and Materials for Recording Australian Languages', *Oceania*, 1945, Vol. XVI, pp. 144–76).

There is a very real need for conformity of orthography in regard to Australian Aboriginal languages, and this can be achieved only by the use of standardized symbols. Thus *j* is generally used with its Continental value of *y*. The use of the *y* initially or within a word is too loose even in anglicized spelling, while *j* is a much more accurate rendering of the native sound.

It is hoped that future workers in Arnhem Land, or for that matter in other parts of Aboriginal Australia, will build on the orthographic foundations being laid to-day by anthropologists and linguists in Australia. It is partly on this account, the unwillingness of some field workers to conform, that Aboriginal terms and concepts are often hard to identify as between different authors. When reference is made to the work of Professor Lloyd Warner, *A Black Civilization*, and native words are quoted, his rendering is given alongside of ours. Recent anthropologists like T. G. H. Strehlow, *Aranda Traditions*, have also adhered to the use of the *j*.

[2] The Yirrkalla songs are on the whole longer than those from Milingimbi. The latter cycle continues the travels of the Djanggawul to Balbanara; this place is between the Blyth and Kupangu Creeks and the Liverpool River, inland from about the centre of Boucaut Bay, west of Milingimbi. A volume (entitled *Daughters of the Sun*) containing and discussing the Milingimbi version of the Djanggawul has now been prepared for publication.

Foreword

Djanggawul ritual and interpretation bring a new perspective to bear on this phase of their life: dreams express individual attitudes towards the cult, and often show distortion of conventional ritual behaviour. In addition, there is the women's attitude towards the Djanggawul ideology, their ritual behaviour, the songs and stories they know, and their place in the general configuration.[1] Also available is a comparatively large series of stringy bark and brown paper drawings relating to the travels of the Djanggawul.

In conclusion, we must consider the question of whether or not the Arnhem Land Aborigines will themselves benefit from a study of this type. It is our belief that understanding of the fundamental issues involved in a religious cult like that of the Djanggawul will (or should) persuade administrators, missionaries and teachers to adopt a more tolerant attitude towards Aboriginal indigenous life. Through it they may glimpse the complexity of its organization and the simplicity of the basic theme: they will understand too the inter-relationship of Aboriginal life with the natural environment, the natives' dependence on the resources available to them, and their faith in the divine nature of the great Ancestral Beings. Through this medium they may, perhaps, come to know and appreciate something of the Aborigines' way of life.

There has been much discussion among anthropologists regarding the mingling of basic research results with applied anthropology.[2] We believe, however, that the anthropologist who over a period has worked with a particular group of people, who has learnt their language, has come to appreciate their way of life, has become in some degree absorbed (as far as this is possible for a stranger and a European) into the society, and has become interested in and emotionally attached to them, discovers sooner or later that he feels morally obliged to aid them in some practical way. Professor Herskovits has commented on this obligation: 'It is the nature of the case that the anthropologist is best fitted to see the strains and stresses of underprivileged groups, or of natives who no longer control their own lives. He sees these stresses and strains from the less pleasant, under-side of the situations in which they live. He sees the problems of the natives as no administrator, however gifted, can possibly see them. When, then he is in a position to aid in obtaining for the natives he knows some reinstatement of the human rights they have been deprived of, he customarily welcomes the opportunity . . .'[3] This is what the

---

[1] This latter section will be treated later in some detail by Catherine H. Berndt.

[2] *Vide* E. E. Evans-Pritchard, 'Applied Anthropology', *Africa*, 1946, Vol. XVI, pp. 92–8, and Melville J. Herskovits, *Man and his Works*, 1949, New York, pp. 650–3.

[3] M. J. Herskovits, *op. cit.*, p. 652.

Foreword

anthropologist feels in Australia to-day, for most Australian Aboriginal groups are in varying degrees of contact with Europeans, while the coastal Arnhem Landers have had a long history of contact with aliens.[1] While realizing our obligations to the people with whom we work, the Aborigines whom we have come to know and respect, becoming perhaps more deeply concerned with local problems than with world-wide issues, we should not, of course, lose sight of the debt we owe to our own culture, or of the wider issues of anthropology. To quote once more: 'Science would hold that knowledge about that (Indian) tribe is less important than knowledge about all Indians (e.g.), or generalizations about human nature and society . . . It is a misapprehension that the anthropologist is primarily concerned with the community he is studying. Typically, and ideally, he is not. He studies that community to gain understanding of all communities, and of culture and society in general.'[2] Not all anthropologists, however, realize these implications. To balance the above quotation, one should add that such objectivity is rarely obtainable, and that the anthropologist's knowledge of culture and society in general should also be applied to the particular problems of a specific community or tribe. For if we owe a debt to the science of Anthropology itself, we owe an even greater debt to the native peoples who have supplied the material upon which that science has been established.

I wish to acknowledge first my own personal debt to the many Arnhem Land Aborigines who have supplied the substance of this volume. Had it not been for their patience and tolerance, our knowledge of this particular cult would be considerably poorer. Reliable data cannot be obtained by an anthropologist simply through entering an alien society and living among its representatives: some sympathy and rapport is essential between anthropologist and informant, and the degree of intimacy attained helps to determine the quality of the material.

I wish also to acknowledge my indebtedness to Professor A. P. Elkin of the Department of Anthropology, University of Sydney, without whose active help and constant encouragement this field work and 'writing-up' could not have been accomplished. I thank also my wife, Catherine H. Berndt, who has helped greatly both on the field and in the preparation of this manuscript for publication.

RONALD M. BERNDT,

Department of Anthropology, University of Sydney.

[1] R. and C. Berndt, *Arnhem Land—Its History and Its People.*

[2] S. Tax, 'Anthropology and Administration', *Américan Indígena*, 1945, Vol. V, pp. 26–7, 28. *Vide* M. Herskovits' discussion, *op. cit.*, pp. 642–55.

Chapter One

SIGNIFICANCE OF THE DJANGGAWUL

D JANGGAWUL, used collectively, is a name given to three Ancestral Beings; alternatively, it may be Djangga or Djangg'gau. Usually it refers to two Sisters and a Brother, although in the Milingimbi version the latter is not mentioned.[1] In north-eastern Arnhem Land, as in the version presented in this volume, the Brother and his two Sisters are always represented. The Brother, known by himself as Djanggawul, is also called, less frequently, Ganjudingu.[2] His 'inside'[3] name is Gundanguru, which means the 'nail' or spike of a 'nail' fish; an alternative 'inside' name is Balwadjar, which has a similar meaning. The elder Sister is Bildjiwuraroiju (or Bildjiwuraru), a name derived from the sacred term *duldjijuldji*, meaning the point of the sacred *mauwulan rangga* emblem.[4] She has the alternative names of Reiwurjun, meaning, 'getting tired (after long paddling)', and referring to the Djanggawul's paddling from Bralgu to the Australian mainland; and of Ganinjara, which means also the point of the *mauwulan* (its point enters her vagina, for the *mauwulan* is a symbolic penis).

[1] The presence of the Djanggawul Brother is not mentioned by L. Warner, *op. cit.*, pp. 333–40.

[2] The Milingimbi version calls the elder Sister Djanggawul (said to be a derivation of the name Gurulgurul, belonging to a *wongar* Dreaming man at Bralgu); the younger Sister is said to be called Ganjudingu (meaning the fin of the barramundi fish). Collectively they were also called Maijilwara, which is a 'big' name.

[3] The use of 'inside' terms is confined to sacred songs; they may also be called on the sacred ground during ritual. Normally, they are used only by men fully acquainted with the relevant ideology, and very rarely in ordinary conversation.

[4] Also said to mean 'a long clitoris dragging'.

Significance of the Djanggawul

The younger Sister is usually called Miralaidj, Malalait or Mandalaidj, which means the 'younger' green-backed turtle called *deirei*. She is also called Djurdjunga, 'clouds coming up', or Balmabalma, which means a 'sacred shade' used on the ritual *nara* ground; this latter has the 'inside' name Mal'marangu.

In the north-eastern Arnhem Land version these three are accompanied by Bralbral (or Barabara), who stands in relationship to them as *waridj* or *mari*, a mother's mother's brother's son's son. He has no other name, and appears only at the beginning of the myth and the song cycle.

Although these three principal Ancestral Beings are brother and sisters, one version of this story tells that the Brother Djanggawul had in the beginning only one Sister, Bildjiwuraroiju and that it was through his incestuous intercourse with her that Miralaidj was born. Miralaidj did not, however, call Bildjiwuraroiju and her brother mother and father: instead she called them respectively elder sister and brother. That is, 'one Sister came out from the big Sister; and this younger one called the other one sister because she came out first, long before Bildjiwuraroiju gave birth to the children who are said to be the direct ancestors of the Aborigines living to-day'. But Djanggawul had coitus with the younger Sister who actually, according to this version, is his own daughter. This incestuous behaviour is nothing unusual, for in the myth the Brother often has coitus with his two Sisters. To all intents and purposes, Bildjiwuraroiju and Miralaidj are treated as Sisters.

These Beings came from a far distant country, and on the way to the Arnhem Land mainland stopped at Bralgu, the *dua* moiety island of the dead. Bralgu is a mythical place, but some native informants say that it may perhaps be an island near Mornington (one of the Wellesley Islands in the Gulf of Carpentaria), or alternatively an island off the Cape York Peninsula.[1] To-day its geographical position remains unclarified, and it is still the Home of the Eternal Spirits, the spirits of departed ancestors as well as of those Beings who were there when the Djanggawul themselves visited the island. It is said, too, that the Djanggawul possessed at that time a far greater number of sacred objects, but because they had only a bark canoe to get to the Australian mainland they were obliged to leave many behind.

The ultimate origin of the Djanggawul is now shrouded in antiquity, and it is fruitless to hypothesize. They are said, however, to be closely associated with the Sun. One myth tells that the Sun,

---

[1] Or, at Milingimbi, said to be near Mapoon Mission station off Cape York Peninsula. This place was suggested by informants who were attempting to place Bralgu in relation to some known site, indicating that it was somewhere in that direction.

Significance of the Djanggawul

a woman, possessed two daughters who were later to become the Djanggawul Sisters. But while the Yirrkalla myth and song cycle do not refer directly to them as Sun daughters, many symbolic references are made to the sun and to its warmth; in fact, the whole concept of the myth, with the growth of human beings and trees, and so on, depends on the presence of the Sun, through the agency of the Two Sisters. In the Milingimbi version this aspect is treated in great detail, if somewhat symbolically; one is left in no doubt as to who the two Sisters really were, and their affinity with the Sun. For example, the feathered strings from the *lindaridj* parakeet which they carried were symbolic of the sun's rays; they travelled from east to west, as the sun itself travels, and from their vulvae the sun's rays spread, while to-day one name for the disc of the midday sun is *dagu, ganbai* or *dala*, meaning the Djanggawul Sisters' vulvae or vaginae.

There is little doubt, then, that the Sisters, if not the Brother, are projections of the Sun. If they are not Sun Goddesses themselves, they are closely linked with the Sun. The question of whether or not it is legitimate to describe certain Aboriginal Ancestral Beings as gods and goddesses raises, of course, a number of problems. Nevertheless, these particular Ancestral Beings are themselves divine in that they possess creative abilities, and are sacred in the full sense of the word. From this point of view, the appellation 'god' or 'goddess' is in order; but by using it we do not in any way imply that these Aboriginal Ancestral Beings, or the sacred emblems they brought with them, are worshipped in the Christian sense. The concept of 'worshipping' is far removed from conventional Aboriginal religious thought: things or Beings are held in reverence, or even in awe, but never worshipped in the way that we understand the term. Our choice of a title for these Beings, however, endowed as they are with all the attributes which go to form the idea of Godhead, is primarily a matter of terminology.

These Beings brought with them to the Arnhem Land coast a variety of sacred emblems, which are material symbols of their cult. First and foremost was the *ngainmara* mat, alternatively called *muralungul, dalwuldalwul* or *wagulwagul*; the latter term applies particularly to the mat's 'mouth' or opening. *Ngainmara* is a secular term, with *nania* as another alternative. This mat is the symbolic uterus of either Sister, but it may also mean the whale, or simply a mat. Its attributes were so sacred, representing as it did the Uteri of the Djanggawul, that it is no longer endowed with ritual value; it has passed generally into the society, and is used primarily by women. That is to say, its sacredness was of such intensity that it could not be kept for use in ceremonies alone, but became an

3

article of everyday use. Moreover, since it is symbolically associated with females, their use of it is not incongruous. The mat, conically shaped, is plaited from split and dried pandanus fibre, and usually has a fringe symbolizing the Sisters' pubic hair. Adult women and children still shelter under such mats from time to time. A child, for instance, may curl up asleep beneath one, completely hidden from view; and then he, or she, may be likened to the sacred *rangga* emblems which in the mythological period were kept within the mat.

The Djanggawul brought with them, too, a dilly bag woven from pandanus fibre interlaced with red breast-feathers of the parakeet, with feathered pendants attached. This is the sacred dilly bag or spirit bag called *jelagandja*, or *mundaidjngu*. It is sacred because it is worn by men during certain ceremonies, particularly the *dua nara*, and contains part of their spirit self; for this bag is also a symbol of the uterus, from which (or, alternatively, from the *ngainmara*) men and women came forth in the beginning. Waxed knobs fastened at intervals along the feathered string may contain foreskins, said to be an allusion to fertility. These bags, although highly sacred, are not kept on the ritual ground, nor are they regarded as secret. Worn by men in the camp, they are seen by all, and women too may use them at times. In fact, their making is often entrusted to women, who in the Milingimbi area also prepare the beautiful feathered string (although in the north-eastern area this particular variety is made by men). It is only when the bag is almost finished that it is passed over to the men, who ritually, to the accompaniment of sacred invocation and singing, cut the loose fringe (the pubic hair or, alternatively, the clitorises of the Two Sisters)[1] and attach the red feathered pendants (the rays of the sun from the Djanggawul). The bag is then returned to the women, who complete the edging and attach the handle of jungle twine. The men who have cut the fringe, because they belong to *dua* moiety groups responsible for the *nara* Djanggawul rituals, are termed 'the Children of the Djanggawul'—like the children who came in the beginning from the sacred uteri of the Sisters (*vide* the myth and the songs).

The Djanggawul also carried with them sacred poles, known as *rangga*. These poles are very sacred; they are used only on the ritual ground, and are seen only by fully initiated men or by neophytes. Women, however, know of their existence and can describe their shape and decoration, and discuss their meaning.

---

[1] The basic symbolism of this, as an umbilical cord, will be discussed later in this volume.

Significance of the Djanggawul

There seem to have been, originally, several basic types: the *djuda*, or tree *rangga*, from which trees sprang up when the *rangga* was plunged into the ground by the Djanggawul; the *mauwulan*, or stick used by the Djanggawul Brother as a 'walking stick', which he plunged into the ground so that spring water gushed forth; the *ganinjari*, 'yam' or walking stick (sometimes confused with the *mauwulan*), carried by the Sisters, and used for obtaining water in the same way;[1] and the *djanda*, or tail of the goanna, with the same function as the *mauwulan*, derived from the goanna seen by the Djanggawul on arrival at Jelangbara, Port Bradshaw.

These original forms have been elaborated into a variety of *rangga* emblems. They include various poles or objects of totemic *wongar* origin, related directly or indirectly to the Djanggawul: *rangga* symbolizing vulva or vagina, penis or testes; stone *rangga*, derived from a stone which was removed from the vagina of the younger Sister; and conventionalized representations of the Djanggawul themselves, for example, the *wirlgul* (younger Sister) *rangga* or the *gungman* (elder Sister) *rangga*. All of these are decorated with clan patterns derived from those originally given by the Djanggawul[2] to the 'new generation' which emerged from the Sisters' uteri; and most have attached to them feathered string— the red parakeet feathers symbolizing the rays of the sun, the red sky at sunset, or blood from the Sisters. They are used in dancing on the sacred ground, and in posturing before the sacred shade or hut; the latter symbolizes the uterus or *ngainmara* mat, and in it *rangga* are stored just as were the first *rangga* in the beginning. Parakeet feathered string was also among the objects brought by the Djanggawul.

All these objects, then, have symbolic significance, and relate to the basic theme of Djanggawul ritual and mythology. This theme is fertility, manifested in the perpetually pregnant Women, the Two Sisters, in the growth of trees and foliage, in the creation of running springs, and in the abiding and life-giving warmth of the sun's rays. It reflects the Aborigines' fundamental reliance on the products of their natural environment, and their emphasis on the procreation of human and animal life, the continuance of their own species and of the food which supplies them with sustenance. They see the theme of fertility mirrored in their surroundings, and in the rhythmic sequence of the seasons, and recognize their own dependence on these and on other natural phenomena for their very being.

[1] The two Sisters are also said to have urinated in various places, making sometimes small streams, and sometimes pools or wells: in the latter case, the well itself is often likened to their vaginae.

[2] *Vide* A. P. Elkin, R. and C. Berndt, *Art in Arnhem Land*, pp. 28–41.

Significance of the Djanggawul

These material objects, then, such as the sacred *rangga*, bag and mat, are focal points, or symbols, through which we may grasp the significance of the concept as a whole. The mat is a uterus symbol; so is the whale, although used in this sense only incidentally. Here is the source of all life, for it was from the Uteri of the Sisters that the first people sprang. Moreover, these Aborigines have recognized the importance of the sexual act in causing conception and pregnancy. This natural sequence of events has many parallels in the animal life they observe about them. Throughout the myth direct references are made to sexual intercourse, while symbolic references in both the myth and songs are numerous. The *rangga* poles, the yam stick, *mauwulan*, *djuda* and *djanda* are themselves penis symbols, an interpretation made quite frankly by the Aborigines themselves. The poles, for instance, are kept hidden within the *ngainmara*, and removed from time to time for drying, thus symbolizing coitus (penis in vagina as a projection of the uterus), and drying the penis after intercourse when it has become 'wet' with semen and vaginal juices. Or the *mauwulan* is plunged into the earth, so that water gushes forth at its removal; this is compared to coitus, the removal of the penis from the vagina, and the subsequent flow of seminal and vaginal juices when the Sisters stand up again. Waterholes themselves are vulva symbols, used frequently in Aboriginal song and mythology, while trees (for example, the *djuda*) are penis symbols, and their roots are called by the term used for penis (*vide* songs). A great deal of this erotic symbolism is expressed in sacred ritual, in posturing and actions.

From this we see something of the importance of sexual intercourse. To the Aborigines, as to us, sex and food are basic drives. Whatever subsidiary drives exist, these two are fundamental, for upon them human life, as they know it, depends. The Aborigines are apt to stress the importance of the sexual drive. 'How else', they say, 'can we continue as a group? By what other means can we obtain food except by its natural increase?' Thus even certain forms of plant life are divided into male and female sexes. Sexual intercourse is felt to be necessary for survival, in so far as the human and animal world is concerned, although this survival depends ultimately on forces beyond the Aborigines' control—on seasonal fluctuation, and on the sun, and so we come back to the significance underlying the Djanggawul. The Aborigines of north-eastern and north-central Arnhem Land consequently pay much attention to sexual matters, and their attitude towards this subject is one of utmost frankness.[1] To them, sexual intercourse is an essential

[1] *Vide* Introduction to *Sexual Behaviour in Western Arnhem Land* (R. and C. Berndt), Viking Fund Series in Anthropology, Yale University, 1951. No 16.

preliminary to pregnancy. Children in this area, for instance, are called *judu* (*jutu*, usually employed in a singular sense), or *djamarguli* (plural). The former word means 'semen'; that is, the child originated from the semen. The latter means 'through (or from) work'; to 'work' (*djama*) a female is to have coitus, and *djamarguli* is literally the 'result of working (or coitus)'.

Erotic references, then, in the Djanggawul cult merely conform to the accepted pattern. To say that the Aborigine is concerned unduly with the subject of sex, and derives a morbid satisfaction from constant direct or symbolic reference to it, it to distort the actual position. He is frankly interested in the workings of the human body, and in the satisfaction of its basic needs; and he recognizes the fundamental importance of the act, not only in ensuring the continuation of life, but also in helping to stabilize relations between members of both sexes, through their very inter-dependence. It is not unexpected, therefore, to find manifestations of this interest in Aboriginal religious emblems and mythology, ritual and song. Indeed, what more obvious means of expression could a simple group of people have? Here, in the Djanggawul doctrine, are crystallized their hopes and desires, related to their fundamental drives, co-ordinated with the natural resources and phenomena and with the environment which they know.

Numerous references are made to the removal of the *rangga* from the *ngainmara*, a symbolic allusion also to the removal of children from the wombs of the Sisters: for *rangga* are likened to children, or human beings, and men and women may use this term to refer to their bones. The spiritual content of the bones is the same as that of the sacred *rangga*, and has, moreover, been passed on from their ancestors—those who were originally removed from the Sisters. When, for example, postulants enter the sacred hut (= *ngainmara* = uterus) on the ritual ground, they are like *rangga* being hidden away within the *ngainmara*. In a polygynous marriage, too, the wives are said to be like *rangga*: their husband has collected them into a group, and has a monopoly over them as a man has over his individual *rangga*. This likening of women to sacred *rangga* is interesting, but probably derives from the fact that women themselves are said to be the source of ritual knowledge,[1] and consequently sacred.

There is much stress, too, on the maternal qualities of the Djanggawul Sisters, although the Brother himself is of considerable importance. The Two Sisters are mentioned far more frequently, particularly in the Milingimbi version of the cycle, although this

[1] *Vide* Chapters 2 and 3. (See also M. Mead, *Male and Female*, London, 1950, pp. 102–3.)

7

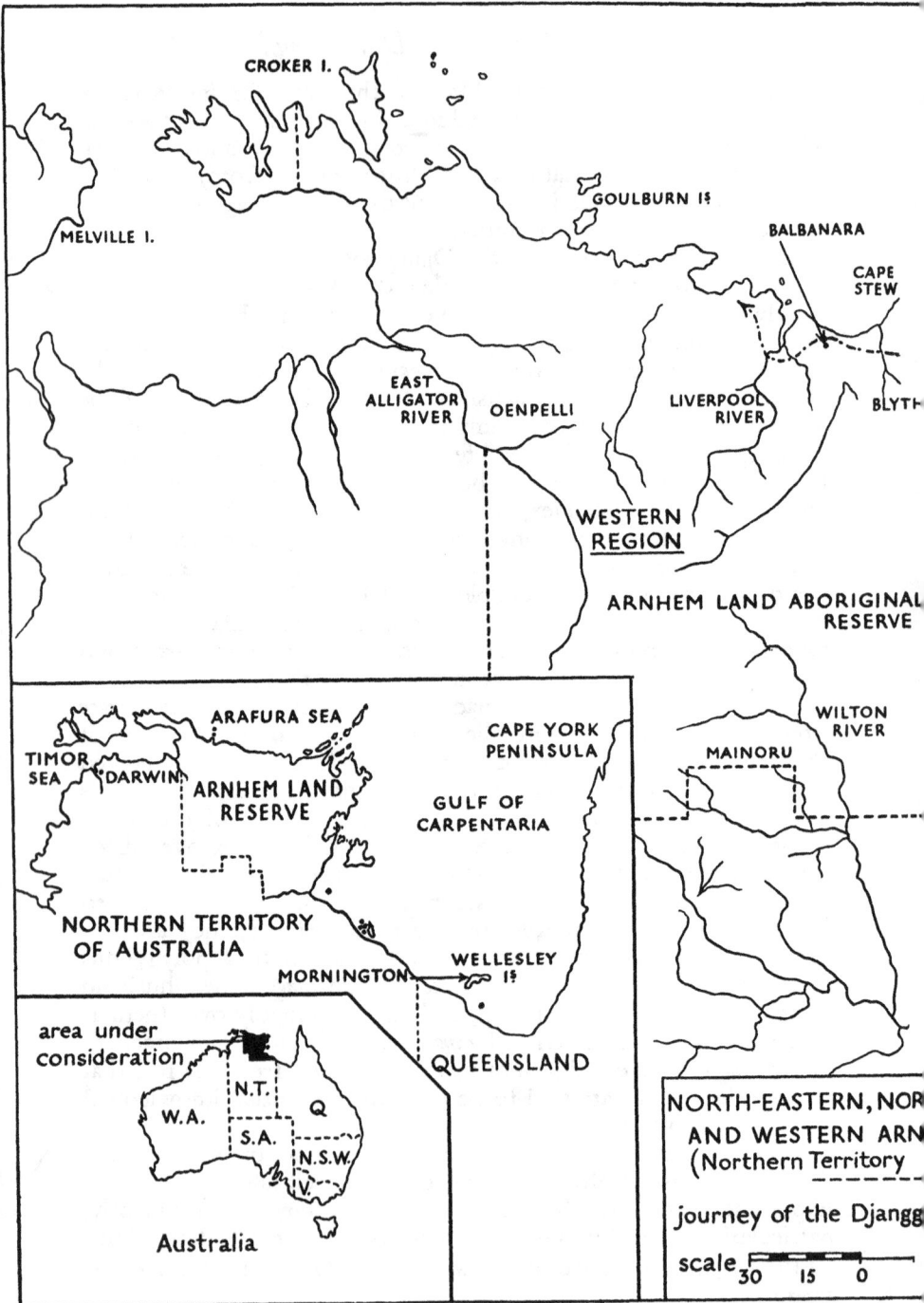

CROKER I.

GOULBURN I$

BALBANARA

CAPE STEW

MELVILLE I.

EAST
ALLIGATOR
RIVER

OENPELLI

LIVERPOOL
RIVER

BLYTH

WESTERN
REGION

ARNHEM LAND ABORIGINAL
RESERVE

WILTON
RIVER

MAINORU

ARAFURA SEA

CAPE YORK
PENINSULA

TIMOR
SEA   DARWIN   ARNHEM LAND
RESERVE

GULF OF
CARPENTARIA

NORTHERN TERRITORY
OF AUSTRALIA

MORNINGTON

WELLESLEY
I$

area under
consideration

N.T.

Q

W.A.

S.A.

N.S.W.

V.

QUEENSLAND

Australia

NORTH-EASTERN, NOR
AND WESTERN ARN
(Northern Territory

journey of the Djangg

scale
30   15   0

8

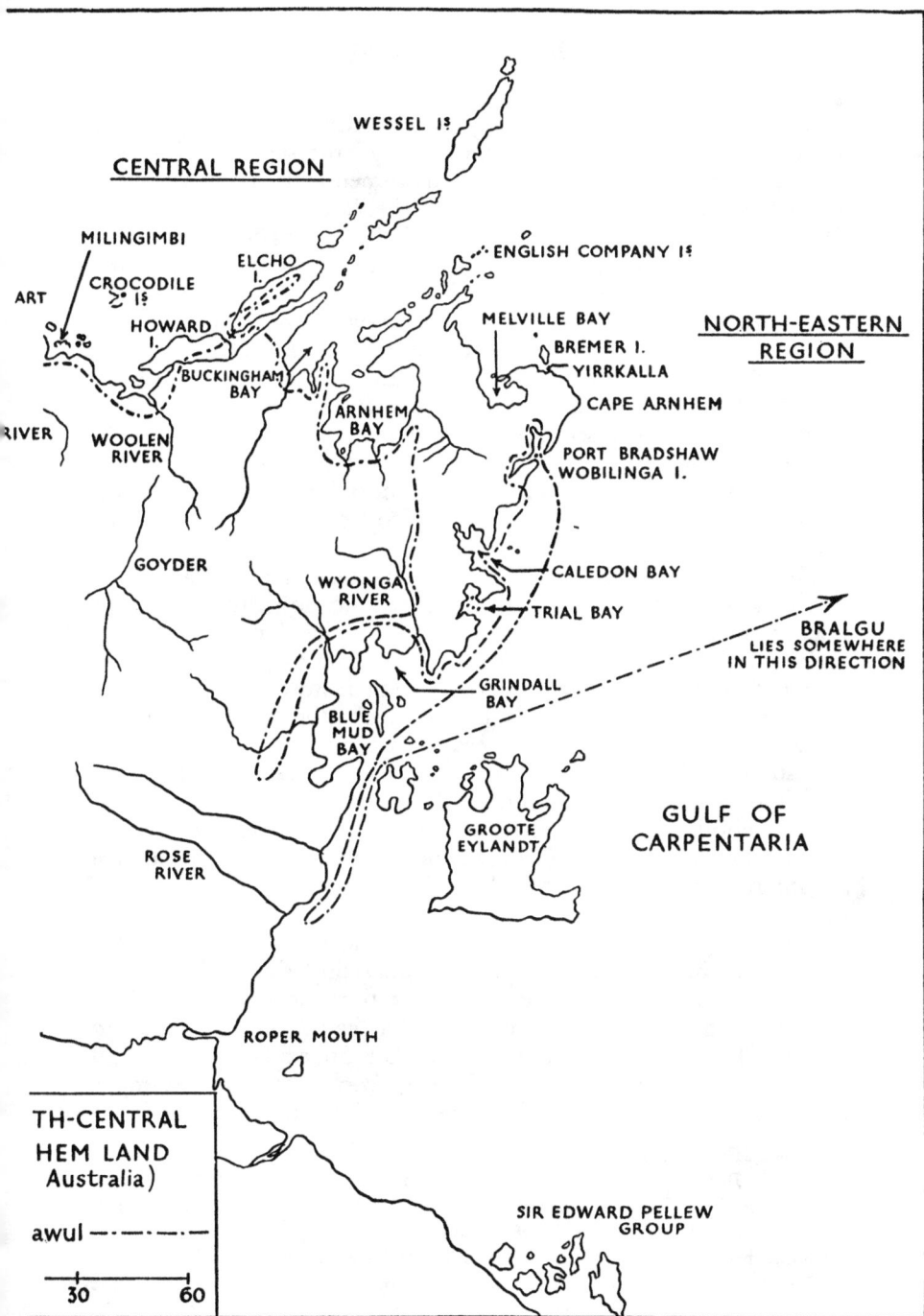

CENTRAL REGION

WESSEL IS

MILINGIMBI

CROCODILE IS

ELCHO I.

ENGLISH COMPANY IS

MELVILLE BAY

BREMER I.

YIRRKALLA

NORTH-EASTERN REGION

ART

HOWARD I.

BUCKINGHAM BAY

ARNHEM BAY

CAPE ARNHEM

RIVER

WOOLEN RIVER

PORT BRADSHAW
WOBILINGA I.

GOYDER

WYONGA RIVER

CALEDON BAY

TRIAL BAY

BRALGU
LIES SOMEWHERE
IN THIS DIRECTION

GRINDALL BAY

BLUE MUD BAY

GULF OF CARPENTARIA

GROOTE EYLANDT

ROSE RIVER

ROPER MOUTH

TH-CENTRAL
HEM LAND
(Australia)

awul — · — · —

30   60

SIR EDWARD PELLEW GROUP

9

Significance of the Djanggawul

is a predominantly patrilineal society. The Two Sisters are Original Mothers of the various *dua* moiety clansfolk, as well as of the *jiritja*. They are Mother Goddesses in the true sense of the term, for although they were allegedly instrumental in populating the greater part of eastern Arnhem Land, they are responsible also for all subsequent fertility. Aborigines call the Sisters 'Our Mothers'. When men cut the fringe of their sacred dilly bags, or perform ritual, they are the 'Sons of the Djanggawul'; when they enter the sacred ground, marked out in a special way, they are returning to their Mothers' uteri; when they enter the sacred hut on the ritual ground, they are also returning to their Mothers' uteri (or uterus, when one hut is used, referring to the elder Sister). The same theme is expressed symbolically in a variety of ways. The whole concept of the return to the Mother on ritual occasions is particularly interesting;[1] but we shall not digress to discuss the theoretical interpretation, as favoured by some modern psycho-analytic schools of thought.

The most important focal point of interest in the Djanggawul myth and songs is procreation, and its ramifications. In some drawings from Yirrkalla the Two Sisters are depicted with people (or children) 'flowing' out from their vulvae. Their legs are apart and flexed, their eyes open with tears running from the pain of child-birth. This concept of people flowing from the Mothers' uteri is used in western-central Northern Territory in reference to the Kunapipi Mother,[2] who is also said to 'let postulants out from her womb during ceremonial time'. (This same theme is expressed, both symbolically and directly, at Yirrkalla and Millingimbi.) The relationship between the Djanggawul and the Kunapipi Mother is an interesting question, which unfortunately cannot be treated here.[3]

The Djanggawul were possessed of abnormally long genitalia. The Brother had an elongated penis, emphasizing, through exaggeration, his masculine function in the fertility scheme. The Two Sisters had abnormally long clitorises,[4] a feature more difficult to explain. The Aborigines themselves offer no explanation, except that the *rangga* may have been derived from them. For example, when the penis and clitorises were eventually foreshortened, the

[1] *Vide* R. Berndt, *Kunapipi.*

[2] *Vide* R. Berndt, *op. cit.*, Chapters II–IV, IX, and R. and C. Berndt, 'The Eternal Ones of the Dream' (being a discussion of Dr. G. Róheim's book of that name), *Oceania*, Vol. XVII, No. 1, pp. 67–78, three plates.

[3] Some mention has been made of this in *Kunapipi*, Chapters I *c* and III.

[4] *Vide* Chapters 2 and 3. The significance of the Sisters' clitorises is revealed in the songs.

Significance of the Djanggawul

severed parts became *rangga* or feathered strings, which are also regarded as *rangga*. An interesting interpretation was made by one informant, himself a ceremonial leader. Within historic times, he said, a certain man was born with both vagina and penis, and with breasts like a woman; he was bi-sexual and produced a child, after which he died. Commenting on this example, which was told to him by a grandparent, the informant suggested that these Djanggawul Sisters may have originally been bi-sexual, so that their clitorises were actually penes which they used to impregnate themselves by inserting into the vagina; for the 'clitoris-penes' were sufficiently long to curve round and use for coitus. The same informant stated that the Djanggawul Brother may possibly have been introduced later. This is, however, the tentative interpretation of one man, and does not represent group opinion.

The presence of elongated clitorises can possibly be explained in terms of the tendency to accentuate a female organ (as has been done in the case of the male); or they may, symbolically, represent the umbilical cord (as in the Song Cycle). The former explanation seems to be more probable, for much stress is placed on the erectness of a woman's clitoris during coitus,[1] while the clitorises of many Aboriginal women are fairly well developed; they are played with and handled by women from pre-adolescent days, in an endeavour to increase their size, so attracting the attentions of men and heightening their sexual satisfaction. In other drawings from the Yirrkalla area, the Djanggawul Sisters have long clitorises, dragging on the ground. In one illustration we see the Two Sisters with elongated clitorises, and the Brother with his long penis; they are holding *rangga*, and people are coming out to be placed on a *ngainmara* mat. The same drawing shows the Wauwalak Sisters,[2] who are the daughters of the Djanggawul, while the Brother puts his hand into the Sisters' wombs to remove the people. The Brother's inserting his hand into the uteri, to remove the people (children), is compared with his putting his hand into the *ngainmara* to remove the sacred *rangga*. Further, it suggests that the Sisters did not invariably give birth to such people in the normal way. The Brother's action in inserting his hand merely accentuates the theme by introducing a further point, which can be more easily represented in symbolism—that is, by the *rangga* and *ngainmara*, illustrating the phenomenon of childbirth.

Professor Lloyd Warner was the first to note the presence of the Djanggawul (which he called Djunkgao) cult, presenting this

[1] *Vide* R. Berndt, *Love Songs of Arnhem Land*, for publication.

[2] The Wauwalak Sisters sponsor all *Kunapipi*, *ngurlmag* and *djunggawon* ritual. *Vide* R. Berndt, *Kunapipi*, Chapters I *c*, III and IV.

Significance of the Djanggawul

material in his book, *A Black Civilization*.[1] The content of the myth which he presents will be discussed in the following chapter (3); here we are concerned with his analysis. He treated the Djanggawul in the same manner as he did the Wauwalak constellation. His opinion was that the Djanggawul cult was not so well integrated as that of the Wauwalak; and he wrongly assumed that it was merely one part of a larger cycle of stories centring around the movements of the ocean tides, and the floods of the rainy season.[2] This misinterpretation seems to have resulted from inadequate documentation. The myth and rituals, as he describes them, are incomplete, and the great song cycle is virtually ignored. However, even if we cannot accept Warner's assumptions concerning the significance and fundamental meaning of the cult, we must recognize the value of his descriptions, particularly as regards observational material, relating to the rituals.[3] Comparing the Djanggawul with the Wauwalak,[4] Warner concludes that both are very much the same in content. We, on the contrary, contend that although both have the same basic significance, stressing fertility, and being concerned with sexual functions and with peculiarly female characteristics, the relevant 'plots' are in themselves dissimilar.[5] They differ in many important details, which need not be tabulated here.

The essential distinction between the two is the fact that the Djanggawul are concerned with procreation, while the Wauwalak are, so to speak, interested in maintaining the *status quo*. The Wauwalak are not assumed to have 'brought into being' all life, as are the Djanggawul; they symbolically re-enact the situation, but are not the creators of it. In native epistemological doctrine this distinction is clearly defined. The Djanggawul came first, the Wauwalak later. It is, nevertheless, a debatable point whether or not the Djanggawul have influenced Aboriginal behaviour more than the Wauwalak. True, the latter have inspired at least three separate rituals; but to counterbalance this the Djanggawul remain aloof in inspiring the great *nara*, which in the ritual sense is much 'higher' than any of the Wauwalak ceremonies.

Warner, however, stressed the 'identification of the two myths and the fundamental sameness of the two rituals.'[6] The rituals do

[1] W. L. Warner, *op. cit.*, pp. 335–56, 399–403, 406–7.
[2] W. L. Warner, *op. cit.*, p. 335.
[3] W. L. Warner, *op. cit.*, pp. 340–56.
[4] W. L. Warner, *op. cit.*, pp. 399–403.
[5] Compare the full Djanggawul myth presented in Chapter 2 of this volume with the Wauwalak mythology set out in *Kunapipi* (R. Berndt), Chapter III.
[6] W. L. Warner, *op. cit.*, p. 399.

Significance of the Djanggawul

differ considerably, as do elements in the myths, but each does help us to understand the deeper significance of the other. The many totems that appear in the Djanggawul, and also in other myths, serve, as Warner also noted,[1] as concrete expression of the underlying concepts of Arnhem Land society, in its relation to nature and to its own institutions; and we find that these concepts are deeply embedded in the myth. They are thus part of the myth, and so subject to interpretation through ritual. But in Chapter 3 we shall discuss something of the Djanggawul's association with totemism. Totemism is relevant, but subsidiary, to the basic significance of the myth. The point that totemism is a philosophy and not a religion, that its manifestations in the ritual provide material crystallizations of religious concepts, must be kept in mind.

That the Djanggawul myth should express the fundamental idea of the backward and forward movements of the tides in the spring floods, either in the present era or in the mythological past,[2] is not made clear in Warner's discussion. The presence of water in the myth is quite a logical feature, for salt and fresh water, like tides and floods, are part of the environment; they are important in much the same degree as other natural phenomena. All of these are drawn into the underlying theme of the Djanggawul, for it is intimately concerned with all fertility, and with all the elements that make possible the continuance of the state of existence known to the Aborigines. That is to say, to bring about fertility (an aspect which, expressed consciously or otherwise, seems to predominate both in the minds of the natives and in their ritual symbolism), the sequence of the seasons must be assured; and this assurance, or the desire to attain it, is expressed symbolically in both myth and songs and materially in totemic manifestation. Warner suggests[3] that the rise and fall of the water in clan wells 'is something more than the symbolization of the flood as male and spiritual'. It is, according to him, 'an actual outflow of water from the sacred centres of the land, which causes the growth of new plants and animals and the refertilizing of the earth. It is the male principle fertilizing the earth.' This aspect receives some treatment in the myth and songs; and excluding his flood concept, and the idea that the male alone is 'spiritual' (a word, incidentally, which needs definition), this is very much what is actually involved. Warner, however, influenced by Durkheimian theory, by his ideas about ceremonial purification, and woman's ritual uncleanliness, has confused the

[1] W. L. Warner, *op. cit.*, p. 401.
[2] W. L. Warner, *op. cit.*, p. 402.
[3] *op. cit.*, p. 402.

issues. The concept that woman is profane, in comparison with man the sacred, is not a feature of eastern Arnhem Land religious or lay thought.

The symbolism in the myth and songs makes clear the intentions of the relevant ritual. In the *dua* moiety *nara*, as an expression of the Djanggawul ideology, the major incidents of the myth are re-enacted in symbolic form. Much of this ritual is taken up with totemic dancing; and the animals, birds, reptiles and vegetable matter danced are totemic in so far that they relate directly or indirectly to the dominant theme. Further, these totems are not used only in relation to the Djanggawul, but are part of the spiritual heritage of the *dua* moiety linguistic groups and clans, which in turn are associated with the Djanggawul.

Dua nara rituals are all inspired by the Djanggawul, although at times irrelevant elements enter; for example, other *dua* spirits or Ancestral Beings of minor importance become associated with the main theme, or *jiritja* moiety elements appear from time to time in the myth. But the Djanggawul are *dua*, and their ceremonies are solely of the *dua nara*, and not (as Warner mentions)[1] of both *dua* and *jiritja*. The latter are inspired by their own separate ideology, and by the Laintjung and Banaitja Ancestral Beings; and although similar in many points, they are basically different. However, it is the practice for some *jiritja* men (maternally related to the *dua* moiety) to help out *dua* postulants, or vice versa: and it is usual for both moieties to hold their own particular rituals at approximately the same time. At Yirrkalla, separate ceremonial grounds and separate huts are used by each moiety; but in the western Arnhem Land variant of the *nara* rituals the same ground is used, although each moiety has its separate hut (or shade), which may or may not adjoin that of the other. In eastern Arnhem Land, the ritual demarcation between the moieties is particularly noticeable.

The *dua*, and for that matter the *jiritja*, *nara* are the most important religious ceremonies of eastern Arnhem Land. Being far more important that the *kunapipi*, *ngurlmag* and *djunggawon*, they are not concerned with age-grading in the same sense that other initiation rituals are. They are primarily revelatory in character; and although novices are received, they are rather neophytes who are already fully initiated into manhood, and already possessed of a certain amount of religious knowledge. By the time a man sees his first *nara* he is well past adolescence, and usually married; he would normally be expected to have already seen the *ngurlmag*, and to be taking a major part in *djunggawon* dancing, as well as in that of the *kunapipi*, although the latter is optional.

[1] *op. cit.*, p. 340.

Significance of the Djanggawul

Long before the actual rituals commence, men go out to the sacred ground to prepare the objects. The wooden poles and posts are removed from their hiding places in the water or mud, and weeks are spent in re-painting them. Women are asked to prepare long feathered strings, which are never directly given to the men, but always 'stolen' by them. This is conventional behaviour, and relates to the Djanggawul Brother and his companions' stealing the sacred *rangga*, bags and so on from the Two Sisters in the beginning (see Chapter 2). The preliminary preparations take weeks, and are accompanied by singing and invocations. Neophytes are brought in from time to time, and their chests painted with sacred clan designs: they continue to wear these when they return to the camp, and never wash or rub them off, but allow them to fade naturally. In this way the neophytes contract many ritual obligations, since they must recompense their 'initiators'—that is, those who are revealing the mysteries to them. They must also observe a number of tabus relating to their general behaviour, and to the partaking of food.[1] Later, the same neophytes are shown the *rangga* emblems and their designs, and the meanings are explained to them.

By this time, the neophytes have reached the stage when they are regarded as being eligible to witness the first ceremonies. The sacred ground has been prepared, the shade erected and the objects completed. A sacred aura is now said to pervade the ritual ground, and the spiritual presence of the Djanggawul is assured.

The ceremonies which now begin are not seen completely by those neophytes who are brought to the ground for the first time. Years may pass before the complete series has been revealed to them, and it is not as a rule until they have reached middle age that they may take an active part in the ritual. Sometimes, however, younger men who show particular aptitude for religious discussion, dancing and singing, are accepted much earlier. There is always a need for young and energetic dancers and actors; and the older men, by allowing the younger men a degree of active participation, cement their adherence to the cult and so reinforce their own position. But even when younger men dance or act, older men are the organizers, and it is their duty to show the way to the other. They, the older men, are always acknowledged to possess greater knowledge of these matters, to be in a position to impart that knowledge. The older men, when they do dance or act, are almost invariably more proficient than the younger men; and although there is a tendency to-day to allow the younger men a greater measure of participation, it still takes years before a neophyte may be legitimately classified as an initiate.

[1] The economic aspect of the *nara* rituals cannot, unfortunately, be dealt with here.

Significance of the Djanggawul

Warner has already set out briefly something of the procedure in this *nara* ritual;[1] although his descriptions are based on observation of these twenty-one years ago, to-day they appear to have been little changed. Although in this volume we are not concerned primarily with the ritual expressions of the Djanggawul myth and songs, it is nevertheless necessary to present briefly the sequence of the ritual and its significance. This will throw the rest of our material into relief, and serve to accentuate basic meanings.[2]

a. The sacred ground is formed, the shade constructed, and various members and ceremonial leaders of the *dua* groups prepare the *rangga* emblems. (See above.) The shade of branches on a framework of wood symbolizes the *ngainmara* or uterus of either Djanggawul Sister (it is said to signify, in one, the uteri of both the younger and older Sisters). The initiates themselves are symbolically *rangga*, or 'the Children of the Sisters'; they represent too the Brother and his companions (who were themselves the Sisters' children). The ground is also a projection of the uterus concept.

The first dances are always those relating to the rise and fall of the surf, and the sound of the sea. These refer to the Djanggawul's paddling across the sea from Bralgu to Port Bradshaw, and are treated in the myth and songs. At intervals throughout this dancing, and during all the *nara* ceremonies, invocations (*bugali*) are called. These, by the terms used, bring into perspective relevant sections of what is being enacted. Furthermore, they are thought to create an aura of sacredness, by spiritually conjuring up the Djanggawul themselves, and their pervading power. All *bugali* invocations are made up of sacred 'inside' words,[3] and numerous examples exist in the song cycles (see, for example, textual material treated separately in Volume 2 of this work). The same participants leave the ground and enter the main camp, and again call out invocations within the hearing of all. Women are said not to know the hidden meanings, but are quite well aware of much of their significance: *vide* Djanggawul myth relating to the loss of the *rangga* and bags by the Sisters. Women feed the men, who then return to the sacred ground. The rôle of the women during this part, and during the whole ritual series, is to provide participants and postulants with food: traditionally, this is cycad palm nut 'bread', supplemented by a variety of edible meats, vegetables and fruits. This is in accordance with the rôle undertaken by the Two Sisters after their

---

[1] *op. cit.*, pp. 340–56.

[2] Full descriptions of the *dua nara* will be presented later. Compare the differences between these rituals and those associated with the *kunapipi: vide Kunapipi*, Chapter IV.

[3] W. L. Warner, *op. cit.*, p. 341: this writer calls these 'power' names.

1. Postulants emerge from the sacred shade, carrying emblems.

2. Embracing the *rangga* emblems on the sacred ground.

3. *Rangga* folk emerge from the Djanggawul Sisters.

4. Various phases of the *nara* Djanggawul ceremonies.

sacred possessions were lost, a rôle which before this loss belonged to the men.

The sequence of the preceding ritual depends on the completion of the many *rangga*, the availability of men and neophytes, the abundance of red ochre and parakeet breast feathers, and the amount of food collected by the women. Although much of the latter is collected throughout the ceremonies, cycad 'bread' is stored, and its preparation commences weeks before the first rituals begin.

Just after the first ceremonies, people from other groups come to the main camp where the *nara* is being held. They have been summoned by specially designed message sticks, feathered string, or miniature copies of *rangga* objects moulded from wild honey wax. Ideally, at this point, all the *rangga* should be ready; but in practice, painting of the objects usually continues for some time, and visitors make and paint additional emblems. All these *rangga* relate to various features of the Djanggawul myth: the *rangga* brought by the Djanggawul; representations of the Djanggawul themselves, or their separate organs; natural phenomena; or totemic objects and species associated with the Djanggawul. Incidentally, the majority of the dances enact something of the behaviour of totemic species, and are carried out with the *rangga*.

When initially, at the onset of the ritual, the *rangga* are removed from the water or mud they are said to be like, firstly, *rangga* removed from the *ngainmara*, and secondly, children removed from the Sisters' wombs. Placing one's arm (or hand) into the water or mud to remove the *rangga* is like the Djanggawul Brother's inserting his hand into the vaginae of the Sisters to remove the children. The sacred clan patterns drawn with ochres on the objects are derived from water marks, which the Djanggawul's original *rangga* acquired during their journey in the bark canoe from Bralgu. Alternatively, these patterns symbolize 'womb marks' on a new-born child. Ochre is symbolic of blood, or the sun's rays, or the warmth of a fire: blood from afterbirth, rays of sun from the *dagu* vagina disc of the sun, and fire (warmth) from the sun. The red breast feathers of the parakeet are symbolic of the sun's rays, of blood, or of an umbilical cord. The reiteration of dancing associated with the sea in every case signifies the great importance of the Djanggawul's landing at Jelangbara, which is one of the most sacred sites associated with these Beings. The singing of water from the sacred waterholes refers to these Beings inserting their *rangga*, and removing them so that water will gush forth; this is symbolic of coitus, and the rise of water is the flow of semen which fertilized both human beings and the earth. It represents, too, the coming of the heavy rains of the wet season, which is viewed as a period of fertilization.[1]

b. The first ceremonies which take place after the arrival of the visitors are related mainly to totemic species, and do not usually involve use of the *rangga* emblems, which are nearly always retained till later ceremonies. Older men organize all these rituals and instruct neophytes. When actors are not carrying out the traditional actions with sufficient skill, they often take over themselves to demonstrate just how it should be done. Both *dua* and *jiritja* neophytes are present. There is also a ceremonial shaving of facial hair; older men leave short tufts or beards that symbolically represent the fringe of the *ngainmara* mat (= pubic hair of the Sisters), and attach red parakeet feathers, like the *rangga* pendant strings. (That is, as the *rangga* have feathered pendants attached to them, so also do men, because they approximate *rangga*—see above.)

c. In the main camp women and young children, and uninitiated youths, gather in a cleared place where they are covered with *ngainmara* mats. This symbolically represents the unborn children of the Djanggawul Sisters, lying in the uteri (or children in the *ngainmara*, or *rangga* hidden in the *ngainmara* or bags; *vide* myth and songs). The men dance from the sacred ground and surround them, carrying spears, womeras and sticks. Invocations are called, most of which refer to places where the Djanggawul Sisters gave birth to the people; they include also sacred 'inside' terms for the *ngainmara*, and for the sacred wells, billabongs or waterholes, for the *rangga* objects, and for the spears and sticks which the men carry. Ancestral names are called too, as well as the 'inside' names of various men taking part in the ritual. Surrounding the people covered by the *ngainmara* mats, the men poke them with their spears and sticks, and they wriggle in response.

The men then dance, calling out sacred *bugali* terms for childbirth, sexual intercourse and so on. Then the women, children and youths emerge from their *ngainmara*, and sit watching the men. Final calling of *bugali* completes the ceremony.

Interpreting this ritual, Aborigines say that the women crouching under the mats are the children of the Sisters; they are 'poked' by the men and wriggle 'like children in a womb'. The poking with spears and sticks signifies the Djanggawul Brother's penis, which causes the pregnancy of his Sisters and the subsequent 'wriggling' of the children. Alternatively, the spears and sticks symbolize the *rangga*, and the 'poking' their replacement in the *ngainmara*. The casting aside of the *ngainmara* represents the birth of the children of Djanggawul, or conversely, the removal of *rangga* (symbolically,

[1] *Vide* W. L. Warner, *op. cit.*, p. 343.

the birth). Or again, the fact that the women are covered by the *ngainmara* refers to the Djanggawul's placing all females, at birth, beneath the *ngainmara* for protection. The men are left out because they were originally placed by the Djanggawul in the coarse grass, and were unprotected: *vide* myth, Chapters 2 and 3. Underlying this ceremony is the idea that the symbolic act of childbirth will be imitated and repeated in real life, so that universal fertility may result.

d. More totemic dances take place on the sacred ground, and continue for some weeks. Various sections of the myth are enacted; for example, there are all the natural species seen at each place through which the Djanggawul passed (see myth). Two or three weeks may be given over to the performance of all the events that happened at one place. During all these ceremonies, the women provide food for the men. Outstanding dances are those of the *djanda* goanna, the *djalga* water goanna, the *lindaridj* parakeet, and spring water, the latter deriving from the *rangga*'s being plunged into the ground by the Djanggawul. At this stage certain *rangga* are used in dancing or posturing. The major, or fundamental *rangga* brought by the Djanggawul from Bralgu, are used by individual dancers, or by groups of actors who writhe along the ground with the *rangga* clasped to their bodies or held in ritual ways. All the dancers emerge from the sacred shade in which the *rangga* are kept, to the accompaniment of singing, or simply to the rhythm of the clapping sticks. Some of the most important emerge in silence; intense reverence is shown in all ritual in which the *rangga* are used.

e. Women gather around a tree or forked stick in the main camp. Men come down from the sacred ground, and the women answer their ritual cries. The ceremonial leader climbs the tree or forked stick and to the accompaniment of clapping sticks invokes the sacred *bugali*. In the western variant of this (that is, the Gunwinggu *mareiin* cult), all women and neophytes are 'steamed' over a special structure, but this does not occur in eastern Arnhem Land. The women, all painted, dance around the tree as the invocations are called. Nearly all the *bugali* are related to places and to totemic species. Pairs of dancers then enact various totemic creatures, dancing near the tree or forked stick and in front of the women. That completes the ceremony. This is continued for a period until finally the men come at night to the main camp bearing flaming torches.

The fire symbolizes that which the Sisters thought had destroyed their sacred bags containing the *rangga*, only to find later that they had been stolen by the men (see Chapter 2). Further, it signifies parakeet feathers, or the warmth of the sun, which is not present during the night.

19

Significance of the Djanggawul

The women dancing around the tree or forked stick represent the Djanggawul Sisters, and the tree is the *djuda* tree (of life-giving properties) and also *rangga* (that is, tree = forked-stick = *djuda rangga* = penis). They dance around, inserting their sacred *ganinjari rangga* yam sticks into the ground, so that water may gush forth (that is, symbolic coitus). The dancing of totemic species before the women at the tree or forked stick is like the dancing by the Djanggawul women in their own sacred shade, within the hearing of the men, but without their participation (*vide* myth). Later the men reverse this situation, and it is the men who dance in their own shade, while the Two Sisters go some distance away.

f. At this juncture there is a repetition of the *ngainmara* ritual, when all the women, children and youths are hidden under the mats. The men dance around them, carrying out the same actions as in section *c*, and the ritual has the same significance.

g. More totemic dances are carried out on the sacred ground, particularly in conjunction with *rangga* objects. Young neophytes see only the secondary *rangga* and totem dances; for all these are graded, and it depends on a man's age, his influence, and his degree of acceptance into the cult, whether he sees the really 'high' or most revered *rangga*. The 'high' *rangga* (particularly the elaborately decorated *djuda*, *djanda*, *ganinjari* and *mauwulan*) are lovingly handled, caressed and sung over by ceremonial leaders. Minor *rangga* and dancing viewed by neophytes bring to them simultaneously a series of associated tabus, relating to eating meat or flesh of the totems which they view, and obliges them to present gifts later on to the leaders. Neophytes, when watching these dances, are usually painted with sacred clan patterns. 'They are painted like dead men, for their spirit must enter the eternal stream in which the Djanggawul are an ever-present influence'—an eternal stream, moreover, that has no limitations of time or space, all being merged into one: the Creative Beings themselves, the *wongar* Dreaming Spirits and totems, the ancestors, the recently dead and the living.

h. The next ritual, a group effort, should normally complete the *nara* rituals. This is the ceremonial bathing by men, women and children. In western Arnhem Land, in the *mareiin* rituals (counterpart of the *nara*) it is the terminating rite, but sometimes is omitted altogether. At Milingimbi it may be a terminating rite, or others may follow it. At Yirrkalla it may be omitted altogether, or used as a terminating rite, or it may be followed by further ceremonies. This ceremonial bathing may take place in a billabong, water-hole, river, or in the adjacent sea; that is, it does not seem to be important whether fresh or salt water is used.

Men, representing geese or diving ducks, dance down to the

bank of the billabong or beach; then, followed by all the other members of the camp, they plunge into the water. Each person washes himself (or herself), and invocations are called. They all emerge, and the men dance various totemic fish.

This ritual act symbolically represents firstly the *rangga* (= people) who become wet while being brought in the Djanggawul's bark canoe from Bralgu. Secondly they, the people, are likened to *rangga*, being plunged into the water (that is, when *rangga* are not in use, or at the conclusion of the rituals, they are hidden in the water or mud, and the people's bathing represents completion of the *nara*). It has also been interpreted to mean that the Djanggawul enter the water to collect fish in their net: *vide* myth, when the Two Sisters enter the water and, opening their legs, bend forward to use them as a fish-catchment. To catch fish in this way, using one's legs as a net, is, moreover, symbolic of coitus: the fish caught are penes (penis of the Djanggawul Brother).[1] Thus, men perform the fish dances after emerging from the water. It also represents the *rangga*'s being inserted into sacred waterholes and billabongs, as was the habit of the Djanggawul; 'they put these *rangga* into wells and so on, leaving them for the new generation.'

Warner[2] mentions that the ritual bathing represents the removal of 'semen'; that is, through the 'incestuous rape of the younger Sister'. This latter conception is not found in any of our versions. Nevertheless, water may signify semen, and thus be a symbol of fertility, just as is the 'foam' of the sea mentioned in the Song Series. The assumption that the women cleanse themselves by washing[3] does not follow from our versions; for all people bathe, not only the women. The lay interpretation of any ritual bathing or washing, whether involving complete immersion or just 'baptism' by anointing with water (also fairly common), is cleansing or purification, in the sense that the sacred aura (which is ritually contagious, and can do harm if not controlled immediately after a ritual), is, for the time being at least, diverted back into the 'eternal stream' (see above). All sacred clan patterns painted on men's bodies, and the complementary sacred patterns on the breasts of women, are removed in this way, thus signifying that the *nara* is nearing completion.

i. Again the 'higher' totem dances and *rangga* emblems are shown to various neophytes in different stages of initiation. All these ceremonies are revelatory in character. These rituals then are divided into two main parts—1, those rituals shown to the younger

---

[1] Also used in everyday speech to refer to coitus—thus a woman 'nets a fish'.

[2] W. L. Warner, *op. cit.*, p. 353.

[3] W. L. Warner, *op. cit.*, pp. 353–4.

neophytes, and, 2, those shown only to the older, fully initiated men who are intimately acquainted with all phases of the *nara* and of the Djanggawul doctrine. These latter rituals, involving meditation and theological discussions, are the most impressive of all. At this time, too, the sacred feathered string is removed and presented to members of the opposite moiety, as well as to younger members in the right line of descent from the ceremonial leaders; that is, a *gudara* (sister's daughter's son) gives to a *mari* (mother's mother's brother) or vice versa.

j. This is followed, soon afterwards, by sacramental eating of the sacred cycad palm nut 'bread'. All the preparation of this 'bread' has been undertaken by the women. It is taken out to the sacred ground where it is sung over, and the sacred *bugali* invoked. All the *bugali* of the country through which the Djanggawul passed, as well as their *rangga*, are called. The actual partaking of the 'bread' may be accompanied by the removal of feathered strings from the *rangga* emblems. This symbolizes the meeting of the Djanggawul with Buralindjingu at Dambojowoi (*vide* myth) when, after the Sisters had had their clitorises foreshortened (that is, the removing of the feathered strings from the *rangga*), they were treated as *galibingu* novices, and palm nut 'bread' was eaten sacramentally. But sacred 'bread' has an additional significance. It is a symbol of all food resources; and when the sacred *bugali* are invoked over it, it becomes possessed of a sacred quality which approximates it to a *rangga* emblem. The eating of it (as a *rangga* emblem) means that initiates are absorbing the sacred qualities of their *rangga* becoming themselves 'more *rangga*', more fully absorbed into the Djanggawul ideology. Symbolically they enter (*rangga* = people) the uteri of the Sisters, so that they may subsequently be re-born, when they leave the sacred ground and terminate the *nara*. The eating of the bread creates a strong sacred bond of friendship between all participants: they become as one.

There are, however, many restrictions relating to the eating of this bread. Not all initiates eat from the same bread, but all those eating must be closely related to one another; for *bugali* names have been 'sung' into the bread, and their power remains in it, and cannot be indiscriminately passed around.

After final painting of initiates' bodies, the *nara* is brought to a close.

We see from these examples that ritual is the outward expression of the Djanggawul myth. It is primarily a re-enactment of the principal features of the Brother and Sisters' original journey through north-eastern and north-central Arnhem Land, and an important form of expressing these is the totemic dancing in conjunction with the sacred *rangga*. All these are correlated with the basic theme. The main structure of the ritual refers symbolically to the sexual sequence which culminates in the act of childbirth; and this, in a variety of forms, is the focal point. It is completely orthodox, for in it is contained the core, the basic thesis, of the Djanggawul myth. By re-enacting the primal birth of their ancestors, the Arnhem Landers convey the sense of 'tribal' (clan or linguistic group) continuity: a continuity, moreover, which cannot be broken unless the actual performance of the *nara* rituals is interrupted or halted. That such an event as abandonment of the *nara* could occur, *cannot* enter the minds of initiates, any more than we could fully envisage the total collapse of our society and culture. On the fringe of alien contact, of course, in towns or on mission stations, this possibility may vaguely enter the minds of some; but even these, though they may have taken part in only one *nara*, cannot consider their utter abandonment. If the *nara* are performed more irregularly to-day than two decades ago, the intention is always present in the Aborigines' minds that, if possible, they will be performed more frequently in the future. The Ancestral Beings will continue to live, so say old informants, even if the life that people know to-day should disappear altogether. The Gods are not dependent on man for their survival, and the 'eternal Dreaming stream' cannot be stemmed.

Upon this thesis rests the social aspect of the Djanggawul, for re-enactment of the initial birth of the people expresses their inherent fertility, which by the grace of the Djanggawul can be diffused to embrace a concept of universal fertility. Moreover, it expresses the seasonal rhythm. The coming of the wet season, with its rains, germinates the soil; foliage and vegetable matter, and all the natural species, 'are re-born'. Because of the Djanggawul, the natural resources of the land are ensured. Man, as a social being, may continue the life he knows, in the way dictated traditionally by the Gods. He is assured of survival.

Chapter Two

THE DJANGGAWUL MYTH[1]

Iｎ the beginning there were land and sky, animals and birds, foliage and trees. There was sea, too, in the waters of which were fish and other creatures; and upon the land were beings of totemic origin. All these things were there, as they had always been; but man, as we know him to-day, was not among them.

Far out to sea, out of sight of the Arnhem Land mainland, was an island known as Bralgu (Bu'ralgu), the land of the Eternal Beings, which later became the home of the *dua* moiety dead. It lay to the south-east of Port Bradshaw, somewhere beyond Groote Eylandt.

It was here, at Bralgu, that the Djanggawul were living. They are said to have come from a big ceremony or meeting, in an unknown land far beyond the isle of Bralgu. On their arrival there they held another large ceremony, much larger than the contemporary *dua nara*, and used all their sacred objects. At that time they possessed a great many emblems, but only a few of these could be brought in the bark canoe to the Australian mainland.

They did not, however, spend very long at Bralgu, for it was only a 'half-way' resting place on the journey they were attempting.

There were three of them: Djanggawul himself, his elder Sister, Bildjiwuraroiju, and his younger Sister, Miralaidj. With them, too, was another man, named Bralbral. The Two Sisters and their Brother, however, were nearly always known as the Djanggawul. Djanggawul himself had an elongated penis, and each of the Two Sisters had a long clitoris; these were so long that they dragged

[1] The Yirrkalla version: this varies in certain points from the Milingimbi version, which will be presented later. *Vide Daughters of the Sun* (for publication).

24

upon the ground as they walked (see Sketch 1). The penis of Djanggawul, *gurlga* or *dulparu* (ordinary name for penis) had a long foreskin (*dabin*), suggesting that it had not been circumcised; at various intervals along the penis were notches, or penis 'rings or ridges', as on an ordinary penis towards the apex. These rings

THE DJANGGAWUL (from rough drawings by native informants)

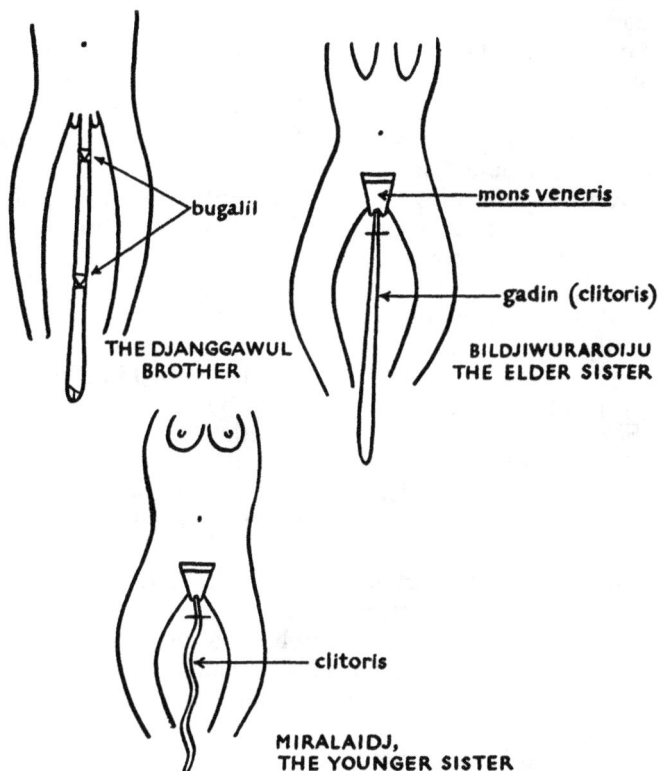

THE DJANGGAWUL
BROTHER

bugalil

mons veneris

gadin (clitoris)

BILDJIWURAROIJU
THE ELDER SISTER

clitoris

MIRALAIDJ,
THE YOUNGER SISTER

Sketch 1.

were called *bugalil*,[1] a term also applied to the sacred invocations at present used among the north-eastern Arnhem Land peoples (*dua* moiety, *bugali*, or *jiritja* moiety, *bugalili*). The elder Sister's clitoris (the ordinary term being *gadin*, and the 'inside' term *ngeribngerib*) was the longer, while the younger Sister's was almost snakelike in appearance.

[1] The secular name for the penis ridge is *balbi* or *bapi*, 'snake'.

The Djanggawul Myth

At Bralgu, as they walked around with these, they left grooves in the ground from their dragging. And when the Djanggawul Brother had coitus with his Sisters, he lifted aside their clitorises, entering them in the usual way. He was able to have incestuous relations with his Sisters, because at that time there were no marriage rules, no moieties, and no prohibitions. Djanggawul was the lawmaker. There is, however, no mention of Bralbral's having sexual relations with the Two Women. Djanggawul had been having coitus with Bildjiwuraroiju for a long time; her breasts had grown large and 'fallen down' with milk, and she had produced many children. Miralaidj, though, was quite young, having just passed puberty, and her breasts were rounded and firm.

They lived at Bralgu for some little time, putting people there, and leaving 'Dreamings' in the form of totemic designs, sacred emblems and body painting. They also instituted their rituals and ceremonies. The Brother's penis and the Sister's clitorises were sacred emblems, like *rangga* poles.

At last they made ready their bark canoe, and loaded it with 'Dreamings', sacred drawings and emblems; the latter were kept in a conically-shaped *ngainmara* mat. When all this was ready they themselves, with their companion Bralbral, climbed into the canoe. Then they paddled out to sea,[1] leaving the island of Bralgu far behind. For days and days they paddled, until they sighted the Arnhem Land mainland. At last they came to it, landing near Rose River. But they soon left this part of the country, and continued paddling along the coast until they reached Jelangbara, Port Bradshaw.

Near Gangudoi Island, while still in their canoe, the Ancestral Beings saw some trees,[2] in the branches of which were perched two *lindaridj* parakeet, drying themselves in the first rays of the sun. As they passed this island, the *djigai* morning pigeon was crying. 'Maybe that bird is crying out on the land,' said the Djanggawul, and so they sang about it. They saw, too, trepang on Bauwuling (or Bauwijara) Islands, and there were many *lindaridj* on Gagubam. A black cockatoo, immediately it caught sight of them, flew over to what are now the sacred sandhills near Ngadibaulwi (or Ngadibalji) rocks.

As the Djanggawul were nearing Port Bradshaw, and while they were still paddling, they could see the white foam from waves breaking around the sacred rock of Gulbinboi, just outside the entrance to the bay. As they looked they saw, too, myriads of small

---

[1] It is said that they came on the crest of a huge wave, but Part 1 of the Song Cycle seems to contradict this.

[2] There are no trees on this island now.

The Djanggawul Myth

lindaridj parakeets flying over the mainland, the sun's rays catching the redness of their breast feathers. There was a constant roar of waves pounding on the beach. They paddled farther into the bay, coming to the Garingan rock, and saw the wide curving beach of Jelangbara. They sang with joy, and allowed the surf to take their canoe into the shallow water.

Then they dragged their canoe on to the beach and unloaded it, making this a sacred place. Jelangbara is the largest Djanggawul centre in north-eastern Arnhem Land and, to-day, the most important.

Here the Djanggawul Brother wished to shorten his Sister's clitorises. But the elder Sister said, 'No, wait till we reach Arnhem Bay. We can have a good rest, and put Dreamings there.' So they walked around, still dragging the clitorises and elongated penis, leaving marks on the ground which may be seen to-day.

Leaving their canoe, the Djanggawul walked along the coast until they came to Ngadibalji, where they saw the *djawuldjawul* mangrove bird. Here too the Djanggawul Brother left his hairbelt, but retained the parakeet-feathered waist-band and arm-bands he was wearing. The hairbelt is now a long sandhill. On the sandhill, were track marks of the *damurmindjari* (*damburindari* or *waburunggu*) wild duck; these birds were eating the *murnji*, or wild peanut roots. On the opposite side was a large barren sandhill, on the surface of which were tracks of the *djanda* goanna, as well as of many birds. A *gamaru* tree with non-edible 'apple'-like nuts was growing there too. This tree is sacred; it is a *jirijiri* bullroarer tree,[1] and to-day only those who are very old may look upon it. Here the Djanggawul paused and heard again the cry of the *ngadili* (*dangadilji* or *rirambung*) black cockatoo. Here too is the sacred waterhole, *milngur*, which the Djanggawul made by inserting the *mauwulan rangga* pole: a spring flows from it down to the beach. It is said that the four Beings entered this hole, and made their camp within.

Later, they walked farther along, and saw two *djanda* goanna resting on the peak of a sandhill. 'Ah,' said the Brother, 'I am very surprised to see this goanna. I had better put it Dreaming (*wongar*) for this country.' *Bangguli* is the goannas' 'inside' sacred name. The goanna crawled up the smooth surface of the sandhill, dislodging the sand. It attempted to climb on to the sacred *djuda* pole (that is, tree) the Djanggawul had placed there, but could not do so, because the Djanggawul were still there. To-day the *djuda* ironwood (or 'black' bark) tree is still there, at Mauwulanggalngu, where it grew from the sacred *rangga*.

---

[1] The connexion with a bullroarer is not clear, for this object is not now used in the *dua nara* ceremonies, but only in the *kunapipi*. *Vide* R. Berndt, *Kunapipi*, Chapters III and IV.

The Djanggawul Myth

After leaving the sandhills the Djanggawul continued walking along. Near the beach at Gumararanggu (named from the *gamaru* tree there), still on the Port Bradshaw peninsula, they heard the noise made by the black *malgu* flying fox, and saw more sandhills and goannas, as well as *gunjan* beach worms.

Coming to Wabilinga Island, which was later to become a large Macassan settlement,[1] they saw the Baijini folk who were working there. They were cooking trepang, where the tamarind trees stand to-day. The Djanggawul were much perturbed and said to the Baijini, 'Baijini, you had better move from here to your own place; for this place must belong to us, and we are going to establish a sacred site.' So some of the Baijini moved to the other side of the island, and some went to Dagu (vagina or vulva) on the mainland. But they left behind them on the island ashes from their fires, the criss-cross elongated bars on which their trepang was left to dry, some huts, and a *djiru* trepang-stirring 'spoon' or ladle. Djanggawul picked this up and looked at it. 'Ah,' he said, 'this is a good colour. I shall have it for myself.' The *djiru* was black, a colour that the Djanggawul now used for the first time, together with blackness from the charcoal in the ashes of the Baijini fires. In this way, the locality became partly *dua*, from the Djanggawul, and partly *jiritja*, from the Baijini.

Another *jiritja* moiety Ancestral Being, named Laintjung, was also present at this site. He exchanged gifts with the Djanggawul, and in return for some red parakeet feathered string gave them some black clan patterns, and opossum fur string. That is why, to-day, each moiety has something belonging to the other: the *jiritja* took from the *dua*, and vice versa. Laintjung was also given a red parakeet feathered *jiridbald* waist-band and some *judumiri* arm-bands. He possessed, too, a piece of cloth[2] which he had obtained from the Baijini, but the Djanggawul refused to take any of this. The Djanggawul had apparently come prepared for this meeting with people of the *jiritja* moiety. They had half expected trouble from them when they requested the Baijini to move, and carried in readiness *gundmara* ('inside' name) fighting dilly bags.

Leaving Wabilinga Island behind them, the Djanggawul moved to Gagubam, where they heard the *djawuldjawul* mangrove bird

[1] It was on this island that pottery was found a few years ago: *vide* R. and C. Berndt, Discovery of Pottery in North-Eastern Arnhem Land, *Journal of the Royal Anthropological Institute*, 1950, Vol. LXXVII, No. 11, pp. 133–8.

[2] That is, according to the great Baijini Song Cycle, cloth woven by the Baijini themselves on the Australian mainland on a primitive hand loom. *Vide* R. and C. Berndt, *Arnhem Land—Its History and Its People*.

calling out in the early morning. After this they heard 'people and children' crying; and here spirit footprints of children may be seen on the rocks. These are the spirits who are as yet unborn, and remain in the uterus of the elder Sister, Bildjiwuraroiju. After leaving Gagubam the Djanggawul passed Bauwuling (or Bauwijara) where they saw *bauwaldja* catfish swimming after small fish and *bunabi* trepang slugs. And above Bauwuling, in the fresh water well on dry land, surrounded by mangroves and salt water, was *biabia* refuse from the trepang.

After spending some time in the Port Bradshaw country, establishing sacred sites, they decided to walk down the beach towards Caledon Bay; but there were so many totemic folk in those parts that they again got into their canoe and paddled down to Gambuga-(wi) at Caledon Bay, in territory of the Karlpu linguistic group. There they are said to have made a sacred place, and put special *djuda*. These were *rangga* emblems which, with others, they had carried from Bralgu in the *ngainmara* mat, and trees sprang up as they were pushed into the ground.

When they had done this they looked up, and saw a big dry weather cloud or mirage, called *wulma*. It was coming from Buguwolumiri, in the country of the Djapu linguistic group, towards the 'bottom' (or southern part) of Blue Mud Bay; so they travelled towards that place, and put more dreamings there. Their clitorises and penis were still dragging on the ground.

Then they saw another *wulma* towards the 'top' of Blue Mud Bay, at Bugalji, in Djarlwak linguistic group territory. They paddled around the coast to that place, and left dreamings there. Then, abandoning their canoe, they went on foot through the bush until they came to Balimauwi; this is also in Djarlwak country, on the northern side of Rose River. They made a big camp, building a number of different 'shades' or huts, which to-day are paperbark trees; and there they also placed many dreamings.

Thus through the greater part of the country about Port Bradshaw, below Jelangbara almost to Rose River, all along the coast and even a little way inland, the Djanggawul left special drawings symbolically related to themselves and to totemic beings. They left, too, sacred *rangga* emblems, such as the *djuda*, the *djanda* (goanna) and *mauwulan* (associated with water springs), as well as sacred baskets. At all those places, moreover, they established their cult, with the singing of songs and the ritual of the *dua* moiety *nara* ceremonies.

While at Balimauwi, they looked up into the north western sky and saw a great *wulma* hanging over Ngaluwi ('inside' name Waguralgu) at Arnhem Bay, in the territory of the Ngeimil and

The Djanggawul Myth

Dadawi linguistic groups. The Djanggawul eventually reached this place and made a camp, putting many dreamings there. They made a fish trap and caught many fish to eat. They also put the wild banana palm, and Djanggawul with his *mauwulan rangga* poked holes in the ground from which water flowed.

After a time they left Ngaluwi, walking along until they reached Gulugboi(wi), where they made a big 'shade'. They pushed their *djuda* into the ground, and trees sprang forth; and they put the *banggada* plants there.

At Daramur (or Darar'woi), inland from Arnhem Bay, the Djanggawul saw a *djanda* goanna in a fresh-water swamp that was covered with wild banana *dara* leaves; this was in Ngeimil territory.

Farther on at Mingu well, also in Ngeimil country, a *djanda* emerged from an open well which contained partially submerged banana foliage: new shoots had come up, completely covering the surface of the water.

Passing on to Djaddjananggu (also Ngeimil), they found a swamp where they saw *warugai* or *marabinj* fish; here too they saw lily roots and foliage, with flowers, and many ducks. Close by was the Maijulwi billabong where the *dadam* lily, with its round edible bulbs, was growing in great profusion. The Djanggawul Brother himself declared part of Maijulwi sacred, so that to-day only two tracks, one at each side, lead down to its banks; women may go down one of these only to get water, and must always return by the same road.

Continuing on, the Djanggawul reached Nganmaruwi, where they erected another large 'shade'. During all the time they had been on the Australian mainland, there is no mention of the Brother's having coitus with his Sisters; but while they were living here, he said to Bildjiwuraroiju, 'I want to copulate with you, Sister.'

But the elder Sister was shy. 'Why?' she asked him.

'I want to put a few people in this place,' the Brother replied.

So he lifted her clitoris, and inserted his long penis. He did the same with Miralaidj. So they continued living there, and he copulated as a husband does with his wives.

After some time, Bildjiwuraroiju became pregnant, and her Brother said to her, 'Sister, may I have a look at you?'

'What for?' she asked.

'Because I want to put some people in this place.'

'All right,' she replied. She opened her legs a little, resting her clitoris on her left leg. The Brother sat before his Sister and placed his index finger into her vagina, up to the first joint.[1] Then he

[1] Tip of finger, *darir*; from tip to first joint, *dariribulungun*.

pulled it away, and at the same time a baby boy came out. Bildjiwuraroiju was careful to open her legs only a little; if she
had spread them out, children would have flowed from her,
for she kept many people stored away in her uterus. These
people (or children) in her uterus were like *rangga* emblems kept
in the conical- shaped *ngainmara* mat, for the latter is a uterus
symbol.

As the baby boy came out, the Brother stood listening to hear
the sound of his cry. As soon as he heard this, he took hold of the
child and put him on to the grass near by. Then he returned to his
Sister, and saw a baby girl coming out. After she had cried, he
lifted her gently and placed her under the *ngainmara* mat, which
served to shelter her from the sun. The crying of a male child is
rirakai'dugung, a forceful 'heavy' sound; while that of a girl is
rirakai njumulgunin, a 'small sound'.

Then another male child issued from the elder Sister, and was
put into the grass by the Brother. She continued giving birth to
children of both sexes; when she had finished she closed her legs,
and the Djanggawul Brother said to her:

'Sister, these little boys we will put in the grass, so that later,
when they grow up, they will have whiskers; those whiskers are
from the grass. We will always do that when we remove male
children. And these little girls we have put under the *ngainmara*
mat, hiding them there. That is because they must be smooth
and soft and have no body hair, and because girls are really
sacred. They must be kept under the *ngainmara*, just as the *rangga*
emblems are kept. We will always do that when we remove female
children.'

The Djanggawul then left this place. The children they had
produced grew up and married, and were the progenitors of the
present Aborigines of those parts. From this time, too, the Two
Sisters remained always pregnant, from having coitus with their
Brother.

They walked along Arnhem Bay until they reached a place
named Gangangu. Here they saw red parakeets, and put a number
of dreamings in the swamp: that is, they hid in its waters some
sacred *rangga* and clan patterns. Then they went on until they came
to Madi or Mugarei (in Ngeimil territory). Here they decided to
make their home, and they put a lot of dreamings. Up to this time
the three of them had slept separately, the Brother calling one of
his Sisters over to his side when he wanted coitus.[1] At Madi, however, they decided to lie together, the Brother himself sleeping

[1] No further mention is made of Bralbral; after his arrival on the mainland he seems
to disappear from the story.

The Djanggawul Myth

between the Two Sisters.[1] But the *djalngin* leech bit them repeatedly, as they waded in the waters of the billabong, and so they continued on to Wulmawi (Walmali or Wulma, meaning a cloud).[2] They lived there for a time, putting many dreamings, as well as a special dilly bag and *djuda* tree *rangga*. The Djanggawul Brother poked the ground with his *mauwulan rangga*, making one hole after another, and calling at each the sacred invocations, so that water came gushing forth.

'This well is for the Ngeimil,' he said, drawing his *mauwulan* from the ground, and letting the water flow.

'This well is for the Riradjingu, this one for the Djapu, this for the Dadawi, this for the Djambatpingu, this for the Djarwak, this for the Marangu, and this for the Marakulu.'[3] He left special dreamings too from Wulmawi to Mudumli, at Arnhem Bay in Ngeimil country. In this way, he put his *mauwulan rangga* into every well in that region.

When they reached Mudumli, the Brother and Sisters saw the *mudum*, a small fresh-water fish. The Brother wanted to sit down here,

[1] In one version, it is said that more children are left at Madi, but not in the same way as described in the main myth. After they had lain together, the Sisters grew large in pregnancy: they went down to Madi pandanus swamp and put into the water their *ngainmara* mat (also said to be a dilly bag), from which came people.

Now these Sisters 'just dropped' (that is, gave birth to) all the people, and their Brother is here said to have been unaware of their actions 'for only women know'. Near the pandanus swamp is a large mud bank, which is the *ngainmara* they used; and since this was made from pandanus leaves, great numbers of these palms grow hereabouts.

This version too declares that it was Madi, and not Nganmaruwi (as in the above text), where the male and female children, after being removed from the *ngainmara* (uterus), were put for the first time in the grass and under the mat respectively. It is said too that the Sisters did not tell their Brother that they did this; 'they themselves only knew about it'. Thus when the Brother came to collect all the *rangga* and put them away in the *ngainmara* mat, he saw that there were many 'people' (also synonymous with the *rangga* emblems). He counted them, before putting them away, and as he did so, he said to himself, 'Ah, this is a man, this is a woman'. There are, therefore, male *rangga* (penis and foreskin *rangga*) and female *rangga* (*gungman*, a woman who has produced a child, and *wirlgul*, adolescent girl, *rangga*). Then the Brother put them back into the *ngainmara*, hiding the women from the men. Those he left behind were called Madjara, which means 'half the group', and those who were left in the mat (bag, or uterus) were Malei'arangu, while all of them together were Madjaramala'bunginbungin. In this way people were left from Blue Mud Bay to Milingimbi, and inland to the sacred billabong of Muruwul (of Wauwalak fame: *vide* R. Berndt, *Kunapipi*, Chapter III).

[2] Also in Ngeimil country, but affiliated with the Riradjingu linguistic group.

[3] *Vide* A. P. Elkin, R. and C. Berndt, *Art in Arnhem Land*, pp. 22–5, for clan and linguistic group terms and organization.

5. *Rangga* emblems displayed on the sacred ground.

6. The Djanggawul Brother and younger Sister at Jelangbara.

7. Sacred *rangga* at Port Bradshaw.

but his Sisters protested that they didn't want to put people in this place.

'May we live here, Sisters?' asked the Brother.

'No,' they replied, 'You may only sing here. We are not going to put our people in this place.'

So they walked along until they reached Dalwirgauwi (in Ngeimil territory). This place takes its name from a water worm or leech (*gauwigauri*), and when they saw it, they sang about it. As they were singing, they looked up and saw a water goanna (*djalga*, 'inside' name; *wonggawa*, 'outside' name) perched on a tree near the billabong. They began to sing about it, and as they did so they killed it, roasting it over the coals. When it was cooked, they cut off its tail and head, and hid the verterbrae under the ground after removing the fat and meat. The hidden verterbrae became a *rangga*.

Leaving this place, they continued on to Woiwiwi (Wuwul or Wulwi), so named because of the tears shed by the Djanggawul; the trio had been walking for a long time, and the sun and the stinging sand had made their eyes smart until the tears ran. Here, too, the Djanggawul Brother persuaded his elder Sister to open her legs so that some children could be left. In much the same way as before, she opened her legs, resting her clitoris on her left leg, while her Brother inserted his index finger into her vagina so that it went up to a point between the first and second joints (this point is called *nabunga*). When he pulled out his finger, children of both sexes came forth; the boys were placed in the grass, and the girls under the cover of the *ngainmara*. These children grew up to become the progenitors of the Aborigines of this region, which was still Ngeimil territory. The Djanggawul also put four *djuda* there, and many dreamings. All these things they left for the children whom they had put there, so that when they grew up they and their descendants could look after them.

At all the places through which they passed, the Djanggawul Brother had had coitus with his Sisters, and the three had dragged their genitalia along the ground, while the Two Sisters continued to be pregnant.

They continued to Ngainmaruwi (or Ngainmaralji), so named because the Sisters had their *ngainmara* mats full of children— that is to say, their uteri were full. Here they saw wild duck tracks, wild peanuts and their foliage, and some *djanda* goanna; but the goanna were frightened on seeing the Djanggawul, and ran away. They made camp here. On one side they placed the *ngainmara* and on the other grass, and in between sat the Brother with his Two Sisters. He lifted Bildjiwuraroiju's clitoris, and again inserted his index finger up to the second joint (*bulungun*); as he pulled it out,

The Djanggawul Myth

both girls and boys came forth one after the other. The girls he put on one side, under the *ngainmara* beside the Sister, and the boys on the other, among the grass, next to himself.

As Djanggawul was occupied in helping to remove the children, he heard a big noise in the distance. This was the sound of new spring water running. He spoke to the two women: 'Sisters, if you will look after our children, I shall go myself to look around and see the water, which should be coming up.'

Leaving his Sisters, he walked along the swamp called Ngudbarei (the 'inside' name of Ngainmaruwi), and he put all the dreamings into its waters for the Ngeimil people. When he had done this he returned to his Sisters, and spoke to the female children. 'I have put our things into that swamp,' he said. 'You must not go there, but when you grow up you can drink water down there away from that sacred place.'

They had all been living there for some time, when one day they saw a *wulma* spreading across the sky. Then the Djanggawul left their children and continued on their journey, walking along till they came to mangroves which belonged to the *jiritja* moiety. As they skirted these, they heard the noise made by a big river running towards the sea from the highlands.

'Look, Brother,' said Bildjiwuraroiju, 'We had better not go through that water (of the *jiritja* moiety); it is running too strongly.' She was referring to the Ngurumuruwoi river, in Dalwongu linguistic group territory.

They listened there, beside the mangroves, and heard the Baijini people talking. These Baijini were making a lot of noise, singing and playing, among their houses.

'Well, Sisters,' said the Djanggawul Brother, 'the Baijini are there. We had better go farther up the river.'

So they continued to Daranga-dabareigarei, which means 'running water from rain', and is in Djambatpingu territory. They went on until they reached Grogula, where the yellow snake had made its camp.

'Look, Sisters,' said the Brother, seeing the yellow snake at this place. 'Look, he blocks our track.' So they went round and past the snake. They had not gone far before they reached Brubari, the place of the Thunder Man, and saw him there; but the Djanggawul Brother said, 'We will leave that *dua* Thunder Man, and go on.' So they went past him too, and continued on their way.

They went on walking until they came to Milguli (named from the *milgu*, mangrove worm). Here two *jiritja wongar* people, belonging to the Kupapingu linguistic group, were collecting these worms.

34

The Djanggawul Myth

'Some one blocks our road again, Sisters,' said the Brother, 'these *jiritja wongar* man and woman.' They listened and heard them chopping wood, removing the worms. So they by-passed the two *wongar*, and continued on until they reached Damijagaiju, in Djambatpingu country, so named because the black *ngadili* cockatoo swooped down and alighted at this place.

When the Djanggawul heard the cry of this bird they were happy, and began to sing. And Bildjiwuraroiju said to her Brother, 'Perhaps we will live at this place. This is our place, and the cockatoo's cry makes us all happy, Brother.' Here too, there were edible *winigamu* roots (called 'jungle tucker'); so they collected these, and sang about them. In the branches of a tree they hung a special dilly bag; and they constructed two large shades, one for the Two Sisters and one for the Brother. The latter, using his *mauwulan rangga* pole, made many wells thereabouts, and he also put many *djuda* trees.

When this was done, the Djanggawul Brother said to his Sisters, 'That is enough for this country. We have to go on now.'

So they went on their way again, but camped only a short distance from Damijagaiju.

It was here that a *wongar* 'enemy' man, or sorcerer, surprised Miralaidj when she was walking by herself. He had come really to kill the Djanggawul Brother, but failing to see him concentrated on the younger Sister. This sorcerer made her unconscious through magic, then inserted *rigal* bones vertically into her body behind the collar-bone, cut her across the cheeks at each side of the mouth and pulled down her jaw. Finally, after copulating with her, he made cuts from the vulva upwards at each side, outlining the mons veneris and pulling the flesh up to bare the pelvic bone. He replaced the flesh, and put her jaw into position, and left her lying on the ground. Some time later she regained consciousness and returned to her Sister and Brother, but the next morning she died. That same day she was buried at Damijagaiju. They erected a post over her grave, and hung upon it two special dilly bags. The elder Sister and Brother were anxious to leave this country; and since they had no intention of returning, they did not place the dead Miralaidj on a platform for decomposition and eventual bone-collection.

Miralaidj, however, miraculously reappears in the story, and accompanies her Brother and Sister on their journey.

They had not gone far when they saw another *wulma* spreading across the sky. They walked towards it, and came to Ngulmamiriju (so named because of the *wulma* or *ngulma*). Here they heard a great many *jiritja wongar*—the fire from Caledon Bay, the 'sugarbag' bee, and so on. The Djanggawul, however, did not stop; they went

35

on, hearing the *jiritja* bee which came from the Kupapingu and Lialaumiri territories. Passing through densely covered bush country, they eventually reached another Ngainmaruwi, in Djambatpingu country, on the western side of Arnhem Bay.[1]

Here the Djanggawul Brother inserted his *mauwulan* into the ground, and withdrawing it made a well. He made a camp, and put many dreamings; and he hung a sacred dilly bag in the branches of a tree. Here, too, he persuaded Bildjiwuraroiju and Miralaidj to give birth to a number of children, in much the same way as before. This time he put his index finger into their vaginae up to the knuckle (*dajalwajun-bulungun* or *deijalwadunju-bulungun*).

Then they left this place, and went on to Balgaimi, where the Djanggawul urinated. They were still dragging their clitorises and penis, and at last they reached Wobilangoii (which is named after Wobilinga Island in the mouth of Port Bradshaw harbour, on the eastern side of Arnhem Land). Here they sang, and put many children. This time the Djanggawul Brother put two fingers into his Sisters' vaginae, the index and middle fingers. He did this each time children were taken out, gradually putting in additional fingers until at last he was inserting his whole hand, and finally his whole arm.

At Wobilangoii the Djambatpingu shark blocked their road to the west, so that they had to make a bark canoe. They hid their sacred emblems within the *ngainmara* mat, and paddled out to sea.

At last they came into Milmindjalboi and drew up their canoe on to the beach. The Djanggawul disembarked, and put a *mauwulan* point into the ground to form a well; but as the water gushed forth the *jiritja* Ancestral Being Banaitja, son of the great Laintjung, came out too. The name of the place is derived from this incident. Since Banaitja was there, the Djanggawul just put some of their dreamings and continued on to Buangura, where they made camp.

Here they heard the *ngadili* black cockatoo crying out. 'Ah,' said the Djanggawul, 'this is the special bird for us. It looks as if we should camp here.' And they began to sing.

Then they heard the *Wurulbaralb* mangrove bird, so they sang about that too. When they had finished, the Djanggawul Brother took his *mauwulan* and poked it into the ground, but it sank right in ('diving right down'). He tried another place, with the same result. Then he walked to the summit of a hill and put it into the ground there; just below the surface it struck black rocks, but a little water gushed forth and ran down the hillside at Bunangura. Then he tried elsewhere, but the *mauwulan* did not go right down.

[1] This place has the same name as the one mentioned before, and means the place of the *ngainmara* mat.

The Djanggawul Myth

He returned to the camp, and put his index, second and third fingers into his Sisters' vaginae, removing a number of children, whom they left at this place.

Continuing their journey they reached Jagajawula, where the Djanggawul Brother inserted his *mauwulan* in a likely spot; but when he withdrew it, no water came out. Farther up he tried again, and again, with the same result. No water appeared.

'I don't know what we are going to do, Brother,' said the Sisters. 'We are growing thirsty, and no water comes out when we withdraw the *mauwulan*.'

They walked along until they came to Dunawi (so named because they put the *mauwulan* in there). Here they saw plenty of *waluwon* mangrove shells, and sang about them. Still they walked on, until they reached Galgidjboi (or Duwalgidjboi), where they saw geese, from which the place takes its name. Here, too, they saw the Thunder Man; but they sang only about the geese. The Djanggawul put two *djuda*, crossed together and standing up.

While they were walking along, the Brother and Sisters tripped over a *wulimu* 'grape' grass creeper, which became tangled about their feet. As they fell, the Brother accidentally pushed his *mauwulan* pole into the mud; and straight away a big sea came up and flooded this part of the country.

The Djanggawul talked together about this, 'What shall we do? We'd better go back the way we came, for we don't want to go through all this mud.' They turned back, and went along the river bank until they reached Daraweimirangu, so named because the Brother and Sisters took a fire-stick and tried to twirl it to make fire; but they did not succeed.

They left this place, then, and walked along the cliffs until they reached a river. Here the tide was very strong and the river was deep, because of the water which had risen when the Brother accidentally pushed in his *mauwulan*. They tried to cross, but when they could not do so they continued along the bank until they came to Djulngeijari. There they made posts and rails to form a large fish catchment; they saw many varieties of fish and crab, including the *bigun* grass crab, and they sang about these.

Near this place they were able to cross the river. They had not gone far, when they looked up and saw a spreading *wulma* rising from the mainland opposite Elcho Island, in Djambadpingu country. Going towards this, they eventually reached Maidjalngari, where they sang about some wild ducks they saw flying. Bildji-wuraroiju looked up and saw the *ngadili* bird, and sang about that too.

It was here that they made a big camp; and the Djanggawul

37

The Djanggawul Myth

Brother examined the clitorises of his Sisters, wanting to shorten them. But they would not allow him to do so. 'No,' they said, 'we will go farther on, for we must first fill up this country with people. It is a bit cold here, too; it is better that we should have warm country where we cut our long clitorises.' So they left Maidjalngari behind them and came to Gulibangaru, also in Djambatpingu country. There they saw and sang about the *gabila* mangrove 'nail' fish, from which the place takes its name.

They waded in the water among the mangrove roots, trying to catch these fish by blocking channels with their hands. The 'nails' of the fish pierced the Sisters' hands and opened them (*gonglaidjung*)[1] so that the blood ran. So they sang about the fish, and the running blood.

They left this place, and came to Mialbungara ('inside' name, Marabai), where they put a number of sacred dilly bags: Marabai is one of the big sacred places of this region.[2]

'Look, Brother,' said the Sisters, 'I think we can leave these dilly bags in this shade; and we can put all the dreamings in here, because it is a big country.'

'Yes,' the Brother replied. 'I am pleased to hear that.'

So they hung up the dilly bags, first one belonging to the Riradjingu, then the Dadawi one in the middle, and the Djambatpingu one at the end. Then they camped in their sacred shade, and the Djanggawul Brother put his hand, up to a point (termed *malnguraga*) between the knuckles and the wrist, into the elder Sister's vagina. He withdrew a great number of children. A lot of people came out, men, women and children, and they were all crying; there were big groups of them. Then the Djanggawul made three shades, one for each of the three linguistic groups mentioned above, and an additional one for the Djarlwak. While they were living there, the elder Sister said one day to the younger, 'We had better put our dilly bags in this shade, and leave them here for a while.'

'What are we going to do?' asked the other. 'If we put them here, what then are we going to do?'

'Well,' replied the elder Sister, 'we can look around for mangrove shells.'

So they both left their camp to collect *mingaul* and *waluwon* shells.

While they were away, the Djanggawul Brother and his companions, men who had come out of the Sisters, but called the

---

[1] Some versions say that the fish 'cut' the Sisters' hands, dividing the fingers and thumbs, whereas before the fingers of each hand had been joined together.

[2] The Two Sisters took from Madi to Marabai one woman, whose name is unknown Between Madi and Marabai are many wells, made by the *mauwulan* of the Djanggawul.

The Djanggawul Myth

Djanggawul 'brother' and 'sisters', were hiding in their big shade.[1] In the myth, these are called the Djanggawul Brothers. The women who came out of the Sisters are assumed to have gone out foraging for food in another direction.

Meantime, the Two Sisters had collected a lot of shells. When they waded back to dry land, they heard the whistle of the *djunmal* bird (a black, green and yellow mangrove bird), warning them that something was wrong. At once they knew that something had happened to their dilly bags, which contained the sacred *rangga*.[2]

'You know that *djunmal*, Sister,' the younger Sister asked. 'What is it crying for?'

'That bird cries to let us know,' answered the other. 'Perhaps something has happened to our sacred dilly bags. Maybe the fire has burnt them. We had better go back and look.'

They left what they were doing, and ran back towards their shade. The dilly bags were gone, and on the ground about the shade were the tracks of the men who had stolen them.

[1] That is, the Djanggawul Brother had a shade or hut, similar to that used on the *dua nara* ground, although he himself ' "made " no dreaming'. All 'the beginning' belonged to the women, the Two Sisters, and all the dreamings really belonged to them. The Djanggawul Brother and his 'brothers' sat down at their shade and made fire ready to cook their food, for at that time it was the men's duty to collect all the food, and to prepare it for the women as well as for themselves.

In another version, we are told that the men and the Brother just sat there; for the Two Sisters and their 'sisters' (that is, women from their uteri) were holding a *mareiin* sacred *nara* ceremony, which was their 'own business', to which the men could not come. The women, however, were fairly close to the men, for it is said that the men 'came over by themselves on top of the women's tracks', and entered their separate shade.

In their own sacred shade the women made fire, *rindjarei*, the sacred fire dreaming, for fire comes from the redness of the women's vaginas. The twirling firestick in its groove is symbolic of coitus, because a man is warmed by lying between a woman's legs just as he is by a fire, since a woman's vulva is always 'hot'.

After their ceremony the women hung their fighting dilly bags, decorated with tasselled pendants of red parakeet feathers, on the limb of a tree, and went out to collect shell-fish. (Here the main text takes up the story.)

[2] The men sat listening in their shade; and when they heard no noise, no singing or dancing, they said to one another, 'All right. It is no good that we are men. It is no good that women should have that sacred bag and all the dreamings, and we should have nothing. We'll take over from those women.' They all agreed, 'Yes.'

So they came up to the women's sacred shade and went inside; and there they found all the dreamings, all the *rangga* and clan patterns. They began to dance and sing the sacred songs which they had learnt by listening to the women, and which are still sung to-day in the *dua nara*. As they sang, they looked in the direction the women had taken, but saw no sign of them. Then they took down the sacred dilly bag of the women and danced with it.

The Djanggawul Myth

'Sister, look!' called the younger Sister. 'What are we going to do now? Where are our dilly bags?'

'We had better go down and ask the men,' said the other, 'it's nothing to do with them.'

They hurried off, down towards the men. As they came running, the Djanggawul Brother and his companions looked up from their shade and saw them.

'What shall we do?' thought the Brother. He picked up his *jugulung* singing sticks, and began to beat rhythmically upon them, while they all sang.

As soon as the Sisters heard the beat of the singing sticks, and the sound of the men's singing, they fell down and began to crawl along the ground.[1] They were too 'frightened' to go near that dreaming place, the shade of the Djanggawul Brother. They were fearful not of the men, but of the power of the sacred songs. The men had taken from them not only these songs, and the emblems, but also the power to perform sacred ritual, a power which had formerly belonged only to the Sisters. They had carried the emblems and dreamings in their *ngainmara*, which were really their uteri; and the men had had nothing.

The Two Sisters got up from the ground, and the younger one said to the elder, 'What are we going to do? All our dilly bags are gone, all the emblems, all our power for sacred ritual!'

But the other replied, 'I think we can leave that. Men can do it now, they can look after it. We can spend our time collecting bush foods for them, for it is not right that they should get that food as they have been doing. We know everything. We have really

---

[1] In another version it is said that as the Two Sisters saw the men in the shade, and heard the clapping of their sticks with the rhythmic rise and fall of the song, they stopped running and said, 'They take place for us (that is, take our part). Shall we leave them alone?' asked the younger Sister. 'We'll have to take back that bag, because it does not belong to them.'

'If we do that, we'll have to go inside the shade,' replied the elder Sister. 'All right, we'll do that,' said the other.

They began to run again, towards the shade. But the men made a big noise, with their dancing and singing. This halted the Sisters. They bowed their heads and said to the men, 'Forgive us. Our "fathers" can now look after all those dreamings, perhaps better than we can.' (The women substitute the word 'Fathers' for 'Brothers'; it is used here as a term of respect.)

Then the Sisters turned back from their shade and hid in the bush, 'for it is not right that women should go towards the men's sacred place'. This is the beginning of the men's sacred ritual. 'Women should really be the Ceremonial Leaders, for everything belonged to them; but the men stole it all. But really we still know that they are the real leaders.'

It was the men, however, who introduced the drawing of sacred designs.

The Djanggawul Myth

lost nothing, for we remember it all, and we can let them have that small part. For aren't we still sacred, even if we have lost the bags? Haven't we still our uteri?' And the younger Sister agreed with her.

In this way, the Two Sisters left all their dreamings at that place. They put a lot of people there too, while the Djanggawul Brother and his companions sang songs and performed ritual of the *dua nara* ceremonies. The Sisters also made a very sacred well, so sacred that none but those with white hair may go near it. This is the sacred well of Marabai.

After a time, they and their Brother continued on their way[1] and eventually reached Baldangaru, named from the white liquid which poured from the vaginae of the Sisters. This liquid came from them because they had been putting out too many children in that country. They lived for a while at Baldangaru. One day they looked back towards the east, the direction from which they had come, and saw the sun's disc rising and its rays lighting up the country; and so they sang about it.

While they were there, the Djanggawul Brother was sitting with his Sisters, whose clitorises were resting on their legs. He looked at Miralaidj and saw her vulva, for her legs were slightly apart. He began to put his penis out, and gradually it became erect (*laldjunba*) like a sacred emblem pole; he bent forward and took hold of his Sister making ready to insert his penis. But the elder Sister spoke to him. 'No,' she said, 'you are not to do it yet, she is far too young.' (This contradicts previous statements that the Brother had been engaging in coitus with both his Sisters.) 'This is cold country, and you can't put it up properly (that is, erect penis); the hot country is much better. If you wait till we are farther up in the hot country, the skin will be different.' So instead of copulating, they put many dreamings there.

They walked further on to Djauwadad, so named because the Djanggawul slipped a little as they walked along. They were still dragging their elongated genitalia. At last they came through plain country to Dambala(nguru), the 'inside' name, or Greidjaru, the 'outside' name, meaning 'the cutting place of the clitorises and penis.'

Here they made a large shade, and the Djanggawul Brother spoke to the others. 'Sisters, I want to look at you both now, and see what you're like. This is a good place, and I'm going to cut you both.' First he lifted the clitoris of the elder Sister and cut it, leaving only a small clitoris which reached to her thigh. Then he turned to the younger Sister, and cut off her clitoris in the same way.

---

[1] In one version it is said that they went to Muruwul, the sacred waterhole where the Julunggul Snake lives, and where the Wauwalak Sisters were swallowed; but this is not confirmed. *Vide Kunapipi*, Chapter III.

41

The Djanggawul Myth

'Ah,' said the Brother, 'Now you look more like proper women and it is easier for me to see the slit of your vulvae. Let me try them out.' First he copulated with the younger Sister. 'That feels nice,' he said. Then, turning to the elder Sister, he copulated with her too. 'That's very enjoyable,' he told her. 'I can feel the short end of the clitoris touching my penis, as I couldn't before.' The long clitorises the Brother had cut off were like *rangga* poles. He placed these in the sacred shade so that they could always be there for the people to use in generations to come. It is also said that from the cut clitorises, the Djanggawul made a special feathered string used to-day to decorate sacred *rangga*. When this was finished they hung it from the limb of a tree near the shade.

'Sisters,' said the Brother, 'I have made your clitorises shorter. We shall leave a great number of people here, for now that you have short clitorises we can make more people come out from you.'

(It is said in the myth that this is the first time Miralaidj brings people from her uterus; but previous references contradict this.)

The younger Sister opened her legs and a few people came out of her. There were not many, because she was said to be still small.

The elder Sister helped her, by letting out a few from her own uterus. The Djanggawul Brother himself had not yet cut his own elongated penis; he carried it now by swinging it over his shoulder, and wrapping it around his neck.

Leaving Dambala(nguru) the Djanggawul walked along until they heard the sound of running water. Coming nearer, they traced the sound to the waters of Waruwi, as they ran down towards the sea. Waruwi river belongs to the Kupapingu, Waramiri and Ritarngu linguistic groups of the *jiritja* moiety.

'Look,' said the Brother and Sisters, 'the *jiritja* waters block us. We shall walk fast and pass them.'

When they had gone past Waruwi, they heard the sound of the *jiritja* honey bee.

'Ah,' said the Sisters, 'another *jiritja* blocks us! What are we going to do now?' Then the Djanggawul Brother replied, 'I think we will just go past, and not bother about that.'

The continued walking till they heard a wild *boda* duck, who was dancing and singing there. The three Djanggawul began to sing too, and called the name of that place Bodangura (from the duck); this is in Djambatpingu territory.

At last they reached Manbui, which was named after the younger Sister. The Djanggawul stood considering his two Sisters, looking at their clitorises, which now extended to their thighs. 'I must cut them more,' he said. So he cut their clitorises, until each Sister had only a small piece left in her vulva, no longer than women have

42

The Djanggawul Myth

to-day. From the ends that were cut off they made feathered string, and hung it in a sacred shade.

The Djanggawul Brother opened Miralaidj's legs a little, and kneeling before her inserted his penis into her up to its first notch or 'ring' (see Fig. 1). Then he ejaculated, and as he withdrew his penis, people too emerged from the uterus. This was just like the Brother's poking his *mauwulan* into the ground, so that water gushed forth. However, not enough people came from her, so Bildjiwuraroiju helped her. Miralaidj was not yet big enough in the belly, and had insufficient children inside her to fulfil the needs of this country. Nevertheless, most of the people came from her, and only a small proportion from the elder Sister.

At last the Djanggawul reached Gwroidjura (meaning 'to hold and copulate with her'); the Brother grabbed his elder Sister and opened her legs, holding her as he inserted his penis so that half of it went into her vagina. Then he ejaculated, and as he withdrew it people came flowing out.

They continued on until they reached Walinjina, where the Djanggawul Brother poked his *mauwulan* into the ground making several wells. To-day, there are three ordinary waterholes, and four tabu-ed ones.

The three Djanggawul walked towards them and sat down, beginning to dig for the lily worm (*wida* or *gwoiida*), and singing about it.

Then they went on until they reached Maiilwi, where they heard the big *dua* flying fox. The Brother turned to his Sisters, 'You two Sisters, you can wait for me,' he said. 'I am going down to see what's there.' He walked away from them, to a place where he saw all these flying foxes hanging in a special tree. Then he returned to the Sisters. 'I saw a lot of flying foxes there, Sisters,' he said. 'What shall we do, leave them?'

'Let us just sing about them,' replied the Sisters.

But the Brother asked, 'Do you think we can get them all, kill them?'

'No,' insisted the elder Sister, 'we don't want to get them.' She turned to Miralaidj. 'What do you think, young Sister?'

'No,' agreed Miralaidj. 'We will leave them, because they are our own special flying fox.'

'All right,' answered their Brother, 'we shall leave this place.'

They went on, and as they approached Dambojowoi they heard the sound of water (from which the place takes its name). When they reached there they saw Buralindjingu, a very old dreaming man of the Maidjara linguistic group. He was sitting down meditating, but looked up and turned round when he heard the footsteps of the Djanggawul. 'Well, you three,' he said, 'you two women

The Djanggawul Myth

and one man, you'll have to drink at that outside waterhole, and not at this special water where I am; for it is sacred.' Saying this, Buralindjingu took up his *jugulung* singing-sticks, and began to sing. The song and the rhythm were quite different from those used by the Djanggawul: but Buralindjingu was not pleased with it. Turning again to the Brother, he said, 'I'm not much good at singing, *gudara* (son's son). You had better take the singing-sticks.'

So the Djanggawul Brother took the singing-sticks and he and his Sisters began to sing about their journey by canoe from Bralgu, their landing at Jelangbara, and their subsequent adventures right up to their meeting with Buralindjingu. They went on singing their 'travelling story' all night, until the dawn came; and Buralindjingu listened with pleasure to their tale.

The Djanggawul Brother sang also for those two *dalibingu* or *galibingu* (young novices for circumcision, but in this case the Two Sisters). They painted the Two Sisters with sacred clan designs, and smeared red ochre over their bodies; they were *galibingu*, like novices who have their foreskins cut, for they had had their clitorises shortened. So the singing continued until the sun was in the middle of the sky. Then Buralindjingu gave cycad palm nut 'bread' to the Djanggawul, and they ate it sacramentally before continuing their journey.

At last they came to Galiwinggo Island (Elcho Island), where the Sisters produced more people. Camping at Ba'rarabu, the Brother put a number of dreamings, which belong to different *dua* groups.

At Nguruninana (or Wuruninana), near where the Elcho Island mission garden is to-day, they tried to make their home. But *jiritja* spring waters came bubbling up and forced them to leave this place, although the Djanggawul had left *dua* drawings and dreamings there.[1] The red ochre dreaming was the most important: the Djanggawul had brought this from Bralgu, and were forced to leave some at that spring. They then went farther along the Island

---

[1] It is said that the spring waters, which were on *dua* territory, moved to the *jiritja* side and gave the Djanggawul no alternative but to leave.

This *jiritja* water had travelled from the southern shores of Blue Mud Bay to Duwalaba at Arnhem Bay, and then went underground, until at Nguruninana it came gushing out into the Djanggawul's camp. When it reached the Djanggawul, the *jiritja* water said, 'Give me more room! The *jiritja* dreaming told me to come up to you,' (that is, Laintjung had told it to come).

But the Djanggawul replied, 'We'll just put our dreaming in here for the *dua* side, and then we'll go.'

This *jiritja* water dreaming also went through from Grindall Bay north of Blue Mud Bay and northwards through the Bush; it just 'looked' at the second big river (unnamed) in western Arnhem Bay, and then continued to Elcho where the Djanggawul met it. From there it went down a creek to Howard Island and on to Milingimbi, where it came out at Macassar Well.

The Djanggawul Myth

and left deposits of red ochre[1] at Warnggawoi and Gulmanbi spring.

Before the Djanggawul left Nguruninana, two novices were circumcised, a *mora* and a *gurlmu*. These two boys[2] were sitting in a big shade undergoing the circumcisional rites. When cut in the camp they were called *gamajadi*, and then, on being taken out to their seclusion shade, they were called *galibingu*. This was the first time circumcision had been carried out in that region. Afterwards it became a general practice, because the Djanggawul had 'made it a big dreaming.'[3] But the Djanggawul Brother himself was never 'cut' or circumcised in this way: he only shortened his penis. He is said to have circumcised the young boys 'because he didn't want the youths' penes to grow long like his'. He made this law for the new generation only, 'a new law for new people.' And he spoke to them, saying, 'It doesn't matter for myself, but it must be a new law for all my new people, all those I have put in this country.'[4]

[1] This red ochre is called *murunggun*, from which the local linguistic group takes its name. The Djanggawul are said to have spoken here: 'We leave this red ochre, so that all the people may get it from us.' Red ochre is symbolic of the afterbirth blood shed by the Two Sisters, or is a 'condensation' of the sun's redness, as symbolized in the red chest feathers of the *lindaridj* parakeets. Today red ochre from Elcho Island is traded far inland, and all along the coast.

[2] Also termed *muraloi* or *mulaloi*. The old term used to describe this stage was *galibingu* or *galinguru*: the novices are called by this term, or *galamunja* (referring to their penes), while undergoing the rites, and cannot use their real names. The real names of these two were, however, Nganangu and Bralbral, both of the *dua* moiety. The latter is said not to be the same as the Bralbral who accompanied the Djanggawul from Bralgu. These two novices went back and forth from the general camp to their sacred shade. (Among the north-eastern Arnhem Landers there is not the strict seclusion of circumcision novices found in most other parts of Australia.)

[3] In another version it is said that a son of the Djanggawul, a *marlgu* flying fox, was circumcised at Blue Mud Bay; his foreskin was kept and waxed into a feathered string pendant attached to a sacred dilly bag, as is the practice to-day. The reason given for the circumcision is that the Djanggawul Brother discovered that his children (those removed from the Two Sisters) were sleeping together, and indulging in incestuous relations with one another (as the Djanggawul themselves were in the habit of doing). At first he did not realize what they were doing, but one day he found them copulating together. Then he 'changed his mind' and cut (circumcised) the penes of the young boys (his sons), 'because they had slept with their sisters: that was their punishment'.

[4] Informants remark, 'He had been going on in the old way until that time, just like those people at Goulburn Islands, and the Gunwinggu, and others of western Arnhem Land. All those people haven't adopted the new law. If the Djanggawul Brother put it at those places, the people there have missed the law—but we, the north-eastern and north-central people, did not miss his law.'

Another version states that the Djanggawul started circumcision 'because he was pushed out by new people' (in the dreaming concept of *jiritia*, spring water).

45

The Djanggawul Myth

Before they left Nguruninana, the Djanggawul Brother awakened one early morning to see the sun rising.[1] He called to his Sisters; they all sat up, feeling its warmth. The sun's heat caressed his shoulders, and turning around the Brother saw it rising from Djalwalauwa,[2] or as it is also called, Djanggawul, on the Wessel Islands. As he looked, he sang. The Djanggawul then went over to the Wessels, and at Jalarula are the Brother's knee marks.[3]

When the *jiritja* spring water caused the Djanggawul to move, they crossed the strait to the top of Howard Island, and looked around for a place in which to build their camp.

Then they went on to Dariwi, where the *jalbin* wild honey was; but they did not stop here, for the Djanggawul said, 'Something blocks our way.' They walked along to Galguwiri, where they made camp, erecting a large shade; and the Brother, using his *mauwlan*, made a number of special wells. They also went to the top of Galguwiri, where the Brother made another well, and put his hand, up to the wrist, into the vagina of the young Sister. When he with-

---

[1] It is said in this version that this was the first time the sun rose. However, there are many references to the sun before this, and the reader must bear in mind the connexion between the sun and the Djanggawul.

[2] The place of the Djanggawul is the sun's place. As the Djanggawul looked to the east, in the direction of the rising sun, they thought of their home at Bralgu.

At Djalwalauwa the sun left its mark on the ground; this place is also said to be the 'home' of the red *lindaridj* parakeet, which belonged to the two 'daughters of the Sun'.

Walu, the Sun, had two daughters named Barinangu (counterparts of the Djanggawul Sisters). Originally they accompanied their Mother across the sky so that there were three suns; but their Mother said to them, 'You will have to go back to the Spirit Country of Bralgu, because it's no good for us all to go this way; it would be too hot for the people.' So they went back to Bralgu, and later came with the Djanggawul Brother to the Australian mainland.

But another inconsistency appears. The Mother speaks as if there were people already on the mainland, before the visit of her two daughters. One version tells that while the Djanggawul Brother and his Two Sisters were on Elcho Island there were three suns in the sky (that is, the Mother Sun and her two daughters), and that is why the Djanggawul got very hot; and it was then that the Mother Sun sent her two daughters to Bralgu, so that only one sun remained.

According to Warner (*op. cit.*, p. 537) the Sun woman is the wife of the Moon.

A 'play' or secular story (*wagal dau*) of north-central and north-eastern Arnhem Land declares that the Sun woman, who has one daughter, carries with her across the sky the sacred *mauwulan* and *ganinjari* sticks, and feathered string from the *lindaridj* parakeet (who calls her 'mother').

[3] There is little evidence relating to the Djanggawuls' visit to the Wessel Islands. Several versions insist that they did not go there, and that the places there are associated with them 'only through the song side'. The various groups on the Wessels always came to the mainland to celebrate the *dua nara* Djanggawul rituals.

46

drew it he listened, and heard the children coming out. The little boys came first, and these he threw into the grass. Then he listened again, and heard a little girl crying; he pulled her out, and placed her under the *ngainmara*. Other girls, too, came out from the young Sister.

When the Djanggawul Brother placed his hand into his Sisters, he used his right hand and arm (*dunabangu*) for Miralaidj, and his left hand and arm (*wilgurdei* or *djalbudei*) for Bildjiwuraroiju.

The three walked on until they came to Barangal (where the yellow snake was), and there they heard the *dalba* snake. 'Something blocks us here,' the Two Sisters said to their Brother. 'We will go past.'

They went on to Ngaladjalg (or Ngaladjeigan-djeiginli) which is on an open bay east of Milingimbi, in country of the 'light' Djambatpingu language group. Finally they reached Djiriliwuramaiju (or Djiriliwiriju), known by the 'inside' names of Maluwa or Magulmaguli. There they made a big shade, and sat down to dig for *ragai* roots.

While the Two Sisters were sitting in the waters of the billabong collecting these roots, their legs were apart and the water entered their vaginae. With the water came leeches. As soon as this happened the Sisters got up, and felt the leeches and the water inside their uteri. While they stood with their legs apart, out rushed the water, the leeches, and some children. The water and leeches had made them too heavy, and that is why the people came out too. So a great number of people were put here; and at the same time, the Djanggawul sang.

Coming on to Jalwuljalwul they made camp, the Two Sisters constructing their shade at one place and the Brother making his a little distance away. Later on he came down to where his Sisters were, and saw a child issuing from Miralaidj. He cut its umbilical cord, saying, 'This is my boy; he must go into the grass.' And he tossed it among the coarse undergrowth. Every day he visited the Sisters, and watched them bringing forth children. Each time a boy came out he put it into the grass; but the girls he deposited carefully in a clean soft place, hiding them under the *ngainmara*.

At every place they went to, the Djanggawul Sisters brought out children who grew to adulthood; and in this way the Djanggawul Brother was able to name all the various linguistic groups and clans.[1]

[1] There are some inconsistencies in respect of this. On the one hand, according to the mythological text, all the clans and linguistic groups had a common origin, all having the Djanggawul for their parents. On the other hand, it is said that these clans and linguistic groups were of the *dua* moiety, while other Ancestral Beings, such as Laintjung and Banaitja, originated the *jiritja* moiety linguistic groups and clans.

Only the *dua* clans and groups, however, are mentioned; and in order to propagate,

The Djanggawul Myth

Leaving Jalwuljalwul[1] the Djanggawul continued on their way to Balmargi, in the country of the Wulagi people, on the mainland opposite Milingimbi. Here they put many dreamings and a number of people; and they left in the mangroves the *lindaridj* feathered strings, which are now parakeets. The Brother shortened his long penis, and with the piece that was cut off he made a *rangga* emblem.

This completes the myth in so far as the Yirrkalla people are concerned.[2]

When the Djanggawul Beings first landed at Jelangbara they spoke Riradjingu; then, when they went to a Karlpu place, they spoke Karlpu; at Bulmawi they spoke Djarwak; when they reached the eastern shores of Arnhem Bay they spoke Ngeimil, then, as they journeyed on, Dadawi, until they reached the western side of the Bay when they spoke Djambatpingu, as they did also at Elcho Island. At Djiriliwuramaiju they spoke Guruguru. That is, they usually spoke in the dialect of the linguistic groups through whose country they passed, and it is implied that they left these dialects for the people who were removed from the Sisters' uteri.

the original members of these (the children of the Djanggawul) would of necessity be obliged to carry out incestuous relations. Earlier we read (that is, Footnote 3, p. 45) that the Djanggawul Brother punished his son (or sons), by circumcising them, because they slept with their sisters. Aborigines rationalize by saying that although the Djanggawul children were the first human beings to be placed on the mainland, and from them the *dua* clans and groups were formed, other *jiritja* people were not long in coming, and were placed there by the *jiritja* Ancestral Beings. Some informants, however, prefer the theory that all people, both *dua* and *jiritja*, sprang from a common source, the uteri of the Two Sisters.

[1] This marks the termination of the north-eastern and north-central cultural bloc.

[2] Other versions take the myth farther into western Arnhem Land, and as far as the Goulburn Islands. It is said that at the latter place the Djanggawul gave birth to more people, and that there attempted to circumcise two novices. They made a big shade and danced, as at Elcho Island, but after being circumcised the two youths died. Then the Brother said 'Leave them. If you cut those of the new generation here, they will die.' That is why these people do not practise the rite of circumcision.

Chapter Three

THE CONTENT OF THE MYTH

THIS myth is further extended and elaborated on its arrival in the Milingimbi region; but since we are considering only the Yirrkalla version, the former will be retained for later study.

Professor Lloyd Warner's version of the Djanggawul myth[1] does not conform either to the Yirrkalla or to the Milingimbi version, as recorded in song and in linguistic text from a wide range of informants. It does, however, more closely approximate the latter, for there, as in Warner's version, only Two Sisters are mentioned and not the Djanggawul Brother. Apparently most of the beginning of the Djanggawul myth was unknown to Warner's informants, for their important journey from Bralgu and landing at Port Bradshaw are omitted altogether.

However, we shall treat first the points which bear some similarity to those mentioned in Warner's version. It is stated that 'our grandfathers came out from the wombs of these women',[2] by 'grandfathers' the natives meaning their original ancestors: but the significance of this remark is not noticed, and the theme of perpetual pregnancy is not treated. The section which relates how the Djanggawul Sisters lost their sacred emblems agrees in most major points, and in this way Warner's version helps to stress the important place held originally by the women, that is, their possession of all the sacred objects and of the power to perform all sacred ritual. This aspect is of fundamental importance when we consider the basic theme of the Djanggawul myth.

[1] L. Warner, *A Black Civilization*, pp. 336–40.
[2] L. Warner, *op. cit.*, p. 337

The Content of the Myth

The statement that the Two Sisters 'hit themselves on each buttock so they could make plenty of people and their vaginae would grow larger'[1] is quite different from what was mentioned in the Yirrkalla version. The point that their vaginae were small, and not large enough for sexual intercourse, is not found in the above myth. Warner mentions[2] that before their coming there was no land at all, and that they were responsible for making all the islands on the northern coast of Arnhem Land. This again does not conform. Nor does the section relating the incestuous 'rape' of the younger Djanggawul Sister; during the writer's recent work at Milingimbi, Aboriginal informants knew nothing of this. In the Milingimbi version, however, a certain amount of attention is paid to the stone *rangga* which was lodged in the vagina of the younger Sister.[3]

A most important point does appear in Warner's version, where he states that the Two Sisters, when they first came, carried the sun. 'They were the leaders of the sun'; it was just as though it belonged to them. 'In the beginning we had the sun, the water and those Two Women—nothing more.' The sun was first.[4] A close association is inferred here between the Djanggawul Sisters and the Sun (or suns)[5]; and this becomes clearer in the Milingimbi version which we shall present later. The fact that the two daughters of the Sun Woman may be the Two Djanggawul Sisters is further borne out by the sun's association with the red breast feathers of the *lindaridj* parakeets in which is symbolized the redness of the sun. Moreover, the sun's full disc at midday is termed *dagu, ganbai*, or *dala*, vagina or vulva, and it is from the vulvae of the Sisters that the sun's rays come (*vide* Milingimbi version of the Djanggawul).

The dominating feature of the Yirrkalla myth is fertility, the fact that the Djanggawul were responsible for producing the original ancestors of the present Aboriginal people of Arnhem Land. This was their main function; but in treating it the myth offers a great deal of symbolism, in the way of mats, baskets and *rangga* poles, and emblems of male and female organs of generation. All the objects which the Djanggawul brought with them from Bralgu possessed life-giving qualities: the *ngainmara*, the eternally full uterus from which the people came; the *mauwulan*, which when plunged into the ground caused water to flow; and the *djuda* poles, from which grew flourishing trees. Associated with all these *dua* moiety emblems were strings of *lindaridj* breast feathers, symbolizing

[1] L. Warner, *op. cit.*, p. 337.
[2] L. Warner, *op. cit.*, pp. 336, 338 and 340.
[3] L. Warner, *op. cit.*, p. 339.
[4] L. Warner, *op. cit.*, p. 340.
[5] *Vide* Footnote 2, p. 46; see also L. Warner, *op cit.*, p. 537.

the warmth of the sun, which made it possible for all things to live and grow.

Apart from the significance of the myth as a whole, there are several interesting features. Throughout this version the incestuous relations of the Djanggawul Brother with his Sisters are acknowledged, and repeatedly mentioned. It is said that when the Djanggawul roamed Arnhem Land, there was no marriage system. The Djanggawul themselves possessed no moieties; it was only later, when their adventures became a matter of mythology, that they were classified as belonging to the *dua* moiety. Informants point out that the Djanggawul made their own laws, and are acknowledged as law-givers. It was through their incestuous intercourse that the Two Sisters were able to produce human beings, to populate the country through which they passed. Even at that early period, the importance of sexual intercourse in relation to pregnancy must have been realized, for the part the male plays in this activity is heavily stressed: the emphasis is such that it cannot be a mere projection of present-day knowledge.

Later in their travels, however, when the Djanggawul arrived at Blue Mud Bay and also at Elcho Island,[1] the Brother seems to have altered his attitude towards incest, and to have 'punished' his sons, by circumcision, for having coitus with their sisters.

It was, nevertheless, the Djanggawul themselves, answerable to no one, who determined their own law, and continued to cohabit together. The present marriage rules of local Aborigines are said to have been instituted by the Djanggawul; apart from sacred ritual, they created and gave to their people the complete structure of their social organization, with its associated culture. Some Aborigines, however, while acknowledging the primary importance of the Djanggawul, hold that other Ancestral Beings and Spirits were responsible for instituting certain features. Other religious cults have indeed come into being, among them the important Laintjung-Banaitja constellation. The Djanggawul, however, are considered responsible for establishing the fundamental pattern of this Aboriginal society.

To-day, when that society and culture are taken for granted by its members, the major importance of the Djanggawul lies in their sacred ritual and in their doctrine, which, regarded superficially, comprises merely the outline of their travels around the Arnhem Land coast. Underlying that story, however, is a vast wealth of symbolism and allusion, which will become more apparent after we have presented the great song cycle. It is this symbolism which is expressed in sacred ritual to-day, finding expression in song and

[1] *Vide* Footnote 3, p. 45.

The Content of the Myth

dance, and in the *rangga* emblems and sacred baskets. The *rangga* poles, although modern in manufacture and decoration, are still the 'same' as those used by the Djanggawul, and contain the very spirit that possessed them in that mythological time: they retain the sacred aura of the Djanggawul.

There is no explanation in the myth for the elongated penis and clitorises of the Djanggawul,[1] except that this special feature makes them unique among Ancestral Beings and Spirits of this area. When they had been cut, the severed fragments were treated as *rangga*, or as feathered pendant strings. Some informants insist that the original *rangga* mentioned in the myth were actually the genitalia of the Djanggawul.

Another interesting point raised in the myth is that the Sisters, when having their clitorises cut by their Brother,[2] were treated as circumcisional novices. Immediately afterwards followed the circumcision ceremony at Elcho Island, said to be instituted by the Djanggawul Brother himself. To-day, however, no circumcision ceremony is associated with the *dua nara* rituals; this feature is relegated to the *djunggawon* and *mandiela*, sponsored by the Wauwalak mythology.[3] The *dua nara* is not age-grading as the myth suggests; but since these rituals appear to be more purely indigenous than, for example, the Wauwalak ceremonies, it is possible that they were originally designed for this purpose. In the course of time the initiatory elements have disappeared from the ritual, but remain in the myth; and to-day the ceremony is revelatory in function.

Some inconsistencies appear in the myth, but this is not unusual in mythology which has been handed down through the generations by word of mouth. It is something which must be considered: we must allow for differences in theme, for a variety of versions, and for a considerable range in interpretation. Mythology presented verbally in story or song, no matter how conventional the structure of the society, shows a certain amount of flexibility, since the only means of presenting, and thus of preserving it, must be the individual members of that society. The narrator of a story may stress some particular aspect, elaborating it perhaps to the detriment of others. This process, gradual as it is, has cumulative effects; when, as apparently here, it has been continuing for centuries, we may suppose that the myth, for example the Djanggawul, has altered considerably from its original form. This must be taken into account in our analysis of the myth, and in our interpretation of its meaning.

The fact that the Aborigines pay so much attention to tradition

[1] *Vide* R. Berndt, *Kunapipi*, Chapters I *c* and IV.
[2] The symbolic significance of these has been treated in the Song Cycle.
[3] *Vide* R. Berndt, *op. cit.*, Chapters I *c* and IV.

The Content of the Myth

may serve to minimize the number and extent of such alterations and deviation, as found in their mythology. On the other hand, especially on the north-eastern coast of Arnhem Land, these people have been subjected in varying degrees to the infiltration of new ideas.[1] Their society, or for that matter their culture, has not remained static through the ages, while they were experiencing various forms of alien contact. Without elaborating on the subject here, however, it seems safe to say that, whatever the extent of past alien contact in Arnhem Land, the majority of these Aborigines appear to have retained, as far as we can tell, the fundamental elements of their traditional outlook. Even if the Djanggawul saga has been considerably altered from its original, we have now no means of discovering what that original was like. We must, then, be satisfied with what knowledgeable Aborigines tell us to-day, learning their interpretations, and the apparent intent of contemporary *nara* rituals.

The original theme of the Djanggawul was possibly similar in many points to its modern counterpart, for the basic theme of fertility is heavily emphasized, and constantly expressed in symbolism: and symbols to these people provide the material basis upon which they have elaborated their religious thought and ritual.

We shall return to this point in a later chapter. At present we are concerned with inconsistencies; and a possible explanation for these may be found in the fact that tradition, orally transmitted, is not static, but is inevitably dependent on individual variability.

The most obvious inconsistency arises from the statement, at the beginning of the myth, that before the arrival of the Djanggawul in Arnhem Land there 'were only land and sky, animals and birds, foliage and trees . . . and beings of totemic origin.' The Djanggawul, we are told, were responsible for the creation of human beings as we know them to-day. Throughout the myth, however, mention is made of other people, as well as Spirits, with no indication of their having sprung from the Djanggawul. It seems then, that, in addition to totemic beings, there were others who came into contact with the Djanggawul. Aborigines say that before the Djanggawul came there were only 'bird people in the land'; the latter may be taken to mean 'totemic beings' of animal, bird, reptile, fish or vegetable origin. Again, although these natural species were present, the Djanggawul are said to have 'made them *wongar*, or 'dreaming'. 'Dreaming' is totemic in the sense of being specially

[1] *Vide* R. and C. Berndt, *Arnhem Land—Its History and Its People*; and also R. and C. Berndt, 'Secular Figures of North-Eastern Arnhem Land,' *American Anthropologist*, 1949, Vol. 51, No. 2, pp. 213–22, with plates.

possessed of an aura, or spiritual substance, which has been directly obtained in 'the beginning' (that is, in the mythological era) from the Creative Beings (for example, the Djanggawul). The concept of *wongar*, then, rests on the fact that a particular natural species came into association with an Ancestral Being, and was declared sacred by that Being: it became incorporated in the mythology related to that Being, and through this divine connexion became totemic. This process seems to account for the majority of such *wongar*. For example, the Wauwalak tried to cook some animals and vegetables in their fire, at the sacred billabong of Muruwul; but these sprang from the ashes and rushed away, diving into the waters of Muruwul and becoming *mareiin*, sacred, as well as *wongar*.[1] When the Djanggawul reached Arnhem Land, however, they found that some *wongar*, mostly belonging to the *jiritja* moiety, had preceded them. The concept of *wongar*, of course, is not confined to the natural species; it includes all natural phenomena and physiographic features, as well as human beings, in most cases Spirits who through divine association have become *wongar*.

Now the Djanggawul, of super-human ability, making their own laws, creating their own pattern of behaviour, and possessing the power of giving life, were in no sense *wongar*, although the term *wongar* is used loosely in referring to them. They were not in any way totemic, and this is an important distinction. Totemism is merely incidental to them; it is a philosophy embedded in the traditional religion, and not a religion itself. Totemism seems to be an instrument wielded by these Beings to express focal points in their religious ideology, and used extensively to provide symbolic representations.

The Djanggawul, on arrival at Port Bradshaw, were thrown into immediate association with the *jiritja* Beings, Laintjung and the Baijini.[2] Laintjung is the *jiritja* male counterpart of the Djanggawul; he, with his son Banaitja and certain associated females, is often said to have been responsible for bringing into being the ancestors of the *jiritja* moiety people. This aspect has never been treated in such detail in the *jiritja* scheme of creation as it has in the *dua*; nevertheless, Laintjung himself was not totemic, but was creative in the same sense that the Djanggawul Brother was. Laintjung, then, is legitimately contemporaneous with the Djanggawul; but

[1] *Vide* R. Berndt, *Kunapipi*, Chapter III.

[2] *Vide* R. and C. Berndt, 'Sacred Figures of Ancestral Beings of Arnhem Land', *Oceania*, Vol. XVIII, No. 4, pp. 309-26, plates and figures; 'Secular Figures of North-Eastern Arnhem Land', *American Anthropologist*, Vol. 51, No. 2, pp. 213-22; A. P, Elkin, R. and C. Berndt, *Art in Arnhem Land*, pp. 28-31; and R. Berndt, *Kunapipi*, Chapter I *c*, as well as *Arnhem Land—Its History and Its People*.

this does not apply to the Baijini, who are said also to have been present on the Djanggawul's arrival.

The Baijini, although partially mythological are, rather, historical; for they are said to have been the pre-Macassans, primarily traders and aliens to the coast, and not in any way creative as were the Djanggawul. They are, however, treated in the myth as if contemporary with these Ancestral Beings. This inconsistency, which does not conform to other data relating to the Baijini, seems to be a projection of the historical into the mythological past, and for this the necessity for oral transmission, with its reliance on individual narrators, must be held partly responsible. Although an interesting feature, and one which illustrates the flexibility of traditional mythology handed on in this way, contrary material shows that it must be regarded as an introduced element. This being so, one may wonder how many other elements, not apparent to the anthropologist, have been incorporated through the centuries. Alien words or concepts, of course, may be found in many traditional songs and stories, and are not especially apparent in the great Djanggawul cycle. The inclusion of the Baijini, and for that matter of Laintjung, is quite logical from the Aboriginal point of view. It widens the sacred perspective of the *dua*, bringing it, so to speak, up to date; for their religion is a living faith, the scope of which must be broad enough to include all facets of the contemporary situation. Moreover, it serves to explain why the *dua* may use black charcoal when painting their sacred clan designs, and why the *jiritja* may use certain *dua* possessions, such as red feathered string from the *lindaridj* parakeet. In this way it correlates *dua* and *jiritja* belief; and it gives sacred sanction to the *dua* for their use of black colouring, an important consideration from a ritual point of view.

There is another inconsistency, too. We are told that the Djanggawul are creative, and thus 'super-human': they are, virtually, Goddesses and a God; and yet they behave in very much the same way that human beings do to-day. They are, that is, made in the image of man; but they are not answerable to man. When they behave in a super-human way—in their creative feats, in the miraculous reappearance of the younger Sister after being killed by sorcery, in their possession of elongated clitorises and penis—they are projections of human wishes and ideals, possessed of qualities which these Aborigines find particularly attractive or important. Such projection, however, may take place only at a subconscious level; the repressed desire for incestuous relations, for example, severely prohibited in everyday life, finds an outlet in mythology. The Djanggawul Sisters represent an ideal of Arnhem Land womanhood —ever bountiful, ever fertile: for this aspect is paramount in the society of north-eastern and north-central Arnhem Land, which places considerable stress on female fertility among both human beings and natural species.

On the whole, however, the Djanggawul are very much like ordinary mortals. They depend on natural resources for food and sustenance; they must walk in order to traverse the country, and use canoes to cross the sea and rivers; they enjoy the satisfaction of coitus, the warmth of the sun and of fire; they sing and perform ritual. Moreover, their super-human powers do not seem to avail them when forced to alter their direction because of a *jiritja* moiety dreaming, or to move their camp, as in the case of the *jiritja* spring water at Elcho Island; or in the case of sorcery, as when Miralaidj was killed. The myth, then, deals with Beings whose behaviour, although they are super-human, approximates that of ordinary man. The myth is correlated with a way of life that the Aborigines know and appreciate, and consequently has a greater hold on their emotions; it involves a faith of which the adherents include all members of the society. The sacred aura of the Djanggawul extends over man, woman and child, bringing them all within the sphere of its religious expression, as manifested in the songs and the ritual.

Another feature is the segregation of the sexes when, in the myth, female children are placed under the *ngainmara* mat, and male children in the coarse grass. This reflects the Aborigine's assumption that man's rôle in life is rough, his activities are more strenuous than those of women, he takes the initiative in fighting, and altogether carries out the heavier work. His skin too is coarser, from his original exposure by the Djanggawul, while the contact with grass resulted in his growing facial hair. Women, on the other hand, were handled with greater care, protected from the harsh glare of the sun, from the rough ground and the grass. Because of this initial treatment, they are supposed to-day to be soft and yielding, with no facial and the minimum of body hair; and they are not, in theory, expected to carry out strenuous work. In reality, however, they are not the demure and submissive creatures idealized in this section of the myth. When the occasion demands, they can undertake equally difficult and strenuous activities, and possibly have greater endurance than men over a period. Nevertheless, the myth implies that they should in some measure conserve their strength to expend in sexual intercourse and childbearing. This twofold distinction between the sexes, on both physical and psychological grounds, is fundamental in local thought, with important effects on expected and actual behaviour. It is most interesting that we should find it expressed, in these terms, in a myth which purports to offer explanations of basic drives in Aboriginal society.

The Content of the Myth

The rôle of women in sacred ritual receives attention in that section of the myth which describes their losing to the men the sacred dilly bags and *rangga* emblems. This has considerable bearing on the concept of what is rightly sacred and what profane; the theory that women are profane because they do not take an active part in many religious ceremonies has been the subject of much discussion.[1] Although it is not the place here to discuss the question in any detail, a few points are worthy of notice.[2]

The north-eastern and north-central Arnhem Landers' conception of sacred life, as mentioned, encompasses all members of the society, irrespective of sex. The 'aura' of religion, as they know it, permeates all cultural institutions, from the most simple or mundane to the most complex. According to the Djanggawul ideology woman, in the shape of the Two Djanggawul Sisters, was the source of all religious ritual, a fact which becomes apparent after studying the symbolism of the songs. At the same time, man's complementary part must not be underestimated. It might be suggested that because to-day the myth and associated ritual, with the songs, are now largely in the possession of men, the peculiar reproductive function of females has been more strongly stressed. It is reasonable to suspect, also, that if the Djanggawul had not lost their bag and *rangga* emblems, so that all ritual had remained in the hands of women while men continued to play a subordinate part, the emphasis would have been on the procreative abilities of the male sex.[3]

It is possible to conjecture that, by and large, members of one sex would be more intensely interested in the procreative and sexual function of the opposite sex than in their own. Whether or not the stress on female fertility was an 'original' manifestation,

[1] *Vide* B. Spencer and F. J. Gillen, *Native Tribes of Central Australia*, 1938, p. 464; P. Kaberry, *Aboriginal Women, Sacred and Profane*, 1939; C. H. Berndt, *Women's Changing Ceremonies in Northern Australia*, L'Homme, Cahiers d'Ethnologie, de Géographie et de Linguistique, I, Paris, 1950.

Émile Durkheim, in *The Elementary Forms of the Religious Life*, 1926, acknowledged that women's part in Aboriginal sacred life was greater than his direct references would imply (p. 138, footnote 6).

[2] *Vide* A. P. Elkin, R. and C. Berndt, *Art in Arnhem Land*, 1950, pp. 28-33, and R. Berndt, *Kunapipi*, Chapters I c, III and IV.

[3] *Vide* M. Mead, *Male and Female*, London, 1950, pp. 102-3, in respect of some New Guinea tribes. 'The basic theme of the initiatory cult . . . is that women, by virtue of their ability to make children, hold the secrets of life. Men's rôle is uncertain undefined . . . man has hit upon a method of compensating himself for his basic inferiority . . . Behind the cult lies the myth that in some way all of this (ritual behaviour) was stolen from the women . . . men owe their manhood to a theft . . .' This is a particularly interesting thesis, which would repay further detailed attention.

57

The Content of the Myth

as the myth would tend to explain, it is now almost impossible to tell. We can say, however, that on the authority of the myth, the ritual and the songs, together with certain emphases and attitudes current in contemporary Arnhem Land society, it does seem that the source of this religion may be found in female fertility. At the same time the peculiar function of the male, in the sexual act and in procreation, is treated in much symbolic detail. Summing up the relevant treatment of male and female in the Yirrkalla version of the Djanggawul myth, we arrive at the conclusion that both played an equally important part. In the Milingimbi version of the same myth, however, woman's part is stressed to such an extent that the Djanggawul Brother makes no appearance at all in the story.[1]

In the myth the Djanggawul Brother and his companions brazenly stole the bags and *rangga* from the Sisters, offering no compensation in return. Their separate rôles were then automatically reversed, so that women instead of men were obliged to collect food. The crux of the situation, however, is apparent from the remarks made by the Sisters immediately after their ritual exclusion. 'We know everything. We have really lost nothing, for we remember it all, and we can let them have that small part. For aren't we still sacred, even if we have lost the bags? Haven't we still our uteri?' This is still the attitude of the women.[2] Woman herself is still sacred— not merely her procreative organs, her menstrual and afterbirth blood,[3] but herself as a member of the female sex. She did not contest the action of the Djanggawul men because her rôle in society is conventionally one of submissiveness, arising from her treatment when removed from the Djanggawul Sisters' uteri.

However, the whole problem of respective male and female sacredness is too complex for the cursory attention which is all it can receive here. To examine it in detail, from the point of view of north-eastern and north-central Arnhem Land society, would necessitate the presentation of the Wauwalak Song Cycle, an examination of *kunapipi*, *ngurlmag* and *djunggawon* rituals,[4] and a

---

[1] Milingimbi version to be presented later. *Vide*, for example, L. Warner, *op. cit.* pp. 336–40.

[2] My wife's work among Yirrkalla and Milingimbi women bears out this statement. Their knowledge of sacred ritual is far more extensive than we have been led to believe, while their active participation is far from insignificant. The same holds good for certain other areas, for example, western Arnhem Land and Central-Western Northern Territory. See C. H. Berndt, *Women's Changing Ceremonies in Northern Australia, op. cit.*, 1950.

[3] There is a cultural stress on these features in Arnhem Land society. See *Kunapipi*, Chapter III.

[4] This has been treated briefly in *Kunapipi*, especially Chapter III.

discussion of contemporary behaviour and attitudes. Nevertheless, it is one of the most important issues raised in the myth, and fundamental in our conception of Arnhem Land religion. By admitting the place of women in ritual life, we extend the function of religion so that it is not solely, or even partially, the prerogative of man. Each sex has its definite and traditionally defined rôle; and by accepting this premise we realize the potential greatness of a faith which has meaning for all the members of the society.

Chapter Four

THE DJANGGAWUL SONGS

T HE songs of the *dua nara* include some of the most beautiful literary efforts of Aboriginal Australia. They are poems set to traditional tunes, outlining the activities of the Djanggawul. In essence, they represent the original songs sung by these Ancestral Beings in the Dreaming Times; but through the ages they must have undergone a certain amount of alteration, a process to which they are vulnerable on account of their length. This is not to suggest that their content has necessarily been distorted, but merely that, through the course of generations in a non-literate society, they have not come down to us with exactly the same form and content as when they were sung by the Djanggawul.

The songs of north-eastern Arnhem Land, of which some examples have been set out elsewhere,[1] have a unique place in Aboriginal Australia, for they are longer and expressive of greater detail than those found in other areas. In structure and approach they differ from those of, for instance, southern Arnhem Land,[2] or Central-Western Northern Territory.[3]

These songs are poetry in their own right, and express the spirit of the culture to which they belong as, perhaps, no other

[1] See R. Berndt, 'A Wonguri-Mandjikai Song Cycle of the Moon Bone', *Oceania*, Vol. XIX, No. 1, pp. 16–50; 'Badu, Islands of the Spirits', *Oceania*, Vol. XIX, No. 2, pp. 93–103; C. Berndt, 'Expressions of Grief Among Aboriginal Women', *Oceania*, Vol. XX, No. 4, pp. 286–332, and 'A Drama of North-Eastern Arnhem Land'.
Also see R. Berndt, *Love Songs of Arnhem Land*, for publication.
[2] *Vide* R. Berndt, *Kunapipi*, Chapters VII, VIII, X, XI.
[3] C. Berndt, *Women's Changing Ceremonies in Northern Australia*, L'Homme, 1950.

medium can do. In this respect they are inseparable from that culture, expressing as they do something of the Aborigines' sense of the beautiful, their feeling of strength and sureness in the essential goodness and vividness of their own way of life. This is an important point, for as these poetic songs stand to-day they represent the achievement, not of individual men or women, but of the community as a whole. Moreover, this achievement does not belong to any one era, but is the culminative result of centuries of effort—how many, we shall probably never know.

The songs are an integral part of the Djanggawul myth and of its ritual, for these three elements are interdependent. The Djanggawul myth, as set out in Chapter 2, is rarely told by a story-teller; it is, rather, sung out, in the manner of the songs presented here and in following chapters. What is more, no *nara* ritual is performed without the accompaniment of these songs.

These songs are not merely traditional; they are also sacred, because each is essentially of divine 'composition'. They set out to describe in detail all the incidents that took place during the wanderings of the Djanggawul, from the time they left their spirit home at Bralgu until they reached the neighbourhood of Milingimbi.[1] There is a certain amount of repetition, beloved of the Aboriginal song man; there are 'inside' and 'singing' words, alternatives to those in everyday use, and a wealth of symbolic allusions. The language of the songs is not archaic or highly specialized, as found in some areas in reference to sacred singing, but is for the most part the ordinary language spoken by the people. This is interspersed with occasional sacred words, 'singing' words, or invocations used only in this context; but essentially the songs are constructed in such a way that all may understand them. They are sung according to a defined traditional rhythm, the words being abbreviated, lengthened or elaborated to meet the requirements of the tune, while the development of the theme proceeds graphically with the help of considerable detail.

These Djanggawul songs express the essence of ceremonial behaviour, and of the relevant mythology, and through them we understand the significance of the *dua nara* and of the Djanggawul cult. To appreciate them fully, it is necessary to understand thoroughly both the ritualistic background and the mythology, in conjunction with other facets of the cultural pattern of this area. While the song is in progress, participants and onlookers alike are reminded of the intent of the ritual—but not of that intent alone, for these sacred

[1] As mentioned elsewhere, this journey is extended in the Milingimbi version of the Djanggawul cycle.

songs are possessed of a sacred power peculiar to the Djanggawul.[1]

The songs, since they 'belong' to the divine Beings, give the ritual an atmosphere of reality, in the sense of veracity, and a deep consciousness of affiliation and continuity with these Beings themselves. Sacred songs, sung on the ceremonial ground by hereditary leaders, in conjunction with ritual and dancing, and in the presence of religious symbols or emblems, vividly reflect and re-inspire the religious emotions of all who hear them.

The songs presented here are translations, and have inevitably suffered in the process. To appreciate all the subtle turns of phrase, the abundant allusions and so on, one should read them in the original, interlineally translated, in conjunction with copious notes.[2] It is only through understanding of the language that we can derive the fullest benefit from these songs.

Nevertheless, we have adhered strictly to the literal translation of all words in the songs, endeavouring to retain the beauty of the original. Difficulty has been experienced, however, in finding satisfactory English equivalents for certain words. The translation errs, perhaps, on the side of restraint, for many of the English words used (unlike those in the Aboriginal text) may appear prosaic and lacking in poetic value. The different words referring to sounds of various kinds, for instance, are not easy to transcribe: and 'noise' is a poor, although often necessary, substitute.

No attempt has been made to conform to the original rhythm and metre, since this would involve manipulating the translation at the expense of its actual content. The arrangement into lines conforms to the pauses made by the Aborigines themselves when singing or reciting.

Comments or notes are not attached to each song, as in the case of the originals, but any points that seem to need discussion have been referred to in the section immediately following each part of the cycle. For convenience, and to facilitate the gradual development of our analysis, we have set out ten parts to this epic, corresponding to various stages in the travels of the Djanggawul.

As the songs progress, from one stage to another, we may follow the symbolism and intent which have already been indicated in earlier chapters. The significance of each part will be treated briefly at its conclusion, so that at the end of the epic the whole may be viewed in proper perspective.

---

[1] In *Kunapipi* (*op. cit.*, Chapter VII) it was said that 'the songs are the echo of those first sung by the Ancestral Beings: the spirit of the echo goes on through timeless space, and when we sing, we take up the echo and make sound.' This applies also to the Djanggawul songs.

[2] These are to be published separately through the journal *Oceania* as a monograph, on account of the great number of phonetic texts. The serious reader or student is advised to read these in conjunction with the translations set out here.

Chapter Five

THE DJANGGAWUL SONG CYCLE

PART ONE

In which the Djanggawul cross the sea from Bralgu Island, and eventually reach the Arnhem Land mainland for the first time.

Song 1

ALTHOUGH I leave Bralgu, I am close to it. I, Djanggawul,
    am paddling . . .   1
    Paddling with all the paddles, with their flattened taperin
  ends.
Close I am coming, with Bildjiwuraroiju,
Coming along from Bralgu. We splash the water as we paddle,
  paddling wearily,
With Miralaidj, undulating our buttocks as we paddle.   5
We paddle along through the roaring tide, paddle a long way.
I am paddling along fast, through the rough sea . . .
Beside me is foam from our paddling, and large waves follow us.
With Bralbral, we move our wrists as we paddle, making noise as
  we go through the sea . . .
We, Djanggawul, are paddling along, lifting our paddles, slowly
  going along . . .   10
All the way we have paddled. I rest my paddles now, as we glide.
On the sea's surface the light from the Morning Star shines as we move,
Shining on the calmness of the sea.
Looking back I see its shine, an arc of light from the Morning
  Star. The shine falls on our paddles, lighting our way.
We look back to the Morning Star and see its shine, looking back
  as we paddle.   15

The Djanggawul Song Cycle

Star moving along, shining! We saw its disc quite close,
Skimming the sea's surface, and mounting again above Bralgu.
Close to us it rises above the expanse of sea; we look back, seeing
  its shine.
Morning Star, sent by the dancing Spirit People, those people of
  the rain, calling out as they dance there with outstretched arms.
They send it for us, that we may travel along its shining path from
  Bralgu.   20
Close, its 'feathered ball' appears above Dangdangmi! Close is the
  Morning Star, on the end of its string and pole!
Close is the Morning Star, stretching from its pole, extending out
  from its string . . .
Shining from Bralgu, as we paddle through the sea.
Bubbles rise to the sea's surface; our canoe is carried on the crest
  of waves. Ah, *waridj* Bralbral!
Sound made by our splashing paddles, and the sea's roar as we rise
  to the crest of a wave!   25
We make our paddles sound, with the noise of the sea, sound that
  is heard far away at Bralgu.
We, the Djanggawul, make sound with our paddling, make spray
  as we paddle fast . . .
The salty smell! The roaring sea, and its foam! Its wide expanse
  behind us!
We paddle, with Bildjiwuraroiju, following the waves along,
Pushing our way through the waves that block us   30
Sound from our sacred *ngainmara* mat! Noise as the waters surge
  around it!
Sound, as the sacred poles are moved about with the rolling of
  the canoe!

Song 2

We Djanggawul saw the Morning Star shining . . . ,   1
Saw its shine on the green-backed turtle, lighting up its throat . . . !
Paddling, we saw that turtle: saw its eyes open, its flippers out-
  stretched as it floated.
Sea water lapped at its shell, spreading across its back.
Making a sound as it rose above the surface; see the dilly bag at
  its back!   5
It swam through the sea, with shell like a rock, hiding the bag
  under its flipper.
'I have another basket' (the turtle says). 'It is the cuttle fish.'

64

The Djanggawul Song Cycle

Song 3

Paddling we hear a sound;   1
A fish jumped to the water's surface;
A catfish! a sawfish! For us that fish jumps!
A flying fish, making a noise as it jumps, splashing the water . . .
A sawfish beside us; for it hears the sound of our canoe, the canoe
    of the Djanggawul.   5
Fish jumping! Sawfish, splashing the water with its nose!

Song 4

I, Djanggawul, am leaving Bralgu, paddling away from there,
    paddling fast.   1
The sweep of the paddle of Miralaidj, out in the deep sea, far from
    the mainland!
Paddling fast as we smell the Baijini from far away.
Sound within the water, as we pull on our paddles! Bildjiwuraroiju
    paddling . . .
Coming close to the mainland, splashing as we skim through the
    open sea . . .   5
See the shine of the Morning Star, as we look back, shining from
    Bralgu.
Sound of our narrow paddle . . . paddling along.
Spray falls across the canoe, coming strongly in from the heavy sea.
Close up! Paddling against the strong high tide; waves spread out
    as we go, waves from our paddling:
Waves that roar as they spread—coming from us, from our canoe. 10
Spraying like rain, churning to foam. The smell of the sea!
We paddle fast through the sea, for we hear the distant sound of the
    Baijini,
Sound and sea smell from them, from far away, spreading across
    the sea's expanse . . .
Carefully we must go, for the sea is rough, Miralaidj. Let us rest
    on our paddles, Bralbral. (They are speaking to one another.)
Sound of the sea from the Djanggawul's paddling!   15

Song 5

What is that we hear? A sea goose skims the water's surface.   1
It is for us, *waridj*! (They say as they paddle.) It comes from
    Buragumi, from the mainland.

As we paddle, what blocks our way? Flocks of sea geese alight on the water before them,

Hearing Bralbral and the Djanggawul talking. Flocks of birds alight on the water.

Flocks of birds, like hordes of people, people whom we shall put on the mainland.   5

Paddling we see them skimming the sea's surface, in the glistening rays of the Morning Star:

Resting on the sea's surface, from their home at Port Bradshaw.

See them as we move our arms in paddling, paddling slowly.

Grey crested birds . . . emerging from the mouth of the *ngainmara* mat!

They see the Djanggawul, paddling along . . . beautiful birds! As Bildjiwuraroiju, Miralaidj and Bralbral paddle.   10

We see the shine of the Morning Star, as we look back,

See the shine that radiates from its disc; we turn as we paddle . . .

It shines on the ebbing tide, shine reaching out from Bralgu.

As we paddle we see the shine moving . . .

As we paddle through the glistening water, it follows us . . .   15

Going through the great wide sea . . . through the path of light . . .

Morning Star suspended on end of string, from a sapling pole,

Its 'feathered ball' close to us: now skimming the sea's surface, now rising once more. Shining on us!

Song 6

What is that which blocks us? The whale!   1

As we paddle, we see its gaping mouth. What is that?

Spray and sea splash as it moves.

We paddle gently, for we see the open mouth of the whale.

What is this swimming? Our *ngainmara* mat, swimming under the water!   5

Water swirling! We hear the noise of the water, and of its spray.

We saw it out at sea, a long way from Bralgu—spray from the swimming whale.

Water rises and swirls, with noise caused by the whale: spray and foam from the whale . . .

As we paddle, we see it swimming. Bralbral calls to the Djanggawul,

It is our mat, our basket! Let us take some. The others we leave in the sea!   10

Waves rise from the large *ngainmara* mats that they leave behind, swirling waters spraying from them!

66

Water comes in from them, coming to us: foaming, spraying and roaring, out on the sea!

Song 7

Splashing, a fish swishes its tail as it rises, close to the whale's 'whiskers'.   1
A splashing catfish, turning over on to its belly . . .
From Bralgu, from the mouth of the whale . . .
It splashes, its spike protrudes as it swims before the gaping mouth of the whale,
Splashing and chasing it. 'I (says the whale) am splashing. I chase this fish, under the water.'   5
Touching the fish with its 'whiskers'. The catfish splashes . . .
Splashes before the open mouth of the whale,
Spraying, dragging its spike through the sea . . .
  And the noise of the sea, being churned up . . . !
Waves rising and splashing, caused by fish . . .
Noise of the water and foam from that fish . . .   10
Waves spreading out, spraying and splashing, caused by the fish . . .

Song 8

What is that? A sea egg!   1
We must paddle with care, with the spade paddle, dragging it through the sea as we rest.
Oh *waridj* Bralbral! Oh *waridj* Miralaidj! It is a stranger to us, from Bralgu.
Sea eggs forming in lines, with their spiny 'hands',
Drift with the waves in the calm sea, spread with the moving waves,   5
Drift on the surface, glistening in the shine of the Star.
The continuous lap of the sea, and its waves! Lines of sea eggs spreading across the sea!
Strangers! At the fringe of the shine of the Star from Bralgu, they spread out in the rising waves . . . The sound of the sea . . . !
Paddling, the Djanggawul see these eggs, as they move their shoulders . . .
Their heads are grey. They have paddled far, and the salt water has whitened their hair.   10
They are tired from paddling.
They pause as they see the eggs . . .

Drifting in the calm sea, their lines spreading, their short 'hands'
    moving:
Sea eggs we see as we paddle. Gently we drag our paddles along,
    as we rest them.
We paddle through the shine from the Morning Star, from Bralgu,
    slowly along as we see these eggs.   15

Song 9

What is that, *waridj* Miralaidj? Drag our paddles carefully.   1
See them, as the Djanggawul paddle fast.
They see them emerging from the water, coming up from Bralgu . . .
A green turtle we see in the water, making a sound . . . ,
See it through the shine of the Morning Star, shining on its throat
    as it swims . . .   5
See it moving its shoulders; see its shell . . .
We see it rise to the water's surface, its flippers 'paddling'.
Carefully we are moving our shoulders, as we are paddling. Let us
    rest, *waridj* Bralbral.
They see its shell shining as slowly it rose, catching the rays from
    the Star . . .
Floating on the crest of a wave, and making a noise,   10
Close to them as they paddle . . .
The Djanggawul move their buttocks, paddling fast. Noise from
    their paddle movements!

Song 10

What is that blocking us, *waridj* Bralbral? Carefully we must
    paddle.   1
Resting on paddles, dragging them, we see that stranger from
    Bralgu,
Stranger drift-wood, revealed in the shine of the Star . . . ,
Carefully moving our arms, we see it drifting by . . .
Making sounds as it drifts, splashing and making waves,   5
This stranger from Bralgu: drift-wood, drifting and splashing . . .
Pushed by the waves, and making a noise, drifting, and sending
    out foam . . .
Spray from the sea! Spray from away at Bralgu . . .
Foam all over the sea, stretching out from Port Bradshaw . . .
'I leave the foam on my body,' says the drift-wood. Foam stretching
    from Walbinboi Island!   10

The Djanggawul Song Cycle

We see it close as we paddle. Drag our paddles, *waridj* Bralbral, *waridj* Djanggawul.
Foam and spray spread all over the sea, stretching out from Port Bradshaw . . .
See our heads! Grey from paddling, from salt and foam!
The Djanggawul are tired . . . See Bildjiwuraroiju paddling carefully, Bralbral undulating his buttocks.
It (the wood) is a stranger from Bralgu, from the source of the Star's shine. 15

Song 11

What is that crying? Careful! We must rest from paddling, *waridj* Bralbral. 1
We hear a sound. What is that now? A plover, *waridj*, hovering above the drifting timber.
It has seen our canoe, and circles about it.
It cries as it circles about the drift-wood, goes soaring cloudwards,
Cries as it swoops about the drift-wood. *Waridj*, it circles round and round our canoe. 5
Paddle carefully, Djanggawul, rest on our oars.
Its screeching cry sounds over the waters from Bralgu, mingling with the roar of the sea, spreading across it.
Sound as it skims the sea's surface, sound from its splashing; and foam!
The birds and clouds leave that cry for us, *waridj* Bralbral. It is a message for us . . .
Its cry echoes back from the clouds, as it circles around and cries through its beak: 10
Screeching that comes through its beak, up from its throat, reaching up to the sky.
Its eye is keen; it sees our canoe, and all within it, and sees the drifting wood.
Up and down goes its cry. The bird flies with hanging claws. Its eyes are closed, but the eye of its anus is open.
See, a message for us, *waridj* Bralbral!
The noise of its cry, as it circles! Foam covers the sea! It cries as it circles, away out from Port Bradshaw. 15

Song 12

We paddle fast, *waridj*, moving our arms. Bralbral, we paddle fast. 1
We have come far from the island of Bralgu. What is that shining, *waridj* Miralaidj?

69

The Djanggawul Song Cycle

The Morning Star shines on us, as we paddle along. See the Star
    shining!
Lift up the paddle carefully, *waridj!* Bralbral paddles, moving his
    buttocks.
Now we are paddling fast, moving our shoulders, lifting the
    narrow paddle: 5
Swaying our hips as we paddle. We have left Bralgu behind us,
    waridj Djanggawul.
We follow that Baijini sound, smelling the mainland, and paddling fast.
We must rest on the paddles, *waridj*. Going along, we hear the sound
    of the Baijini talking.
We paddle in on the morning tide, in through the breakers . . .
Our water is rushing onwards; from somewhere it must be ebbing. 10
Sound of the surf: waves from our paddling: splashing—foam
    from the surf !
Waves arise from our paddling, *waridj* Bralbral . . .
We are paddling fast along, sweeping our paddles . . .
Tired from paddling, with head grey from the foam . . . Oh
    Bildjiwuraroiju!
We are paddling fast, we are close to land, to Port Bradshaw.   15

Song 13

What is that, *waridj* Bralbral? Carefully drag the paddle, resting it
    on the canoe.   1
What is that, moving there? Those, *waridj*, are sponges, spreading
    their formless 'arms'.
We see them as we rest on our paddles, scratching ourselves from
    the sponges . . .
The Djanggawul are tired. This is a sponge, *waridj*! We saw the
    formless 'arms' moving along . . .
Paddling along, we see the ebbing tide. We saw the sponges, and
    heard the roar of the sea.   5
I am tired, like these drifting sponges, *waridj*; so let us rest our
    paddles . . .
We paddle fast when we hear the sound of the Baijini: the smell
    of the sea!

Song 14

We are paddling fast, *waridj* Djanggawul, moving our arms fast
    as we paddle.   1
We lift up our paddles, swishing quickly along . . .
A black porpoise follows our paddling and splashing.

70

The Djanggawul Song Cycle

Carefully, *waridj* Bralbral, rest your paddle, dragging along. Water
swirls from our paddling,
Spray follows behind us. We smell the Baijini, hear the sound that
they make.   5
We paddle fast as we hear the Baijini; and the smell of the sea,
from their fires.
Carefully, *waridj* Miralaidj, we move our arms, paddling quickly,
swaying our hips,
Lifting the narrow paddle. We are reaching Port Bradshaw.
Soon we shall leave behind us the noise from our swishing paddles.
Spray and surf on the rolling tide, white foaming breakers, all
from our paddling, *waridj* Bralbral, *waridj* Djanggawul.   10
We paddle in through the big waves, through the roar of the surf
caused by our paddling.
We rest on our oars. Foam from our swishing paddles stains and
patterns our bodies from Bralgu, far out at sea.

Song 15

What is that, *waridj* Bralbral? Carefully rest your paddles. What
is blocking us?   1
A huge black sawfish, seen in the shine of the Morning Star,
Sawfish with gaping jaw and barbs, seen through the shine of the
Star.
What is that, *waridj*? Two sawfish swimming, long black sawfish.
Carefully we go, letting our paddles drag through the water.   5
The Djanggawul, tired from travelling, see them through the shine
of the Star.
We paddle quickly, and see the sawfish rise, with a loud noise as
they turn in the water.
Loud noise from that, *waridj*! And water comes up. The jaw of
the fish pushes the waves along, and makes spray.
Where is this spray coming from, *waridj*? We are paddling fast,
swishing along through the water.
We move our arms carefully, *waridj* Bralbral, swaying our buttocks,
making a noise as we paddle fast . . .   10
So we may reach Port Bradshaw . . .
Paddling quickly, we move our arms; and our heads are grey . . .

Song 16

What is that drifting along by us, *waridj*? Carefully we rest our
paddles, dragging them through the sea.   1

The Djanggawul Song Cycle

Bralbral, it is a small sawfish, seen in the shine of the Morning
Star . . .
Carefully we are paddling, swaying our buttocks. Djanggawul,
this is a fish blocking us . . .
Paddling we see its back, and its saw, and the ripples it makes on
the water. Paddling we see the sawfish.
Carefully we must go, *waridj* Bralbral, swaying our buttocks
gently.   5
What is blocking us now? Its tail blocks us, 'paddling' and lashing
the water.
We hear the roar of the sea from Bralgu across to the mainland.
We paddle, hearing the sawfish splashing and churning the water,
fighting smaller fish.
We are smelling the sea and paddling fast. We saw the tide flow in,
and the waves breaking.
We paddle, hearing the noise of the fish, and the waves breaking. 10

Song 17

Carefully rest the paddle, *waridj* Bralbral. What is this blocking us,
Oh *waridj* Djanggawul?   1
A young porpoise, a stranger from Bralgu, we see through the
shine.
Porpoise born in fresh water. It splashes, turns on its side, hitting
the sea with its tail: veins in its tail . . .
Carefully we drag our paddles through the sea, splashing towards
Port Bradshaw, smelling the sea . . .
Its jaw protrudes from the sea: young porpoises come swimming
behind the canoe . . .   5
Coming from the fresh water, *waridj*, from Bralgu, from the land
of the Spirits.
They made a crying sound, through the fat of their heads, spouting
up sprays of water . . .
Swimming from Bralgu as they hear the paddling, the moving of
shoulders.
Carefully we must paddle, *waridj* Djanggawul, lifting the narrow
paddle, and moving fast . . .
Moving our buttocks, swaying our hips as we paddle. We saw the
porpoises, heard the noise of their spraying,   10
Sound of the water, with foam from the splashing of young por-
poises,
Chasing fish, which circle around, swimming under the water.
We see them as we paddle, through the shine of the Morning
Star . . .

The Djanggawul Song Cycle

Song 18

What is that blocking us, *waridj* Djanggawul? Carefully rest our
paddles, *waridj* Bralbral.   1
It is a bird, that cries as it swoops along, circling about our canoe,
waridj Miralaidj.
It stretches its neck as it cries, gliding with outstretched wings,
waridj, giving us strength for paddling.
Our seagull dives to the water, sending out spray with its beak
as it skims the surface . . .
That bird, *waridj*, goes flying up and down, shaking itself dry: 5
Carefully we paddle, dragging the paddles along, as we hear that bird.
The female gull, with its beak, cries out as it sees the dark rain
clouds rising.
The seagull cries out at the time of the wet season: it thinks of nesting.
Gliding along, it thinks of its home at Bremer Island.
Diving it skims the water, sending out spray. Its eyes can see in
the night. It shakes itself dry.   10
We paddle fast as we smell the sea, smell where the Baijini are.
The seagull splashes the water, making a noise, giving us power
to go quickly.
We move our wrists fast, swaying our hips as we paddle.
We are moving fast, *waridj* : hear the swish of our paddles.
Our heads are grey from the foam . . . we are tired from
paddling.   15

Song 19

What is blocking us? Carefully drag our paddles, *waridj* Bralbral
(says Djanggawul).   1
An immense sawfish! Carefully rest our paddles Djanggawul. It is
a large sawfish.
What shall we do? We shall continue to paddle.
See its saws and its gaping mouth! *waridj*, are those its teeth?
Leave it swimming behind, for it whips up the sea with its jaws . . . 5
Carefully, *waridj*, let us paddle quickly and go. We saw it through
the shine of the Morning Star.
Carefully swaying our buttocks, we leave it behind, lying under
the surface . . .
There, near Port Bradshaw, it swirls the water, making a hollow
noise:
We paddle fast as we smell the sea . . . Bones of that fish, large
verterbrae like an expanse of sea.
Waridj, we move our hips as we travel fast, leaving it lying there, 10

73

The Djanggawul Song Cycle

Where it lives in the rough sea, for it is ferocious: it carries a 'poison
   bag'. The sawfish clan is always wanting to fight,
Always looking for trouble, always ferocious. It swims along
   with its bag of poison, that enters the teeth of its saw . . .
'I (says the fish) make the sea rough from my anger. No canoe may
   come hear me, or near my saws. I make the sea rough, I have
   poison!'
Let us paddle fast, *waridj*, it may attack us. Go fast, *waridj* Bralbral . . .
Shoulders moving, we plunge down our paddles. We, *waridj*
   Djanggawul, drag on our paddles and rest them.   15
Hear the sound of the incoming tide, *waridj*, let us go fast!
The high tide is flowing and roaring, ebbing from somewhere:
We see that fish in the shine of the Morning Star . . .
We plunge down our paddles, paddling fast, moving our buttocks,
   waridj Djanggawul. Smell the sea and hear the Baijini sound . . . !

Song 20

What is that, *waridj*? Carefully sway our buttocks, Bralbral, with
   dragging paddle.   1
This is sea-weed floating, a mass of sea-weed floating . . .
Waridj, it is a stranger from Bralgu, this floating weed, with fragments dislodging and drifting away.
It drifts into rows spreading out with the waves. Blown by the
   wind, it drifts backwards and forwards—spreading across the water.
Roar of the sea as it carries the weed on the incoming tide, and the
   spray of the surf!   5
We saw it through the shine of the Morning Star, there on our
   way to Port Bradshaw from Bralgu.
Let us go fast, *waridj* Djanggawul. Moving our arms quickly and
   swaying our buttocks, we lift up the paddles.
Far we have paddled. Is that spray, rising before us?
Is that the sea smell we follow? Is that the Baijini sound we hear?
Let us paddle fast, *waridj*, quickly, moving our buttocks, as the
   waves rush in, the high tide breaks on the beach . . .   10
Carefully, *waridj*. Djanggawul, moving his buttocks, lifts up his
   narrow paddle.

Song 21

What do we see, *waridj*, as we look back?   1
Paddling, we see the shine of the Morning Star.
Yes, *waridj* Bralbral, paddling we see it close to us. The Morning
   Star sends out its rays as it rises near us:

74

The Djanggawul Song Cycle

It skims the water, shining across the sea, the Bralgu Star, its rays shining near us.

It skims the sea, from Bralgu, shining upon us, on the end of its string, attached to a young sapling.   5

Another Star, *waridj*, a feathered ball held by the Spirits . . . Close is the Morning Star . . .

It shines near, as we turn to see it. Oh, Morning Star, Oh pole and strings . . .

The Star and its rays rise gradually for us, *waridj* Miralaidj; we rest our paddles, dragging them through the sea.

See the shine from the disc of the Star, close to us, *waridj*.

The Bralgu Spirits are dancing, sending the Star . . .   10

Rain people, the stamping sound of their dancing . . . ! Dust rises, *waridj*, from under their dancing feet . . . !

There from the fresh water place, from the Spirit country.

The shine falls on us, from Bralgu, covering us with its shine . . . Close, it shines across to the mainland, to Port Bradshaw.

The morning Star shines, bringing the dawn . . . putting an end to the night . . .

Close to us, ending the darkness, bringing the dawn . . .   15

It pierces the darkness, that Star, sent by the Spirits. The sound of their dancing!

The morning Star shines from Bralgu, shines like the *mauwulan* pole . . .

It rises from the sandhills at Bralgu, where the Spirits dance, *waridj*, for us.

We move fast with the narrow paddle; we hasten, moving our wrists, as the tide roars in.

For the daylight is on us, the dawn, before the cry of the morning pigeon. The Star still shines for us, *waridj* Djanggawul.   20

Our hips and buttocks are swaying. Let us go carefully, because of the water,

It is rising for us, and roaring, with foam and spray of the surf.

We push the water along with our canoe, our paddles swishing.

Waves come up, with the rising tide. Spray comes from our swishing paddles. From us the tide is flowing.

Is that the mainland we are approaching from Bralgu?   25

Is that the mainland, Port Bradshaw, we are approaching . . . ?

The smell of the sea! *Waridj*, we paddle fast, quickly moving our wrists.

We lift up the narrow paddles—*waridj* Bralbral, our paddles . . .

We lift up the big paddles, moving fast, swishing the paddles . . .

Our paddles! We drag them along, the flat and the narrow paddles . . .   30

The Djanggawul Song Cycle
Song 22

What is that, *waridj*, in front of us? We rest, dragging our paddles. 1
There ahead of us, *waridj* Bralbral.
That is the morning pigeon. Darkness goes, with its cry!
We saw darkness only towards the west . . .
Bird that 'twists' its tongue as its whistles! Daylight comes with
    its cry. 5
We saw the calmness of dawn (no sound but the pigeon's cry).
It ruffles itself, *waridj*, crying, and shaking its feathers. Its cry goes
    out to its nestlings.
The small clear cry of that pigeon and of its nestlings . . .
Talking fast from their nest . . . The pigeon flies down from the
    smooth inside of the nest. Their cries reach us, 'twisting' their
    tongues . . .
We saw the Morning Star ending the darkness. Then, the cry of
    the pigeon! Cries like the speech of different linguistic groups,
    like the Madarlpa dialect! 10
The bird talks fast, a sound like the Dalwongu dialect . . .
If flew across from its nest in the 'arm-band' bushes . . .
It teaches that cry to its young: the nestlings ruffle themselves.
Teaching that cry! It calls from the limbs near its nest. They are
    'twisting' their tongues . . .
We saw it, flying down, as the darkness was clearing, 'twisting'
    its tongue and whistling. 15

Song 23

We paddle fast, moving our buttocks, *waridj*. We lift up the narrow
    paddle . . . 1
We paddle fast, with the narrow paddle . . . We speed along,
    waridj Djanggawul . . .
Wei! What is that, *waridj*? We rest our paddles, Bralbral, and drag
    them.
That, *waridj*, is the long drawn cry of the black bird.
Crying out, for it saw the darkness clearing . . . 5
What is that? The sound of the black bird, long drawn as the
    darkness clears.
It saw the coming dawn, and the calmness.
What is that, *waridj*? A black bird crying, at dawn, and the cry of
    the nestlings!
Crying with mouths agape, as they hear the roar of the waves, and
    smell the sea,
As they hear the noise of the water, the foam and the spray. 10

76

The Djanggawul Song Cycle

'I (says the bird) heard the noise of the water rising, the incoming
tide . . .
I draw out my sound, it reaches out to Port Bradshaw . . .
A long cry, moving my head, as I see the water rising, and see the
spray . . .
Nesting among the limbs of the "coffee" tree, of the *djuda
rangga* . . .'
It grasps the tree with its claws, crying from that sacred tree,   15
Sending out its cry, as the big waves rise and spray.
The sea roars as the bird cries, and the sound reaches up to the
clouds,
A long-drawn sound entering the banking clouds, the cloud-
flecked sky.
A long cry, as it saw the tide roaring in, with its spray
'I saw the spray. I cry out as the waves come splashing together.   20
I saw the water, and saw them paddling fast. The smell of the sea!
I saw the tide coming up. The Baijini sound, the smell of the sea!
I saw the water, roaring, as the waves came in at Port Bradshaw,
coming from Bralgu.'
Foam coming up, and spreading. The bird cried as it looked at
the water.
The crest of the surf shines in the light of the Morning Star. The
sea roars, and the waves are splashing together.   25
The bird saw the darkness clearing, uttering its long cry as the dawn
came,
The cry in the stillness, as the darkness cleared (with the light)
from Bralgu!

Song 24

What is that, *waridj* Bralbral? We rest our paddles at the cry, and
drag them along.   1
We look round to see the cry. It comes from Bralgu. It's close
to us!
It is coming up, moving along. The sun, with its *mauwulan
rangga* emblem!
As it rises, its rays warm the Djanggawul's backs. It comes rising,
close to them.
The sun, with rays emerging before its disc! Close, it shines on the
water, warming our backs, *waridj* Djanggawul.   5
Close it is rising, from the sand, from the sea into the sky.
Hot sun, burning our backs, its rays leading back to Bralgu!
Rising sun, reflected in the sea! Sun for us, with its heat!
Rays of the sun emerging, *waridj*, leaving its home beneath the water!
Sun coming up close, with spreading rays!   10

The Djanggawul Song Cycle

For us, *waridj*, it leaves its home under the sea.
Its rays touch us like hands; their reflections shine in the water.
We go fast. Paddling along we see the rays touching us, so that the
    sweat comes out.
The sun comes up for us, leaving its home; the glare is hurting our
    eyes.
It comes closer, rising above the sea, burning our backs.   15
The smell of the sea! It leaves its home in the water, and warms
    us . . .
We paddle fast, to Port Bradshaw, to the Place of the Sun, to where
    the Baijini are.
Reflections shine in the sea. The rays warm us, on our way to
    Port Bradshaw.
We lift up our paddles, *waridj*, we go fast but carefully, moving our
    arms and our buttocks.
The sun reaches us, with its rays. Its red glow, *waridj*, for us, from
    the sacred parakeet feathers!   20
We rest our paddles. It is for us! We paddle fast, *waridj*, and
    carefully.
Our buttocks are moving. It is for us, *waridj* Djanggawul! We
    paddle fast!
Our hips sway as we paddle along, lifting the paddles,
On our way to the Place of the Sun, at Port Bradshaw.
The sun's rays touch us, warming our backs . . .   25
Rays like the parakeet-feathered string of our *rangga*! Feathered
    string like our child! Red glow of the sun.
Rays warming our backs, like feathered string! Like feathered
    rangga!
That sun rises above us, burning our backs, going to the Place of
    the Sun.
It burns our backs, and it shines on the water at Lilildjang.
Its warm rays touch us, stretching to Arnhem Bay . . .   30
It leaves its home in the water, and rises, burning.
Warm rays touching our backs, touching our *rangga*! Shining, and
    making the mainland clear to see!
For us it shines on the sacred sandhills at Port Bradshaw . . .
Stretching out its rays, warming our backs, illuminating the water-
    holes at Arnhem Bay . . .
That sun, sending out its rays to Elcho Island,   35
Burning our backs, from the red ochre there . . . at Elcho
    Island . . .
That sun sends out its rays to shine on the sea, *waridj*, on the main-
    land near Milingimbi . . . ,
Warming our backs, as it reaches west to the wide Barara country.

The Djanggawul Song Cycle
Song 25

We go fast, moving our wrists, and lifting our paddles.   1

We paddle along, *waridj* Bralbral, as the sun's rays touch us, and touch our paddles.

Our buttocks and hips sway, as we paddle along:

What is that? What is that cry?

Flying foxes, suspended there in the tree, *waridj* Djanggawul, crying out from the tree.   5

We saw the sacred tree, the sacred *rangga*. Flying foxes, in the sacred tree!

Little flying foxes crying, as they hold that sacred tree . . . !

They cry from their home, where they hang among the branches of the sacred tree,

Cry from the topmost branches, from all the branches of the tree . . .

They cry from their home: crying, *waridj*, from the sacred Leichhardt fig tree.   10

Song 26

We go fast, lifting our paddles, moving our wrists . . . we are close to our country.   1

We go fast, moving our buttocks; for we hear the roar of the sea, the spray of the surf,

Coming up from our paddling! Foam from our paddling!

Wai! *waridj* Bralbral, carefully drag the paddles, for they are splashing up foam.

What has happened? Sea smell, and splashing!   5

What, *waridj*, is that? Wai! Our feathered arm-bands!

What has happened? They are wet from that foam.

We are all getting wet! What shall we do? Throw away the wet *rangga*?

They are wet from that foam, our *rangga*, *waridj* Bralbral: wet from lying in water! We are nearing Port Bradshaw.

Shall we, *waridj*, undo it, then throw it away? No, let the sacred mat with the *rangga* sink down, near the Place of the Sun.   10

We shall not untie its 'mouth' . . . Let it sink down into the sea, outside Port Bradshaw . . .

Sacred invocations to the *rangga* and *ngainmara* . . . ! We invoke the *bugali* as it sinks . . . , calling the sacred names.

They sink down, making a noise as the sea covers them.

The Djanggawul Song Cycle
Song 27

Let us rest on our paddles, *waridj*, for I (Bralbral) am tired.   1
Stop paddling, *waridj*.
What is happening there, *waridj*? (Bralbral says) My body aches
with tiredness.
Tired, because you are worrying (about the mat containing the
rangga).
I am worrying (says the Djanggawul Brother) about the *rangga*.
(Why didn't we open the mat?)   5
I am just tired! That was why, *waridj*, we threw away the sacred
rangga and mat.
We are coming close to the mainland: our journey, our paddling,
is done.
We land on the beach at Port Bradshaw.
That is our country! We plant our *mauwulan* here.
We have arrived, oh *waridj*!   10

8. The Goanna Tail *rangga* shown by Mauwulan, a ceremonial leader.

9. Postulants dancing the Incoming Tide, entering the sacred ground.

10. Calling of invocations before the emergence of sacred emblems.

Chapter Six

COMMENTS ON PART ONE OF THE SONGS

THIS first section of the saga introduces us to the Djanggawul and their companion Bralbral, and sets the stage for succeeding parts. It purports to show their immediate origin, and tells how the sacred *rangga* emblems and the mat were brought to the Arnhem Land coast.

The Djanggawul leave the Spirit Land of Bralgu, and paddle across to Port Bradshaw in their bark canoe. They are guided by the rays of the Morning Star, and in the light from this they see various creatures; it is only in the final songs (21–4) that the Star light gives place to that of the sun. In these colourful songs, the north-eastern Arnhem Landers suggest that the Djanggawul have travelled all the way from Bralgu in a kind of twilight, but as they reach the mainland the sun arises, warming them and illuminating various sacred sites (Song 24). This implies, subtly, their association with the sun.

Song 24 treats the sun as a separate identity, although we have seen (in Chapters 2 and 3) that there is, in fact, a close association, if not complete identification. Line 20, Song 24 speaks of 'Its red glow . . . from the sacred parakeet feathers . . .' This refers to the red glow below the sun, seen as it rises. It is said that the sun is a *dua* moiety woman, and this glow is from her waist-band of human hair string (*ngadiba*) into which are woven red breast feathers from the *lindaridj* parakeet. They were given her by the Djanggawul Brother himself, and when in the sky she always wears this belt. The Djanggawul Brother calls her *gadu* (that is, daughter, man speaking), although in other versions the Brother may call her *ngandi* 'mother', for the Sun Woman's two daughters may be

Comments on Part One of the Songs

identified with the Djanggawul Sisters (*vide* Chapters 2 and 3). The red parakeet feathered string is a material representation of the sun's rays, which it symbolizes when attached as a pendant to a *rangga*, and spread out like the rays; the red feathers are said to represent the heat of the sun. The Sun Woman not only wears the feathered waist-band; she also travels across the sky with the aid of the *mauwulan rangga* (see Song 24, line 3), which she uses as walking sticks, and to which are attached feathered pendants. Identification of these red parakeet feathers with the sun's rays extends throughout the cycle. It symbolizes the concept of fertility, for the small red breast feathers are said to be like children, each individual feather being a 'child'; and they represent the warmth necessary for natural increase to take place.

Lines 26 and 27 of the same song (24) express this idea—'Rays like the parakeet-feathered string of our *rangga*! Feathered string like our child! Red glow of the sun. Rays warming our backs, like feathered string! Like feathered *rangga*!' That is, the parakeet-feathered strings are attached to the *djuda rangga* pole and likened to (or identified with) the rays of the sun. The sun is said to 'carry the *djuda* (tree) *rangga* always, as if carrying a baby.' This reference expresses the underlying theme of the Djanggawul doctrine. The *rangga* object is regarded as a child, and is here called *wagu* (that is, *guliwona wagun*—*vide* text), which is the term used for sister's child (man speaking), or own child (woman speaking). That is to say, the Djanggawul Brother is calling the *rangga wagu*, the child of either Sister, Miralaidj or Bildjiwuraroïju; and they call the *rangga* by the same term. The *rangga* are carried in the *ngainmara* mat, symbolically the uterus of either Sister. They are the Djanggawul's children, by virtue of their presence in the wombs of the Sisters (that is, *rangga* kept in the *ngainmara*): *rangga* approximate children or people (see previous chapters). The *djuda rangga* are sacred poles, from which spring living trees: the association of the sun with these (that is, their feathered strings, likened to sun's rays) suggests how essential the sun is to the growth of trees and foliage. When the sun extends its rays to various sacred sites, lighting up the whole country of north-eastern Arnhem Land (see Song 24) it leaves its material substance at Elcho Island, crystallized in the form of red ochre (line 36). It extends as far as the western tribes on the boundary of the north-eastern-north-central Arnhem Land cultural bloc (lines 37–8), to country on the mainland behind Milingimbi, in the Barara *mata* ('Seagull' linguistic group) of the Bara *mala* ('North-west wind' clan), covering territory known as Burulmura. It reaches out, lighting up and warming all the places through which the Djanggawul are later to travel.

82

Comments on Part One of the Songs

Although most of the songs are self-explanatory, they need some additional comments and, as mentioned, should ideally be read in conjunction with the interlinear translations and accompanying notes. Throughout these songs there is a delightfully smooth rhythmic sequence. In Song 1 the Morning Star rises, guiding the Djanggawul on their journey, and providing an ever-present link with Bralgu Island, the place which they have left. They see a green backed turtle (Song 2) glistening in the rays of the Star; and various fish emerge from the sea as they paddle along (Song 3). Geese settle on the surface of the sea (Song 5) and are likened to the hordes of people to which the Djanggawul Sisters will later give birth, after reaching the mainland. Then a whale appears (Song 6), symbol of both the *ngainmara* mat and of the uterus. A catfish swims before the mouth of the whale (Song 7), and barely escapes being swallowed. Sea eggs float in great numbers on the surface (Song 8), and in Song 9 a green turtle appears to feed on them. Drift-wood (Song 10) floats by, with plovers swooping around it and sitting upon it (Song 11). The Djanggawul continue along the path of light sent by the Morning Star; and their paddling, like the movements of the various marine creatures, creates waves, spray and foam. Sponges appear floating (Song 13) and porpoises race behind the canoe (Song 14). A monstrous sawfish protrudes itself from the sea (Song 15), followed by a smaller one (Song 16), and by more porpoises (Song 17) with their young, spraying and splashing, making foam. Seagulls (Song 18) swoop to and fro, heralding their approach to the mainland, and lending impetus to their paddling. Again an immense sawfish appears (Song 19); it is viewed apprehensively by the Djanggawul, who fear that their canoe may be overturned. As they come near the mainland, they see floating masses of seaweed (Song 20). The last rays of the Morning Star continue to guide them, and now they are not far from Port Bradshaw (Song 21): its rays are driving away the darkness, bringing the day. Gradually the dawn appears, heralded by the morning pigeon (Song 22); but still there is darkness in the western sky. The cry of the pigeon is followed by the long drawn sound of a black bird (unidentified), Song 23; the Morning Star has almost set, drawn away by the Spirit people at Bralgu.

Then the red glow of the sun appears in the east (Song 24). Gradually its rays spread, and its disc rises above the horizon, casting reflections on the sea, illuminating the mainland, warming the Djanggawul and all the land. Flying foxes screech, in the sacred *djuda* trees on the mainland (Song 25). The Djanggawul discover that their *ngainmara* mat and *rangga* are sodden with sea water (Song 26); they throw some away as they enter Port Bradshaw, so

Comments on Part One of the Songs

that to-day a reef lies there. Finally, we are told that they are worrying about the *rangga* and mat they have thrown into the sea (Song 27); they are exhausted after their long journey. They beach their canoe, and exclaim that at last they have reached their own land.

In Song 1 (*et. seq.*) Bralbral[1] and the Djanggawul call each other by the kinship term *waridj*; this is equivalent to *mari* or *gudara* (mother's mother, mother's mother's brother, mother's brother's son's wife, mother's mother's brother's son's daughter, wife's brother's wife, mother's mother's brother's son's son, etc.).[2] The term *waridj* is also commonly used at Yirrkalla (although not at Milingimbi) to signify a non-tabued 'mother-in-law' (mother's brother's wife), a relative who, if actually a wife's mother, would be *mugul rumarang*. Bralbral continually asks questions, intimating that he is less knowledgeable than the Djanggawul; and he has little or no handling of the *rangga*.

The Djanggawul and Bralbral rest on their oars when they are tired (for example Song 1, line 11), or when they fear a marine monster (Song 15, line 1) and must go carefully. As they paddle they undulate their buttocks, swaying their hips, as they stand and dip their oars from side to side.

Throughout this Part of the cycle references are made to the Morning Star, which provides a definite link with the island of Bralgu. It is said that as the Djanggawul look back, seeing the arc of light made by the Morning Star (for example Song 1, line 14), they are able to gauge the distance they have come, as well as the distance they have yet to go. The Star's disc is an 'eye' (line 16) which is said to 'swim' along through the water (line 17) and mount into the sky; it cannot rise too far, for it is held at the end of a string and must remain over Bralgu. The Morning Star is really a ball of seagull feathers attached to a long string, which in turn is tied to a paperbark sapling; there is not only one Star, but many (see latter part of Song 1). The Spirit people at Bralgu hold a ceremony each night and early morning. They dance with arms outstretched (line 19), and sing. As they pound their feet upon the ground, great clouds of dust rise upwards and bring the dusk which, as their dancing intensifies, turns to night. They then manipulate their long dancing pole (the paperbark sapling), with the long string to which feathered balls are attached (line 21). Each 'ball' represents a Morning Star, which the Bralgu Spirits send out towards a particular place on the mainland; it is one of these Morning Star 'balls' which guides the Djanggawul on their journey across the sea.

[1] Bralbral's name is used to designate a clan in the Wessel Islands—the Barabara or Ba'ralba'ral; the clan is also termed the *babaru* (father's clan) of this Ancestral Being.

[2] *Vide* texts and notes in proposed *Oceania* monograph.

Comments on Part One of the Songs

This subject is treated in some considerable detail in the secular Bralgu Song Cycle, associated with the Morning Star ceremony (used during mortuary rituals, for Bralgu is the *dua* moiety home of the dead), when a long pole with string and feathered balls is used, and dancing imitates that of the Bralgu Spirits.

The paddling of the Djanggawul in their canoe, and the roar of the sea, are re-enacted in the *dua nara* (see Chapter 1). A spear-thrower is dragged along the ground symbolizing the paddling. The dancers cry *ei ei a:!* which is the sound of the sea, *a:!* being the dull roar as the waves break. Then they lift up their legs, representing the rising waves which carry the canoe to their crests (line 24, Song 1) and then collapse downwards.

Lines 31-2, Song 1, refer to the *ngainmara* and to the *rangga*, which are carried in the bottom of the canoe (*vide* Song 26, in reference to their being sodden). The *rangga* are stored within the mat (= uterus, with children within), and include the *mauwulan*, the yam stick, *djuda* and *djanda* poles. As the canoe rolls, they move about in the mat and rattle (line 32).

In Song 2 (lines 5, 6 and 7) the green-backed turtle is said to possess a dilly bag: this may be seen from the mark of this bag on the turtle's under shell (its 'chest'); it holds its bag under one flipper, as a man holds his dilly bag when walking or dancing. The cuttlefish is also said to represent the bag of this turtle.

Many references are made throughout the songs, in this section of the cycle, to the Baijini folk (for example, Song 4, line 3)—that is, 'Paddling fast as we smell the Baijini from far away.' Several words used in the text are said to be directly associated with these alien people of the *jiritja* moiety: for example, *buragoimin*, 'sea smell' (line 3), which is also said to mean the smell of the smoke from the Baijini fires, at their settlement at Port Bradshaw. The Djanggawul see the smoke rising in the distance, and know that they must be drawing close to the mainland. The Two Sisters talk with their Brother. 'What do we see? What blocks (or obstructs) our passage? There are strangers in that place! They are blocking us, so we shall sing about them. But as soon as we reach Jelangbara (Port Bradshaw) we will move the Baijini: they can't stop, where we intend to have our sacred camp.' As they draw closer, they hear this word, *buragoimin*, drifting over to them, and for that reason it is included in the song.

Nevertheless, as mentioned in Chapter 3, there is a certain amount of rationalization here. The Djanggawul are frequently said to have been the first 'human' beings to land on the mainland; and yet this contradiction appears in the actual traditional texts, which infer that the *jiritja* Baijini have already settled at Port

Comments on Part One of the Songs

Bradshaw. This is a problem which cannot be solved, and we may only conjecture as to the true state of affairs. However, in the Song, the fires of the Baijini, their talking, and the sea smell from their fires, all incite the Djanggawul to paddle faster, in order to reach the mainland in the shortest possible time.

The reference to careful paddling (see Song 4, line 14) suggests the roughness of the sea, and the Djanggawul's anxiety lest they should inadvertently upset the canoe, and so lose the mat and sacred *rangga*. This care is particularly evident when a marine monster appears; but despite it they eventually get their *rangga* and mat wet, and decide to throw them away (Song 26).

The 'sea goose' mentioned in Song 5 is not really a goose, but merely resembles one: it has white chest feathers, the rest of its body being bluish grey tinged with red. Normally it lives among the swamps, but occasionally flies far out to sea. The introduction of such a bird into this section of the cycle suggests that the Djanggawul are nearing land. The geese come from Buragumi (line 2), a place comparatively close to Port Bradshaw, but occupied at that time by the Baijini. The word *mala* is used in reference to flocks of these birds, as they settle on the water before the paddling Djanggawul; *mala* may simply mean a 'crowd' or a 'lot', but here it refers to a 'clan', that is, a clan of geese. The word *madjara* (line 3), or *maidjaraua* in Song 1, line 32, is used in reference not only to a flock or clan of geese, but also to sacred *rangga* emblems; another example of this is *jandaljandalju* (Song 5, line 3), or *jandaljandalwa* (Song 1, line 32), a term which refers collectively to the emblems. This usage is fairly common in the songs, when 'inside' terms refer to different things and must be explained in context. On the other hand, such words with multiple meanings are used symbolically, like (for example) the word *ngainmara*, a mat, bag, uterus, or whale. The flocks of geese suggest the idea of plenty and fertility: 'They are like the many people we shall soon put on the mainland' (say the Djanggawul). *Vide* line 5, 'Flocks of birds, like hordes of people, people whom we shall put on the mainland.'

The word *bongunbongun* (*bunginbungin*), Song 5, line 4, although referring to the *mala* of these sea birds, is to-day used to classify all the Aborigines from the Cape Stewart region, a little west of Milingimbi, across to Darwin: that is, people who do not belong to the north-eastern Arnhem Land cultural bloc. In line 4 (*vide* original text) the word *ereingu* (or *jereingu*) is used, and translated as 'half the people in here', referring to the people who are to be removed from the Sisters' uteri and left at various places. The same theme is extended in line 5; this refers to a large group of people towards Arnhem Bay, and to the Gurwia *mala*, a group

86

Comments on Part One of the Songs

who were south-west of Yirrkalla in the bush. All, however, are symbolized in the flocks of geese seen by the Djanggawul. The symbolism is extended in line 9: 'Grey crested birds . . . emerging from the mouth of the *ngainmara* mat!' that is, like people issuing from the Sisters' uteri, the mat.

In Song 6 we are told of the whale which intercepts the paddling of the Djanggawul, and causes large waves which threaten to overturn the canoe; it is called by the term *ngainmara*, mat or uterus. Its gaping mouth, *dalwuldalwul* (also *wagulwagul*), is equivalent to *dalwuddalwu* (Song 1, line 31), the 'mouth' of the *ngainmara*, conversely vulva or vagina. The Djanggawul observe it in the sea—' '. . . Our *ngainmara* mat, swimming under the water!' (Song 6, line 5); that is, it is like the *ngainmara* they carry in the canoe. Translators comment, 'there is the whale in the sea; it is really the mat. When the Djanggawul Sisters give birth to female children (*vide* Myth, Chapter 2), these are put under the mat, or into the belly of the whale (through the *dalwuldalwul*).' In line 10 reference is made to the Djanggawul's taking some baskets (= mats), and leaving others in the sea to form whales. The Djanggawul and Bralbral are talking: 'Some baskets we can take with us,' they say, 'and some we can leave in the sea water, like the *ngainmara* whale.' That is to say, the Djanggawul leave the whale 'basket' (as the mat is called) in the sea, and take the 'ordinary' *ngainmara* with them (line 11).

In Song 7 a catfish comes to the surface and 'plays' before the gaping mouth of the whale (line 3). The fish is like a *rangga* about to be put inside the *ngainmara*, or a penis entering a vagina (gaping mouth). The 'whiskers' of the whale touch the fish (lines 1 and 6); they are like the pandanus fringe of the *ngainmara* mat (= pubic hairs of the Sisters). These whiskers are referred to by the same word as that used for the greyish feathers of the sea goose (Song 5), inferring that they also are greyish in colour.

In Song 8, the Djanggawul observe sea eggs for the first time; they are 'strangers' (line 3) from Bralgu, having drifted from there to the mainland. In line 10 (*et passim*), the Djanggawul are said to have grown grey: 'too long they sat down at Bralgu, collecting a lot of *rangga* emblems; and so they became grey.' What is suggested, however, is not so much the greyness of age, as the whiteness of the sea water and foam which has splashed up from their paddling and stained their hair. They are, moreover, stained with sea and foam markings all over their bodies, and these form patterns which will afterwards be used as clan designs.

In Song 9 a turtle emerges to the surface, for it smells the sea eggs; its shell reflects the rays of the Morning Star (line 9).

Comments on Part One of the Songs

In Song 10 drift-wood appears floating near the canoe. Sometimes this comprises merely odd pieces of tree limbs or trunks, but occasionally planks (from wrecks and so on) wash down to north-eastern Arnhem Land from Cape York, the Torres Straits, New Guinea and even, possibly, from the East Indies. Carved or painted planks were sometimes used as *rangga* emblems by the Arnhem Landers. The drift-wood speaks (there is a tendency to personalize, in this way, various birds, animals and objects), 'I leave the foam on my body'; (line 10) that is, foam accumulates on it, forming patterns that resemble totemic designs.

Black birds, plovers, hover around the drifting timber (Song 11); their cry echoes across to the rising clouds. This cry is said to be a 'message' for the Djanggawul (line 9), telling them that they are not far from Port Bradshaw. Reference is also made to 'message clouds', that bend down from the main mass. In Song 13, line 3, we read that the Djanggawul scratch themselves. The 'singing' name of the sponge means 'scratching', for as the Djanggawul rest on their paddles the Brother leans forward and picks one up; idly he squeezes it, then throws it back into the sea. Later he rubs his hands on his thighs, but some unidentified substance from the sponge sets up an irritation on his skin, causing the Brother to scratch. Another 'singing' name for the sponge means 'children playing', suggesting that children play with these dry sponges when they are washed up on to the beaches. In Song 14, line 12, we are again told how the foam from the pounding surf puts patterns on the shoulders and bodies of the Djanggawul, to be used later by them as clan and linguistic group designs.

The (unidentified) sawfish mentioned in Song 15 is also said to be a 'long nosed small black whale'; it is called *deimiri*, and from native drawings appears to be a species of sawfish. Many stories are told of its ferocity, of how it rises erect from the water and falls upon a canoe, breaking it up; alternatively, it may swallow the canoe and its contents completely. Smaller sawfish (Song 16) also appear, fighting smaller fish. The Djanggawul paddle very carefully, for the movement of all these fish causes waves and splashing, making the sea rough. Song 17 brings the porpoise into the picture which is gradually built up by these songs. Reference is made (line 5) to the young porpoises, who are said to have been born in the fresh-water creeks at the island of Bralgu. Aborigines say that the water which they spurt out, as they race behind a canoe or play in the sea, goes in through their mouths and out through the aperture in the back of their heads, 'in much the same way as a human being urinates'.

In Song 18 a seagull swoops towards the oncoming canoe of

the Djanggawul; it gives 'power' to their paddling, and enables them to reach the mainland quickly (line 3). It is said that 'when you are tired from too much paddling (as the Djanggawul were), this gull circles around the canoe, and as you see it, it gives you renewed energy'. The country about Yirrkalla is totemically associated with this bird, from whose cry the Riradjingu linguistic group derives its name. Line 7 refers to the fact that the female gull lays its eggs at the onset of the wet season; thus it ' . . . cries out as it sees the dark rain clouds rising', ' . . . Cries out at the time of the wet season: it thinks of nesting' (line 8). A popular nesting place for seagulls is at Bremer Island (line 9), which may be seen from Yirrkalla.

Song 19 introduces us to the ferocious *marabinjin* sawfish, so fierce that it attacks any other fish, and any canoe; and there are tales of its even having capsized Macassan craft in the old days. This fish whips up the water (line 5), making it very dangerous for the Djanggawul. In its body it carries a 'poison bag' (lines 11 and 12), from which, when it is 'angry', poison is transmitted to the barbs or teeth of its saw. The fish itself speaks in the song, boasting that it makes the sea rough, and that no canoe may go near where it swims (line 13). The Djanggawul paddle in great haste, trying to leave it far behind.

Song 21 includes all the main elements in Songs 1, 4 and 12; it is the final song in which the Morning Star supplies the dominant theme. We are told again how, sent by the Bralgu Spirits, it has guided the Djanggawul on their journey to Arnhem Land; but now it is gradually sinking, heralding the dawn (lines 14, 15 and 16): 'The Morning Star shines, bringing the dawn . . . putting an end to the night . . . Close to us, ending the darkness, bringing the dawn . . . ' In line 17 the Morning Star is said to shine like the *mauwulan rangga* pole, decorated with red breast feathers from the parakeet; this suggests (see Song 24) that the Star is possessed of some of the sun's substance. However, the feathered 'ball' which is the Star is made solely of white birds' down: the feathered jungle string to which it is fastened is intertwined with red parakeet feathers. Conversely, the feathered parakeet pendants attached to the *mauwulan rangga* (and also to other *dua* moiety *rangga*) have white down terminals; the above line refers to this feature.

Before the dawn, while the Morning Star is sinking (drawn back to Bralgu by the Spirits), comes the sound of the morning pigeon (Song 22). 'Darkness goes, with its cry!' (line 3), which is heard in ' . . . the calmness of dawn . . . ' (line 6). This pigeon is said to be a yellow or brown swamp bird, of the jiritja moiety. Reference is made to its teaching its young to utter the same cry (lines 8, 13 and 14), and its peculiar whistle is said to be from 'twisting its tongue'. The pigeons' nests are in the 'arm-band' bushes on the mainland, which provide pliable cane for the manufacture of armlets like those worn by the Djanggawul (*vide* Song 26, line 6). Such nests are noted for their inner smoothness (Song 22, line 9), and the alternative term used for them is *dagawal* or *dagu*, meaning hole or vagina. The birds[1] nesting within are like *rangga* within the *ngainmara*, symbolically representing children in the uterus (here, again, we have the predominating theme of the cycle). The bird is described by the term *dulboingu*, referring to the Gumaidj *jiritja* linguistic group at Caledon Bay; and its cry 'sounds like' the speech of the Madarlpa linguistic group, as well as like that of the Dalwongu.

Following the pigeon are unidentified black birds of the *dua* moiety (Song 23); these live in the jungles adjacent to the sea coast, and fly out to sea. The Djanggawul have now almost reached Port Bradshaw. This bird, too, cried out as it '. . . saw the darkness clearing' (line 5). Its young are mentioned (line 9), and its nests in the 'coffee' trees (line 14); the word referring to this tree also refers to the sacred *djuda rangga* emblem. Although no *djuda* have as yet been 'planted' on the mainland, it is implied that they will be (for example, in Song 25, line 6, in reference to the flying fox).

Song 24 brings us to the sun, which gradually emerges from its watery home below the sea (lines 6, 9, 11). (*Vide* Chapter 2, where reference is made to the sun.) It beats on the backs of the paddling Djanggawul, as they travel westwards; the term *bialdan* means 'burns their backs'. The importance of the ideas brought out in this song have already been noted, and need not be reiterated. The sun's rays are 'caught' or symbolized in the beautiful red breast feathers of the parakeet birds, and the long strings or pendants of these feathers are themselves the very essence of the sun, of its warmth and fructifying qualities; this is a feature that appears throughout the cycle. As the sun beats down on their backs, the Djanggawul sweat (line 13) from the unaccustomed warmth, accentuated by their vigorous paddling. The word used for 'sweat', *ngeingeijun*, also refers to grass dried up by the hot sun: that is, all the moisture is drawn out, and the inner part or body becomes dry. So strong is the glare from the sun that the Djanggawul are obliged to close their eyes (line 14). The Morning Star has disappeared; the cry of the morning pigeon or of the black bird is heard no longer. The mainland is clearly seen, and their destination is in sight.

[1] The bird calls its nestlings *wagu*, a term used by a mother when addressing her children, or by a man to his sister's children.

Comments on Part One of the Songs

Song 25 suggests that the Djanggawul are close to the mainland: the flying foxes are crying from their trees, which are said to be *djuda rangga* (lines 6, 7 and 8). In Song 26 the travellers discover that the *rangga* and mat(s) they have carried in their canoe have become sodden with salt water and spray. Bralbral asks the Djanggawul what they intend to do with the wet *rangga*, tied up in the basket (mat)—line 8, they decide to throw the basket away with the *rangga* inside. On second thoughts, the Djanggawul Brother says, 'No! We will have a look inside first, before they sink down into the sea.' The Two Sisters, however, object. 'No, you are not going to open (or untie) it. You can just throw it into the sea, because it has all got wet.' Since the Sisters are the real custodians of the sacred *rangga*, the decision rests with them; the Djanggawul Brother and his companion Bralbral can do nothing. They therefore throw the *rangga* over the side of their canoe, so that they '. . . sink down, making a noise as the sea covers them' (line 13). Some *rangga*, however, have been kept. It is not clear whether the basket (or mat) containing the *rangga* is thrown overboard, or whether the *rangga* are removed and then thrown out of the canoe. A native drawing (*vide* original text and notes) shows the *rangga* being removed from the *ngainmara*. Not only are the *rangga* wet, but their decorations, like the fibre of the mat, are stained with spray and foam. One part of the original text suggests that the mat is first undone (its 'mouth' opened), and then turned upside down so that the *rangga* fall out one by one into the water; finally, the mat itself is 'put into the water'. The *rangga* make a reef outside the entrance to Port Bradshaw, while the mat turns into a whale (*vide* Song 6). The text, however, indicates rather that the 'mouth' or aperture of the mat was not undone, and all the *rangga* were just dumped overboard. As they are thrown into the sea, the Djanggawul call the sacred invocations (line 12); see Chapter 1.

In the last song (27) of this section, we are told that the Brother and Bralbral regret having thrown away the *rangga* and mat without first looking at them. 'I am worrying (says the Djanggawul Brother) about the *rangga*. (Why didn't we open the mat?)'—line 5. They attribute their carelessness to their being tired—'I am just tired! That was why *waridj*, we threw away the sacred *rangga* and mat.'—line 6. They are very weary, for they have travelled such a long way; and at last they have reached Port Bradshaw. 'That is our country!' (line 9) they exclaim, as they beach their canoe, 'We have arrived, oh *Waridj*!' (line 10). The Djanggawul step on to the shore, and insert their *mauwulan rangga* into the ground; at its withdrawal water gushes forth, leaving a permanent spring.

In commenting on these songs, we have mentioned only the

outstanding details. Many interesting features are revealed in the phonetic texts, and these are discussed elsewhere. We can see, however, how well controlled is the theme, how ideas follow in sequence, and how behind all the various incidents a definite structure or pattern is evolved and retained. Certain points are constantly reiterated throughout most of this section. This is a common practice in most song cycles of north-eastern and north-central Arnhem Land, where it is apparently felt that repetition gives background and atmosphere to the separate songs. The paddling, the Morning Star, the roar of the sea with its spray and foam, appear again and again. There is a feeling of movement and action which lends veracity to the saga; the eternal movement of the sea, its constant roar, and ever undulating waves, are said to have been caused not only by the paddling of the Djanggawul, but by the marine creatures which they meet on their journey. Wherever possible too, the underlying pattern of the Djanggawul ideology is linked to various incidents and themes: the flocks of birds and nests, for instance; the rolling *rangga* in the mat, rattling with the movement of the canoe; the whale *ngainmara*; the *rangga* and feathered string, and the rays from the sun; the throwing overboard of the *rangga* and mat, and so on; all intrude themselves to express the symbolic significance of the Djanggawul's journey.

Chapter Seven

THE DJANGGAWUL SONG CYCLE

PART TWO

In which the Djanggawul land at Port Bradshaw, and walk around in its immediate vicinity.

Song 28

W E reach the shore! We leap from our canoe, oh *waridj* Miralaidj! 1
 Shall we put in the *mauwulan rangga* here, *waridj*? Not yet! That (string) must first be attached.
I myself (says Miralaidj) put feathered pendants from my arm-bands on the *mauwulan* emblem. Myself, *waridj*, I put them . . .
Try plunging the point of the *rangga* into the ground, making a well.
Put the *mauwulan* in for us, *waridj* (say the Djanggawul Brother, and Bralbral) . . . 5
Yes, all right, *waridj* (says Bralbral). You do it for us.
I am doing it for us (says the Djanggawul Brother); for us, Bildjiwuraroiju, I put the *rangga* point into the ground.
It's all right! Water, fresh water, is surging up for us!
For us, water surges up in the well, from our *mauwulan* point . . . !
Go on, *waridj*, taste it! Taste that well water! 10
It is surging up at Port Bradshaw, at the Place of the Mauwulan.
It is good, *waridj*, the water that rises up?
Yes, this is good, *waridj*! But first it was salt to the taste.
You, *waridj*, taste with your tongue, just on the tip of your tongue.
I'll put on my tongue just a drop from that well. Ah! It tastes good, for us, *waridj* Miralaidj. 15

Indeed, this is good! When we have finished here we shall cover
it up.
Our well, and its water, are sacred!

Song 29

Waridj Djanggawul, shall we put out the *rangga* to dry? They are
wet from the foam and the spray.   1
We spread them out, to dry in the warm rays of the sun.
The sun looks on us, warming us. We are hot, very hot, oh *waridj*
Djanggawul . . . !
Spread them to dry as the sun's disc rises, growing hotter, so
sweat comes out.
Spread them thus, to make them good, to dry them in the rays of
the sun, *waridj* Djanggawul!   5
Thus we spread them out to dry, for the sea has soaked them
through.
The sun will make good again their feathered strings. Red feathers
shining in the sun, feathered pendants like the sun's rays . . . !
Thus we make them good, putting them out to dry. Feathered
rangga, our children, from the *ngainmara* mat!
Feathered strings on the *rangga*, feathered arm-bands! We make
good again all the feathered pendants . . .
Thus we make dry the arm-bands, feathered strings like the rays
of the sun.   10
Thus we straighten the feathered strings, stained and wet with
foam, so they may dry in the sun.
Let them stay there, spread out to dry at Port Bradshaw, at the
Place of the Sun.
Watching the sea. It is roaring. The noise of the spray!
We make them good, we dry them, our strings and *rangga*. They
are wet, after their long journey from Bralgu.
Foam from out on the sea has splashed them, foam from afar!   15
We make them good, putting them out to dry—our feathered
pendants, our children!
What shall we do, *waridj?* Shall we sit down here? No, this is close
to the sea. We'll go somewhere else,
We'll move away to another place, a place that is dry.
There we shall live, making a sacred shade to store our *rangga* . . .
Yes, *waridj*, it is agreed; that is where we shall go.   20
We shall move there, and among the arm-band bushes we'll make
a large shade, with gaping mouth.
Yes, indeed, *waridj* (says Bralbral), it is agreed; I was just wishing
to ask you . . .

The Djanggawul Song Cycle

Song 30

We walk along, making the country, with the aid of the *mauwulan*
  rangga.   1
We put the point of the *rangga* into the ground and sing all the way
  along, swaying our hips.
Oh, *waridj* Miralaidj, our heads are lolling in weariness! Our bodies
  ache, after our long journey from Bralgu!
We are making country, Bildjiwuraroiju, the large sandhill at the
  Place of the Mauwulan!
We Djanggawul, walking along, see clouds coming up in the
  distance . . .   5
See those spreading white clouds, that rise above Wobilinga
  Island,
See them rising over Bilari Hill. Clouds coming up for us,
  waridj!
We plunge the *mauwulan* point into the ground, making it good.
We shall put it in at our sandhill, for us, *waridj* Bralbral!
We are clapping our sticks and singing, to make ourselves strong,
  swaying our hips as we walk.   10
We saw the clouds, there, above Ganjumingalei,
Saw those clouds coming up, behind Port Bradshaw;
Rising for us, rising to guide us, *waridj*.
Ourselves we are making the country, making it around Port
  Bradshaw: the Place of the Sun, the Place of the Mauwulan
  Rangga!
For these are the places which we saw first of all!   15
There are clouds coming, from the country at Arnhem Bay!
Clouds we saw, making us feel good as we walk, swaying our
  hips, oh *waridj* Djanggawul!

Song 31

What is that, *waridj*? That is a black cockatoo.   1
Why is it calling out, from the sacred tree, with a feeble cry?
The sun is hidden: cloud shadows fall on its body, making it
  cold:
It grasps the tree, scratching, and pecks it, as the *mauwulan* stabs
  the ground,
There at the Place of the Mauwulan, with its long beak, up in the
  topmost branches.   5
A long-drawn cry comes from the top of the tree. Why does it
  peck, like the *mauwulan*?

The tree is its shade, a *rangga* shade. It cocks its head from side to side, watching them from the tree,
Up in the leaves of the topmost branches, hearing the roar of the sea.
Scratching, it grasps the limbs of the sacred tree.
What is that long-drawn cry, that low cry? It has heard the sea, pounding at Luringei beach (beyond the Island).   10
A long cry comes as we first make the country, calling the place names, at Wobilinga.
A long cry from its open beak, its claws grasping a branch of the red-blossomed trees among the mangroves.
What is that cry, as the bird looks back at us, prodding the ground with our *mauwulan*?
It has seen the Ngadibalji rocks there, on the beach, from the Brother's waist belt!
Uttering its long-drawn cry, wearily, watching the clouds rising at Bilbam.   15
Watching the clouds rising up from the Place of the Ngainmara, out in the sea.
It saw the clouds rise there, at the Place of the Star, clouds above Bilari Hill!
Giving its long-drawn cry, as we walk with the aid of the *mauwulan*, making country!
It saw the water. The roar of the rising tide!
Crying out, as it saw the spreading foam! A long cry from its *rangga* shade, from the topmost branches!   20
Scratching, the bird utters its long-drawn cry, calling the sacred names of the *rangga*, and of the *djuda* tree!

Song 32

What is that, *waridj* Bralbral? It is a duck.   1
Yes, *waridj* Djanggawul, a duck! Flapping its wings, and quacking!
Ducks clustered, eating, around red *munji* berry bushes!
Their tracks on the sandhill! Heads and tails erect, they are going in search of berries . . .
Tracks leading this way and that—into the *nara* shade! Into the shade, to the sacred *rangga* place!   5
White feathers like paint on its breast—foam from the sea, foam which has stained it as it came flying from Bralgu!
From the open sea, leaving marks of white clay; it came from Bralgu to the Place of the Sun.
It leaves white clay at that place, along the Port Bradshaw coast!

11. The Djanggawul Beings on arrival at Jelangbara, holding *rangga* emblems.

12. A ceremonial leader (Manimbar) represents the Djanggawul Brother as he tastes water on arriving at Port Bradshaw.

13. Sacred sites at Port Bradshaw; showing *rangga* folk left by the Djanggawul.

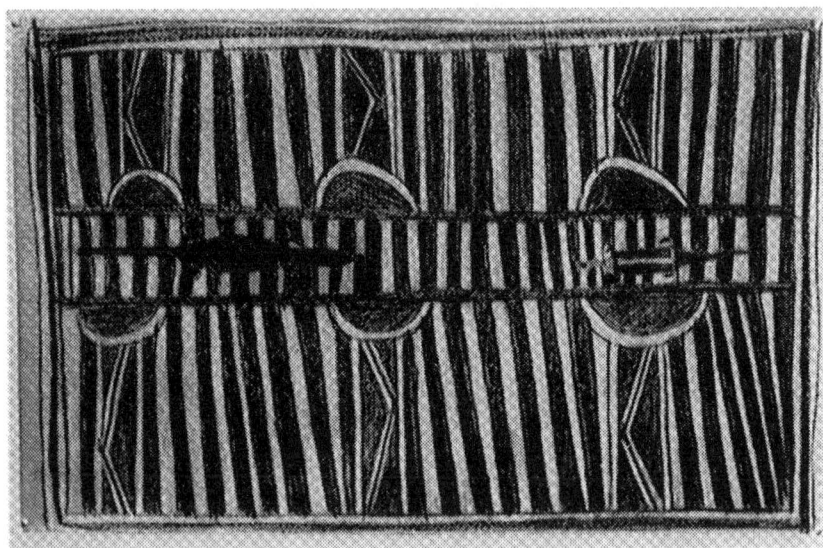

14. The sacred goanna at the Place of the Mauwulan.

The Djanggawul Song Cycle

Spray splashes on to the ducks, leaving marks of white clay,
Putting it on at Bilabinjang, *waridj*, for us! We sing as we clap our
    sticks! 10
Ducks cluster about the red *munji* berry bushes, *waridj*, for us!
With swaying hips we hear their cry, *waridj*, for us!
We hear the sound of wings, beating fast! Tail feathers blown in
    the wind! Noise of a flock of ducks, flying above us!
Step by step, *waridj*, we leave behind us the sound of the swift-
    flying ducks, the sound of their cries;
Leaving them, alone by themselves, there at that sandhill, at the
    Place of the Mauwulan Rangga. 15

Song 33

What is this crying, *waridj* Djanggawul? *Waridj*, it is a parakeet, 1
Calling softly from the sacred tree, its red breast feathers glistening
    in the sun.
It grasps the *rangga* tree, watching them, cocking its head from side
    to side as if it were weary.
It ruffles its breast feathers, making them dry. Trilling and calling,
    with head moving, grasping the sacred tree!
Softly, it calls the invocations of the sacred tree. 5
There, on the tree, it saw the sun's rays and the glowing sunset
    sky,
Saw the rays of the sun setting, in the west beyond Milingimbi.
Drying its red feathers in the glow of the sun, it clasps and scratches
    the tree with its claws . . .
It watched the sinking sun, saw the last rays shining at Arnhem
    Bay,
Saw the red glow spreading over Arnhem Bay, multi-coloured
    rays of the sunset! 10
Shining into the sacred shade, lighting it up, away towards Arnhem
    Bay!
Calling softly, it watched the sun setting at Bulibuli,
Looked at the sun, and spoke: 'I am drying myself, my red breast
    feathers, my *rangga* feathers—my children!'

Song 34

Oh, what is that? We shall sit down, *waridj*, at our Place of the
    Mauwulan. We Djanggawul, we shall make camp. 1
In this place, where we sit, we leave the mark of our buttocks.
We shall make our camp here, our sacred shade.

It is our own shade, on its frame of branches. We name the places,
at the sacred sandhill.

We shall put the sacred *rangga*, the *djuda rangga*, into the mouth of
the shade.   5

We shall put in the sacred *rangga*, calling the sacred invocations of
the *djuda* tree . . .

We shall put in another *rangga*, *waridj* Djanggawul, put the sacred
rangga emblems into the mouth of the shade . . .

We call the sacred invocations of the *djuda* tree, the elbow-like
limbs of the *djuda*!

We put in the *rangga*, calling, invoking their spirits . . .

Leaving the *rangga* erect, because we are invoking the sacred names.
Trees shoot up from the *rangga* poles!   10

We put in the sacred *rangga*, the jutting limbs like our elbows,
calling the sacred names!

Into the sandhill, *waridj*, we put the sacred *rangga*, at the Place of
the Mauwulan Rangga, the Place of the Sun.

Another *djuda*, *waridj*. Bralbral! We'll put in the sacred *rangga*, put
it into the shade, calling the invocations!

Calling the sacred names of the *djuda*, putting the *mauwulan* in,
calling the invocations!

Trees shoot up, with branches and leaves, when we put in the sacred
rangga—the sacred trees!   15

We fasten on to the *rangga*, to make them strong, the red feathered
strings from the parakeet.

Another sacred *rangga*, *waridj* Djanggawul, we put there, calling
the invocations,

Calling the sacred names as we put in the *rangga* . . . and trees
spring up.

We put in that *rangga*, *waridj*, at the Place of the Sun, so it may look
at the sea,

Hear the roar of the sea, from the Place of the Mauwulan. The
djuda growing there, in sight of the splashing foam,   20

So it may look at the rough expanse of the sea.

We take the *djuda*, the *rangga*, from the mouth of the sacred *ngainmara*,
putting them there, out of the sacred mat.

The *rangga* stand there, feathered strings drying, stretched out like
yam foliage, on that sacred tree.

It is from the *mauwulan*, *waridj* Bralbral. *Waridj* Djanggawul, we
put the sacred *rangga* at the Place of the Sun, at the Place of the
Mauwulan.

We walk with the aid of the *mauwulan*, plunging in its point. Shall
we put *rangga* here?   25

Put the point of the *mauwulan* in there, *waridj* Djanggawul.

The Djanggawul Song Cycle

Song 35

Wei! What is that blocking us, *waridj* Djanggawul? 1

It is a *djanda* goanna, *waridj* Miralaidj. We walk along swaying our hips, and singing.

A *djanda* goanna! We leave it there crawling; by itself it is making country, putting the sacred sandhill.[1]

There with its body, its fat, and its verterbrae!

We leave it behind, *waridj* Djanggawul. It has made tracks on the sandhill, crawling and making country, at the Place of the Mauwulan. 5

We are clapping our sticks and singing, watching it crawling. We walk with the aid of the prodding *mauwulan*, making the country.

We are tired. We, ourselves, see that *djanda* goanna entering the mouth of the sacred *ngainmara* mat!

We shall cover it up (with the mat), *waridj* Djanggawul, for that goanna is fat, it is sacred!

We put it into the sacred well, as a *rangga*, at the Place of the Sun, the Place of the Mauwulan!

We leave it crawling! For we saw the sea, the roar of the incoming tide, as the water rose up in the well! It splashed in the well, making foam, like foam on the sea. 10

Water rising, high tide coming up, as the goanna kicked in the well; and the splashing spray!

It was moving its claws, and foam splashed as it dived.

We seized it as it came from the mouth of the *ngainmara* mat, *waridj* Bralbral, out of the sacred mat.

We leave it crawling along, by itself it is making country, putting the sacred sandhill.

We put it into the well, at the Place of the Mauwulan. 15

It can stay in there, that *djanda* goanna. Ourselves, *waridj* Djanggawul, we walk along with the aid of the *mauwulan*, swinging our thighs, clapping our sticks and singing.

We can see it, *waridj*, as we go making the country. We see clouds building up as we stab the ground with the point of the *mauwulan rangga* . . .

Bildjiwuraroiju, Miralaidj, Djanggawul! As we walk along shadows are cast on us, *waridj!* Shadows cast by the clouds, massing above the sea.

---

[1] Rationalization on the part of the Djanggawul. They themselves 'made' the sandhill, as they are said to have made other parts of the country.

The Djanggawul Song Cycle
Song 36

That is a yam plant, *waridj* Djanggawul. Shall we put it here?   1

It can see the water, hear the roar of the sea! We spread out the feathered strings, *waridj* Bralbral, the creepers, to make them strong.

Creepers and leaves of the yam grow from those feathered strings, for we spread them out on the ground.

Yam creepers and leaves, like feathered parakeet string, stretching out its 'arms'!

Looking back towards Bralgu those 'arms', growing strong in the sun! Stretching to Bilabinjang!   5

We make those creepers strong and good, *waridj*. Thus let them stretch, to Luringei!

We make them good, putting them down, the feathered-string creepers. Thus let them stretch, to Ngadibalji, the Place of the Djanggawul's Hair-Belt.

Let it stay strong and good, reaching to Bilbam rocks.

This is the yam foliage, *waridj*. We put it down. Let it stretch to Wobilinga Island!

Creeper runners, runners of feathered string! Cover them up, *waridj*, for us, at the Place of the Mauwulan.   10

These are creepers: we put them down. Thus let them stretch, to Jelangbara!

This foliage, *waridj*, we put it down. Thus let it stretch to Ngain-maralji, the rock, the site of the sacred mat!

Feathered strings, these are the creepers. Thus let them stretch to Balibingu Island!

Feathered string runners, we put them down to grow strong, stretching to Gularungngai!

We put creepers, *waridj*, this spreading foliage, looking back to Walbinboi Island, white as a sail!   15

These we put down, to grow strong, towards Gagubam Island.

Yam foliage lying there, seeing the water and spray, the roar of the incoming tide!

These, *waridj*, we put down thus, stretching to Birimalei.

Another leafy creeper we put down thus, towards Bilari Hill;

Then another leafy creeper to Birimalei.   20

Another good creeper of feathered string leads to south Port Bradshaw beach to Maldjalji.

And another yam creeper thus, *waridj*, let it stretch to Grurun-dei.

These creepers reaching to Marimidjalijuma, place of the Fighting Weapons!

Another feathered string we spread out here, yam creepers stretching
   into the Place of the Star.
This yam foliage, we put down. Thus let it stretch, towards
   Ngogawei!   25

Song 37

What is that, *waridj* Djanggawul? It is a blanket lizard, scratching
   the tree as it climbs, *waridj* Bralbral.   1
We are clapping our sticks and singing. Its head is poised, watching us,
As it climbs up, in among those trees, on those sacred *rangga*!
   Poised with protruding backbone, quietly watching!
Its frill is erect. It scratches the tree as it climbs, *waridj*, the sacred
   rangga! Grasping the tree, which is the sacred *rangga*!
Quietly it watches us, *waridj* Djanggawul, walking along with the
   aid of the *mauwulan*, swaying our hips.   5
Walking along, plunging the point of the *mauwulan* into the
   ground . . .
Why do we do it? So that there we may see the clouds coming up,
   for us, *waridj*, as we are walking along.
Clouds casting shadows over us, hiding the sun, as we prod the
   ground with the point of the *mauwulan*, putting the sandhills.
We walk along, *waridj* Miralaidj, Bildjiwuraroiju; we are weary.
   We hear the sound of the water, our water, as we make wells
   all along our way.
We leave behind that blanket lizard, watching us from the tree.   10
We poke the *rangga* into the ground, and they grow into trees,
Djuda trees, for us, *waridj* Bralbral, as we quietly walk along.

Song 38

What is that, *waridj* Djanggawul?   1
Yes, something is blocking us, *waridj* Bralbral. What can it be?
   Listen, is that the sound of the Baijini talking?
Are those their words that drift from the roofs of their huts, from
   the young Baijini playing?
We hear the noise, *waridj*, of their talking together.
Yes! That is the shine of their light skin! They are standing about,
   and working the trepang.   5
Yes, because they belong to the Djanala clan.
What can we do, how can we make them move?
We, *waridj*, shall quietly chase them away; they can't stop there!
Why can't they make their place at the other side, by themselves,
   waridj Djanggawul? They can make a big camp there.

But here, they make the place pale as they stand about together, at
  Bauwijara, at Janimbilnga (among their huts and their trepang
  camps).   10
We ourselves shall go there, when they have left, walking along
  with the *mauwulan*.
We ourselves shall go there, *waridj* Bralbral, go by ourselves,
  putting our footprints all along the beach.
We ourselves are making the country, putting a sandhill there,
  putting our footprints.
We hear the roar of the sea, and the spray wets us. *Waridj* Djanggawul, we are putting our footprints here.
The roar of the sea! Its foam and spray! We plunge in the point of
  the *mauwulan*, making wells . . .   15
This is for us, *waridj*, this trepang ladle left by the Baijini. We
  hide it, within the mouth of the *ngainmara*. Put it with care,
  waridj Bralbral!
Ourselves we are putting the country, hiding the ladle beneath
  our arm. It is sacred!
Yes, *waridj* Djanggawul, and we ourselves are sacred! We shall
  hide it, putting it in with the sacred *rangga*, *waridj*.
We plunge in the point of the *mauwulan rangga*, *waridj* Bralbral, for
  it can see the water, and hear its sound . . .
We quietly plunge in the *mauwulan* point, and there we see water
  come bubbling up.   20
Like spreading waves, water comes gushing forth.
Waridj, this is a *djuda* tree springing up, where we quietly plunged
  in our *rangga*, in there, at Wobilinga Island.
There, *waridj*, it stands, with feathered strings.
Quietly, we put in the sacred *djuda rangga*, with feathered strings,
  that grow into trees.
There the tree may see the foam and spray, feel the splash of the
  water.   25
We shall quietly put in those feathered strings, calling the sacred
  names, calling the invocations, so they will grow.
They are standing about, *waridj*, where we have left them: at the
  Place of the Mauwulan Rangga, the Place of the Sun.
So they may see the foam coming up, the rough expanse of sea.
Foam and spray coming up, from the plunging point of the *rangga*.

Song 39

We shall hang the sacred basket on that *djuda* tree, *waridj* Miralaidj, 1
Hang it on the sacred *rangga* tree, calling the invocations . . .

Hang the baskets on that tree, for we are weary: among the topmost
    branches of the *djuda* . . .
Wearily, we put them in the topmost branches of the *rangga* tree . . .
Baskets, with feathered pendants: we shall hang them in that shade,
    oh *waridj* Djanggawul . . .   5
Another basket, quietly we hang it, *waridj*: putting these baskets
    within our sacred shade.
We put them there, for they are in our *djuda* trees, our shade!
We put them in there to dry, *waridj* Bralbral, into the mouth of the
    shade,
Into the mouth of the shade, of the sacred *ngainmara* mat.
From within the fringe of the *ngainmara* mat, *waridj* Miralaidj, they
    can see the water at the Place of the Mauwulan, at the Place of
    the Sun, hearing its roar.   10
We put in these baskets, with feathered pendants. Why *waridj*?
    We leave them there, for drying.
Within this shade, we are drying them . . .
So we may hide them again, within the mouth of the mat,
Hide them in there, *waridj* Djanggawul, making them sacred.
For these we are hiding are stained, splashed with salt water and
    foam.   15
Salt water marks from Bralgu, from the open sea.
We ourselves are made sacred, *waridj*! We call the sacred invoca-
    tions . . .
We are putting the *rangga*, *waridj*, into the mouth of the *ngainmara*,
After drying them in the rays of the sun, putting on the feathered
    strings;
And we, ourselves, are stained with the sea.   20
We hang out the feathered arm-band pendants, putting them on
    the sacred *djuda* trees;
Drying the feathered strings on the *djuda* trees.
Rays of the sun touch them. We saw the rays making them warm
    and dry.

Song 40

That is an ordinary dilly bag, *waridj* Djanggawul.   1
We hang it up on the sacred *djuda* tree, with roots fast in the
    ground.
Let it dry, by itself, as we call the sacred invocations . . .
We put feathered string on that tree (which bears fruit for the
    sacred parakeet); there they may dry.
We saw them clasping the tree, like the parakeet. Calling the
    invocations!   5

The Djanggawul Song Cycle

We put the bag on that sacred *djuda* tree, that *rangga* with feathered pendants.
Another basket, *waridj*, we put there, to dry in the sun, calling the invocations!
Putting feathered strings on the tree, calling the *bugali*!
Let them dry there in the heat of the sun's rays, as we call the invocations!
They see the water at the Place of the Mauwulan, at the Place of the Sun!   10
The rays of the sun reach out to them, drying them in the warm glow of the sunset.
We hang them carefully on the tree, calling the invocations. They see the wide stretch of the sea, the rising tide, and the waves spreading . . .
From within the mouth, and the fringe, of the *ngainmara* mat.
We are drying them, for they are stained with foam and spray, straightening them out.
And putting the feathered pendants back into the *ngainmara* . . . 15

Song 41

That is a bird, *waridj*, a parakeet there for us, *waridj* Djanggawul: as we sing going along, clapping our sticks.   1
It is upon the sacred *djuda* tree, clasping the tree with its claws . . .
Let the parakeet stay there! It saw the sun's rays, and the glow of the sunset reflected in its feathered breast.
It calls softly: like red feathered pendants, perched at the top of the tree, crying, moving its head from side to side.
Drying itself and its children, its red breast feathers!   5
It saw the sun, its glowing rays at sunset:
Clasping the tree, like feathered string pendants! It looked at the rays of the sun, in the red sunset:
The bird on the sacred *djuda* sees the water, cries as the tide comes up.
It saw the rays of the sun, with its glowing redness, the spreading glow as it sank beyond Milingimbi.
Feathered string pendants drying, red breast feathers! 'Myself (says the bird) I am drying them, my children.'   10
It sees the red sunset sinking at Arnhem Bay,
There, in the Arnhem Bay country, the sun is setting.
Saw the feathered pendants glow, in the sunset redness from Arnhem Bay;
Saw the sun sinking there, at Ngubarei, its rays shining into the mouth of the sacred shade.

The Djanggawul Song Cycle

The parakeet called out, watching the bright sunset there at Dulabei,
    Arnhem Bay.   15
Let us leave that parakeet, like a feathered pendant, hanging on the
    sacred *djuda* tree . . .
Calling the sacred *djuda* invocations, drying, moving its head from
    side to side . . .
Clasping the limbs of the tree, calling the invocations for the sacred
    djuda, the sacred feathered pendants.

Song 42

We walk along, *waridj* Bralbral, with the aid of the *mauwulan rangga*,
    prodding the ground with its point: 1
With hips swaying, clapping our sticks as we sing, making good
    country, plunging in the *mauwulan* point.
Making the country for us, with Bildjiwuraroiju, with the
    mauwulan.
Ourselves, *waridj*, we lean on the *mauwulan*, going into Birimalei.
Yes, *waridj* Djanggawul, thus we plunge in our *mauwulan* point,
    into Gauwara (Place of the sacred sandhill) . . .   5
Why, *waridj*, shall we put in here the point of the *mauwulan*?
We shall plant here the roots of the sacred *djuda* tree, *waridj* Bralbral,
    putting in the point of the *mauwulan* . . .
There it stands, that *djuda* tree. We invoke the sacred *bugali* (that it
    may grow) . . .
For it sees the water, *waridj* Djanggawul, at the Place of the
    Mauwulan.
We put in the *djuda* roots, planting the *mauwulan* point.   10
The feathered pendants, the rooted *djuda* tree, can see the water,
    the tide coming roaring in.
Yes indeed, *waridj* Djanggawul, let us leave it standing there.
We shall leave it alone there, where it looks at the water.
We, *waridj*, continue on about the Place of the Mauwulan, with the
    aid of the *mauwulan rangga*,
Making country, as cloud shadows fall on our bodies.   15
Shadows upon us, long shadows cast on us by the massing
    clouds.
Waridj, we walk along step by step, putting the country, into
    Bilari Hill.
We are walking: our heads are grey!
We sing, *waridj*, clapping our sticks, making the country.
Carefully, *waridj* Miralaidj, put in the point of the stick: for here we
    shall rest and make camp.   20

No, we shall put only *djuda* here, putting the *djuda* roots, from the mouth of the sacred mat.

Carefully open its fringe, and take out the *djuda*:

For, *waridj* Djanggawul, we put it in here, with the sacred feathered pendants.

And these feathered strings, *waridj*, shall we undo them?

No, leave them in here like that! Let them stand, so they see the rising tide and the foam.   25

Now we put them back into the mat so no one may see them, at the Place of the Mauwulan.

Ourselves, *waridj* Bralbral, we invoke the sacred names for the *djuda*.

It sees the water, the tide rising and roaring. We are calling the invocations!

Waridj, we go along clapping our sticks and singing, poking the ground with the point of the *mauwulan rangga*.

Our foreheads are whitened with foam, coming from Garidbing: 30

Marks from the salt spray, from the sea on our journey from Bralgu.

For ourselves, we are making the country, at Bilari Hill.

Shadows fall on our bodies, from passing clouds.

With swaying thighs we are walking along, *waridj* Djanggawul,

Making country with the point of the *mauwulan*, around Bilari Hill.   35

Where shall we rest? In here? Why not here, so we may build a shade?

We must sit down somewhere, *waridj*, so we may open the mouth of the *ngainmara*, parting its fringe,

For shall we not put the roots of the *djuda* here, *waridj* Djanggawul?

No, not here shall we put our pendants, our feathered strings.

Song 43

It stands there, that *djuda* tree, *waridj*, for we call out the invocations, as we are planting its roots.   1

Yes indeed, *waridj* Djanggawul! Let us plant another *djuda* here, with the *mauwulan* point!

Let it stand where the foam comes up, like the foam which marks it, from Bralgu, at the Place of the Sun, by the open sea.

It stands with its roots, with its feathered pendants: parakeet feathers, and darker feathers, fat of the *djanda* goanna!

We put in the *djuda* roots, and the feathered strings—spreading them out to dry.   5

The Djanggawul Song Cycle

Ourselves we put them. They see the water, the tide flowing in,
and rising, at the Place of the Mauwulan.

I ask you, *waridj* Miralaidj: Shall we part the fringe at the mouth
of the sacred mat?

I ask you, *waridj*: Shall we insert our *mauwulan* point? Will you
allow us to do so?

I listen, *waridj* (awaiting your answer)!

Chapter Eight

COMMENTS ON PART TWO OF THE SONGS

THIS section is concerned primarily with the arrival of the Djanggawul and their companion at Port Bradshaw, or Jelangbara (its general name). They move about for a while in this area, where much of their time is taken up with drying the feathered strings and *rangga*, which have been damaged by salt water on the way from Bralgu. They also 'make country', and create wells by plunging in the point of their *mauwulan rangga*. They 'plant' trees, too, which spring up from the *djuda rangga*; and they come into contact with the Baijini folk.

As in Part One, a series of incidents may be traced, in sequence, through the songs. Song 28 tells of the Djanggawul's arrival, and of their making a well; this is their first action, for they are thirsty after their long journey. Then the sea-splashed *rangga* are laid out in rows, and the feathered strings too spread to dry in the sun (Song 29). They are arranged in such a way that they are 'watching the sea. It is roaring. The noise of the spray!' (Song 29, line 13). This theme appears in various songs throughout the section, suggesting the intimate association of the *rangga* with these natural elements: for they have been stained by the sea, and their feathered strings are likened to the glow of the sun. It reflects, too, the seasonal fluctuations: the rising tide symbolizes the wet monsoonal season, and the spray the rain fertilizing the ground, while the foam is life-giving semen.

In Song 30 the Djanggawul are walking about the country; but they are tired, and as they walk they move their heads from side to side (Song 30, line 3). A cloud rises, and guides them on their way. A black cockatoo appears; and its pecking a tree trunk

(Song 31, line 4) is likened to the Djanggawul's prodding the ground with the *mauwulan rangga*, which they use as a walking stick. This bird too is compared to a *rangga* (totemic manifestation); and the tree in which it perches is its *nara* (ritual) shade, which has sprung from a *djuda* planted by the Djanggawul. It, too, looks seawards. Ducks cluster around a berry bush (Song 32), and again we find association with the sea: 'White feathers like paint on its chest—foam from the sea . . . ' (Song 32, line 6).

Song 33 concerns the *lindaridj* parakeet, whose breast feathers reflect the sun. It ruffles its feathers, drying itself in the sun, as the Djanggawul dry the feathered pendants. Also it moves its head from side to side (line 3), as the Djanggawul do (Song 30, line 3).

In Song 34, the Djanggawul desire to make a *nara* shade, into which they will put the dried *rangga* and feathered strings; they also 'plant' *djuda* trees, where they may look at the sea (line 19). A sacred *djanda* goanna appears in Song 35. It is treated as a *rangga*, of which it is a living representation, and is put into a well— '. . . It splashed in the well, making foam, like foam on the sea' (line 10). Then, in Song 36, the feathered lengths of string are compared to the foliage of the yam, for they do eventually turn into this plant: 'creepers and leaves of the yam grow from those feathered strings, for we spread them out on the ground' (line 3). These strings lead to various places, as they grow 'good', strong, in the sun. Then a blanket or 'frilled' lizard (Song 37) appears on a *djuda rangga* tree: it, too, is totemic, and synonymous with a *rangga*. As a diversion from the central theme, the Baijini folk appear in Song 38, and the Djanggawul obtain from them a trepang ladle, which they declare sacred. The Djanggawul also take over the Baijini site, which they make sacred to themselves. Song 39 returns to the subject of the sacred dilly bag, which is hung on a tree to dry—for it, too, has been splashed by salt spray and foam. The *djuda* have grown to trees, forming a *nara* shade among whose branches the bags are hung. Ordinary dilly bags are treated in the same way (Song 40).

As the section draws to a close, Song 41 returns to the *lindaridj* parakeet, drying itself in the last rays of the setting sun. It perches on the *djuda* tree like the feathered strings which have been hung up to dry. This bird is a focal point of beauty, in ritual and song, and symbolizes one of the most important elements in fructification. Song 42 returns to the Djanggawul, walking along with the aid of the *mauwulan* (line 1), making wells as they go (line 5), and planting *djuda* trees (line 7). They are looking for a place where they can put up a *nara* shade, and Song 43 continues the theme: trees are planted and they search for a place where they can open out their sacred *ngainmara* mat.

Let us now consider these songs separately, elaborate their contents in some degree, and so reveal their symbolic significance.

Line 2 of Song 28 reads in translation: 'Shall we put in the *mauwulan rangga* here, *waridj*? Not yet! That (string) must first be attached . . .' The original text reads: 'not finished that . . .' That is to say, the 'Djanggawul are not finished with this *mauwulan rangga*.' He, the Djanggawul Brother, intends to use it to make a well (line 4). His companion, however, persists in asking the Djanggawul, 'May we put it in here?' The Djanggawul Brother answers, 'No, I am not ready to do that yet. We must carry it farther up the beach. It is no good putting it near the sea. We must go farther up.' Aborigines say that the Djanggawul are the leaders of the sacred *rangga*, and Bralbral always defers to them. Bralbral, that is, serves as the 'foil' for the Djanggawul, the one who always asks questions to which they supply the answers. The latter part of line 2 refers to the younger Djanggawul Sister's giving the *mauwulan rangga* to her Brother, so that he may poke the ground with it and make a fresh-water well. Before he can use it in this way, feathered pendants must be attached. The Sisters, therefore, remove the long pendant decorations on their arm-bands, and fasten them to the *mauwulan*. Here it is inferred that (as mentioned) the Sisters themselves are the real custodians of the *rangga* emblems, while the Brother (but not Bralbral) merely uses them. 'I am doing it for us (says the Djanggawul Brother); for us, Bildjiwuraroiju, I put the *rangga* point into the ground' (line 7).

Symbolically, the Djanggawul Brother is asking the Sisters' permission to have coitus with them. The *mauwulan* is his penis, the feathered pendants, in this context, the Sisters' clitorises. He, the Brother, inserts his *mauwulan* into the ground and creates a well—symbolic coitus. The *rangga* is withdrawn—'. . . Water, fresh water, is surging up . . .' (line 8), implying penis removal, with seminal and vaginal flow, after coitus. The word used for well is *mil(ngu)*, which also means semen.

Line 6, 'Yes, all right, *waridj* (says Bralbral). You do it for us' may be elaborated as 'Shall we poke a hole in the ground with the *mauwulan*? Shall I do it? asks the Brother. To this, Bralbral agrees. 'Yes, this is good, *waridj*! But first it was salt to the taste' (line 13). At first the gushing water tastes salty; but Bralbral kneels down beside the well. He touches the water with the tip of his tongue, to see if it is good for drinking. They express pleasure, and then declare that 'Our well, and its water, are sacred!' (line 17).

The *rangga* are placed in a row so that they may dry in the warmth of the sun (Song 29); they are arranged according to the different linguistic groups and clans to which they will later belong. The Djanggawul call the sacred names of the totemic species—the fish, birds, animals, and the sacred emblems themselves. These are the *rangga* that were splashed with sea spray on the journey from Bralgu, and retained in the canoe while others were dropped into the sea (*vide* Song 26). The Djanggawul turn them over to dry them.

Line 8 reads, 'Thus we make them good, putting them out to dry. Feathered *rangga*, our children, from the *ngainmara* mat!' and 'We make them good, putting them out to dry—our feathered pendants, our children!' (line 16). Here we return to the underlying theme. The pendants, *ju(wul)dun* (*vide* Song 24; from *judu*, meaning 'child'), likened to the sun's rays, are attached to the sacred *rangga* as hanging pendants. Aborigines say, 'this string is like a baby. They never lose it, and always carry it as if they were carrying a baby.' This refers to the carrying of the *rangga* and feathered string in the *ngainmara* mat (= uterus). The word *wagu* (own child, woman speaking; sister's child, man speaking) is also used to describe the feathered string. The *rangga* and the string are like the children which the Djanggawul Sisters will remove from their wombs and leave at various places, so that they may become the ancestors of the present-day Arnhem Landers. The reference to their drying in the sun implies their maturing in the uteri, awaiting their birth. Line 12 of the original contains the word *baima* 'let (them) stay there', 'always there', or 'stay(ing) behind': thus, 'Let them stay there, spread out to dry at Port Bradshaw, at the Place of the Sun'. This implies a sense of permanency and immutability, and is linked with the concept of dreaming—the idea of continuum, manifested in the 'eternal dreaming stream', where there is no division between past, present and future. In this case, it is a symbolic permanency. The feathered strings are drying in the sun, reflecting the sun's rays: they are a crystallization of the sun's essence. Later, as in Songs 33 and 41, the feathered strings themselves may not be there, but are represented by the parakeet birds which ruffle their breast feathers in the rays of the setting sun. They are perched on the sacred tree, on the *rangga djuda*, and are like the pendants attached to the *rangga* itself. Moreover, even when they themselves are not there, the sun's rays continue as an 'eternal' symbol of the ritualistic emblems. In this context, that is, *baima* signifies to the Aborigines something essentially indestructible.

The latter part of Song 29, lines 17–22, indicates the Djanggawul's desire to construct a sacred *rangga* shade ' . . . we'll make a large shade, with gaping mouth' (line 21).

Comments on Part Two of the Songs

In Song 30 the Djanggawul continue 'making the country, with the aid of the *mauwulan rangga*' (line 1). This savours, to some extent, of rationalization, for it is apparent that the land as such was already there when the Djanggawul reached Port Bradshaw. Their 'making the country', in this context, refers to their making wells, and certain physiographic features, and planting trees. As they walk along, they use the *mauwulan rangga* as walking sticks, prodding the ground (line 2). The picture presented in parts of these songs is one of the Djanggawul and their companion, bent in weariness, helping themselves along with the *mauwulan*. They wear arm-bands with long feathered pendants, and waist-bands of hair string, with dilly bags swinging at their backs. The Two Sisters carry the *ngainmara*, containing the *rangga*; while attached to their beards the men wear strands of feathered string (indicating that they, themselves, are sacred). Their hair and foreheads are stained with sea foam, encrusted with whitish-grey salt, giving the appearance of age. Wearily they move, or loll, their heads rhythmically from side to side to the clapping of beating sticks, swaying their hips as they sing their sacred songs. Except for their decorations they are naked, their brown skin whitened with salt water. None of them is old: Miralaidj has only just reached puberty, and is capable of childbearing; Bildjiwuraroiju is an older woman in her prime; and both men are approaching middle age.

A black cockatoo, with red markings on the underside of its tail, appears in Song 31. It is perched on the *djuda rangga* (line 2), pecking at the tree trunk in imitation of the Djanggawul, as they poke the ground with the *mauwulan*. The *djuda rangga* has grown to a tree, the leafy branches of which are the birds' shade (that is, like a *rangga nara* shade). The bird cocks its head on one side, peering at the Djanggawul; it hears the sound of the surf on the other side of Wobilinga Island, where there is a long stretch of beach. 'A long cry comes as we first make the country, calling the place names, at Wobilinga' (line 11). The same bird perches on a red-blossomed tree growing among the mangroves, where the red flowers symbolize the parakeet-feathered strings (line 12). Finally the sacred invocations of the *djuda* are called. These invocations or *bugali*, as mentioned, contain spiritual power whereby it is possible for the Djanggawul to make their *rangga* spring into living green trees.

In Song 32, long-necked wild duck appear, clustered eating around the *munji* berry bushes; these berries (or flowers) are red, and again symbolize the red breast feathers of the parakeet. 'Tracks leading this way and that—Into the shade, to the sacred *rangga* place!' (line 5). It is suggested that the duck is like a *rangga*, and therefore may be placed within the *nara* shade (= *ngainmara* = uterus), because of its association with the Djanggawul during their journey from Bralgu. For example, we read: 'White feathers like paint on its breast—foam from the sea . . . ' (lines 6 and 7). The bird's white breast feathers are likened to white pipeclay markings, the result of the sea foam which splashed it on its way over from Bralgu—suggesting that it was a *rangga* carried in the *ngainmara*. Concerning the last lines (14 and 15), Aborigines say that the Djanggawul leave this bird because 'he was by himself, no one with him; that is why he sings as he goes along' ('We hear the sound of wings, beating fast!' line 13: the flapping wings are likened to clapping sticks. *Vide* Song 30, line 10).

Song 33 concerns itself with the *lindaridj* parakeet, source of the colourful feathers for the sacred strings and pendants. These birds perch on the sacred *djuda* tree ' . . . red breast feathers glistening in the sun.' (line 2); they are like feathered string attached to the *rangga*. Each parakeet is ' . . . cocking its head from side to side, as if weary . . . ' (line 3), just as the Djanggawul move their heads from side to side as they walk along (*vide* Song 30, line 3). The whole song stresses this bird's association with the feathered pendants and the *djuda rangga*. 'Softly, it calls the invocations of the sacred tree' (line 5): the invoking of the power *bugali* transposes the erect *djuda rangga*, with feathered pendants, into a live tree with birds perching upon it—or vice versa, according to ritual context.

The Djanggawul have built a sacred *nara* shade, and the sun's rays enter its aperture—'Shining into the sacred shade, lighting it up, away towards Arnhem Bay' (line 11). The parakeet may thus look into the sacred shade. In the last line (13), the bird itself speaks, ' . . . I am drying myself, my red breast feathers, my *rangga* feathers—my children!' It likens to its children (that is, *wagu*, daughter or son, female speaking; sister's daughter or son, male speaking) the red feathers of its breast, while it also symbolizes the feathered decorations of the *rangga*, which are said to be like *wagu* to the poles (*vide* Song 29, above).

Song 34 returns to the Djanggawul's desire to make a *nara* shade in which to store their *rangga* (lines 1–7). In line 6, 'We shall put in the sacred *rangga* . . . ' the word used is *gurlga* (or *gulgai*) *jibdumana*, translated here as 'put in *djuda rangga*.' This refers to the roots of the *djuda* tree, for *gurlga* means 'penis', and is used generally to mean tree roots—that is, the 'penes of the tree', the part which enters the ground (symbolically representing coitus). Putting the *djuda rangga* in the shade symbolizes the penis entering the vagina, and refers to the Djanggawul Brother's copulating with his Sisters:

his penis is itself a *rangga*. Trees shoot up as the *rangga* are plunged into the earth—'Leaving the *rangga* erect, because we are invoking the sacred names. Trees shoot up from the *rangga* poles!' (line 10) or 'Trees shoot up, with branches and leaves, when we put in the sacred *rangga*—the sacred trees! (line 15). 'We put in the sacred *rangga*, the jutting limbs, like our elbows . . .' (line 11): the word *ligan*, elbow (or something shaped like an elbow) refers to jutting limbs, or the 'elbow' branch, of a tree. The Djanggawul said, 'I put that *ligan* from that *djuda* to my body, for it is copied from my own elbow, because I belong to *djuda*.' This is particularly important. The Djanggawul identify themselves with the *djuda rangga* tree, and its jutting limbs are like their own elbows. The simile becomes clear when one recalls that the north-east and north-central Arnhem Lander considers his bones to be *djuda*.

The sacred invocations mentioned here, and elsewhere, refer in this case to the *djuda* tree (for example, lines 6, 8, 9, 10, 11, 13, 14, 17 and 18). Many and varied are these *bugali*, and each may refer to the complete *djuda*, to a special part of it, or to the roots. In addition, each belongs to a specific *dua* linguistic group. For example, *jilbunbangala*, line 6, is the complete *djuda*; so are *gulimboinga, gunidjbilnga, milgunmirin*, and *wirilwuma*. In line 8, *gwowadmina* belongs to the Ngeimil-speaking group; *gambrulngan* is an 'inside' *bugali* for the *djuda*, and *gambuldji* simply the *djuda* itself. *Gondura*, in line 10 is a *djuda* invocation associated with the 'bottom' Ngeimil-speaking group; *jareijarmiri* belongs to the Gwolamala Ngeimil; *guluddumbir* (line 11) is a 'singing' invocation of the 'bottom' Ngeimil; *djudjungan* (line 13) is for the Dadawi-speaking group and *madangalang* a 'singing' name for this; *birwongan* (line 14) belongs to the Dadawi, as do *balgdungan* and *galalwungbaingnga*. *Wongidnga* (line 17) belongs to the Djambatpingu-speaking group, as does *geiawarngurun*; *milnganjingangan* is a Djambatpingu invocation for a *djauwalani* tree (line 18); so are *guligulin* and *djauwulgurungangin*. That is to say, all the *djuda* were originally *rangga*, like the *mauwulan*. The Djanggawul put them into the ground, where, after the invocations had been called, they shot up as trees.

Geimanangala or *geimalangana* (lines 15 and 18) is the whole tree, trunk and branches, freely translated as 'tree itself'. It is either of two trees—the black plum ('outside' term *ganmarug*), with thick leafy branches providing a large shade, or the *djauwalani* or *buwolawal* tree, with large leaves, and thick clusters of fruit resembling Leichhardt figs. The fruit is called '*lindaridj* (parakeet) food', for large flocks of these birds collect in its branches. ' . . . The *djuda* growing there, in sight of the splashing foam' (line 20). The *djuda*, planted by the Djanggawul, grow up as trees; from where they stand, their branches may look at the sea water, the foam and splashing waves on the coast; they can hear the continual roar of the sea and the sound of breaking waves—in memory of their journey from Bralgu. Line 22 refers to the *djuda* being removed from the sacred *ngainmara* mat (= uterus): lines 25 and 26 refer to Bralbral, speaking to the Djanggawul Brother: 'How shall we carry ourselves?' (referring to the *rangga*). 'You just put them there; we have a lot in the *ngainmara*,' answers Djanggawul. Symbolically, this refers to children removed from the Sisters.

In Song 35 a sacred *djanda* goanna makes its appearance: it is itself a *rangga*, become alive. Line 5 reads: '. . . It has made tracks on the sandhill, crawling and making country, at the Place of the Mauwulan.' This refers to the long level sandhill, through which the Djanggawul have made a track, while at each side are the claw marks of the goanna. The goanna goes into the sacred mat (line 7): the Djanggawul follow its tracks, and find them leading to the mouth of the *ngainmara*, in which it had originally been hidden on the way from Bralgu. Fully grown *djanda* goanna may not be killed at this sacred place at Port Bradshaw; only small ones, the 'children' of the *djanda*, may be killed and eaten there. Line 8 refers to the goanna being covered up: 'it is sacred, and nobody may have it.' The goanna is then removed from the mat (line 9) and put into a sacred well. It dives into the well and, as it hits the water, makes a noise; spray splashes up and foam appears on the surface of the water (line 10). At the same time, the high tide comes up on the beach, and water rises simultaneously in the well. The well is subject to the underground movements of the high tides (lines 11 and 12). This refers also to the seasonal fluctuation of the tides during the wet monsoonal period, when the earth is being fertilized: symbolically, the goanna is the *rangga*, and *rangga* after ritual use are put back into the sacred wells, or into a swamp, and covered with mud (*vide* Chapter 1). Or the goanna may be the penis, the well the vagina, the spray the ejaculation, and the foam the semen—referring to the sexual act carried out by the Djanggawul, or, alternatively, to the fertilization of the earth. That is, 'We seized it as it came from the mouth of the *ngainmara* mat' (line 13).

Song 36 relates to yam foliage and runners, which have originated from strands of parakeet-feathered string laid out on the ground to dry (lines 1–4). The Djanggawul spread out feathered strings from the *mauwulan rangga*, to dry in the sun; they grew into *banggada* yam plants. These strands of string are referred to as *barlga* 'arms', which are the creepers or runners of the yam. They spread out in such a way that each strand points in a certain direction, for example, '. . . stretching to Bilabinjang' (line 5). All the places mentioned are associated with the Djanggawul: for example, Ngadibalji, line 7, where the Djanggawul Brother left his hairbelt; Ngainmaralji, line 12, the reef of the metamorphosed *ngainmara* mat; Galibingu, line 13, a small island which in the Djanggawul's time was inhabited by two male *galibingu* circumcision novices and six women, all of whom came from the Sisters; Maljalji, line 21, meaning 'take it away', for the Djanggawul Brother put his *mauwulan rangga* into the ground there, but withdrew it again, and then gave the place its name; Grurundei, meaning 'reaching there', for the Djanggawul came to this place, a little south of Port Bradshaw (line 22); Marimidjalijuma, line 23, meaning 'danger long', referring to a spear and fighting dilly bag, the former having been thrown a long way; and Ganjumingalei (or Ganjingialangei), the place of the Morning Star, south of Port Bradshaw (that is, from Bralgu; *vide* Part One of the cycle).

A blanket lizard appears in Song 37, perched on a sacred *djuda*, which has grown from the Djanggawul's *rangga* (line 3): that is, line 4, the Djanggawul are singing, and at the same time the lizard climbs the tall tree, which is really the sacred pole. Line 8, '. . . as we prod the ground with the point of the *mauwulan* . . .' '. . . as we make wells all along our way' (line 9). The *mauwulan* point is plunged into and out of the ground (*dalwuljalbunara*), making wells, all along the way. This is again symbolic fertilization, as in line 11, when the *djuda* are put into the ground and from them grow green trees: that is, *gurlga* (or *gulgai*)-*jibdundanga*, all the roots growing from it, as a penis, fertilizing (see above).

Song 38 brings in the Baijini folk whose talking is heard by the Djanggawul (line 2). The Baijini's association with the Djanggawul has been mentioned (Chapters 1 and 3). The sound of the Baijini's speech drifts over (line 3) from where they are erecting a hut, putting on its roof. They are not, apparently, as dark as the Djanggawul, being described by the term *ridjun* (line 5), which may be translated as the 'shine' of the 'pale' skin of a number of Baijini together. A crowd of them is standing about on rocks, on roof tops, and so on: and *ridjun* is the combined paleness or whiteness of their bodies.

It is quite possible that this Baijini element has been superimposed on the original theme, for in contradiction to what is given here, the Aborigines stress that the Djanggawul themselves were the first visitors to the Arnhem Land coast. From this point of view, it seems incongruous that the Baijini should be collecting trepang there (line 5). The song, however, indicates that the Baijini were already firmly entrenched when the Djanggawul arrived; although the latter contemplated moving them, so that they themselves could establish a sacred site (lines 7, 8 and 9). Although no mention is

made of the actual eviction of the Baijini, and of the way in which
this was done, lines 12–16 infer that the Djanggawul were successful;
for example, 'This is for us, *waridj*, this trepang ladle left by the
Baijini . . .' (line 16). The ladle, described by the term, *djirunma*,
often used for a paddle, is a stirring 'spoon' used by the Baijini
in curing trepang. The Djanggawul pick it up and hide it, and later
put it carefully into their sacred *ngainmara* mat, treating it like a
rangga (lines 16, 17 and 18). They are attracted by its black colouring
(*vide* Chapter 3), and use it as a secondary sacred object. The rest
of the song refers to their making wells, and planting *djuda* trees:
the symbolism of this has already been treated.

Song 39 concerns the sacred dilly bag, which is closely woven
from pandanus and has feathered pendants. (See Chapter 1, where
reference has been made to their making and significance.) These
special baskets are still carried by the Sisters, and not by the men,
who have ordinary dilly bags; they are symbolic of the uterus, and
approximate the *ngainmara*. The baskets are hung on the *djuda*
(line 2), and when in this position their feathered pendants are 'like
the parakeets', shining in the sun (line 19). They are not only hung
on the *rangga* (or trees), but placed in the branches used in constructing the sacred *nara* shade (line 6); and they are also put in the
ngainmara (lines 9 and 10). 'From within the fringe of the *ngainmara*
mat . . . they can see the water at the Place of the Mauwulan . . .'
The very act of hiding them in the mat makes them *mareijin*, sacred
(line 14). Song 40 tells about the ordinary undecorated dilly bag.
'We hang it up on the sacred *djuda* tree, with roots fast in the
ground' (line 2): the roots of the tree are like penes, protruding
into the ground. Here, as in other songs, a number of invocations
are used; and the symbolism of the red breast feathered string is
elaborated, for this will later be attached to the ordinary dilly bag.

Song 41 brings us back to the parakeet, perched on the *djuda*
(line 2); *vide* Song 33. The rays from the setting sun fall on the red
breast feathers of these birds, which catch and reflect the glow of
the sunset (line 3). '. . . its children, its red breast feathers!'
(line 5): that is, *wagu* (children, woman speaking; sister's children,
man speaking), or *judu* (line 10). The latter word is commonly used
when referring to 'children', usually as a singular noun, but it means
'semen'; the parakeet's breast feathers are said to be like children.
(Alternatively, the word *djamarguli*, children, may be used, meaning
'a result of coitus'.) The bird itself speaks: 'Myself, I am drying
them . . . !' (line 10).

Song 42 continues the Djanggawul's travels about the Port
Bradshaw region, walking with the aid of the *mauwulan* (line 1),
and making wells (line 3). With the point of the *mauwulan* they make

a hole in the ground and insert *djuda* (line 7) 'planting' them (the word used here is *didunga*, to plant, or to put something into a bag). Lines 7–13 refer to a large *djuda* tree which stands at Port Bradshaw, its branches spread out to form a shade, within which are many *lindaridj* parakeets. These may not be disturbed or caught, for they are on the sacred *djuda*, just like feathered string pendants on the *rangga* emblem. The rest of the song is a repetition of the same theme. Bralbral and the Djanggawul discuss the matter of erecting a *nara* shade, in which they may undo their *ngainmara* and remove the *rangga* and pendants. This symbolizes their uncertainty as to whether they will leave people (= *rangga*) from the Sisters' uteri (that is, 'undo their *ngainmara*') at this place (lines 36–9).

The final song (43) of this section is really a continuation of the preceding one. The last three lines (lines 7, 8 and 9) refer symbolically to the Djanggawul Brother's requesting Miralaidj for intercourse.

This section, then, continues the theme which has been presented in the first section of the epic, and which becomes more apparent as we proceed.

Chapter Nine

THE DJANGGAWUL SONG CYCLE

PART THREE

In which the Djanggawul continue their journey through the Bush country behind Port Bradshaw in a north-westerly direction until they reach Banbaldji, at Arnhem Bay on the north coast.

Song 44

WE walk along by ourselves, *waridj*, step by step, with the aid of the *mauwulan*, plunging in its point . . .   1
Hips swaying, we ourselves are making country along the way, with the *mauwulan rangga*:
Moving our arms as we lift the *rangga*, swaying our hips, clapping our sticks and singing.
Our bodies are covered by shadows of passing clouds, at the place of passing clouds: clouds rising and looming!
Clapping our sticks, we sing as we walk, *waridj* Bralbral, to Nuga-wong, beyond Port Bradshaw.   5
May we sit down there? (asks Bralbral) No, replies the Djangga-wul . . .
Here we may only wait to plunge in our *rangga* pole, making a sandhill.
Why shall we not undo the mat, *waridj* Djanggawul, parting its fringe?
No! Somewhere else we shall go, to dry the *rangga* emblems:
Here we shall just sit down (for a while), for fast we have come from the Spirit Country.   10
We sing as we go. All the way from the sea we have walked, moving our arms as we use the upright *mauwulan*.

Yes indeed, *waridj* Djanggawul, we are making the country,
   plunging in the *mauwulan rangga*:
Walking with hips swaying, *waridj*, Our heads grey from the foam
   which splashed us on our journey from distant Bralgu.
Here we must sit and make our camp—our sacred *nara* shade!
Here we shall dry the feathered strings on the *djuda*, and all the
   sacred *rangga* . . .   15
Yes indeed, *waridj*. I am asking you, Djanggawul, listening: shall
   we open the mouth of the mat?
Come, shall we take them out from within its fringe?
We are drying them in the sun, in the heat of its rays.
They grow dry on that tree, *waridj* Bralbral, at the mouth of the
   sacred shade:
For they have been splashed with white foam from the Place of
   the Sun, from Bralgu.   20
We make them dry, hot in the burning glare of the sun, soaked
   in its warm rays.
Here we insert the *djuda* roots, and hang the feathered arm-band
   pendants:
In there we put the feathered strings, standing, always there in
   the bush behind Port Bradshaw.
They may look back at the water, the surf roaring at the Place of
   the Mauwulan.
They are drying in there, on the tree at Buginja.   25

Song 45

We walk along, *waridj* Miralaidj, step by step, with the aid of the
   mauwulan, plunging in its point . . .   1
We walk along with hips swaying, making the country. Our bodies
   are shadowed by passing clouds, clouds rising and looming!
We are making country, Bildjiwuraroiju, with the *mauwulan* point.
Yes indeed, *waridj* Djanggawul. Where, then, may we rest?
At Laleidjajiginmil! Carefully, *waridj*, we put in our sticks as we go,
   for our heads are grey.   5
We shall sit here to rest. Yes indeed, *waridj* Djanggawul; here we
   shall make our camp, erect our shade.
Yes indeed, *waridj*, I always listen to what you say. We shall plant
   the *djuda* roots here.
We remove the feathered strings from the mouth of the mat,
   waridj, out through its fringe.
Ourselves we put in the *djuda* roots, taking them from the mouth
   of the sacred mat.

The Djanggawul Song Cycle

Yes indeed, *waridj*. I am asking you, *waridj* Djanggawul. Shall
    we plant the roots in here, oh *waridj* Miralaidj . . . ?   10
We put in the djuda roots, calling the sacred invocations . . . ,
So that they stand within the mouth of the shade . . .
There we put in the roots, and the feathered strings to dry.
They are drying there in the hot rays of the sun.
They are stained from the sea, on their way over the sea to the
    Place of the Mauwulan, the Place of the Sun.   15
Rays of sun touch them, hot in the burning glare of the drying sun . . .
Our feathered strings, our basket pendants, hanging up on the
    tree by the mouth of the *ngainmara*!
At its fringe, by its transverse fibre—the sacred *ngainmara*!
Yes indeed, *waridj* Djanggawul, I always listen to your word.

Song 46

We plunge in the *mauwulan* point as we walk, *waridj* Djanggawul,
    planting the roots with the *mauwulan rangga*.   1
There is feathered string, like yam foliage.
Yes, put it there, so the sun may look on it, burning and drying,
For foam has splashed upon it, coming from Bralgu, to the Place
    of the Sun.
The hot rays of the sun look on it, burning, drying those feathered
    strings.   5
We put all the sacred *rangga* within the mouth of the *nara* shade,
So the rays of the sun may see them, with rising heat, in the fringe
    of our sacred mat.
We put in the *djuda* roots, so they may look back towards the water
    at the Place of the Mauwulan,
Calling the sacred invocations for that *djuda* . . . !
Let them dry there in the heat, those feathered strings and pendants.
Ourselves we put them within the mouth of the shade.   11
Let them dry as they stand. Heat rising from the mouth and the
    fringe of the *ngainmara* mat!
Sacred is this! Sacred to us is the *ngainmara*'s mouth!
Yes indeed! I am asking you *waridj* Djanggawul (says Bralbral),
    waiting to hear your word, *waridj* Miralaidj!
We put down the yam creepers, and spread them.   15
Take them from within the mouth of the mat! We spread out the
    feathered strings, the yam creepers.
Carefully we spread out the creepers, the strings, so they look back
    to the Place of the Mauwulan.
Feathered strings from our arm-bands! Carefully we spread out the
    creepers, so they may see the water—the rising tide!

The Djanggawul Song Cycle
Song 47

We go along, making country, with the aid of the *mauwulan rangga*; 1
Going there, to where the white clouds are rising, our hips swaying.
Step by step, we sing as we go, making the country, inserting the
   mauwulan point.
Walking wearily. Our heads are grey, stained with the sea foam,
   like clay on our foreheads—from Bralgu.
We are walking along, oh Bildjiwuraroiju, oh Miralaidj, oh *waridj*
   (Djanggawul)!   5
We see the clouds spreading, rising there above Bunjinina, above
   Galdjurandu, near Caledon Bay.
Large clouds bending down, for us, *waridj* Miralaidj!
Carefully plunge in our *rangga* pole, making country: holding its
   head, inserting its point.
Travelling into the bush, with the aid of the *mauwulan*: singing as
   we go!
Shall we sit down here? Shall we make our *nara* shade here?   10
Shall we erect our shade, here at Bunjinina, putting in the *djuda* roots?
Yes indeed, *waridj* Djanggawul. I listen to your word . . .
Shall we sit here, *waridj*, and open the *ngainmara* mat?
Yes, we part its fringe: we put the *djuda* and roots within the mouth
   of the shade.
Let it stand in the shade! We put in the roots of the *djuda*, there,
   at Bunjinina.   15
It looks at the water, the rising, foaming tide:
The sacred well, when the *djuda rangga* are planted.
We call the sacred invocations, planting the *djuda* roots.
We invoke the names! For the *djuda* limbs gaze on the sea, at
   Bunjinina, at Galdjurandu!
Another, *waridj* Miralaidj! Put in the fringe, into the mouth of the
   mat.   20
We shall put *djuda* roots at the Place of the Mauwulan, and into
   Bunjinina, into the mouth of the shade.
For we are calling sacred invocations! Come, Miralaidj, put in
   another *djuda*!
From the fringe of the mat, we put in the roots at Bunjinina,
Calling the sacred invocations . . .
There it may look at the water. We erect the *djuda*, calling the
   sacred *bugali*.   25
Come, *waridj* Miralaidj, plunge in the *mauwulan* point, erect the
   djuda! Bildjiwuraroiju, put in the roots with its point!
We are drying the *rangga* posts, *rangga* from the Spirit Country,
   from Bralgu.

For the foam has stained them, coming over the sea.
The rays of the sun look on them, the rising heat of the sun!
Sun's rays, touching and drying them! The burning sun looks on
   them, drying the feathered strings at the mouth of the mat.   30
We are drying them, *waridj*, from within the *ngainmara*, in there
   at the sacred shade.
We are drying them there, *waridj* Miralaidj, at the mouth of the
   shade.
Come, let us put out the feathered strings to dry! Feathered arm-
   band pendants, feathered *rangga* string, let them stay here at
   Bunjinina!
For the foam has splashed and stained them, on the sea journey
   from Bralgu, towards the Place of the Sun . . .
Come, *waridj*, plunge in the *rangga*, so we may dry the feathered
   pendants and strings.   35
Let them dry in the scorching heat, drying the damp foam on the
   feathered strings.
Wet feathered strings like ourselves, from Bralgu: sacred, as we
   are, *waridj*!
We are drying them, calling the invocations:
Drying them there at Bunjinina, where they may see the water,
   the sacred well.
We invoke, calling the *djuda*, the feathered pendants and strings. 40
The warm sun looks on them: for we are invoking . . .
We dry them, at Bunjinina, calling the invocations.
We dry them: the sun looks on them, with rising heat.

Song 48

We look back, as we make the country, using the *mauwulan* point. 1
Waridj, we saw a cloud coming up. Whence is it coming, from
   Bulibuli?
Yes indeed, *waridj* Djanggawul. We shall put in our *mauwulan* all
   along the way, dragging it, Bildjiwuraroiju, with hips swaying.
We plunge in its point as we walk along, making country, with
   hips swaying, clapping our sticks and singing.
Our bodies are shadowed by the rising clouds.   5
Our heads are grey, splashed with foam marks, like white clay—
   foam, coming from Bralgu!
We leave them on us (those marks)—heads grey from the foam, *waridj*.
Step by step, we plunge the *mauwulan* point into the ground . . .
We see the clouds spreading, rising above Banbaldji, casting
   shadows over the sacred well.

We walk along, ourselves, with the aid of the *mauwulan rangga*,
making country.   10
Yes indeed, *waridj* Miralaidj, I always do as you say. I always
follow you; always listen to you.
For you are my leader (says Bralbral)—you, *waridj* Djanggawul,
our leader!
We move our bodies, hips swaying, making country, up to Bulibuli
at Arnhem Bay.
These clouds are rising upwards from Guminjungli.
Yes, let us go now, *waridj* Miralaidj, go on to Banabaleia. There
we shall see the message clouds.   15
There we shall sleep. Yes, there we shall put our camp; in there
we shall rest.
Shall we put our camp in here . . . ?
No, we shall only sit to rest, for we have been walking fast, making
the country.
Yes indeed, *waridj*, I always listen to you—to your word, *waridj*
Miralaidj!
Shall we open the fringe, the mouth of the *ngainmara* mat? Shall
we leave the *rangga* here?   20
No, we shall just sit resting, for we have put the *mauwulan* all the
way! (We have not yet opened the mat.)
From the mouth of the sacred mat a goose cries out!
It wants to come out: let us part the fringe of the mat!
We lay the geese on the water's surface. Their feathers flutter down,
as they take to the air together—geese, like *rangga*!
For they have been covered up in our sacred *ngainmara*.   25
Their spirits are left by the water: water splashing, foam from the
sea coming up at the Place of the Mauwulan, at the Place of the
Sun.
We lay them on the surface of the water: geese, like *rangga*!
They are flying over and swimming, in clans together, like the
people we shall put (in this country)!
Yes indeed, *waridj* Miralaidj, I listen to your word: for you are my
leader—you, yourself, *waridj* Miralaidj!
I follow your every desire: 30
We open, again, the fringe of this sacred mat, *waridj* Miralaidj.
Shall we put in the *djuda*?
No, we shall just sit here and rest. Somewhere else we can plant
the roots of the *djuda*.
Yes indeed, *waridj* Miralaidj, I may only ask you. Show us what
we shall do.
You may not live here, *waridj*; we must close again the open mouth
of the mat, covering the mat and its contents, for it is sacred! 35

We just place the *rangga* geese on the water's surface, for they want
to come out:

These sacred emblems we must cover up, within the *ngainmara*
mat, beneath its transverse fibres—all those sacred *rangga*.

Yes indeed, *waridj* Miralaidj, we must move on, making country,
inserting the *mauwulan* point.

Oh Bildjiwuraroiju, big clouds are rising for us—spreading over
the sky, and bending down.

Yes indeed, *waridj* Miralaidj! For us, as we walk along, singing. 40

Our bodies are shadowed, as the clouds hang close. Carefully, we
put in the point of our *mauwulan* all the way, going into Bulibuli
and Banbaldji.

Our bodies are shadowed at Buginja. Indeed, we shall continue
to plunge in the *mauwulan*!

Swaying our hips, we insert the *mauwulan* point.

We are weary, walking along with the aid of the *mauwulan*, singing,
as carefully we plunge it in.

Our heads are grey, and our hips swaying: oh Miralaidj, oh
Djanggawul!   45

Ah yes, that place, Banbaldji, it is for us!

In there we shall sit and rest. Yes, indeed, ourselves we shall make
the sacred *nara* shade, and put out the *rangga*.

Yes, *waridj* Miralaidj. I listen to your word.

We make our shade in here; laying out the branches at Bulibuli,
at Banbaldji.

There it can see the water rising up in the sacred well . . .   50

Yes, *waridj*, that is good: I wish to follow you, when you sit down
here to rest.

Song 49

What is that, *waridj* Miralaidj? What is this fish? A small yellow-
tailed fish.   1

Come, truly I want it! We must hide it, cover it up in this sacred mat,
waridj Bralbral, for us!

For we must put it into our sacred shade . . .

Yes, that is good! Ourselves we cover it up, making it sacred,
waridj, hiding it within the mouth of the mat.

There is another, *waridj* Miralaidj! What fish is that, we have caught
in our fish trap, our mat?   5

That is mine, *waridj* Bralbral! I must cover it, hide it within the
closed-up mouth of the mat!

Yes indeed, *waridj*, we ourselves are concealing them.

For this is our sacred shade: it is within our shade!

We cover up its mouth with the sacred branches.
Ourselves we declare it sacred, that fresh-water fish, so no one
may see it.   10

Song 50

What is that fish, *waridj* Miralaidj? Ah, *waridj*, it is a 'nail' fish.   1
Come, let us, ourselves, declare this 'nail' fish sacred:
We shall cover it up, hiding it in the mouth of the mat. Open
    the mat and put it beneath the transverse fibre, declaring it
    sacred.
Yes indeed, *waridj* Miralaidj, we shall put it into our shade . . . We
    sing about that 'nail' fish, going along.
For this is our shade, and we put the fish within it, within its
    mouth . . .   5
We hide that fish, covering it up within the *ngainmara* mat—that
    fish, *waridj*, bearing our sacred name!
'Nail' fish, swimming along! It is ours, we shall get it! For it carries
    its 'spike' like a *rangga*!
It goes into the sacred mat, beneath the transverse fibre; we cover
    it up inside the mud, like a *rangga*.
It will swim into the mouth of the sacred mat.
Within the shade, the sacred shade . . .   10
That fish is not for us! Here is another one. What fish is this?
Come, let us hide it within the mouth of the mat, within its fringe.
What is this one? A whiskered fish. We shall make it sacred, we
    must cover it up.
What is that, *waridj*? It is a whiskered fish . . . !
Here is another, *waridj*. Come on, this one is called a large 'nail'
    fish.   15
We shall hide it, *waridj* Miralaidj, making it sacred, that large 'nail'
    fish.
We shall hide it, cover it up in the mat. You, *waridj*, open the
    mouth of the mat, to receive our 'nail' fish!
What is the name of these fish? Their clan is truly sacred, *waridj*,
    to us!
This large 'nail' fish is sacred to us: we hide it within the mouth of
    our sacred mat.
You, *waridj*, part the fringe of the mat, so we may cover it up
    within.   20
What is that, something else? Where is it, *waridj* Djanggawul?
Ah! Yes, *waridj* Miralaidj! This is a water goanna.
A *djalga* water goanna; what shall we do with it . . . ?
Yes indeed, *waridj*, we shall put a sacred *djuda* in here:

Yes, we shall leave it behind, grasping this sacred *djuda*; for it is
  ours, *waridj* . . .   25
We can sing about it, going along: the *djalga* goanna, perched on
  the sacred *djuda*!
It is hanging there on the forked *djuda*; calling the invocations!
Hanging there on the *djuda* limbs, invoking!
It clasps the limb of the *djuda*, scratching, calling the invocations!
It hangs there: we see it diving into the sacred well, and the water
  comes splashing up, at Banbaldji . . . !   30

Song 51

We are going along, *waridj*, near Bulibuli . . .   1
Yes, indeed, I listen to your word, for I always follow you . . .
We walk along with the aid of the *mauwulan*, making country,
  inserting the *mauwulan* point, our hips swaying.
Carefully, *waridj* Djanggawul, we put in the *mauwulan*, drag it along.
We are walking with grey hair, stained by the splashing foam,
  from the Spirit Country, from Bralgu.   5
Stained with salt and foam from the sea, splashing at the Place of
  the Sun, the Place of the Mauwulan.
Our bodies are shadowed by clouds as we walk, at Buginja:
With hips swaying, our bodies shadowed, as the clouds come rising
  and spreading for us, *waridj* Miralaidj!
Step by step we walk along, making country, inserting the *mauwulan*
  point.
Hips swaying, we walk along, dragging our *rangga*, and plunging
  it into the ground, making the country . . .   10
We reach Bulibuli. We are tired, *waridj*, but we sing as we go along!

Song 52

Shall we sit here, to make our sacred shade?   1
Yes, indeed, *waridj* Miralaidj, we shall rest here in the shade, opening
  our sacred mat.
We shall put it within the mouth of the leafy shade, our mat with
  the *rangga* emblems.
Yes indeed, *waridj* Miralaidj, I listen to your word, for you are
  my leader: I always listen to you.
We shall dry them in there, for us, within the mouth of the shade   5
The feathered strands of the *djuda*, within the mouth of the shade!
We put them there to dry, removing them from the mat . . .

They see the sacred well water at Banbaldji—rising and roaring!
We shall dry them in there, all the *rangga*; and there we shall put
    people:
We put them there, within the mouth of the shade.   10
Yes indeed, *waridj*, I follow your desire! I am awaiting your
    words . . .
Thus you speak to me, *waridj* Miralaidj . . . If you wish, you
    will put (people) in there . . .
Into my sacred shade . . .

Song 53

We shall just plunge our *mauwulan* point in, making country,   1
Making a sacred well for ourselves . . .
Yes indeed, *waridj*, at Banbaldji we put in the point of the *mauwulan*,
    making ourselves a well.
When this is done, we withdraw the *rangga*; and our water comes up
    from the well:
Comes rising up, spray splashing! Water coming up from that
    mauwulan point!   5
Yes, *waridj* Miralaidj, leave it now. This well is ours! We must
    cover it up: it is sacred!
No one may see it, that sacred well, no one come near it!
For the water comes roaring up, spraying and swelling.
From putting in the *mauwulan* point, water rises, splashing and
    foaming, from inside the spring.
It is our well water that roars; *waridj*, we cover it up for us.   10
Yes, indeed, that is good. Thus we shall go along, making the
    country.
Water from within that well is sacred like a younger sibling! We
    must cover it up.
Spray comes up for us there: for you yourself, Bildjiwuraroiju,
    have plunged in the point of the Goanna Tail *rangga* . . . !
Water rises and flows, and spray splashes for us!
This we sing as we go along, singing about that water: 15
We ourselves made it sacred, covering it up, *waridj*, so no one may
    see it, no one may touch it, for it is tabu.

Song 54

Come, *waridj* Miralaidj, open the mouth of this *ngainmara*, part its
    fringe!   1
We must put in the roots of the *djuda*, the sacred tree, calling the
    invocations.

We must put them into the mouth of the shade, so they may see
    the rising well water at Banbaldji . . .
Carefully, *waridj* Djanggawul, put in the *djuda* roots . . .
We plant the roots, from the sacred mat.   5
Waridj, the hot rays of the sun look on them, drying the feathered
    djuda pendants: the burning heat of the sun!
For they have been stained by that foam on our way from the Spirit
    Land, from Bralgu, where the foam splashes at the Place of the
    Sun, the Place of the Mauwulan.
Ourselves we spread out the arm-band pendants to dry, at Ban-
    baldji:
They look at the water, rising up in the well, and hear its
    roar . . .
From within the mouth of the sacred *ngainmara* mat, beneath its
    transverse fibre.   10
Ourselves we put them into the sacred well, covering them, for
    us, *waridj*, so no one may see them.
The hot rays of the sun look on them with their scorching heat!
We put the string into the mouth of the shade,
Put all the *rangga* within its mouth, to dry in our sacred
    shade . . .

Song 55

Come, *waridj* Miralaidj, let us make more country.   1
Let us open the mouth of this mat, parting its fringe, to put in the
    roots of the *djuda*.
They may see the water, the well at Banbaldji.
We plant the *djuda*, invoking the sacred names.
They may see the water rising, and roaring, where we put in the
    roots!   5
Ourselves, we put these feathered arm-band pendants at Banbaldji,
Calling the sacred *djuda* invocations:
They may see the well water rising at Banbaldji, foaming and
    splashing, surging up like a spring!
We put in the *djuda* roots, to dry in the rising heat. The rays of the
    sun warm them!
The burning sun looks down on the feathered strings!   10
We part the fringe of the mat, covering ourselves.
The hot rays of the sun look down, with scorching heat!
We hide those feathered strings, the 'arms' of the *djuda*, within
    the mouth of the shade.
It is our sacred shade, *waridj* Miralaidj!

Song 56

This is another *mauwulan*, belonging to *waridj* Miralaidj.   1
We shall put the *djuda* roots into the mouth of the shade.
You may open the mouth of the mat, pull back its fringe.
We dry the *rangga*, the *mauwulan* point, Bildjiwuraroiju, in the
  rays of the sun.
The hot rays of the sun look on them: heat from the sun!   5
It dries them, the burning sun: drying the *mauwulan* point, oh
  Bildjiwuraroiju!
It dries them, for they have been within the *ngainmara* . . .
The rising heat dries them: we put in the roots . . .
They may see the sacred well at Banbaldji, with its rising water:
We put them into the well water, covering them, making them
  sacred.   10
Yes indeed, *waridj* Miralaidj, that is good. I always listen to you:
  I follow your desire, for you yourself are my leader.
You, *waridj*, I listen to your word; for I follow you, and only
  you . . .
We are drying the *rangga*, planting the roots: we hide the feathered
  arm-band strings, and the *mauwulan* point,
Hide the *mauwulan* pendants and the *djanda* goanna symbols.
Ourselves we are covering the sacred Banbaldji well, and the
  feathered pendants: 15
We hide them all, from within the mouth of the *ngainmara* mat,
  parting its fringe . . .

Chapter Ten

COMMENTS ON PART THREE OF THE SONGS

T HE Djanggawul have left Port Bradshaw, and travel across north-eastern Arnhem Land until they reach Banbaldji at Arnhem Bay. The same theme already observed in the first two sections is elaborated here.

In Song 44, the Djanggawul look for a place in which to build a sacred *nara* shade, where they may spread out the *rangga* to dry. They sing as they go along, prodding the ground with their *mauwulan*, 'making the country'. The *rangga* and feathered pendants are still damp from salt water and foam. In Song 45, there is more discussion about making a sacred shade. Bralbral continually asks the leaders what they intend to do, and often receives evasive answers: he defers particularly to Miralaidj, the younger Sister, although this emphasis on her rather than on Bildjiwuraroiju is not explained. The Djanggawul plant *djuda rangga*, which spring up as green trees; and the business of drying the *rangga* and the feathered strings receives much attention. Song 46 refers to the spreading out of the feathered strings, which are likened to yam creepers. The white clouds beckon them on (Song 47). The sacred *djuda* are erected, looking towards the incoming tide in memory of their epic journey from Bralgu.

Continuing on (Song 48), they see the clouds spreading over the sky. This is during the hot weather, just before the wet monsoonal season (hence the references to the scorching sun). Bralbral asks whether the Djanggawul intend to build their shade, but they tell him that they will only sit down and rest. Geese, which are really *rangga*, come from within the mat; they are placed on the water of a billabong at Banabaleia, and likened to people who will

131

be put there by the Sisters. The Djanggawul are making for Ban-baldji, where they will make a sacred well and build their *nara* shade; in the distance they imagine that they can hear the rising well water.

In Song 49 they catch a yellow-tailed fish and declare it sacred, putting it into their *ngainmara* mat, which is synonymous with their shade. Other fish too are caught (Song 50); they are all declared sacred, and treated as secondary *rangga*. This is the totemic aspect, which appears throughout the cycle. The fish, reptiles and animals which came into association with the Djanggawul became them-selves totemic, through virtue of the Djanggawul's declaration of their sacredness, and of their being covered up with the *ngainmara* or put into the shade. Most important of these is the water goanna (mentioned in Song 50). It perches on the sacred *djuda*, and becomes the *djalga*, water goanna *rangga*, which is put into the sacred well at Banbaldji—as *rangga* are put after use.

In Song 51 the Djanggawul continue along, making country with the aid of their *mauwulan*, until they reach Banbaldji (Song 52). There they build a shade and place within it the *ngainmara* containing the *rangga*. They remove the *rangga* from the mat, and spread them to dry. The sacred well (Song 53) is made by plunging in the *mauwulan*; the water which surges up is declared tabu by the Djanggawul. They plant *djuda* roots, and put *rangga* from the *ngainmara* into the well after their ritual use. More *djuda* are planted (Song 55), the feathered strands are dried, and the well water surges up; and more *rangga* (in Song 56) are placed in the sacred well.

Now we may turn to the individual songs. Song 44 mentions the appearing clouds which cast shadows over the Djanggawul's bodies. Wearily, Bralbral asks the Djanggawul Brother, 'May we sit down here?' Djanggawul, however, replies, 'No' (line 6). They are still tired, from their long journey, but travel farther on. 'Here we must sit and make our camp—our sacred *nara* shade!' (line 14). The words *jalandu*, *balma*, *balmabalma*, and *ngunamu* are used for 'shade', which is a square hut constructed of boughs, taken from the *djuda* trees; the last term, *ngunamu*, refers to the inner part of the structure, to the rails and inner roofing. The *rangga* are referred to by the term *jandaljandal*, or *maidjara* (line 15), which means all the sacred *rangga* together (the *djuda*, *djanda*, *djalga*, *mauwulan*, *ganinjari*, *ngainmara*, feathered pendants, dilly bags, armbands and so on).

Song 45 is self-explanatory. Line 8, 'We remove the feathered strings from the mouth of the mat, *waridj*, out through its fringe' refers symbolically to attempted coitus by the Djanggawul Brother.

Comments on Part Three of the Songs

The feathered string is here the elongated clitoris which protrudes from the vulva (mouth of the *ngainmara*); while the fringe is pubic hair. Putting *rangga* into the *ngainmara* or shade symbolizes intercourse.

Song 46 accentuates the sun theme. In Song 47, most of the invocations are associated with the Karlpu, Riradjingu, and Ngeimil linguistic groups, and refer to the *djuda* tree. In line 37, the general translation does not give the full meaning. The original reads 'make like water sacred . . . ' That is to say, the *rangga* are moistened with well water, in order to symbolize the initial splashing on their way from Bralgu; this is, incidentally, on of the reasons given for ritually covering up *rangga* in the mud or water (that is, in the sacred well water, as in Song 56) after ceremonial use. Esoterically, however, this refers to intercourse and to fertilizing the earth (see above).

Song 48, which is unusually long, incorporates most of the elements treated in the other songs. The Djanggawul travel along, using the *mauwulan*: and shadows fall on them from the clouds. Bralbral asks whether they will open the *ngainmara*, but the answer is 'No'. However, 'From the mouth of the sacred mat a goose cries out!' (line 22). Geese, sacred like *rangga*, are hidden in the *ngainmara*, like children in a uterus; they have matured in the sun, and are ready to come forth. 'It waits to come out; let us part the fringe of the mat!' (line 23). The Djanggawul have come to a billabong. All the geese are 'talking' in the *ngainmara*, so the Sisters let them out, placing the breast of each goose on the surface of the water (line 24). Leaving the billabong, they fly around in flocks for the first time, so that feathers fall to the ground, just as feathers fall from the *rangga* pendants. These geese are described by terms used for people and for *rangga* (that is, *jandaljandal*, and *maidjara*), 'For they have been covered up in our sacred *ngainmara*.' (line 25). Line 26 refers to the spirits of the geese, being left by the water; the word being used means that the Djanggawul 'make' these birds by the water; for nearly all spirits (those that are to be reborn) seem to be associated with water. Even spirit children are 'made in' or by the water, for they live in it before entering their mothers to animate the foetus. 'We lay them on the surface of the water: geese, like *rangga*! They are flying over and swimming, in clans together, like the people we shall put (in this country)!' (lines 27–8). The geese symbolize the people of that totem put in this place by the Djanggawul.

References such as those made in line 35 (etc.) symbolize as mentioned, attempted or actual coitus of the Brother with his Sisters (that is, the covering and uncovering, and putting into the mouth of the *ngainmara*). In line 37, 'cover up' really means, according to the Aborigines, that the Djanggawul Brother wants the younger Sister to have coitus with him: but she refuses, closing her legs (that is, 'covering up the sacred mat' = uterus = vagina). When reference is made to opening the 'mouth' of the *ngainmara*, to parting the fringe, and putting in *rangga* emblems, it means that one of the Sisters opens her legs, her pubic hair (that is, fringe of the mat) is brushed aside, or her clitoris is put on one side (*vide* Chapter 2), and the Brother's penis (that is, *rangga*) is inserted.

The clouds referred to in this song (48) come up from various places in north-eastern Arnhem Land, and cast shadows as they pass over certain camps. The sketch below, prepared by Aborigines, demonstrates the movement of these clouds across the country.

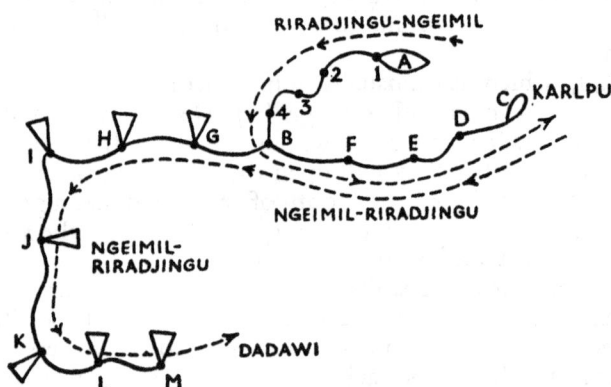

Reference	Places over which these clouds pass
A	Jelangbara, Port Bradshaw
1	Birimala
2	Gudadimi
3	Maldjalji (or Mildjarwi)
4	Grurundei
B	Bilari
C	Bunjinina
D	Laleidjajiginmil (or Lalaidjeiginlji)
E	Buginja
F	Ganjumingalei (or Ganjingialangei)
G	Guminjungli (or Guminjungboi)
H	Miliba
I	Guluboi
J	Didimuru
K	Wilangi
L	Bunawalji (or Bunawauwima)
M	Munadjiwi (or Manmaldji, Munadjing)

Comments on Part Three of the Songs

All these places belong to Ngeimil-Riradjingu linguistic groups. A to B are predominantly Riradjingu, C to F predominantly Ngeimil, while at C they merge with Karlpu. G to M are predominantly Ngeimil, merging at M with Dadawi.

The clouds come up from A, and pass over the places located at 1, 2, 3 and 4 to B, which is on the southern side of Port Bradshaw. They drift from B to C, passing over F, E and D, around Port Bradshaw, to C, at Caledon Bay. D, for instance, is inland from Port Bradshaw, E is still farther inland, and F in the bush between Port Bradshaw and Arnhem Bay.

G is inland from Arnhem Bay, between these two places; I is at Arnhem Bay on the coast, and J also at Arnhem Bay, a little island. K is at Arnhem Bay, near mangrove swamps, L right among the mangrove swamps, and M is on an 'open bay', at the mouth of a creek running into Arnhem Bay.

All these *dua* moiety clouds come up at the end of the dry weather, before the first light showers of the wet monsoonal season. They are 'yellow' and black, as contrasted with the vivid 'yellow' ones of the *jiritja* moiety which follow later, when the new grass shoots appear.

Songs 49 and 50 refer to fish caught in a fish trap, which is made by blocking part of a creek. The fish trap, however, is really the *ngainmara*, and the fish are caught in this. Alternatively, when a woman has coitus she catches a fish (penis) in her net (vagina = uterus = *ngainmara*). The fish caught are declared sacred. 'For this is our sacred shade: it is within our shade!' (line 8). The word here used for the shade, *balbmarangnguwun*, refers specifically to the sacred shade belonging to the Marakulu-speaking people. The 'nail' fish mentioned in Song 50 (line 1) is a species of catfish. Line 8, '. . . we cover it up inside the mud, like a *rangga*', means that the fish themselves are put in the mud. The Djanggawul are described as saying: 'We take out those fish, and put them into the mud.' From this it would appear that they were not caught swimming, but were removed like *rangga* from the *ngainmara*, as were the geese (as in Song 48). However, immediately afterwards (lines 11 and 12) another fish is 'caught' and hidden within the mouth of the mat. It is a 'whisker' fish, also a species of catfish, and is declared sacred. Then a large 'nail' fish appears (line 15); this is another variety of catfish said to be 'like a young shark', and having five spikes instead of one. It is followed by a *djalga* water goanna (line 22), already mentioned: this goanna lives on fresh-water shells. The invocations belong to the Ngeimil linguistic group (lines 27, 28, and 29), while Banbaldji is a Ngeimil camp. The symbolism of the goanna's plunging into the sacred well (line 30) is apparent, and refers to coitus.

Comments on Part Three of the Songs

Song 51 is a repetition of the same theme; but in Song 52 the sacred shade is made. People are then removed from one of the Sisters—'We shall dry them in there, all the *rangga*; and there we shall put people:' (line 9). And 'Thus you speak to me, *waridj* Miralaidj: if you wish, you will put people in there . . . ' (line 12). The word *malarareinguman* is used in line 9, meaning 'put people into there' (that is, into the shade). This, in slightly different forms (as *malajereingoijulman* or *maladareingoijulman*), may be translated generally as 'putting people into this place from either one of the Sisters': from *mala*, clan or group (hence *malara*). This line (12), a continuation of line 11, refers to Bralbral and the Djanggawul Brother deferring to the Sisters. The original reads: '. . . you I (always) follow desire . . . ' The meaning becomes clearer from comments on these lines made by the Aborigines. 'As long as you want (desire), it is all right ("I'll just sit in the shade"),' says the Djanggawul Brother (deferring to his Sisters' opinion). 'I am a man', he tells them. 'If you (women) want to sit down and make a shade (sacred for *rangga*), that's all right, because it is your desire (your own business). That is nothing to do with me, because I'm a man. You two are too happy! For you carry all the people inside your uterus (that is, *ngainmara*). You may put them all the way along (that is, as you travel through the country). When we reach the back of Milingimbi, you may empty out your bellies altogether.' 'That is right, Brother,' say the Sisters. 'We will do that. We are very happy, for we are pregnant. Whether we put people here or not depends on our own wish.'

Song 53 tells how the sacred well is made: 'When this is done, we withdraw the *rangga*; and our water comes up from the well:' (line 4), referring to symbolic coitus. 'Water from within that well is sacred (as are the uteri of the Sisters), like a younger sibling! We must cover it up (for us, *waridj*)' (line 12). The word used for younger sibling is *jugoijugoijuman*, '(make) like a younger brother or sister (*jugujugu*)'. The reference is obscure, and may here refer to the obligations of an older towards a younger brother or sister, or to the fact that the older brother's wife is not accessible to the latter.[1] The goanna tail *rangga* emblem (the *djanda*) is said to be 'just like a brother' (to the Djanggawul Brother himself).

The symbolism of intercourse is continued in Song 54: 'Come *waridj* Miralaidj, open the mouth of this *ngainmara*, part its fringe!' (line 1). 'Carefully, *waridj* Djanggawul, put in the *djuda* roots . . .' (line 4). Song 55 extends the same theme; the invocations (line 4)

---

[1] It has reference to the 'sons of the Djanggawul', who have been removed from the Sisters' uteri; they are called, in some instances, the 'Brothers' of the Djanggawul, because they were the 'first born'. This feature is mentioned later in the cycle.

belong to the Ngeimil liguistic group. Song 56 tells how the *rangga* are finally put into the well, which is then covered up.

Part of the beauty of these songs lies not only in their nostalgic character, but in their clever interweaving of several themes, one with the other. These themes are developed gradually and subtly, each idea connected to the last, and each constantly repeated in a different or in a similar context. In fact the repetitive quality of all these songs creates the desired atmosphere, and conveys to the Aborigines a sense of their reality.

Chapter Eleven

THE DJANGGAWUL SONG CYCLE

PART FOUR

In which the Djanggawul confine their travelling and observations to the region of Arnhem Bay, particularly around Wagulwagul.

Song 57

WHAT is that for us, *waridj*? It is a duck, crying out!   1
Yes, *waridj* Djanggawul. I thought it was a stranger, for
it is flying fast, with flapping wings!
It is ours, this duck, flying to the *munji* berry bushes . . .
We shall sing about it, *waridj* Bralbral, as we go along . . .
For we saw them, those ducks, flying fast as we walked along,
females and males by themselves.   5
They leave tracks behind, everywhere! Their feathers are stained
with foam, from the open sea, from Bralgu!
The heads of these birds are grey . . .
We sing about them as we go along, *waridj* Miralaidj;
Yes indeed, *waridj* Bralbral, we leave them behind. They are flying
wearily with foam marks upon them!
They scratched the ground with their claws as they took to the
air, flying at Banbaldji.   10
Our ducks are flying fast, craning their necks in flight.
Ducks, crying out! We look at them, and leave them to go their
way.

Song 58

What is that crying out, *waridj* Miralaidj? It is the parakeets, calling
softly.   1

The Djanggawul Song Cycle

The birds are in those trees, on the topmost branches of the
   djuda:
Cocking their heads from side to side, and calling—bird with the
   red breast feathers!
We hear them, and leave them behind. There they are always
   ruffling their feathers to dry them: parakeet nestlings!
Let us leave them there! For they see the water rising as they
   ruffle themselves, at Banbaldji.   5
They are calling softly, up in the topmost branches. Their red
   breast feathers!
Up in that sacred *djuda* tree; they are always clasping it:
Calling the invocations for the *djuda* tree . . .
Crying softly, for they saw the sun, at evening: saw the red rays of
   the setting sun.
Birds crying softly, and calling!   10
We sing, *waridj* Djanggawul, clapping our sticks.
Yes, indeed, *waridj* Miralaidj, I thought that sound a stranger!
But these are our young birds, crying out, softly, from the *djuda*,
   always clasping it . . .
Calling the sacred *djuda* invocations!
Clasping the tree, calling the invocations!   15
Clasping the topmost branches, crying, calling the invocations!
Yes, *waridj* Miralaidj, that bird sits in the sacred tree, as a *rangga djuda*
   because of the invocations . . . !
Let us leave them behind, always clasping the sacred *djuda*:
Calling softly, cocking their heads to one side and crying, watching
   the well water rising at Banbaldji.
Crying, watching the sun entering the sacred shade at Dulabei, at
   Ngubarei; rays piercing, lighting up the shade . . . !   20
Parakeets, calling softly, as they saw the warm rays of the sun!
Leave them behind, perched on the topmost branches; parakeet
   nestlings, drying their feathers:
They saw the rays of the red sunset, away beyond Milingimbi,
Saw the rays of the evening sun, as its disc was sinking.
Saw the red rays, the warm red glow of sunset!   25
They cry in the sun's rays, calling softly, clasping the limbs of the
   sacred *djuda*.
We hear them calling softly from the mouth of the *ngainmara*,
Crying softly as they saw the sun, at Marabai:
Saw the warm red rays of the sun, at Bulbulmara:
Saw the red sunset reflected at Jiganjindu, at Dambalang!   30
Crying softly, drowsily, falling asleep.

The Djanggawul Song Cycle

Song 59

We walk along with the aid of the *mauwulan*, step by step, *waridj*
  Miralaidj, poking the ground.   1
Yes indeed, *waridj*, we walk along, to where we see clouds coming
  up from Wagulwagul, the Place of the Mat:
They shadow our bodies, as we walk along with the *mauwulan* . . .
We see those clouds rising, *waridj*, stretching to Didimuru; another
  cloud comes up for us, over the sea . . .
We walk with the aid of the *mauwulan*, Bildjiwuraroiju, poking the
  ground: 5
Using the *mauwulan* carefully, *waridj*, with hips swaying:
We are not tired, walking along, but our hair is grey from
  foam,
From the foam splashing, at Bralgu, the Spirit Land, away over the
  rough sea.
Carefully, *waridj*, we lift up our *rangga* . . .
Yes indeed, all right, *waridj* Miralaidj: you feel unwell?   10
My body is tired from dragging the stick, *waridj*, poking it in so
  carefully.
Turn over the mouth of the mat, come close up into it, *waridj*.
This is our place, at Banbaldji, at Bunawauwima,
Where we may sit and rest.
Yes, *waridj*, indeed! We put it in here, *waridj*, put the *mauwulan*
  point into the left side of that mat . . .   15
Our camp is in the middle.
But I feel unwell, *waridj*. Indeed, I am full of people!
In here are *rangga*-people! Come, open the mouth of this 'mat'!
This basket, which is a uterus!
Yes indeed, *waridj* Miralaidj. You must help me, for you are my
  leader . . .   20
That 'basket', *waridj*, comes from the Place of the Mauwulan!
Yes, that basket is drying from the foam which splashed it at
  Bralgu, the Spirit Land, across the sea:
All its feathers are shining, drying.
Quietly she opens her legs, only a little, opening that 'basket':
Our basket, with its feathered string and its pendants . . .   25
Our feathered strands, which were spread out carefully to dry in
  the sun's rays, at the Place of the Mauwulan.
The hot sun dried them, its rays looking down on them with
  scorching heat: thus we spread out the feathered strings.
Carefully lay out the feathered strings, leading to the Place of the
  Sun . . . !
They see, from the mat, the water and splashing foam!

Carefully lay out the feathered pendants, *waridj* Miralaidj! Take
   them, *waridj*, from here, from within the 'basket'. 30
Feathers like goanna fat! For they have dried in the warm rays
   of the sun at the Place of the Mauwulan.
The hot sun looks on them: they see from the mat the rising well
   water, bubbling.
We dry them, as the hot rays look on them, warming them . . .
They stand there in the heat that rises scorching . . .
Our red feathers look at the splashing foam from Bralgu, the Spirit
   Land, at the Place of the Sun, the Place of the Mauwulan . . . 35

Song 60

We walk along with the aid of the *mauwulan*. Yes, indeed, *waridj*
   Miralaidj, making country! 1
We stretch ourselves after resting, looking about the country,
   waridj, and at our mat.
Hips swaying, we make the country; Bildjiwuraroiju prods the
   ground as we go, with the *mauwulan* point.
Sit down carefully, *waridj*, for you have been carrying all our *rangga*
   across the sea from Bralgu: through the shine of the Morning
   Star, from the Spirit Country!
You are walking along, your hair stained with foam, from the Place
   of the Mauwulan, the Place of the Sun: 5
We have left behind our island of Wobilinga.
Our hair is always grey, like white clay: we have left behind us
   Walbinboi and Gagubam Islands . . .
Greyish, like foam on the rocks at Bauwijara Island, where the
   sea splashes up!
We leave it behind, walking along; we are tired, *waridj* Djanggawul!
Carefully we make the country—carefully, with the aid of the
   mauwulan. 10
We are drawing close to Wagulwagul, the Place of the Sacred
   Mat!
We see the rising clouds, coming up from the Place of the Mat.
Come, *waridj*, let us walk quickly along!
Yes indeed, *waridj* Miralaidj, holding the *mauwulan* at our hips:
For truly, I can walk quickly, but my body is heavy: 15
I grow tired, carrying all those *rangga* inside me, from far away,
   from Bralgu, and the sandy country there!
Yes indeed, let us go, *waridj*, making the country, swaying our
   hips, coming to Wagulwagul.
There they may come out, *waridj*!

We are coming close, indeed, walking quickly with the aid of the
mauwulan:
With hips swaying, and bodies shadowed by the passing
clouds . . .   20
Waridj, let us sit here to rest.
Yes indeed, *waridj*, truly in here we shall sit to rest.
Yes, *waridj* Miralaidj, I listen to your word: for you are my
leader . . .
Here we shall make a shade . . . so it may see the water rising at
Wagulwagul.
Ourselves, we are making our sacred shade . . .   25
Yes, *waridj*, ourselves we are making it good within the branches . . .
In there, *waridj*, we shall put the mat; we take out the *rangga* and
place them on it, by the mouth of the mat:
Where do the feathered strings lie across the ground? At Janeijann-
gauwoi, the place of the feathered string . . .
Where is that place, Munadjiwi? There we shall camp, *waridj*
Miralaidj; that is our camp!
Ourselves we shall camp, *waridj* Miralaidj, at Jigeijarung!   30
What is that other place? It is Dararwoi, *waridj*, or Wandauwi.
Ah, yes, *waridj*, that is our country!

Song 61

What shall we do here, *waridj* Miralaidj?   1
Yes, we shall make a fish trap here, *waridj*. Put it into the well of
Wagulwagul!
Put the *djuda* roots into the mud, into the well, calling the invoca-
tions.
Put in the *rangga* carefully, so that they rise in the well: pushing
the mud (against them), calling the invocations.
There they are coming up for us! Pull the grass, for blocking the
fish trap: we call the invocations.   5
We pull the grass, making the fish trap: putting it into the well
and calling the invocations . . .
Pulling the grass, invoking the sacred names!
There is another well for you, *waridj*. Indeed, put in the *rangga*
there, dragging the grass, making the sacred wells.
Water comes up from them, flowing into the fish trap . . .
Water rising up to the grass barrier, splashing and surging against
it . . .   10
Put them in, calling the invocations . . .
Carefully, *waridj*, indeed, dragging them through the mud:

We are putting the fish trap, making the well at Wagulwagul—
ourselves, *waridj* Miralaidj.
Yes indeed, I am listening to your word!
Ourselves we are making the fish trap, *waridj*, putting grass into
the sacred well at Wagulwagul.   15
Indeed, put it carefully, pushing the mud . . .
There is another well! We put in the *djuda* roots, making a shade,
calling the invocations:
Making a well at Wagulwagul, invoking the sacred names . . .
Making a well there, putting in the *djuda* roots . . .
Water is rising for us, spraying and roaring from within . . .   20
We indeed, *waridj*, have made the well, putting grass in the fish
trap, pushing the mud (against it).
Ourselves we pull the grass, where we put the well . . .
Waridj Miralaidj, I am just asking you, awaiting your word: for
you are my leader . . .
It is our well we are making: we put in the *rangga*, and water comes
roaring up . . .
Rangga dragging in the mud, pulling the grass—the expanse of
water! It is ours, *waridj* Miralaidj!   25

Song 62

Another well we shall make at Wagulwagul . . .   1
We put in the *djuda* roots, pulling the grass, calling the invocations.
Carefully, *waridj* Djanggawul, push mud (about the posts).
Yes, indeed, we are making it, pulling the grass, calling the invoca-
tions . . .
What is happening, *waridj*? Surely, the posts are falling aslant!
Straighten them up, put in the *rangga* roots, calling the invoca-
tions!   5
Carefully put them in, at the well, invoking the names of the sacred
djuda!
Clouds are rising for us, as we swim to straighten the posts:
Clouds are rising for us, from within the *djuda* posts, the posts of
the fish trap.
They are ours, the clouds rising and passing!
Another well for you, *waridj*!   10
Come, let us put in the *djuda* roots, calling the invocations . . .
We make the well, invoking the sacred *djuda* names as we put them
in . . .
They are rising for us, coming up as we plunge in the *mauwulan*,
making a well.

Carefully we put in the *djuda* roots, calling the invocations:
For us, from the *rangga*, the water comes roaring and splashing
    against the fish trap!   15

Song 63

There indeed we shall make another well, *waridj*, at Wagul-
    wagul . . .   1
We pull the grass, dragging it along . . .
Yes indeed, *waridj*, surely we shall put in the *rangga*, calling the
    invocations . . .
We pull the grass, invoking the sacred names.
We put it in, making the well, calling the invocations . . .   5
Making the well at Wagulwagul, pushing mud against the posts,
    as we call the invocations . . .
We put in the *mauwulan, waridj*, making the well, calling the *bugali* . . .
We pull the grass, making the well, putting in the grass and calling
    the invocations . . .
Those are our *rangga* that (seem to) float in the water, like clouds
    coming up:
Clouds (that seem to be) swimming, spreading over the sky and
    bending earthwards: 10
There indeed, *waridj*, we put in our well.
Yes, indeed, I listen to what you say, I await your words . . .
For us the spray comes up from the well, at Wagulwagul . . .
Clouds spreading over the sky, as water surges against the fish
    trap:
Water rising up in the well, swirling with foam: 15
Spray coming up for us, *waridj*, at Wagulwagul, water roaring for
    us, dragging the mud and the grass.
Carefully, we put in the fish trap!

Song 64

Here, *waridj* Miralaidj, let us open (the *ngainmara* mat)!   1
We shall part the fringe of the mat,
We shall look inside, and see the crowd of people.
Let us put them outside the mouth of the mat, turning it over and
    placing them on it!
We put them there, by the fish trap: *rangga* people, clan of the fish. 5
For we flatten the mat to put fish on, *waridj*, smoothing out the
    mat:
We dry them, as they come from the mouth of the mat.

15. Calling invocations before the sacred shade.

16. The Goanna emblem emerges from the shade.

17. Various sacred shades, with the Djanggawul.

18. *Nara* postulants representing male and female Goanna.

Come, part the fringe of the mat, at its mouth! Pull it up, pull it up
    from the water, *waridj* Miralaidj!
Yes, go, pull it up and look! Indeed, pull up both the mats!
Come, be quiet! I see a clan of fish, *rangga* inside the fish trap.   10
Where, *waridj*? Yes, here we see, *waridj*! So come, *waridj*, and here!
    Yes *waridj* Miralaidj, here are more . . .
Yes indeed, go on! For here is another, hidden in the sacred mat.
    Let us cover it, so no one may see.
I am 'jealous' of you. These fish, I make them tabu!
I see them: take them into your hand, put them in the warm heat
    of the sun.
We take them in our hands, watching the sun set!   15
Go, turn back, hide them within the sacred mat, beneath its trans-
    verse fibre, dragging the grass . . .
We hide them beneath the open conical mat, inside the mouth of
    the mat, from within the fish trap:
We put the *rangga* fish, the people, inside it.
Yes indeed, *waridj*, that is our grass (by the trap)!
The sun is setting, sinking down far away!   20
The rays of the sun have vanished beyond Milingimbi.
Carefully, we put them in, making the 'camp'.

Song 65

Come, *waridj*, put in the mat, the fish trap, pulling, dragging the
    grass.   1
Yes indeed, *waridj* Miralaidj, I listen to what you say . . .
Go, put it in, *waridj* Djanggawul!
Yes indeed, carefully put it into the mud.
Yes, *waridj*, the water is rising, carefully, surging up through the
    ground into the mouth of the mat!   5
Yes, go, paint it with mud! Push the mud about it, making a fish
    trap!
Pull the grass, pushing it (into place).
It is finished! Yes, *waridj*, finished indeed!
Come, let us walk along, where we hear the well water rising and
    roaring, from the sacred shade . . .
It is finished! Go, flatten the sacred mat, so we may sleep upon it!   10
Our bodies are tired from pulling the grass: our heads are weary,
    our eyelids heavy.
We rest our heads on the *rangga*, restlessly turning: hearing the
    fish, the roar of the water rising up in the well.
We sleep but lightly, hearing the fish, the 'nail' fish moving within . . .

Yes indeed, we lie half asleep, reflecting. What is that, *waridj*, moving along?

Indeed, *waridj*, it is the 'whisker' fish!   15

What is that, another? A yellow-bellied fish!

We cover it up within the mouth of the mat, beneath its transverse fibre, parting the fringe.

What is that, *waridj*, another? It is a barramundi!

Yes, a barramundi, within that mat, that fish trap. It drew them in, at the well: into the fish trap, dragging the grass, invoking the sacred names.

The fish jumped into the well . . . into the fish trap!   20

Plenty of fish inside, *waridj*, for us!

Shall we go walking on, *waridj*, with the aid of the *mauwulan*?

No, wait a little! We shall leave after the dawn: it is almost daylight . . .

Yes, let us wait until after daybreak, until we see the warm rays of the sun shining upon us.

(When) the sun's disc shines: red glow coming up for us, from the Sun Woman's feathered girdle!   25

We feel the heat of the sun, *waridj*, its warm rays.

We stretch our limbs, *waridj*, rising from sleep.

Well, shall we just walk on, *waridj* Miralaidj? Yes, prodding the ground with the *mauwulan rangga*!

Come on, let us make the country, *waridj*, prodding the ground with the stick.

Bildjiwuraroiju is making country, using the *mauwulan* point! Swaying our hips we walk along, step by step, at Wagulwagul. 30

Yes indeed, *waridj*! Bildjiwuraroiju inserts the *mauwulan* point.

Yes indeed, *waridj*, this sacred mat with its transverse fibre! Go, put it right inside the mat, and we'll turn it over!

It is done. Let us leave the mat in here, at Wagulwagul.

Go, bow your heads! Myself first (says one of the Sisters), I shall look at the country.

Come, *waridj*, now you may see the *rangga* (fish), as we part the fringe of the mat!   35

Come, they are jumping into the fish trap, among the grass!

We see a clan of fish, the sacred *rangga* . . .

This is a large group of fish! We shall just put them into the mouth of the mat:

We cover them up, for these fish of ours are sacred: no one may see them.

Another fish appears from the mud: it is always lying there, covered up by the mud.   40

Put it within the mouth of the mat; hide it, for it is very sacred to us!

Cover it, lying there, with its tail splashing the water!
What is that large fish, *waridj*? It is a 'whisker' fish, putting its
 spike sideways, chasing smaller fish at the mouth of the mat.
Put it in, cover it up within the mouth of the sacred mat, hiding
 it there; it is sacred.
Waridj, truly we make them sacred for us.   45
We hide them within the mouth of the mat, covering them up.
What is that spiky fish, *waridj*, for us?
We saw it lying there, swimming among the *rangga* posts and the
 mangroves . . .
Put it into that mat! We take it and hide it, covering it up and
 making it sacred, within the mat:
Spiky fish that belongs to us, *waridj*, indeed!   50
Yes, indeed, *waridj*, place it within the mouth of this mat, so no one
 may see it.
Here is another, a small 'nail' fish!
Put this fish within the mouth of the mat, to hide it, parting the
 fringe. Cover it up, for it is truly ours!
Yes indeed, I am just showing you this, for it is sacred to us, and
 so we hide it.
What is that? A mangrove goanna.   55
Put it in! It is sacred: for it has fallen down from the tree on to
 the *djuda* roots.
We hide it within the mat: we cover it up, for it is sacred, placing
 it within the mouth of the sacred mat.

Song 66

A bird is calling! What is that, indeed, *waridj* Miralaidj? A goose
 alighting, its breast touching the water, amoung the *djuda* posts
 of the fish trap!   1
Drying itself as it sits on a post, ruffling and plucking at its
 feathers . . .
Within the well at Wagulwagul, clasping the *djuda* roots:
Clans of geese like *rangga*, quietly perched on the *djuda* posts,
 calling the invocations.
In the sun's rays, in the full heat of the burning sun . . .   5
Those goose-people, drying themselves at the well, feathers
 fluttering, calling the invocations!
Drying themselves, as they clasp the *djuda rangga*, in the well at
 Wagulwagul.
Geese like *rangga*, like people! Clans of birds, always clasping the
 djuda, at the mouth of the sacred mat!

They are ours, *waridj*. We cover them up—they are sacred. We put
  them, sacred to us, into that basket!
Yes indeed, *waridj*, they are ours: for we are calling the invocations!   10
We cover them up, hiding them in that basket, that sacred bag,
  calling the invocations . . .
We hide them, invoking the sacred names.
Ourselves we are binding the *rangga*, fastening goose feathers into
  the binding!
Yes indeed, *waridj*, we always cover them up and hide them, for
  they are sacred.
We go along with the aid of the *mauwulan rangga*, making country,
  prodding the ground, at Wagulwagul.   15
Bildjiwuraroiju, using the *mauwulan* point!
Yes, indeed, we go fast with swaying hips, dragging the stick along:
  poking it into the ground, singing away, and making country.
As we walk, our heads are grey, stained with foam from the sea:
Foam that splashed our hair, leaving its salty stain, back at the
  Place of the Mauwulan . . .
At the Place of the Sun, out on the rough sea.   20
Let us leave it! We have come far, from the Land of Spirits, through
  the shine of the Morning Star, from Bralgu, far beyond the
  horizon.

Song 67

Oh! What is this? A small black mangrove bird, *waridj*.   1
Yes, it is a mangrove bird! I thought I heard a strange sound, as
  it cried among the mangroves.
Yes, it saw the daylight coming, the stars fading . . .
This is the mangrove bird: it heard the water rising and roaring,
  with foam splashing:
Crying at the water swirling within the well at Wagulwagul,
  splashing against the mat, the fish trap!   5
So the bird looked back, and saw the daylight spreading from
  Bralgu, driving away the night:
Saw the daylight coming, the darkness clearing away . . .
Looking back, it saw the Morning Star sinking.
Its long-drawn cry echoed up to the clouds—to the woman clouds,
  to the large spreading, pregnant clouds . . .
Sound drifting upward into the message clouds, clouds massing
  together.   10
Its long cry comes from the *djuda* trees, the poles of the fish trap:
  scratching the trunk as it sits clasping the tree . . .
Tired, it cries as the water comes rising up:

148

The Djanggawul Song Cycle

The long-drawn cry merges with the roar of the water . . .
The long-drawn cry, as the water rises, tossing: it grows tired, from
the splashing spray, the rising well water.
With a long cry it clasps the *djuda*, watching the water at Wagulwagul, rising against the mat.   15

Song 68

We walk along with the aid of the *mauwulan*, prodding the ground. 1
Yes indeed, *waridj*, we are making the country, step by step, with
hips swaying, using the *mauwulan rangga*.
Making country: Bildjiwuraroiju pokes the point of the *mauwulan*
into the ground, we sing as we go along.
It is good, *waridj*: I always listen to your words, for you are my
leader . . .
What is that, *waridj*? That is an opossum, scratching its fur.   5
Come, *waridj* Djanggawul, give me the basket, we shall cover it up.
Ourselves we are putting it into the basket, covering it, making
it sacred.
It will hang quietly on the *djuda* tree, as we call the invocations.
We shall bind the *rangga*, invoking the sacred names . . .
Ourselves we shall twine feathers and fur into the binding.   10
Yes indeed, *waridj* Miralaidj, that is agreed . . . no one may see!
We hide it, cover it up within the basket, within the mouth of the
mat, so no one may see.
We shall sit down, fastening feathered strings to the *rangga* emblems:
ourselves, there at Wagulwagul, the shade of the Sacred Mat:
Feathered string from within the mouth of the shade . . .
Yes indeed, *waridj* Miralaidj, I listen to your words, for you are
my leader.   15
I always follow you: it is you I am always asking, for you are my
true leader . . .
Yes, we shall hide it so no one may see: like a younger sibling!
We cover it up, for it is sacred—we make it tabu, for us!

Song 69

What is that, a mangrove goanna? Yes! It is ours, *waridj*: we take
it and put it within the mouth of the mat, making it sacred!   1
We shall hide it within the peak of the mat, the sacred basket,
beneath the transverse fibre.
Cover it up beneath the transverse fibre, parting the fringe of the mat:
we hide it so no one may see, for it is sacred, like a younger sibling.

Ourselves we cover it up, this mangrove goanna, putting it in among
    the *djuda* roots and the trees, the *rangga* poles.
They are just dry ing, those feathers, the fat of the mangrove goanna: 5
On the tree, in the rays of the sun, scratching the *djuda*; in the
    burning heat of the sun.
It clasps the *djuda*, wearily, quietly there on the tree . . .
It saw the water rising up in the wells, splashing and roaring up
    into Wagulwagul.
Yes indeed, *waridj* Djanggawul, I was just asking you this . . .
For it is sacred to us: we cover it up within the mouth of the mat,
    the sacred shade: 10
We shall put it well within the peak of the mat . . .
We hide, it for that mangrove goanna has a very sacred name:
    we cover it up, making it tabu to all but us!
Yes indeed, I listen to your words: I hear what you say.
You are my leader, *waridj* Miralaidj, my great leader . . . !

Song 70

We are walking along, *waridj*, singing, and making country with
    the *mauwulan* point. 1
What is that, *waridj*? A mangrove shell. We must put it within the
    mouth of the mat and hide it, making it sacred.
Indeed, Miralaidj, here is another to put in the basket.
Come, we must cover them up, put them in the sacred basket . . .
What is that there? We saw another! 5
Yes, take it, put it in for us; we hide it within the mat, covering
    it up for us, making it sacred.
We walk on, with hips swaying. What is that? It is another shell.
Go, get it and show me! It looks like a land snail, *waridj*.
Indeed, it is sacred to us. We cover it up with the mat, so no one
    may see it: it is like a younger sibling!
Put it within the peak of the mat, quietly and reverently, for it is
    very sacred: it is attached to the *djuda* . . . 10
We clap the sticks, and sing as we go along, hiding it well within
    the mouth of the shade . . .
Yes indeed, *waridj*. Truly, we put it there, so no one may see or
    go near it:
It is as our younger sibling, *waridj* Miralaidj. It is ours: we cover
    it up within the mouth of the shade, of the sacred mat, parting
    its fringe . . .
Ourselves we hide it, so no one may see or go near it, for it is very
    sacred: there at the sacred well the water is always hiding it.

Chapter Twelve

COMMENTS ON PART FOUR OF THE SONGS

THE Djanggawul have arrived at Arnhem Bay. As they draw near Wagulwagul they hear a duck crying (Song 57); its feathers are stained by the sea foam which splashed it on the way from Bralgu, suggesting that it came to the mainland in the *ngainmara*, in the form of a sacred *rangga* emblem. Here are male and female ducks, crying out on their way from Banbaldji (*vide* Part Three). *Djuda* have been planted, and from the topmost branches the sacred red breasted parakeets cry (Song 58). This song repeats the previous theme; they ruffle their feathers, drying them in the sun.

Clouds appear, rising above Wagulwagul (Song 59), and guide the Djanggawul on their way. They walk on, but the elder Sister feels unwell and cannot walk too quickly. She is pregnant: her uterus is full of people. Towards the middle of the song she is aided by Miralaidj, and the people are removed: they are likened to feathered pendants, and laid out to dry. The whole subject of childbirth is delicately treated in conventional symbolism, and different aspects are linked up with the over-all pattern.

Song 60 repeats the pregnancy theme. The women sit down carefully, for they are tired from carrying such a heavy load in their uteri, and their journey has been a long one. They make an energetic start, but soon tire: they are carrying so many people. They pass through many places, but do not make a sacred shade until they reach Wagulwagul. This is the most important sacred site at Arnhem Bay, taking its name from the 'inside' term for the *ngainmara* mat, whale or uterus.

Reaching Wagulwagul, they put a fish trap at a sacred well

Comments on Part Four of the Songs

(Song 61), and wait for the gushing spring water to bring them fish. Various fish are caught in the trap but not before the rising waters have swept and surged against it (Songs 62–63). Song 64 tells of the fish, which are really *rangga*, that is, people, removed from the pregnant Sisters (see above). These fish are declared sacred and tabu, and covered up within the *ngainmara*. In Song 65, the mat itself is used as a net; and the Djanggawul sleep fitfully, resting their heads on the *rangga* poles which are kept within it. All night long they hear the sound of the fish, caught in the mat trap. A 'whisker' fish a yellow-belly, a barramundi, and many other fish as well as a mangrove goanna are caught; all are hidden in the mat and declared sacred. The Djanggawul make ready to leave this place, but it is too early. They decide to wait until after sunrise, for it is nearly sunrise.

While they wait, a goose makes its appearance (Song 66), alighting first on the water, and then on a *rangga* pole which is part of the fish trap the Djanggawul have constructed. It dries itself in the sun, at the sacred well; its feathers fall as it ruffles and preens them, and the Djanggawul use these in making the feathered string with which they bind the *rangga* emblems. These geese are symbolic of the people that have been removed from the Sisters' uteri: they are declared sacred, and covered up in the *ngainmara* mat. In this way, the totemic creatures are designated.

The Djanggawul continue on their journey, but are not far from Wagulwagul when a mangrove bird cries out (Song 67); it heralds the coming dawn, and delights in the running spring waters where the fish trap has been erected. Large clouds foretell the coming wet season. Soon afterwards, an opossum is seen (Song 68) and is put into a mat, and consequently becomes sacred. Fragments of fur fall down as it scratches itself, and are used in the string with which the Djanggawul bind the *rangga*. In Song 69, a mangrove goanna is seen; this too is declared sacred, and hidden within the *ngainmara*. In Song 70, mangrove shells of various kinds are collected and called sacred, and hidden in the mat.

Returning to Song 57 we see that the ducks are equated with *rangga*, and so with the people to whom the Djanggawul Sisters give birth. Song 58 treats the familiar theme of the parakeets, likened to feathered pendants which are put into the sun to dry; they clasp the *djuda* trees, just as the pendants are attached to *rangga* emblems. The sun enters the sacred shade which has been built; its rays pierce the branches of the shade, and light up the interior. The invocations used here belong to the Ngeimil linguistic group.

Song 59 brings into perspective the pregnancy of the Sisters: it is not made clear whether both or only one are ready to produce the people. 'Yes, indeed, all right, *waridj* Miralaidj: you feel unwell?' (line 10) while she answers, 'My body is tired . . .' (line 11). 'Turn over the mouth of the mat, come close up into it, *waridj*' (line 12), and ' . . . We put it in here, *waridj*, put the *mauwulan* point into the left side of that mat . . .' (line 15). These two lines refer to the position taken by one sister at childbirth, and to the point of the *mauwulan* stick which is placed within her to facilitate delivery. Just what is meant by 'left side of that mat (vagina = uterus)' is not clear, except that the *rangga* pole is inserted from the side. 'But I feel unwell, *waridj*. Indeed, I am full of people!' (line 17). The pains of childbirth are upon her, and she complains that her womb contains so many people (= *rangga*). 'In here are *rangga*-people! Come, open the mouth of this "mat"! This basket, which is a uterus!' (lines 18–19)—(which, interlinear, is: so I feel unwell *waridj* indeed unable to walk far, line 19; in this *rangga rangga* it can open the mouth that mat, line 18; that is basket basket basket uterus, line 19). 'Unable to walk far', refers to one of the Sisters, who is 'too full of people (children)'; that is why they are walking carefully, or slowly. The *rangga*, referred to by the terms *maidjara* and *jandaljandal*, are the people inside the Sister; 'it can open', means that her vulva (vagina) may be opened with the point of the *mauwulan rangga*, in order to let out the people from her mat (that is, uterus). These come forth like *rangga* emblems drawn from the sacred *ngainmara*. 'The mouth' is the vulva; the term 'basket' is an 'outside' word, for an Aboriginal woman's uterus is called the *baidji*, 'basket', while the 'inside' name is *ngainmara*. 'Yes indeed, *waridj* Miralaidj. You must help me, for you are my leader . . .' (line 20): the interlinear translation has here been rendered generally, the literal version being 'yes yes *waridj* Miralaidj I too "frightened" for them yourself say it like my leader.' That is to say, the Brother Djanggawul or Bralbral may not aid Miralaidj at childbirth without first asking her permission for so doing. Aborigines say, 'too "frightened" for them' means 'I am too frightened for them— for all those *mauwulan* and *djuda rangga* emblems (people) inside me.' 'They can't open it (the vulva) without first asking the younger Sister, Miralaidj.' It is inferred that she must be aided by her Sister, and not by her Brother (or by Bralbral), when she 'lets out' the people.

'Yes, that basket is drying . . .' and 'All its feathers are shining, drying' (lines 22–23): this means that the children or people are removed from the uterus, and are drying in the sun (that is, like *rangga*). 'Quietly she opens her legs only a little, opening that "basket" (vulva)' (line 24), is said to mean that 'they open the dilly bag gently'. That is, she opens her legs carefully, so that her vulva opens only a little to let some people out; if she had opened it too wide, too many would have issued forth.

A certain amount of confusion exists as to which Sister is pregnant. In the main version, both Sisters are concurrently pregnant, but in this section stress has been placed on the younger Sister, Miralaidj. As mentioned before, both Sisters carry within their uteri all the people who are to become the progenitors of the present-day Arnhem Landers; they resemble ordinary pregnant women, and their uteri are the *ngainmara* mat or basket. Within these uteri are *rangga*, which are people; in some versions they are said to carry both *rangga* emblems and people, the *rangga* being mixed with the people. The many references, both in this section and in others, refer to the Sisters' uteri being opened to 'let people out', or to 'take out' *rangga* emblems. Although up to this song no mention has been made of the Djanggawul Brother's penis, all references to *rangga* roots and posts infer this organ. For example, the *mauwulan* is really a walking stick, or is used to make wells; the *djanda rangga* is the goanna's tail and the adjoining part of its body; and the *djuda* is really a tree. All, however, are symbolic of the penis of the male Djanggawul. There are other *djuda*, in addition to those specifically used for creating trees, and these are penis or *gurlga* (root) *rangga*. However, the two principal *rangga* which symbolize a penis are the *mauwulan* and the *djuda*—the former because it makes wells, like an ejaculating penis; and the latter because it produces trees (representing vegetable and plant growth and general fertility). The goanna tail motif (manifested in the *djanda rangga*) is commonly a penis symbol; and the word *djuda* is an 'inside' term for a penis.

Song 60 continues the theme. 'Sit down carefully, *waridj*, for you have been carrying all our *rangga* across the sea from Bralgu . . . ' (line 4), ' . . . but my body is heavy . . . ' (line 15), and 'I grow tired, carrying all those *rangga* inside me . . . ' (line 16). 'In there, *waridj*, we shall put the mat; we take out the *rangga* and place them on it, by the mouth of the mat . . . ' (line 27). That is, in line 4, one Sister sits down to give birth to the people they will put there. In line 15 the word *maidjara*, 'clan' or group of *rangga*, is used in reference to the people within her. Line 27 refers to the people's being removed and placed on top of the *ngainmara*. Line 9 mentions the name of the Djanggawul Brother: in the text his name is given as Ganjudingu, 'because he is the "maker" of the sacred mat, the uterus and of the *rangga*.' That is to say, because the Brother is the fertilizer of his Sisters, he 'makes' them big with children. Line 16 ' . . . from Bralgu, and the sandy country there ' (that is, the *rangga* or children have been carried from there) refers to a place at Bralgu named Garwa, which means a desert or sandy country; there are large goannas at that place. Janeijanngauwoi is in the middle of the coast bordering Arnhem Bay, so named from the feathered string; Wagulwagul, the place of the uterus or *ngainmara* mat, is also at Arnhem Bay in Dadawi linguistic group territory; Munadjiwi (Manmaldji or Munadjing) is also at Arnhem Bay; Jigeijarung is localized at a billabong; and Darar'woi is a clay-pan, having the 'inside' name of Wondauwi.

Song 61 tells how a fish trap is made and placed at the sacred well of Wagulwagul. It is constructed from *djuda rangga*, pushed upright into the mud, with cross-barriers formed of grass. When the water flows out and spreads from the wells (for there are many wells at Wagulwagul), fish are caught in these catchments. That is, 'Water rising up to the grass barrier, splashing and surging against it . . . ' (line 10). The significance of the term 'fish trap' has already been mentioned. The invocations used in this song are associated with the Ngeimil, Riradjingu and Dadawi linguistic groups; most refer to the *djuda*, but one invocation in line 18 refers to the foam coming up.

Song 62 continues this theme, but tells that some posts have fallen aslant (line 5); the rushing waters have pushed them over, and the Djanggawul '. . . swim to straighten the posts' (line 7). These are the *djuda rangga* posts, possessed of a sacred quality; and from them 'Clouds are rising for us, from within the *djuda* posts, the posts of the fish trap . . . ' (line 8), 'Clouds are rising for us' (line 7). The wet monsoonal season is upon them, and it is the rains which swell the billabongs and cause the wells to overflow and spread down to the fish trap. 'They are ours, the clouds rising and passing!' (line 9) joyously cry the Djanggawul. The invocations ('bottom' Ngeimil, and Djambatpingu), all relating to the *djuda*, cause the clouds to appear: 'They are rising for us, coming up as we plunge in the *mauwulan*, making a well . . . Carefully we put in the *djuda* roots, calling the invocations . . . ' (lines 13–14) —for they themselves are connected with water (= clouds = rain).

One *bugali* invocation (line 12), *ba'ralgiwul*, is particularly interesting. It is an 'outside' term for a *bugali* invocation, and is also a term used for old or young Djambatpingu women; that is, these women are *ba'ralgi*. For example, should it not be advisable to call a woman by her personal name (it may be tabu-ed to the speaker), her *bugali* name may be used—this is her *ba'ralgi*. All personal names of both men and women stem from their own clan, linguistic group or mythological background, and all have 'inside' and 'outside' equivalents and variants, with relevant *bugali* (or *bugalili*) invocations, or *ba'ralgi*.

Song 63 relates how another fish trap is erected, and the grass barriers put into place (line 2). The *rangga* posts of this trap appear to 'float in the water' (line 9) like the rising clouds (that is, the reflections of the poles in the water): 'Clouds (that seem to be) swimming, spreading over the sky and bending earthwards' (line 10); 'Clouds spreading over the sky, as water surges against the fish trap' (line 14). The spreading waters of the billabong and well, the *rangga* and the fish trap, are connected with the monsoonal rains that fertilize the earth. The invocations mentioned in this song belong to the Gwolamala and 'bottom' Ngeimil linguistic groups, and refer to the *djuda*.

Song 64 tells how the *ngainmara* mat itself is used as a fish trap; but really lines 1–7 symbolize one or both of the Sisters, giving birth to people who are the fish *rangga*. 'Here, *waridj* Miralaidj, let us open (the *ngainmara* mat)! We shall part the fringe of the mat, we shall look inside and see the crowd of people' (lines 1–3). The Djanggawul Brother lifts aside the clitoris and pubic hair (mat's fringe) of one of his Sisters, and looking into her vagina sees the people in her uterus. 'Let us put them outside the mouth of the mat, turning it over and placing them on it! . . . We put them there, by the fish trap: *rangga* people, clan of the fish' (lines 4–5). The *ngainmara* mat is turned over and the people (*rangga* or clan of the fish) are placed within its peak. The word used for clan of fish is *jandaljandal*, the meaning of which has already been discussed. Aborigines say that they 'copy from this' (that is, from its true meaning as *rangga*, or sacred people, within the Sisters' wombs) 'and the people removed are put to the fish group'; this means that totemic beings are created or, alternatively, people are born with whom this totemic species has special ritual associations. Nevertheless, it is said, speaking figuratively, that 'feathered strings' are born. 'We dry them, as they come from the mouth of the mat' (line 7), a parallel to the washing and drying of new-born infants. The theme reverts to the fish trap: 'Yes, go, pull it up and look! Indeed, pull up both the mats! Come, be quiet! I see a clan of fish, *rangga* inside the fish trap' (lines 9–10). The mat is used for catching fish, and when this is pulled up on to the bank it contains a group of 'fish' (see line 10, which is really the same as line 3).

'I am "jealous" of you! These fish, I make them tabu!' (line 13): Aborigines explain this line thus: 'I (the Djanggawul) am "jealous" of these fish,' the Brother tells his two Sisters. That is, he sets the 'fish' aside (fish = *rangga* = penis), declaring them sacred to himself and his two Sisters. The food that has been caught in the *ngainmara* is tabu and sacred: young people to-day may not partake of this *mareijin* tabu-ed food (that is, the fish), for it has been caught in the sacred *ngainmara*.

Comments on Part Four of the Songs

The fish removed from the Sisters (from the uterus or *ngainmara*) are then put into the mud (Song 65, line 4) as are *rangga* after ceremonial use: that is, they are put into the waters within the fish catchment. Then the Djanggawul settle down to rest (line 10), flattening out the *ngainmara* and making it ready for sleeping upon. 'Our bodies are tired from pulling the grass: our heads are weary, our eyelids heavy' (line 11): they are tired from the strenuous work of keeping the spreading water at bay, for it might destroy their fish trap. They lie down, resting their heads on the sacred *rangga*, which serve as pillows (line 12). (The word used for them is *maidjara*.) The Djanggawul sleep fitfully, awakening from time to time as they hear the sound made by the fish (lines 12–13): for these are the *rangga*, the fish which have been caught in the *ngainmara*. In line 14 we are told, 'Yes, indeed, we lie half-asleep, reflecting. What is that, *waridj*, moving along?' '. . . half-asleep, reflecting' is more literally translated as 'head light in sleep' (that is, *bira*); it is at such times, the Aborigines say, that one begins to 'think of things'. The Djanggawul, in this state of *bira*, semi-wakefulness, or the thinking over of things before actual sleep, are lying quietly reflecting on what they have done and what they will do. They are awakened by various fish, which they catch and put into the *ngainmara*.

The well at Wagulwagul is declared sacred, and the *ngainmara* put within it (line 33). 'Go, bow your heads! Myself, first (says one of the Sisters) I shall look at the country' (line 34). The sisters speak to the men, for they themselves are custodians of the sacred objects; the bowed head, with closed eyes, represents the conventional attitude of a young novice brought on to the sacred ceremonial ground for the first time. Presently the men are allowed to look (line 35); 'Yes indeed, I am just showing you this, for it is sacred to us, and so we hide it' (that is, cover up the totemic fish within the *ngainmara*), line 54; 'We hide it within the mat: we cover it up, for it is sacred, placing it within the mouth of the sacred mat' (line 57). The invocations are Dadawi and Riradjingu, and both refer to the special fish trap.

Song 66 concerns the goose which comes to rest on the surface of the billabong where the fish trap is (line 1), and flies up to sit on one of the *rangga* posts (line 2); others flutter over the well (or wells) at Wagulwagul (line 3), clasping the spreading water-washed roots of the trees (that is, *djuda*). 'Geese like *rangga*, like people! Clans of birds, always clasping the *djuda*, at the mouth of the sacred mat!' (line 8): this symbolism has already been mentioned. The Djanggawul pick up the goose feathers which fall from their ruffling (line 2), working it into jungle twine with which they bind the various *rangga* poles, using it for decoration, and for inserting the ends of the pendants.

Reference has frequently been made to 'dragging the stick (*mauwulan*) along' (as in line 17). To-day, in the *dua nara* Djanggawul dancing, neophytes drag sticks along the ground in commemoration of the way in which the Djanggawul dragged their *mauwulan*. On the other hand, the dragging of the sticks signifies water coming in or going out, the ebb and flow of the tide at Port Bradshaw. 'Foam that splashed our hair, leaving its salty stain, back at the Place of the Mauwulan . . . ' (line 19). The Djanggawul still have the salt-water mark on their foreheads and on their hair. At first it was the salt water which left a whitish stain, during their journey from Bralgu. Subsequently, however, during their travels across the mainland, they painted their heads with white clay, to symbolize the initial foam stain. Later still, as they drew near the end of their travels, their hair became grey: and this, too, represented salt-water marks.

Song 67 tells of a small black mangrove bird appearing, crying out as it sees the first glow of morning (line 6): 'Its long-drawn cry echoed up to the clouds—to the woman clouds, to the large spreading, pregnant clouds . . . ' (line 9). These large clouds are termed 'pregnant woman' clouds (*djililg*), for from them come many scattered smaller ones; another larger cloud, *mindjil*, has a small black mark on it, and this too represents a woman. With these clouds above them, the Djanggawul continue (Song 68) until they hear an opossum; this animal is treated totemically, and put within the *ngainmara* (lines 6 and 7). The Djanggawul then sit down in a shade they have built, and decorate their *rangga* (lines 9 and 10), binding them with string intertwined with opossum fur.

Song 69 brings in the mangrove goanna. This is treated in similar fashion, being placed within the *ngainmara* mat and declared totemic, in the sacred sense of the term. The goanna in the mat represents symbolically the penis in the vagina. The *ngainmara* itself serves as a special shade for the goanna (*nara* hut = mat = uterus)—line 10. The shade is similar to that used to-day on the sacred ground. Within this, sacred objects are made. Men have collected *lindaridj* parakeet feathers in readiness, and while they sit making their *djanda* or mangrove-goanna *rangga*, they watch the goanna resting in their shade. Aborigines comment: 'we look at this goanna resting, and copy it in wood; we compare the one with the other.'

Song 70 refers to certain mangrove shells, which are found by the Djanggawul, and made sacred by being put into the *ngainmara* (line 2). 'Put it within the peak of the mat, quietly and reverently, for it is very sacred: it is attached to the *djuda* . . .' (line 10); the word used for 'reverently' is *mareijin reiwuljuma*, that is, sacred, quietly, gently or solemnly. The 'snail' shell is attached to a limb or root of a tree (*djuda*) in the water; when removed from the tree, it recedes farther into its shell (that is, entering its *ngainmara*—being covered up, made sacred). The Djanggawul then continue on their journey.

Chapter Thirteen

THE DJANGGAWUL SONG CYCLE

PART FIVE

The Djanggawul continue their journey along the coast of the mainland, about Arnhem Bay.

Song 71

WE have come to the river crossing, *waridj*. Where shall we cross, there to the other side?　　　　　　1
Go, make yet another well at Wagulwagul: putting the *mauwulan* point in, Bildjiwuraroiju, so that water comes gushing forth!
Dragging the stick through the mud, putting it into the ground!
We walk along fast, using the stick; and here we see a whale!
What is that, *waridj*, blocking us? A whale!　　　　　　5
Yes, a whale is blocking us! Indeed, oh the bulk of its body . . . !
What can we do? The whale is right in the mud before us:
That whale with its huge ribs, its tail flipper . . .
Indeed, *waridj* Miralaidj, its bulky body is ours, as it lies high and dry in the mud.
Oh, Wagulwagul Whale, covered up within it—the *ngainmara*! The Uterus!　　　　　　10
Water is rising up from the mud, mixing with spray from the whale: waves clashing together, water stirred up by the whale . . . !
Foam coming up! Well water rising and roaring, flowing about the whale: by its rib bones, the transverse fibre of the mat, into its mouth!
Water rises, flowing into the mouth of the whale, the gaping mouth of the whale:

19. The Djanggawul Goanna emerges from the shade.

20. Postulants in stylized attitudes, with Goanna Tail emblem.

21. Clapping sticks and blowing the sacred Julunggul drone pipe, above the posturing sacred Goanna.

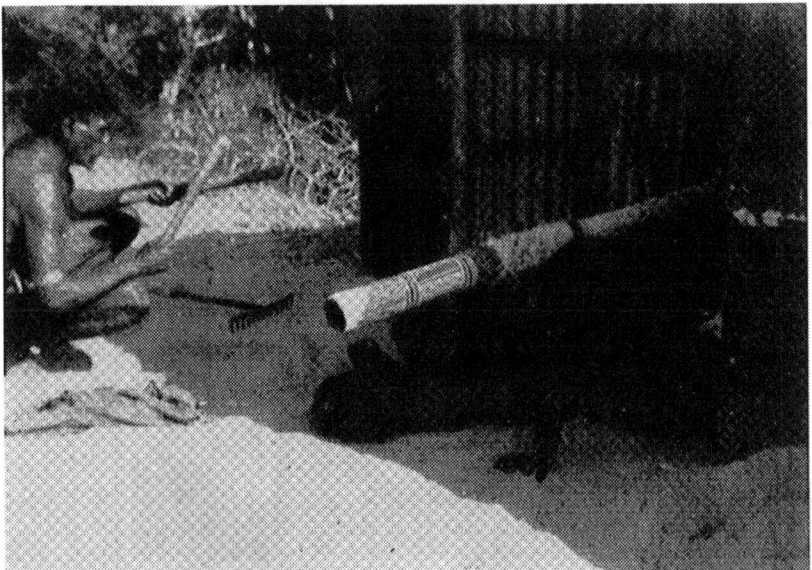

22. The Julunggul Python emerges from the sacred shade: postulants lie on their backs, with the emblem resting upon them.

Mouth of the *ngainmara*, like our *nara* shade!
Water flowing in, roaring: waves spraying and splashing together,
 stirred up by the whale!   15
Spray splashing against the posts of the fish trap, against the
 ngainmara mat . . .
It pushes the grass of the fish trap, splashing and foaming, with
 waves stirred up by the whale.
We see the whale, with its huge body, stranded in the mud at
 Wagulwagul—covered in mud.

Song 72

We are making a fire. Wei! Place it within the mouth of the shade! 1
Yes indeed, *waridj*, all right. Make the fire in the shade, gathering
 wood together, so we may roast the mangrove shells.
Carefully, *waridj*, put in the *rangga* roots.
Go, then, part the fringe at the mouth of the mat, put it within the
 shade:
Turning over its peak . . . ! There within the mat we can hear
 the people, beneath its transverse fibre.   5
Go, put your hand through into the 'mat', removing the mangrove
 shells, putting them into the ashes.
Go, turn it over again, emptying out the shells from the mat, with
 its transverse fibre, into the ashes among the firewood.
Get the beating sticks and clap them: let us sing . . .
As we take them carefully out through the mouth of the mat, its
 transverse fibre—clapping the sticks!
These clapping sticks from far away, from the shine of the Morning
 Star, from Bralgu; coming with the sacred mat.   10
Waridj, do not break open the shells too roughly! Cover them up
 in the ground after we have eaten.
What is that sound, which echoes within the mouth of the mat?
 The sound of the clapping sticks, and the opening of shells.
Do not hit too hard with the clapping sticks, like the feathered
 rangga: only so that the sound drifts into the *ngainmara*.
Come, *waridj*, turn over the mat, carefully part its fringe: feel its
 inner surface, *waridj* Djanggawul!
Yes, yes, indeed! I listen for your word, so I may undo the mouth
 of the mat and part its fringe, putting my hand within to grasp
 that feathered string inside the basket.   15
Come, quickly, pull them out, these *rangga*-people . . .
Let all the *rangga*-people lie down together, in here!
All the *rangga*, the people, within the mouth of the shade . . .

M   161

Into the shade, on the cleared ground within its branches:
For they have come from far away, from Bralgu, across the sea . . . 20
Across the deep sea, glistening in the shine of the Morning Star:
    far away, from Bralgu!
Where the foam comes spraying up at the Place of the Sun, splashing
    us, at the Place of the Mauwulan.
Let them dry there in the sacred shade, as we call the *djuda* invoca-
    tions . . .
They are drying in the warm rays of the sun!
The warm rays dry them, the burning heat and the glare!   25
Reverently we spread them, so they may see the well water at
    Wagulwagul:
Well water rising, foam splashing up on to the feathered strands.
Carefully spread out the feathered strings to dry, so they may see
    the rising water:
Carefully spread out the feathered strings, so they may see the
    burning heat!

Song 73

Here we pull out another: we see the clan, the *rangga* clan . . .   1
We look at the crowd of people, the *rangga*, beneath the transverse
    fibre of the mat.
Yes, yes, indeed, *waridj* Miralaidj. I ask you, I listen to what you
    say! For you are a great leader . . .
We put the sacred *djuda* roots within the mouth of the shade:
Let the *rangga* dry there, as we put the *djuda* within the mouth of
    the shade, among the branches . . .   5
They see the well waters at Wagulwagul . . .
Water rising and spraying: rough waves, splashing and flowing . . .
We plant the roots of the *djuda*, calling the invocations . . .
There are the feathered strings of the *rangga*! We invoke the sacred
    names, the bubbles rising to the surface of the water . . .
We plant the *djuda* roots, calling the invocations . . .   10
For the fire is the spirit of the wood, wood from the claypan tree!
We dry them in the rising heat, in the burning rays of the sun . . .
They see the warm rays, the scorching heat: and the sweat comes out!
Drying in the burning rays, seeing the rising heat!

Song 74

Here is another, *waridj* Miralaidj! Indeed, undo the mouth of the
    mat and remove them, parting its fringe.   1
We shall dry them, seeing the clan of *rangga*, of people . . . !

Yes indeed, *waridj*, I ask you: for you are advising me . . .
We put the *djuda* roots, with feathered pendants, into the well, at
Wagulwagul.
They see the water, rising and roaring, with splashing spray . . . 5
We put the *djuda* roots into the mouth of the well: planting the roots,
as the water sprays.
We cover them up: they are ours, from within the peak of the
ngainmara mat . . .
We dry them in the rising heat, for they are wet.
Yes indeed, I listen to you, for you speak to me as my leader,
waridj Miralaidj . . .
We dry them in the hot rays of the sun, so that the sweat comes
out . . .   10
They see the scorching rays of the sun, the rising heat; we call the
invocations . . .
We put them into the well, covering up the *rangga*, calling the
invocations . . .
Carefully we spread the feathered strings, invoking the sacred
rangga names: the goanna—its backbone, the fat of its tail! The
djuda trunk, and branches . . . !
We plant the roots, calling the invocations . . .
Planting the roots, with the feathered strings from within our
ngainmara mat with its transverse fibre, the mouth of the
shade . . .   15

Song 75

Come, here is another. We pull it out, putting the sacred roots
into the mouth of the shade . . .   1
Part the fringe of the mat, with its transverse fibre.
Yes indeed, *waridj* Miralaidj, I listen to you: I ask only you, for
you are my great leader . . .
We plant the *djuda* roots within the mouth of the shade . . .
among the branches at the back of the shade . . .
We dry them, in the hot rays of the sun: 5
The scorching rays of the sun look down on them, burning hot . . .
We put in the *djuda* roots, with their feathered strings . . .
There they stand quietly, aslant, with their feathered strings . . .
They see the water at Wagulwagul, rising up from the well:
Well water, jumping and splashing, flowing and roaring . . .   10
They stand aslant, quietly, watching the water slowly rising; for
we are calling the sacred invocations . . .
We plant the *djuda* roots at Wagulwagul, putting them carefully,
calling the invocations:

From within the mouth of the mat, its transverse fibre.
We cover them up well within the peak of the mat, parting the
fringe at its mouth as we put them back . . .

Song 76

That is finished. Come, let us hide the *rangga*, the people, cover
them up within the *ngainmara*! Clans of people, like feathered
geese—so many! 1
Put them all back within the mouth of the mat, covering them up
sideways, laying them reverently.
Quietly place them, like younger siblings: hide them within the
peak of the *ngainmara*, dragging it closed:
Carefully, making more room within for the *rangga* people.
We put them within the mat, the shade, past its transverse fibre . . . 5
Carefully we put the *rangga* people, for they have come from far
away—from Bralgu, from the shine of the Morning Star, far
out to sea beyond Port Bradshaw . . .
Ourselves we cover them up, wet from the splashing foam at the
Place of the Sun, the Place of the Mauwulan.
From the sea's smell, and splashing, from the alien sound of the
Baijini . . .
Carefully, we hide them from these . . .
Separately we shall cover them up, reverently, laying them side-
ways, like younger siblings, making them tabu . . . 10
Clapping our sticks, we sing as we go along . . .
We make the country, going along, from the sandhill near Port
Bradshaw, from the shine of the Morning Star, from Bralgu . . .
From the shine of the Star, far away, from the Place of the Morning
Star, the Place of the Spirits, from Bralgu . . .
Moving our buttocks as we paddled, bringing these *rangga*!
Dragging our paddles, resting them on the canoe, bringing these
rangga . . . 15
Foam coming up and splashing, on our journey across the sea from
Bralgu:
Spray on the sea, at the Place of the Sun, the Place of the Mauwulan!
We cover them up.

Song 77

We put this flattened mat into the mouth of the shade, *waridj*
Bralbral. 1
Yes indeed, we shall sleep, for we are very weary:

Our eyes closing, we rest our heads on the *rangga*, within the sacred
  shade . . .
Our bodies, *waridj*, are tired from drying all those *rangga* . . .
Yes indeed, *waridj*: we are lying down, our heads well within the
  shade.   5
Our bodies are weary from all that drying, from spreading out all
  the feathered *rangga*, the clans of *rangga* people . . .
Now we awaken a little! We sit up, wide awake.
We have finished sleeping, our weariness is gone.
Yes indeed, *waridj* Miralaidj, indeed we feel better.
That basket, *waridj*: what about that sacred dilly bag?   10
What is it, that mat like a younger sibling?
Go, *waridj*, it is in there!
Yes, *waridj* Miralaidj, truly you are my leader!
We shall cut the fringe, from within its mouth.
There it hangs in the sacred shade, among the top branches: 15
Go, cut off the fringe! Cut it right off—carefully, *waridj*!
For the feathered strings are in there, and the rangga. Ah, the
  fringe of the basket!
Foam coming up and splashing! Carefully, cut the fringe of the
  basket!
We are calling the sacred invocations . . .
Carefully, *waridj*, invoking the sacred names!   20
Within are the *rangga* people, *waridj*, the feathered strings, the
  sacred Goanna Tail *rangga*.
Yes, yes! Indeed, that is good!

Song 78

We go along with the aid of the *mauwulan*, making country.   1
With hips swaying, step by step, we prod with the stick: dragging
  it, holding it carefully . . .
As we go along, *waridj*, our heads are grey.
We saw the clouds rising and spreading, into Galbara, spreading
  into our shade . . .
Carefully moving our buttocks, wearily, moving our heads from
  side to side: tired from making country, plunging in the *mauwulan*
  point!   5
As we walk, our bodies are shadowed . . .
You, clouds, we saw you rising, spreading into the sacred shade
  at Ngubarei:
Clouds banking and rising, spreading into Wuwul;
Clouds coming over, *waridj*, for us!

Hips swaying, we sing as we go along, with the aid of the *mau-wulan*.   10

We see those clouds rising and spreading, *waridj*, from Muduga-nimi . . .

We walk along, *waridj*, making country: Bildjiwuraroiju, inserting the *mauwulan* point!

Yes indeed, *waridj* Miralaidj. I am listening to your words, asking you what to do: for you are my leader . . .

Clouds are coming up at Ga'ragaranga,

Rising and spreading: we walk within their shadow.   15

Passing clouds are shadowing us: clouds massing and rising, over Djurwarami.

Massing clouds! Here we shall sit at Galbara, where we make a sacred shade . . .

Yes indeed, *waridj*: I feel weary and ill, moving my buttocks slowly, because of the *rangga* people.

Indeed, *waridj* Miralaidj, because you say that to me, let us sit here! I follow your desire.

Here, where ourselves we make a sacred shade, clearing the ground within . . .   20

It is our camp, our shade, with trees standing quietly, aslant . . .

They too are quiet and weary, standing like younger siblings, above the *rangga* people . . .

They see the water, at Dulabam.

Go, quickly, *waridj*, into the sacred shade!

Yes, yes indeed, *waridj* Miralaidj: heap the earth to one side, near the mouth of the shade!   25

Go, place the mat peak upwards within the mouth of the shade:

Oh, the fringe of the mat, the sacred mat!

Within the shade are the clan of *rangga*, the people!

Song 79

What is that, *waridj*? It is the *mauwulan* point.   1

Come, put it in, *waridj*! Put in the *djuda* roots with the *mauwulan* point.

You just put in those roots, with their spreading branches! Bildji-wuraroiju plants them, with the *mauwulan* point.

They come from far away, from the shine of the Morning Star, from Port Bradshaw, from Bralgu, far at sea, to the Place of the Mauwulan:

From the smell of the sea, from the faraway sound of the Baijini talking . . .   5

The Djanggawul Song Cycle

Upon us is foam, that splashed us far out at sea, on the way from
  Bralgu.
Here the *rangga* stand in the shade, shrouded in tabu-ness:
In the shade at Galbara, quietly standing for us.
They are very sacred! We cover them up within the mouth of the
  mat, beneath its transverse fibre, its inner peak.
Yes, yes, indeed, *waridj* Miralaidj. I ask you, for you are my great
  leader . . .   10
Within this shade, *waridj*, we hang up our *rangga* and feathered
  pendants, standing the *mauwulan* upright . . .
Bildjiwuraroiju, it is very quiet: a silence of reverence, tabu-ness.
Our baskets are splashed with foam: stain from the sea towards the
  Place of the Mauwulan, the Place of the Sun.
Here is another basket. Hang it up in there, its red feathers shining:
Quietly, reverently, like a younger sibling.   15
Quietly: it is sacred to us, *waridj* Djanggawul!
Yes, yes indeed, that is true, *waridj* Miralaidj. I was just asking you.

Song 80

Here is another basket, *waridj*!   1
Come, hang it up on the sacred *djuda* tree, from the *mauwulan*
  point.
We dry the feathered strings, spreading them out, because they
  are wet with foam:
They quietly shine as they dry, on this our basket: we invoke the
  sacred names of the *djuda rangga* . . .
It hangs on the upright *mauwulan*, on that *djuda*, for it is ours. We
  cover it up with the transverse fibre, within the mouth of the
  mat, within its peak: it is sacred to us, it is tabu!   5
Here is another basket! Let it dry on the upright *mauwulan*.
It hangs there quietly, in reverent tabu-ness.
The feathered strings upon it grow dry in the heat. The burning
  rays of the sun look down on them, scorching, with rising heat!
The hot sun looks on them, making them dry, rising high the
  haze . . .
For they are wet from the foam that splashed them near the Place
  of the Sun, the Place of the Mauwulan . . .   10
We call the sacred invocations . . .
Our basket hangs here, as we invoke the sacred names . . .
The basket hanging, as we call the invocations . . .
It sees the water rising at Dulabam, coming up from the sacred
  well:

Spray on the water, splashing and roaring.   15
It comes up, in the reverent stillness: up to the mouth of the shade,
    washing into the shade!

Song 81

Here is another basket, *waridj*!   1
Come, hang it up within the mouth of the shade, on the *djuda*
    roots, on the upright *mauwulan rangga.*
It hangs reverently quiet, with feathered strings—like a younger
    sibling.
We put them upon the sacred trees, the *djuda*, removed from within
    the *ngainmara* . . .
They come, these trees, from beneath the transverse fibre, the
    inner peak of the mat.   5
Yes indeed, *waridj*, I just asked you; for you are my leader,
    Miralaidj.
Indeed, quietly we spread out the shining feathered strings,
Quietly, solemnly, calling the invocations . . .
They see the water at Ngubarei! We call the invocations . . .
Carefully hang the feathered pendants, invoking the *djuda*
    names . . .   10
They dry there, watching the well water rising at Galwiang.
Yes indeed, *waridj* Miralaidj, I listen to your word . . .
They are ours! Stained with foam from the splashing spray, from
    Bralgu, from the shine of the Morning Star, near the Place of
    the Sun!
The roaring sea, coming up, where the feathered strings are hang-
    ing, within the mouth of the shade.
Heap up the mound within the shade, like the sacred sandhill . . ! 15

Song 82

Here is a basket, *waridj*! Surely, another basket for us!   1
Come, hang it up on the upright *mauwulan*!
Red feathered strings there, quiet, reverently sacred!
We are drying them in the hot rays of the sun . . .
They see the sun and its rays, the rising heat.   5
For they are stained with foam, that splashed them far out at sea,
    towards the Place of the Sun . . .
Our buttocks swayed as we paddled: paddling and resting, with
    shoulders moving, carefully dragging the paddles . . .

We carried our *mauwulan rangga, waridj*, almost dragging it; upon
  it were hanging the sacred baskets, and all the *rangga* . . .
Yes, *waridj*, we have finished making straight the *rangga* . . .
Quietly, in reverence, they hang on the tree within the mouth of
  the shade . . .   10
They dry in the shade, on the branches above the clearing . . .
Hanging upon the upright *mauwulan* . . .
They see the rising water, spray coming up from the sacred well,
  as we call the invocations . . .
For we are invoking the sacred *djuda* names!
Those hang quietly, in solemn tabu-ness: 15
Upon them the feathered strings dry in the rays of the sun, in the
  burning heat of the sun . . .

Song 83

Here is another basket, *waridj*, for us! Come, hang it upon the
  upright *mauwulan*.   1
Within the mouth of the shade, on its branches above the clearing,
  near the sandhill mound . . .
Quietly, solemnly, red feathers shining, like a younger sibling . . .
Yes indeed, *waridj* Miralaidj, I just asked you, for you are my great
  leader; I listen to your words . . .
You tell me what is right: for indeed, *waridj* Miralaidj, I always
  follow you!   5
We dry it, for it is wet from the foam that splashed us out on the
  sea, towards the Place of the Mauwulan, the Place of the Sun.
They are ours, these feathered strings; we call the invocations . . .
They clasp the *djuda* tree, as we invoke its sacred names . . .
They see the water rising in the well, flowing strongly, foaming
  and splashing:
Spray, splashing and roaring, water pushing aside the mud and
  leaves: water bubbling up in the sacred well!   10

Song 84

What is that crying, *waridj*? The *lindaridj* parakeet, with red breast
  feathers, is calling!   1
Crying, for it saw the red sunset, the warm rays of the sinking
  sun . . .
Saw the hot sun, and the glowing reflections of sunset, in the west
  beyond Milingimbi.

The Djanggawul Song Cycle

Saw the sun's rays, as it clasped the sacred *djuda*, among the small
    twigs: red breast feathers reflecting the glow of sunset!
Cocking its head from side to side and crying softly, clasping the
    djuda—like feathered pendants!   5
Drying itself, ruffling its breast feathers!
'Myself' (says the parakeet) 'I have baby nestling feathers!'
Saw them reflecting the rays of the red sunset in the west beyond
    Milingimbi:
The bright, glowing haze of the sinking sun!
It saw the red glow at Jiganjindu, at Marabai; shining over at
    Bulbulmara, at Arnhem Bay.   10
Parakeets calling softly, clasping the *djuda*, just as the feathered
    pendants cling to the *rangga* . . .
The *djuda* roots well planted, the *djuda* standing: parakeets clasping
    it, calling softly . . .
They see the well water rising and bubbling, splashing and mur-
    muring . . .
Soft cry of the parakeets, cocking their heads from side to side,
    gently twittering!
Drying their red breast feathers, like feathered pendants, like
    nestlings . . .   15
They cry into the rays of the sun, watching the sun sinking:
Their gentle cries fade away, as the last rays shine into the mouth
    of the shade, into the mat:
Crying, as the rays disappear from the inner peak of the mat, from
    its transverse fibre!

Song 85

Come, put the mat down carefully: turn it over, its peak upper-
    most: 1
Prepare and straighten out the mouth of the mat.
Come, sit down by the mouth, open out the mat at the mouth of
    the shade . . .
Yes, it is done, *waridj* Miralaidj: we part its fringe. Come, then,
    let us pull them out!
Pull hard, so that their heads protrude a little . . .   5
Here is another feathered string! Pull hard, *waridj*, pulling them
    from the mouth of the basket, the mat . . .
Another feathered string, *waridj*! Pull it out from that basket, from
    the mouth of the mat, the sacred shade!
Pull out another feathered string! It has come from far away, where
    the foam splashes up, from Bralgu:

Where the spray is splashing, out to sea, near the Spirit Country
 coming up from there, *waridj* Miralaidj!
Just pull out the feathered strings!   10
Yes, yes indeed, *waridj*, I listen to your word, for you are a great
 leader: I always ask you . . .
Come, pull out another feathered string!
Yes, indeed, carefully remove the feathered strings; some are
 caught on the transverse fibre within the mat . . .
Yes indeed, it is done, *waridj* Djanggawul!
Just pull out these! We see the clan of *rangga*, the people . . .   15
They have come from Bralgu, far across the sea, from the shine of
 the Morning Star, from the Place of the Mauwulan, the Place
 of the Sun . . .
Go, put them in the rays of the sun, so they may see the rising
 heat: drying these red breast feathers and those feathered
 strings . . .
At the Place of the Mauuwulan, the warm rays of the sun look at
 them: sweat comes out from the heat, as the sun goes down . . .

Song 86

There is another, Miralaidj! Pull it out from the inner peak of the
 mat . . .   1
Carefully, for it has a sacred name—the goanna-fat feathered string!
Carefully cover them up, within the transverse fibre of the mat,
 these feathered strings . . .
The well waters are rising, *waridj* Miralaidj . . .
Go, put in the *djuda* roots, the *rangga*—the feathered goanna-fat
 strings, the goanna's tail, and its vertebrae . . .   5
Yes, it is done. We have straightened them up, calling the invoca-
 tions . . .
Putting in *djuda* roots from far away, from Bralgu!
Yes, it is done.
Go, put in other *djuda* roots, straightening them thus, *waridj*!
They see the water, from the Place of the Mauwulan: carefully,
 invoke the sacred names . . .   10
Straighten them up, so they do not slant, calling the invocations . . .
The roots are firm: they see the well water rising and bubbling at
 Dulabam.
Rising and roaring, with spray flashing, well water flowing!
Splashing water surges about the upright *djuda*, with feathers
 shining.
They see the water bubbling up in the well, with foam and spray: 15

The Djanggawul Song Cycle

Here is feathered string, with goose feathers . . .
Come, put in more *djuda* roots, with feathered strings, calling the
  invocations . . .
They see the water at Dulabam: *rangga* with shining feathers! We
  invoke the sacred names . . .
They stand at the well, where the water is bubbling and rising . . .

Song 87

Here is another, *waridj*. Come, put in the *djuda* roots, thus, and the
  feathered strings!   1
They may see the well water at Ngubarei:
Their feathers shine as they stand—from far away, from Bralgu!
From far out to sea, from the Spirit Country, towards the Place
  of the Sun, the Place of the Mauwulan,
Where the foam is spraying and splashing: we call the sacred
  invocations . . .   5
They are standing, quietly, solemnly, as we invoke the sacred names . . .
They see the water rising and splashing, bubbling up in the well:
  waves splashing together!
Well water rising and roaring: put in the *djuda* roots, for us!
Yes indeed, *waridj*, I listen to your word, for you are my great leader:
I always ask you, for you are my great leader; I follow your desire,
  waridj Miralaidj . . .   10
Thus we put the *djuda* roots into the well:
In there the water rises, splashing. Carefully put them into the mud;
  clasp the top of the *djuda rangga*, and plunge it in . . . !
We call the invocations, putting in the roots, with the feathered
  strings . . .
They see the well water, rising and bubbling.
Carefully straighten them, so they see the well water rising and
  roaring . . .   15
Put them in carefully, reverently in the quietness!
Foam is splashing and spraying, staining them—from Bralgu,
  from the Place of the Sun, the Place of the Mauwulan!
Carefully do it, as the well water rises.

Song 88

What is that crying? A nestling? A nestling crying out, for it saw
  the sun's rays.   1
Yes, crying softly! Nestling with red breast feathers, clasping the
  limbs of the *djuda* tree as it moves from twig to twig!

172

The Djanggawul Song Cycle

Nestling, crying softly, for it saw the glowing rays of the red sunset,
   away in the west beyond Milingimbi:
Saw the red clouds of the sunset, as it perched in the *djuda* tree . . .
Ruffling and shaking itself, drying its feathers, up on the sacred
   tree . . .   5
Parakeet nestling crying gently, red feathers gleaming in the
   sunset: cocking its head from side to side, perching in the sunset
   glow!
It saw the glowing disc of the sun, half sunk below the horizon . . .
Saw the warm rays, the glare of the sun: heat drying the red breast
   feathers . . .
Drying there, red feathers reflecting the sunset—very quietly,
   solemnly reverent: crying softly at the sunset!
They see the well water bubbling up, roaring and spraying: 10
Splashing spray, water churning and roaring . . .
Well water rising and bubbling, pushing the mud and leaves . . .
Parakeets, clasping the limbs of the *djuda*, crying softly, notes
   rising and falling!
They are always there, on the sacred *djuda* tree . . .
They saw the sunset glow spreading across Bulbulmara: 15
Saw its rays spreading from the west, beyond Milingimbi:
Saw the warm rays of the sun going in below the horizon!
We hear them calling within the mouth of the mat, beneath the
   transverse fibre . . .
Talking there, drying their feathers, within the peak of the mat.
They have gone with the mat—It is done!   20

Chapter Fourteen

COMMENTS ON PART FIVE OF THE SONGS

THIS section relates, directly and symbolically, to the removal of the people from the uteri of the Sisters. Each aspect treated has corresponding elements in Parts One and Two of the Cycle. Song 71 concerns the Djanggawul's departure from Wagulwagul, at Arnhem Bay. They have not gone far when they come to a tidal river or creek, which they intend to ford; but as they cross they see a large whale, stranded high and dry in the mud (line 5). 'What can we do? The whale is right in the mud before us' (line 7); 'That whale with its huge ribs, its tail flipper . . .' (line 8). This song refers back to the whale which the Djanggawul saw on their way from Bralgu (*vide* Part One of song cycle); and they recognize it: '. . . its bulky body is ours . . .' (line 9). Joyously they cry, 'Oh, Wagulwagul Whale, covered up within it—the *ngainmara!* The Uterus!' (line 10).

Wagulwagul is the name, not only of that place at Arnhem Bay (*vide* Part Four), but also of the whale, the uterus (or vagina), the mat, shade, and the basket. The Djanggawul recognize the whale as being their own *ngainmara* mat (*vide* Songs 6 and 26 of Part One), in which the *rangga*, totemic species and people are hidden. As the whale lies there, it stirs, so that water surges up from the mud. This is followed by the incoming tide, with water flowing around it, and then the whale sprays out foaming water (line 11). The theme thus reverts to the rough sea beyond Port Bradshaw, and the foam which splashed the Djanggawul on their journey from Bralgu. This scene symbolizes, too, the *ngainmara* lying in the bottom of the bark canoe on its journey across the sea (*vide* Part One), and the water which splashed in upon it.

174

Comments on Part Five of the Songs

The simile is extended in the next line (12), 'Foam coming up! Well water rising and roaring, flowing about the whale: by its rib bones, the transverse fibre of the mat, into its mouth!' and, in line 13, 'Water rises, flowing into the mouth of the whale, the gaping mouth of the whale.' The rib bones of the whale are likened to the transverse fibre (horizontal threads, *boijuwa*) of the *ngainmara* mat. As the tide rises, the well at Wagulwagul rises also, and the water flows into the gaping mouth of the whale, or the *ngainmara* mat. The whale 'draws in' the water (takes it in, *daijamaijam*); this is, symbolically, an ejaculation into the vagina (that is, *ngainmara*). 'Mouth of the *ngainmara*, like our *nara* shade!' (line 14): that is, the whale's mouth is gaping open, and resembles the opening of a sacred *nara* shade. As the whale stirs, the waves break against it (line 15); the water grows rough, like the sea on the way from Bralgu, and dashes against the fish trap and the grass barriers (lines 16 and 17) mentioned in Part Four. The *ngainmara* had been placed there as a fish trap, and fish were flowing into it: conversely, water and fish are flowing into the gaping mouth of the whale (symbolizing the *ngainmara*). 'Spray splashing against the posts of the fish trap, against the *ngainmara* mat . . .' (line 16), and 'We see the whale, with its huge body, stranded in the mud at Wagulwagul—covered in the mud' (line 18).

This song refers to the low coastal flats at Arnhem Bay, which are subject to inundation by high tides and monsoonal rains. The whale mentioned here has drifted up a tidal creek at high tide: 'as the water comes in, the whale comes in too.' The creek, like the Djanggawul, belongs to the *dua* moiety. The Djanggawul see the whale and sing about it. The whale itself is really of the *jiritja* moiety, but 'went the wrong way' in coming up the *dua* creek; hence it may legitimately symbolize the *ngainmara*. The Djanggawul then 'put the whale right down into the mud of the creek' (*vide* line 7—'. . . The whale is right in the mud before us'), the literal translation being 'put right into'. That is, when the waters subside, the silt covers the whale, so that to-day in this creek one may see only foam and water surging up out of the mud, like the spray or spout of the whale.

Song 72 leaves the whale theme, and reverts to the sacred *nara* shade. The Djanggawul have brought fire with them, and at the mouth of the shade (line 1) they ignite fresh wood, using *rangga* roots from the sacred *djuda* (line 3). In the ashes of the fire, they roast their mangrove shells (*vide* Part Four). Lines 4, 5 and 6, 'Go, then, part the fringe at the mouth of the mat . . . There within the mat we can hear the people . . . Go, put your hand through into the "mat" . . .', significantly suggest the bringing forth of people from the Sisters' wombs; see Chapter 2 in reference to the Brother Djanggawul's putting his hand into his Sisters' vaginae for this purpose. The fire (line 1) in that case is kindled to serve as a source of warmth during the process of childbirth. Conversely, in keeping with the Aboriginal scheme of suggesting events by the use of symbolism, it is said that mangrove shells are removed from the *ngainmara* and placed in the ashes of the fire (line 6). The Djanggawul empty out all the shells (line 7), that is, take out all the people (children). After doing this, the Djanggawul Brother rhythmically beats his clapping sticks (line 9), which came originally from Bralgu (line 10). These same sticks are used to break open the roasted mangrove shells, and the Brother is warned by his Sisters not to hit too hard. They wish to preserve the empty shells—'. . . Cover them up in the ground after we have eaten' (line 11); for these shells, having hidden within them the meat (that is, symbolically the people), are likened to the *ngainmara*. The sound of the clapping sticks and the noise made by the opening of shells drifts into the mouth of the *ngainmara* (lines 12 and 13),[1] and corresponds to the sound of babies within and emerging from the womb. Line 14, 'Come, *waridj*, turn over the mat, carefully part its fringe: feel its inner surface, *waridj* Djanggawul!' again reflects the theme of fertility. The Djanggawul Brother inserts his hand past the pubic hair, feels within the uterus of one Sister, and then removes the people; '. . . putting my hand within to grasp that feathered string inside the basket' (line 16) refers symbolically to pushing aside the elongated clitoris. The people (= *rangga*) are taken out and laid in rows (line 17): the relevant words are those normally employed in these songs to refer to people, *rangga* and so on. They are all placed in the shade (lines 18 and 19). The latter part of the song, lines 20–30, dwells on the origin of the people and the *rangga*, 'For they have come from far away, from Bralgu . . . ' (line 21), and on their drying in the warmth of the sun (line 24). The theme thus reverts to the spreading out of *rangga* and feathered strings to dry in the sun, after being splashed by salt water (lines 28 and 29).

In Song 73, more people are removed from the Sisters: 'Here we pull out another. We see the clan, the *rangga* clan . . . the crowd of people, the *rangga*, beneath the transverse fibre of the mat' (lines 1–2). 'We put the sacred *djuda* roots within the mouth of the shade' (line 4). The Djanggawul Brother peers into the vulva of one

---

[1] The *bilma* clapping sticks 'take part for' (that is, are a representation of) the *mauwulan rangga* pole with its feathered strings. In this song the Djanggawul beat their sticks softly so that their sound does not go too far, and only enters the *ngainmara*.

Comments on Part Five of the Songs

Sister, and then removes the people (= *rangga*): these are put out to dry in the mouth of the shade. The invocations (lines 8 and 10) are Dadawi, and relate to bubbles rising to the surface of the well water.

Song 74 repeats the same theme. '. . . Indeed, undo the mouth of the mat and remove them, parting its fringe' (line 1). After this, *djuda* roots and feathered pendants are put into the sacred well at Wagulwagul (line 4). The symbolism of the well has already been noted. The invocations, mentioned in lines 11, 12 and 14, are Ngeimil and refer to the goanna-tail fat, the goanna vertebrae, and the trunk and branches of the *djuda*.

Song 75 extends the theme: more people (or *rangga*) are removed (line 1), and placed in the mouth of the shade (line 4) to dry in the sun (line 5). The *rangga* are placed upright but aslant, and are hung with feathered pendants (line 8). Finally they are returned to the mat (line 14), a reference to sexual intercourse. The invocations (lines 11 and 12) are 'bottom' Ngeimil, and refer to the *djuda*.

Song 76 suggests that the Djanggawul are, for the time being at least, finished with the *ngainmara* (line 1). All the *rangga* people, the clans of people like geese (referring back to Part One), are covered up: '. . . hide them within the peak of the *ngainmara*, dragging it closed' (line 3). As the Djanggawul pack the *rangga* back into the mat, they make room for others (line 4). Then, 'Carefully we put the *rangga* people, for they have come from far away—from Bralgu . . .' (line 6): the song dwells on the Djanggawul's long adventurous journey (lines 6–8, 12–17), as they carried the people (or *rangga*) whom they have now removed and finally covered up (line 18).

Song 77 tells how the mat is flattened and put into the *nara* shade (line 1). The Djanggawul are exhausted, their eyes heavy with weariness (line 3): for have they not brought out many people? (line 6). Later, however, they feel refreshed (line 9), and propose to '. . . cut the fringe, from within its mouth' (line 14)—that is, of the mat, or sacred dilly bag. They cut the fringe from the *ngainmara* mat, or from the top edging of the dilly bag: 'Go, cut off the fringe! Cut it right off—carefully, *waridj*!' (line 17). This symbolizes the cutting of the Sisters' pubic hair. Aborigines of these parts have an aversion to hairy bodies, and go to great lengths to keep themselves free from superfluous hair. The removing of this 'pubic hair', however, is further symbolic of the foreshortening of the Sisters' clitorises later in the epic. In Djanggawul ritual to-day, as mentioned in Chapter 1, the fringe of a newly made sacred dilly-bag is ceremonially shorn, section by section, to the accompaniment of appropriate singing and the calling of invocations:

'We are calling the sacred invocations . . .' (line 19). In line 16, the word used for cutting off the fringe is *dabi-gulgduwan*. This is the same word used to refer to cutting a boy's foreskin at circumcision; the word *dabi* means 'foreskin', 'basket', 'dilly-bag', 'uterus', 'sun ray', or 'snake'. Care must be taken when cutting the pubic hair (or clitoris), conversely the fringe of the basket, 'For the feathered strings are in there, and the *rangga* . . .' (line 17); 'Within are the *rangga* people, *waridj*, the feathered strings . . .' (line 21). On the other hand, the pubic hair may be woven into a feathered string—for in the Myth (*vide* Chapter 2) it is said that the severed part of the Sisters' clitorises became feathered strings or *rangga*. In line 16 the fringe is referred to by the word *budjei*(*mi*); the explanation of this word tells that the fringe is cut off because it has salt water stains (sea mark); it is the 'inside' name for the fringe of the *ngainmara* or of the basket, and also for the pubic hair. The meaning of this word will be discussed later; it has associations with clitoris, smell, semen and feathers, all relevant to this particular context.

In Song 78 the Djanggawul continue on their journey making towards Galbara, on the eastern shores of Arnhem Bay in Ngeimil linguistic group territory, where they see clouds rising (line 4). They have come so far that they feel tired (line 5), but still the clouds beckon them on to Ngubarei, to Wuwul and other places in Ngeimil territory: 'As we walk, our bodies are shadowed . . .' (line 6). After a while they can walk no farther ' . . . I feel weary and ill, moving my buttocks slowly, because of the *rangga* people' (line 18). They pause, and make a sacred shade (line 20). The ground within is cleared of grass and stones, and earth is piled up around it immediately opposite the mouth of the shade (line 25). This mound of earth represents the sacred sandhill which the Djanggawul made at Mauwulanggalngu, the Place of the Mauwulan, at Port Bradshaw, and upon which the *djanda* goanna rested (*vide* Part Two, Song 35). The conical mat is placed within the shade (line 26), and one of the Sisters is then ready to give birth to more people (line 28).

Song 79 refers to the *djuda* and its roots, which have been removed from the *ngainmara*, and are now plunged into the ground so that they stand upright (lines 2 and 3). The song dwells on their origin, and on their journey across the sea (lines 4, 5 and 6). 'Here the *rangga* stand in the shade, shrouded in tabu-ness' (line 7): the word *milijundaija* is translated in this context as 'shrouded in tabu-ness'. The word has been variously translated as, for instance, 'very quietly' or 'reverently'. It is, however, an 'inside' term referring to a tabu state: Aborigines, in discussing this concept, say that it

178

means 'no one may speak, no one may move, no one may come near.' There is an aura about them, apart from the mere fact of their being 'forbidden' to unauthorized persons.

'They are very sacred! We cover them up . . . ' (line 9); that is, they are *jindi mareijin* (big sacred). In 'outside' speech the *mareijin* pole (or *rangga*) is *duldji* (hence *duldjijuldji mauwulan*), but the 'inside' term is really *djuda*. 'Within this shade, *waridj*, we hang up our *rangga* and feathered pendants, standing the *mauwulan* upright . . . ' (line 11). The *rangga* are put point downward into the ground, so that they stand erect; the feathered pendants and sacred dilly bags are then hung upon them—as in contemporary *nara* ritual, when neophytes dance around them.

'. . . it is very quiet: a silence of reverence, tabu-ness' (line 12); and 'Quietly, reverently, like a younger sibling. Quietly: it is sacred to us, *waridj* Djanggawul!' (lines 15–16). In the first place *reiwul-jungwoijum* means 'very quiet'. *Djalwaijun* is the common term used for 'being tired', while *reiwuljun* means 'tired' or 'quiet', in relation to a reverence associated with an aura of sacredness (surrounding and pervading the *rangga*): *reiwulwolabum* means 'quietly'; *reiwulwuroiljun*, 'moving head from side to side in weariness'. This 'tiredness' is used in a sacred sense: the tiredness of the Djanggawul after performing a ritual duty, or after giving birth to people; the tiredness of the *lindaridj* parakeet as it cocks its head from side to side, crying softly at the sight of the red sunset. It is used here, also, when the ritual objects are placed in a certain way, and regarded by the neophytes in silent contemplation. Their sacredness extends over and pervades the whole sacred *nara* shade, as in silence the neophytes gaze upon the *rangga*. There is no awe, or fear, but simply a sense of ritual well-being and of unity with the *rangga*: for are not the *rangga* symbolic of the people themselves? Are they not all from the same womb?—'like a younger sibling'. The presence of the *rangga*, their state of 'tabu-ness', the reverence in which they are held, the silence, the dead quietness—all these produce a highly electric aura of sacredness which is dynamic. The neophytes become incorporated in what we may call the 'stream of sacredness'. They are united with the Creative Beings— they themselves *are* the *rangga*. The original process of their emission from the Mothers' wombs is, once again, a reality.

Song 80 returns to the hanging of the sacred dilly bags on the upright *rangga* (line 2). The invocations used, creating the desired atmosphere of sacredness, are Riradjingu, Ngeimil, and 'bottom' Ngeimil, and refer to *djuda* and the goanna's vertebrae. Line 5, '. . . it is sacred to us, it is tabu!' means that the sacred baskets and *rangga* may be used only by the ceremonial leaders: it refers to present-day ritual activities, when only the leaders may handle the 'higher' *rangga*.

The use of 'inside' terms (which will become apparent to the reader of the interlinear texts) is said to be derived from the *rangga* or people's being, or having been, inside the *ngainmara* mat, the sacred shade, or the Sisters' wombs. They were originally terms used specifically while inside the mat, shade or uterus, and were consequently held sacred. Hence they may be used to-day only under ceremonial or sacred conditions: for example, on the sacred ritual ground, or during certain singing—even if this takes place in or near the main camp, as when women are wailing the 'clan' songs in mourning. So general has the application of the use of these 'inside' terms become that they are found scattered through songs and so on which cannot, strictly, be termed sacred. Partly because of this, there is no clear-cut demarcation between sacred and profane. The aura of sacredness, as mentioned elsewhere, pervades all aspects of Aboriginal life, so that there is sacredness in the main camp during ordinary mundane activity, as well as on the sacred ground; however, in the latter case, the degree of sacredness is intensified, or its manifestation is different.

There is another explanation of the distinction between 'inside' and 'outside' terms. It is said that as the Djanggawul travelled along through the country they spoke to people of various groups—suggesting that people existed on the mainland prior to the Djanggawul's visitation and to their peopling it with those removed from their wombs; they used not only their own language, but that of the local people. In this way, there was a superimposition of 'new' (that is, introduced) words on the 'old' (that is, local) words. It is repeatedly said that the Djanggawul 'changed their speech as they went along'. Thus the older words became 'inside' words.

This feature is particularly apparent to-day in north-eastern Arnhem Land; in the Macassan Song Cycle, for instance, a great many Macassan (and other alien) words have been used as 'inside', 'outside', or 'singing side' or 'singing inside' words. An explanation may lie, also, in the fact that many dialects have been and are still spoken in the region under discussion, although these belong to the one linguistic division.

Among the Riradjingu-speaking people, the following words signify 'inside' in the sense in which it is considered here: *galangu*, or *murugai* (the latter meaning, literally, 'big'); *djinawugnga*, in the same dialect, means 'very inside', signifying 'so much inside, so sacred, that it is almost beyond the concept of sacredness'. In the Djapu, 'inside' is signified by the term *dumurogngu* (a variation of *murugai*, also meaning, literally, 'big').

Comments on Part Five of the Songs

In Song 81 another basket is hung on the upright *rangga*; and more *djuda* are withdrawn from the mat (line 5). The invocations used are 'bottom' Ngeimil, and refer to the *djuda*. 'Heap up the mound, within the shade, like the sacred sandhill . . .' (line 15) relates, symbolically, to the sandhill on which the Djanggawul saw the sacred *djanda* goanna (*vide* Song 78). Song 82 refers again to the sacred dilly bags, emphasizing their past travels across the sea (lines 6 and 7). Line 8 mentions that the *mauwulan rangga* is held downwards, almost dragging on the ground, for it is very heavy; and when the Djanggawul think of the long way they have come, they grow weary. Actually, however, this signifies the way in which they dragged their paddles through the sea (line 7). Here the invocations are Dadawi.

The same theme continues in Song 83: 'Quietly, solemnly, red feathers shining, like a younger sibling . . .' (line 3); and the Djanggawul Brother defers to his Sisters. In retrospect (line 6), they dwell on the wetness of the foam splashing over the *rangga*, and compare this to '. . . water rising in the well, flowing strongly, foaming and splashing . . . water bubbling up in the sacred well!' (lines 9–10). The invocations are in this case Djambatpingu, referring to various parts of the *djuda* and to the *ba'ralgi* (*vide* Song 62).

Song 84 recalls the presence of the *lindaridj* parakeet, which has been symbolically removed from the *ngainmara* (uterus) in the form of feathered strings (see above). These birds cry as they see the red sunset (line 2), for their breast feathers are its reflections (line 4). 'Myself' (says the parakeet) 'I have baby nestling feathers!' (line 7). This concept has already been discussed: the small downy breast feathers are said to be like young nestlings carried by the mother birds, and also like the eggs inside the female parakeet. The birds' 'gentle cries fade away, as the last rays shine into the mouth of the shade, into the mat' (line 17). It is suggested that this section of the cycle is drawing to a close. The cry of the parakeet fades gradually into the silence of the coming dusk as the sun sets; the last rays of the sun lengthen, illumining the interior of the mat (or basket), and finally the sun sinks below the horizon.

Song 85 returns to the uterus-mat. The day is not yet over; although dusk is falling, there is still time to open out the mat at the mouth of the shade (lines 1–3). 'Yes, it is done, *waridj* Miralaidj: we part its fringe. Come, then, let us pull them out!' (line 4). The people, or *rangga*, are removed: 'Pull hard, so that their heads protrude a little . . .' (line 5); but '. . . some are caught on the transverse fibre within the mat' (line 13), and need special attention. The Djanggawul Brother is told 'Just pull out these! We see the clan of *rangga*, the people . . .' (line 15). Then the song turns, in retrospect, to the journey from Bralgu (line 16). Finally, the *rangga* and feathered strings have all been removed, and are drying in the warmth (and in the red glow) '. . . as the sun goes down . . .' (line 18).

More *rangga* are pulled from the *ngainmara* (Song 86) and carefully covered up (line 3). *Djuda* are put in the sacred well: 'Splashing water surges about the upright *djuda*, with feathers shining' (line 14). This water rises up as the *djuda* roots are put into the well: 'They stand at the well, where the water is bubbling and rising . . .' (line 19). The invocations are Ngeimil.

In Song 87, more *djuda* roots are put into the well at Ngubarei, at Arnhem Bay; the invocations used here are Dadawi and Gwola-mala. The day is almost finished, but still a few rays flicker in the western sky. The rising well waters are compared to the rough sea out from Bralgu; and consequently the well waters roar and rush along, '. . . water rising and splashing, bubbling up in the well: waves splashing together!' (line 7). But although the waters surge around '. . . roaring . . .' (line 15), there is a 'quietness' (line 16); the earth is settling down for the night.

The last song (88) of this part was 'always' sung by the Djangga-wul when they made camp at sunset; as the sun is sinking, they always sing this *lindaridj* parakeet song, which completes their day, just as to-day this is the final song sung in any *dua nara* ritual. It is an elaboration of Song 84, and the theme has already been treated. The *lindaridj* perch in the branches of the *djuda* tree, as the sun goes down. They are ruffling their feathers to dry them before going into the *ngainmara* mat for the night: '. . . crying softly at the sunset!' (line 9); (they) 'saw the warm rays of the sun going in below the horizon!' (line 17).

Then suddenly, the rays have disappeared; the dusk is upon them, and the warmth of the sun gone. The parakeets leave the branches of the *djuda*, and fly into the *ngainmara* mat (line 20). In the original text, the song ends with the exclamation *ridan*! signi-fying that the birds have finally vanished within, and the day is over, and that this section of the cycle is completed. 'Talking there . . . within the peak of the mat (beneath the transverse fibre) . . .' (line 19) refers to the birds in the *ngainmara*; they have returned inside, and rest as feathered strings which symbolize the parakeets: they have returned to the womb.

Chapter Fifteen

THE DJANGGAWUL SONG CYCLE

PART SIX

In which the Djanggawul reach Madi at Arnhem Bay, spend some time there, and continue down the Bay westwards.

Song 89

WE walk along, *waridj*, with the aid of the *mauwulan*. 1
We are going thither, to Madi!
We are making country, Bildjiwuraroiju inserting the
mauwulan point:
Making country, plunging in the point of the *mauwalan* . . .
We saw the clouds coming up, over the shade: 5
Carefully, swaying our hips, carrying our sticks, *waridj*: walking
along with the *mauwulan*, making country.
We are drawing close to our shade, to its topmost branches, its clearing . . .
We shall sit in the mouth of the shade . . . for there is something
within that mat . . .
Yes indeed, *waridj*. My body feels sick and weary, from moving buttocks
all the way, carrying all those *rangga* people, those clans, within . . .
You are my leader, I listen to your words, *waridj* Miralaidj. You
are my leader, my great leader; I always rely on you . . . 10

Song 90

Go, *waridj*, put in the *djuda* roots, with the point of the *mauwulan*! 1
The roots of the *djuda* stand, with feathers shining, very quietly,
solemnly sacred . . .

The Djanggawul Song Cycle

They have come from far away, from Bralgu, from across the
   deep sea, at the Place of the Sun . . .
Sea roaring and splashing, spraying and staining with foam: sound
   of the Baijini talking, the smell of the sea . . . !
Carefully, reverently, *waridj* Djanggawul, straighten up the
   rangga . . .   5
Yes, yes indeed, *waridj* Miralaidj, let the roots stand up. Do it thus,
   turning the *mauwulan* round:
Let them see the water at Dulabam bubbling up from the well,
   splashing and roaring . . .
Water rising up, roaring, with foam spraying, splashing and
   flowing in strongly . . .
Yes indeed, *waridj*, because you told me to straighten up the
   mauwulan,
So they may stand there with shining feathers, solemnly quiet,
   hung with their feathered pendants . . .   10
Then cover them within the mouth of the mat . . .
Carefully spread out the feathered strings, so they point towards
   Wulma, the Cloud Place:
Spread them thus, so they reach to Mudunganingil.
Carefully spread them thus, towards Galwirligal.
Straighten them carefully, so they extend towards Nguwan . . . 15
Put them so they extend to Ngainmaralji, the Place of the Mat.
Spread out the shining feathered strings so they reach towards
   Ngubarei, and the sacred well at Dulabei . . .

Song 91

Here is another *mauwulan* stick. Come, put in the *djuda* roots, the
   mauwulan point, within the mouth of the shade . . .   1
The feathered strings shine as they stand, quietly, reverently:
They stand quietly, shining, on the sandhill mound within the shade:
Hanging quietly, reverently, from the topmost branches.
Plunge in the *mauwulan* point, Bildjiwuraroiju, for the foam has
   left stains upon it: 5
Splashing from far away, from Bralgu, away out on the deep sea,
   out from the Place of the Mauwulan, the Place of the Sun . . .
Water roaring as the foam splashed, staining those feathered
   strings leading this way and that . . .
Now the feathered strings are drying:
Cover them up, from within the peak of the mat, from its transverse
   fibre: they are ours, they are sacred, no one may see them . . .
Spread the feathered strings! Straighten them out, thus, reaching

out to the water, into the shade at Gundangngarul, at Balwal-
djal.   10
Feathered strings! Put them carefully, spreading in all directions . . .
They are covered up on the sandhill mound at the sacred *nara*
shade . . .
Spread the feathered strings, reaching into the water:
Covered up, in the well, with water splashing and rough water . . .
Water rising and bubbling with spray as the waves dash roaring
together . . .   15
Rising water pushing the silt along, flowing strongly!
There they are lying, those feathered strings, from the sacred
basket, from the mat, from the shade, from the transverse fibre,
from the inner peak of the mat . . .
They came from within the sacred mat, from the mouth of the
basket . . .

Song 92

We turn over this mat, carefully, with its peak uppermost . . .   1
Go, turn it over so it becomes conical!
Yes indeed, *waridj*, carefully we put the mat within the mouth of
the shade . . .
Come, we see the clan of people, the *rangga*! Carefully part the fringe
of the mat, with its transverse fibre . . .
Go, put them along! Go, pull them out, putting your hand within
the mouth!   5
Yes, pull out another, and another—one by one!
Pull them out! We see the clansfolk in the mouth of the mat:
Just pull them out one by one. Grasp it and straighten it, pulling
it hard so it comes out head first from this mat . . .
Yes, yes indeed, *waridj* Miralaidj. I just asked you, for you are my
great leader . . .
Here we are putting the sacred *rangga* people from that mat: drying
them carefully, *waridj*.   10
One has been caught on the transverse fibre of the mat! Put your
hand through, grasp and straighten the feathered string!
Now that is done! Yes, finished *waridj*, indeed!
Come, let us take them from within this other mat, where we see
another clan of people:
Come! Quickly, put your hand within the mouth of the mat, within
the sacred shade . . .
We come from far away, from Bralgu, the Place of the Spirits, far
across the sea: from the Place of the Mauwulan, from the Place
of the Sun, from the shine of the Morning Star!   15

There, where the foam splashes and stains!
We plant the *djuda* roots in the warm rays of the sun, invoking the
    sacred *bugali*.
Carefully, put in the *djuda*, calling the invocations . . .
Carefully, let them sit there, as we invoke the sacred names . . .
They stand with shining feathers, quietly, in sacred tabu-ness: 20
Drying there in the hot rays of the sun, the glaring heat.
It looks down on them, and sweat comes from them in the rising heat:
Red breast feathers splashed and stained with foam from the sea
    beyond the Place of the Mauwulan.
Thus we lay them out carefully, reverently,
They see the water rising at Dulabang.   25
The roots are standing within the well, covered up by its waters:
    for they are very sacred.
There, take hold of two of them within the well!
We put in the *djuda* roots, the *rangga* standing erect!
They see the water at Ngubarei:
Water rising and bubbling, splashing and roaring, spreading out
    like the tide . . .   30

Song 93

Here is another feathered string: 1
Come, dry it in the warm rays of the sun!
Go, put the *djuda* roots into this well, at Galwia: for we call the
    sacred invocations . . .
Carefully put another root into the well.
Yes, *waridj*, the goanna *rangga*, the *djuda*, the goanna tail *rangga*! *Rangga*
    with dark goanna-fat feathers, body of the *djanda* goanna!   5
Thus we straighten them up, so they stand in the rising heat,
    sweating in the hot rays of the scorching sun:
The feathered goanna-fat strings look back to the Place of the Sun,
    far away near Port Bradshaw.
The rising heat of the sun beats down on the feathered strings . . .
Thus they see the water at Ngubarei, at Dulabang, at Galwia,
    among the wild banana palms:
Water bubbling up in the well, splashing and roaring . . .   10

Song 94

Come, *waridj*, put in the *djuda* roots!   1
Yes indeed, I was just asking you, for you are my leader . . .
They are standing there, those our *djuda*! We put in the *djuda* roots,
    calling the invocations . . .

They stand, looking over at Dulabang, Ngubarei, Galwia,
Where water bubbles up in the well, roaring and spraying, pushing
    along the silt . . .   5
Well water rising, spray splashing on to the red breast feathers:
They stand with their shining feathers, quietly, reverently, in the
    well:
For we cover them up, for us, from within the mat with its trans-
    verse fibre.

Song 95

Come, *waridj*, another! Indeed, we plant the *djuda* roots in the well. 1
Putting them into the well at Dulabang, and Ngubarei.
For we are calling the sacred invocations . . .
Carefully we straighten out the strings, leading into the sacred well,
    invoking the sacred names . . .
They stand with feathers shining, solemnly and reverently, drying
    in the hot rays of the sun: 5
The rising heat of the sun, beating upon them so that sweat comes
    out . . .
The sun looks on the feathered strings, splashed by foam from far
    out at sea, from Bralgu, from the Place of the Sun:
Splashed by foam from the rising sea at the Place of the Mauwulan!
They see the water as it splashes up roaring . . .
Water roaring up in the well, flowing strongly, pushing along the
    silt . . .   10
They stand with shining feathers, in reverent quietness.

Song 96

Come, put in another, put the *djuda* roots into the well . . .   1
They stand with shining feathers, quietly, our *djuda* from within
    the mouth of the mat:
The roots go down, as we call the invocations . . .
They see the well water rising at Dulabang, at Ngubarei:
Bubbling up, splashing and roaring, pushing the silt along . . .   5
They are drying in the warm rays of the sun, in the rising heat and
    glare . . .
The hot sun looks on them: heat beating down on them so that
    sweat comes out . . .
They stand with shining feathers, in sacred tabu-ness: our *djuda*
    rangga, from within the transverse fibre of the mat.

The Djanggawul Song Cycle
Song 97

Let us put more roots, *waridj* Miralaidj, into the well, making a
   well . . .   1
They come from far away, from Bralgu, from the shine of the
   Morning Star, far out to sea, towards the Place of the Sun . . .
They were splashed by the rising foam . . .
Let them dry in the rising heat, the scorching sun looking on them
   so that they sweat . . .
We call the sacred invocations of the *djuda* . . .   5
They stand with shining feathers, quietly, in solemn tabu-ness:
They see the water in the sacred well, as we invoke the sacred
   names:
See the water splashing and roaring, bubbles and spray rising . . .
Yes, it is coming up, *waridj* Miralaidj! Truly I listen to your words,
For they come from the mouth of the mat, the shade: from its
   transverse fibre, from the inner peak of the mat . . .   10
We are covering our spirit form, so no one may see; making it
   tabu, like a younger sibling.

Song 98

Here is another: come, put the *djuda* roots into the well!   1
We make the well, calling the invocations . . .
Put them in, quietly, with shining feathers, as we invoke the sacred
   names . . .
They see the water bubbling up, splashing and spraying . . .
Quietly they stand, watching the rising water rushing through the
   wild banana palms: 5
Roaring along, pushing the silt, with waves splashing together . . .
They come from within the transverse fibre of the mat . . .

Song 99

Here is another, *waridj* Miralaidj: come, put it in!   1
Yes indeed, I was just asking you, *waridj* Miralaidj:
Indeed we are putting the roots into the well . .
They stand quietly, with shining feathers, drying in the hot rays of
   the sun:
The burning sun looks on them, with rising heat and glare . . . 5
They are our spirits, they are tabu: we call the invocations . . .
We put the roots, the *rangga*, into the well, invoking the sacred
   names:

They see the water splashing and rising, roaring up with spray . . .
Spray coming up as the waves splash together, pushing along the silt . . .
They are drying, from within the mouth of the mat . . .   10
We part the fringe of the mat, covering them up within its transverse fibre, the inner peak of the mat: like a younger sibling.

Song 100

What is that crying, *waridj*? It is a nestling, crying on the sacred *djuda* tree . . .   1
Clasping the limbs with its claws, crying softly . . .
The parakeet saw the glow of sunset shining on its red breast feathers:
Drying itself, ruffling and shaking its feathers: its red feathers reflecting the sunset!
It saw the spreading rays of the sunset: crying, it watched the warm sun setting—rays like roots of the *djuda*!   5
Watched the sun sinking beneath the horizon . . .
Crying very softly, quietly sacred . . .
It saw the red sunset spreading, from far away beyond Milingimbi . . .
Perched there, crying as it saw the mouth of the mat, the sacred shade . . .
Birds, drying themselves from the splashing spray . . .   10
'Myself (said the parakeet) I have children, my feathers . . .'
It clasps the *djuda* tree with its claws, watching the rays of the sunset away beyond Milingimbi . . .
Saw the warm rays of the red sunset, at Marabai:
Red sunset over Jiganjindu, and Bulbulmara: the sun sinking there.
The birds saw the last rays of the setting sun: 15
They ruffle their shining breast feathers, drying themselves . . .
Crying they see the rising water at Dulabang well: crying softly, quietly . . .
Cocking their heads from side to side as they cry, clasping the *djuda* tree . . .
Sitting there, they see the mouth of the sacred mat . . .
See the mouth of the mat, in the light of the setting sun: see its transverse fibre . . .   20
Swooping down they enter the mat, the sacred basket, going right inside to sleep.
It is done!

The Djanggawul Song Cycle
Song 101

We walk along with hips swaying, making country with the aid of
the *mauwulan* point . . .   1
We look at the country as we make it, all the way along . . .
Where shall we go? Into Wulma, Place of the Cloud?
Yes indeed, *waridj* Miralaidj, certainly we shall go with the aid of
the *mauwulan* point.
Bildjiwuraroiju plunges in the *mauwulan* point.   5
Our heads are grey, as we walk along, stained by salt water from
Bralgu, from out to sea, where the foam splashes . . .
We walk in the shadow of rising clouds, spreading and stretching
down: casting their long shadows over the land, thundering in
the distance . . .
We look at the country, with hips swaying, singing as we go: we
are making the country, dragging along our stick . . .
What country is close to us? Wulma, Place of the Cloud.
Carefully, *waridj* Djanggawul, we sway our buttocks, lifting the
mauwulan under our arms: 10
For within us are the sacred *rangga*, the people . . .

Song 102

Yes indeed, *waridj* Miralaidj, I listen to your words, for you speak
as my great leader: I always follow you.   1
Shall we go into Wulma, Place of the Cloud?
Yes, let us sit here and rest, making a sacred shade . . .
Making the mouth of the shade, and its clearing: putting the mound
of earth, the sacred sandhill, and boughs covering the shade . . .
Yes indeed, *waridj* Miralaidj, I always follow you: for you speak
to me as my leader . . .   5
Let us sit in here to rest, for I am feeling ill . . .
I feel tired, from carrying all those *rangga* people within . . .
They can see the sacred well water at Dulabang, at Ngubarei, at
Galwia: rising and splashing, bubbling, foaming up in the
well . . .

Song 103

Come, *waridj* Djanggawul. I am feeling tired. Yourself indeed,
waridj, you must put in the *djuda* roots, the point of the *mauwu-*
lan . . .   1
They stand with shining feathers, quietly and solemnly.

The Djanggawul Song Cycle

Here is another: come, put in the *djuda* roots . . .
For these are our *rangga* from Bilari: plunge in the point!
Straighten them up, for they are aslant: their feathers shine as they
  stand, quietly.   5
They see the water at Ngubarei well, rising and splashing, flowing
  in strongly . . .
See the waves splashing together, roaring, pushing along the
  silt . . .
Another, oh *waridj* Djanggawul: yourself, put in the *djuda* roots!
Bildjiwuraroiju plunges in the *mauwulan* point.
Carefully, straighten them up: 10
Have we finished straightening our *rangga*, *waridj*? Yes, finished
  indeed!

Song 104

Here is a mat, a basket. Take it, *waridj*, shining on the upright
  mauwulan: hang it up on the tree—solemnly and reverently, like
  a younger sibling . . .   1
Let them stay there within the clearing, on the branches at the mouth
  of the shade, near the sandhill mound . . .
Let them stay there, quietly, with their red feathered strings and
  pendants;
They are quietly drying there: for they come from far away, from
  the Place of the Sun, the Place of the Mauwulan . . .
Foam splashed them out on the sea, near Bralgu, the Spirit
  Country . . .   5
We spread them to dry in the hot rays of the sun, in the warmth
  and glare . . .
The burning rays of the sun look on them, and sweat comes out:
  the rising heat, and the haze . . . !
We cover them within the mouth of the mat, within its transverse
  fibre, within the sacred shade . . .

Song 105

Here is another basket: come, hang it on the upright *mauwulan* . . . 1
They are always quiet there, with their feathers shining . . .
For we always cover them up within the peak of the mat, within its
  transverse fibre . . .
They are drying in the hot rays of the sun, watching the rising
  heat . . .
For the foam has splashed and stained them: they are quiet . . . 5

191

They see the water at Dulabang, at Ngubarei, at Galwia.
They are always there, upon them those feathered pendants and
    strings: they are ours!
Yes, yes indeed, *waridj*, they are quiet in their tabu-ness:
They are always drying within the mouth of the sacred shade, by
    the sacred sandhill mound . . .

Song 106

Come, *waridj*, turn over the mouth of the mat, put its peak upper-
    most . . .   1
Go, open it, so we may see the *rangga* clansfolk . . .
Yes indeed, *waridj* Miralaidj, I listen to your words, for you are my
    great leader: I follow your desire . . .
Come, then, put your hand within, and pull them out. Pull hard,
    so that they come head first, so they do not catch on the trans-
    verse fibre: turn them around, and pull them out . . .
Quietly in sacred tabu-ness: for they have been covered up, from
    the Place of the Mauwulan!   5
They are very sacred: for they come from far away, from Bralgu,
    the Spirit Country, far out towards the place of the Sun . . .
Where the sea came foaming up, splashing them . . .
Come, grasp them, pull them out carefully: for one is caught upon
    the transverse fibre of the mat;
Straighten the feathered pendants, so that they may lead into
    various places . . .
Straighten the feathered strands, pulling them through the fringe,
    the transverse fibre of the mat . . .   10
For they have been covered up within the inner peak of the
    mat . . .

Song 107

What is that, *waridj*, crying? That is a nestling. What, a parakeet? 1
Yes indeed, *waridj*. I thought it a stranger crying: heard it talking
    gently, that parakeet, its breast feathers glowing like the red
    clouds at sunset.
Drying itself, as it saw the warm rays of the sunset, the sun sinking
    away beyond Milingimbi . . .
Crying softly, drying itself, clasping the *djuda* limbs with its claws—
    parakeets covering the tree . . .
Drying its feathers: 'Myself (says the bird), I have red breast down,
    my children!'   5

Clasping the *djuda* tree, quietly, solemnly . . .
It saw the red rays of the sunset: saw the sun sinking there at
   Bulbulmara, at Jiganjindu, at Marabai:
Always clasping the tree, at sunset: there we always hear them.
They dive, then, into the well water at Ngubarei, at Dulabang, at
   Galwia;
They go right within, covered up completely within the well. 10
The water roars: we see it rising and bubbling, with foam and
   spray . . .
Water splashing, roaring along, rising up from the well and running
   strongly:
Well water rising and roaring because the parakeets dived
   within . . .
Roar of the water entering the peak of the mat, the sacred basket . . .

Song 108

We see the clanspeople, *waridj*: first undo the sacred mat!   1
Yes, quickly, pull them out, put them there, beneath the trans-
   verse fibre of the mat:
All of them—take them out, and put them aside.
Then take out another, and put it close, this way.
Yes, *waridj*, indeed I undo the mouth of the mat, parting its
   fringe . . .   5
Yes, *waridj*, quickly: put your hand through. Gently, *waridj*, be
   careful! Put your hand within the transverse fibre, parting the
   fringe.
Straighten the sacred *djuda*!
Yes, *waridj*, quickly, straighten another, as you remove it.
You saw water within the sacred well: and there we put in the
   djuda roots:
Go, take them out from within, putting them into the well: 10
Water surges up into the well, bubbles rising, like water foaming up
   from the sea . . .
Go, get two more *djuda*, *waridj*, and put the roots into this well,
   at Ngubarei: calling the invocations . . .
We are invoking the sacred *djuda* names . . .
Carefully straighten them up: let them see the well water at Ngubarei!
Go, put other roots here, into the well, so the water rises, foaming:15
They stand with feathers shining, quietly and solemnly, from within
   the peak of the mat:
From the Place of the Spirits, from over the sea: from the Place
   of the Sun, the Place of the Mauwulan . . .

O

The splashing foam stained them, far away, where we heard the
  Baijini sound . . .
Go, put another *djuda* there, making a well . . .
Carefully, pull out the *rangga*!   20
Yes, quickly, put in more *djuda* roots with their feathered pendants,
  so that water surges up, spraying and bubbling . . .
Straighten the *djuda*, so they may see the water at Galwia.

Song 109

Go on, put in more *djuda* roots, making a well so that the water
  covers them: 1
Turn them, thus, that they may see the water at Dulabang, at
  Ngubarei.
Carefully look after the *rangga*, with the feathered strings upon
  them . . .
For they are ours, from the inner peak of the mat, from its trans-
  verse fibre:
Stained with the foam that splashed them. We call the invoca-
  tions . . .   5
They see the water splashing, roaring as the spray comes up . . .
Roaring as it pushes the silt along, flowing strongly . . .
Well water, bubbling and splashing among the wild banana
  palms . . .
They stand with shining feathers, quietly, reverently, like younger
  siblings . . .
Covered up, from within the peak of the mat, from its transverse
  fibre, from the mouth of the mat, from the fringe . . .   10
Fringe around the mouth of the *ngainmara*. They are ours, *waridj*!
No one may see them. They are our spirits: they are highly sacred.

Song 110

Come, put in more *djuda* roots, making a well. Carefully straighten
  them!   1
Yes, *waridj*, indeed they may see the water at Dulabang:
They shine as they stand, quietly and solemnly; we cover them up
  in the well—carefully, *waridj*!
For upon them are feathered strings and pendants: we are calling
  the invocations . . .
They shine as they stand, quietly: carefully we invoke the sacred
  names . . .   5

They see the well water at Dulabang, at Galwia, at Ngubarei.
Well water rising and bubbling, splashing and roaring; rushing
    through the wild banana palms . . .
Washing down the silt, flowing strongly, with waves rising!
They come from the transverse fibre, from the mouth of the mat,
    from its inner peak: they are tabu.
For they come from far away, from the open sea, from the Spirit
    Country . . .   10
They are splashed and stained with foam from far away, from
    Bralgu . . .
We paddled along with buttocks swaying, and paddles dragging:
    resting our paddles as we came from Bralgu. Our country,
    waridj!
Yes indeed, I listen to you, for you are my leader; I always follow
    you . . .
All right, we shall put them quietly into the well at Dulabang . . .
They see the water at Ngubarei.   15
Carefully, pull out the *rangga* people from within the peak of the
    mat . . .

Song 111

Put in another! They stand with feathers shining, quietly, reverently: 1
Put in the *djuda* roots, *waridj* Djanggawul, straighten them up:
    Bildjiwuraroiju calls the *djuda* invocations . . .
Carefully hold the top of the *rangga*, dragging it in the mud.
They see the well water rising and splashing, roaring up at Dula-
    bang, at Ngubarei . . .
Put them carefully! Yes indeed, *waridj* Miralaidj: feathered strings
    on the *rangga* . . .   5
Go, *waridj* Djanggawul, indeed you must put more *djuda* roots into
    the well . . .
Make the well water rise, so that they stand, shining, watching the
    water . . .
Trees, from within the sacred basket, the transverse fibre of the
    mat, from within the peak, the mouth of the mat, the sacred
    shade . . .
Carefully, *waridj*, for they are stained with foam . . .
They stand quietly and solemnly, with feathers shining, as we
    straighten them . . .   10

Song 112

Here is another *djuda*: come, put in the *djuda* roots, making a well! 1
They stand solemnly, quietly . . .

The Djanggawul Song Cycle

They see the water rising at Dulabang, roaring and splashing:
  for we call the sacred invocations . . .
Carefully, straighten the *djuda rangga* . . .
Carefully, hold the top of the *rangga*, dragging the mud.   5
For we are covering them up: no one may see them. They are
  tabu, like a younger sibling . . .
From within the transverse fibre, from the mouth of the mat, the
  sacred shade . . .
They stand very quietly in sacred tabu-ness . . .
For they come from far away, from Bralgu, across the sea, from the
  Spirit Country, through the shine of the Morning Star . . .
Foam splashed and stained them far out to sea, near the Place of
  the Sun: the sound of the Baijini talking, the smell of the
  sea . . .   10
Carefully, they are standing aslant: straighten them up . . .
Yes, yes indeed, *waridj* Miralaidj. You speak to me as my great
  leader: I always follow you!

Song 113

Another, *waridj* Miralaidj: put in the *djuda* roots, making a well. 1
They stand quietly, seeing the water splashing up, foaming and
  roaring . . .
The sound of rising water, splashing and foaming, rustling the
  wild banana palms . . .
Flowing strongly, roaring and splashing . . .
Carefully, let the *rangga* stand with shining feathers, as we call the
  invocations . . .   5
Put in the *djuda* roots, invoking their sacred names . . .
Carefully, for they come from far away, from Bralgu, from the
  open sea, from the shine of the Morning Star, the Place of the
  Sun . . .
Where the foam splashed up, staining the *djuda*, as with swaying
  buttocks we dragged our paddles . . .
Yes, yes indeed, *waridj* Miralaidj. I always listen to you, for you are
  my leader. I hear your words, for you are my great leader woman:
  I always follow you . . .

Song 114

We walk along, *waridj*, with the aid of the *mauwulan*, poking the
  ground as we go, and making country . . .   1
We plunge the *mauwulan* in, and drag it along, swaying our hips:

196

our bodies are shadowed by clouds, rising and spreading . . .
Bildjiwuraroiju inserts the *mauwulan* point . . .
Our bodies are shadowed by spreading clouds that bend down to
  the horizon.
Carefully, because of the *rangga* clan. Our heads are grey, and we
  move them from side to side: 5
Foam mark from the sea, upon us: foam that splashed us from the
  wide sea near the Spirit Country . . .
Carefully we move our buttocks, for we carry the clans of *rangga*,
  the people . . .
Let us sit down here!
Yes indeed, *waridj*. My body is sick: I feel very tired, from all these
  rangga people. Let us sit here.
Yes indeed, *waridj*, we shall make a shade, a sacred shade . . .   10
Carefully we clear the ground, and arrange the upper boughs;
  carefully we make the sacred shade . . .
Now we have finished, *waridj*. Come, yes, our shade is finished!

Song 115

Go, put this mat down flat beside me. My body feels sick: I am
  very tired: 1
Go, put in the *djuda* roots, Bildjiwuraroiju inserting the *mauwulan*
  point . . .
That is done; indeed, it has come from the transverse fibre of the
  mat . . .
Yes, *waridj* Miralaidj! Go, turn over the mouth of the mat.
Put another, turning over and opening the mouth of the mat, the
  sacred basket, the inner peak of the mat . . .   5
Carefully, from within the mat. Yes, open it out carefully, let it sit
  there, *waridj*:
Indeed, they come from the transverse fibre of the mat.
Yes, undo the mouth of the mat, parting its fringe: from within
  the people, the men, come streaming out . . .
We see the clansfolk, in the well we see them, at Ngubarei:
For we put only half the people there.   10
Come, shall we cut off their foreskins?
Yes, *waridj*, I take a clapping stick, singing as I tap it against the
  mauwulan pole.
Do it carefully, *waridj*! Go, grasp the foreskin . . .
We put the foreskin within the sacred basket:
Pulling the foreskin, cutting it off, as the people, the men, come
  streaming out . . .   15

They play there in the sacred shade, where the *djuda* roots are standing:

They see the rays of the sun spreading from far away, beyond Milingimbi . . .

Playing there, where the *djuda* roots stand, they see the water at Dulabang, at Ngubarei, at Galwia.

They come from within the mouth of the sacred mat, the shade, from its inner peak . . .

They are ours, *rangga* people coming out as she sits with legs apart . . .   20

We put waist-bands on them, one by one, after their circumcision . . .

Yes, go, put on another there: put on the feathered waist-bands . . .

They wear them, those who came from the sacred *ngainmara* . . .

Song 116

Go, sit down with thighs apart!   1

Yes, go, cover up the female children within the mat again, for they are tabu: put them well within the inner part of the mat, beneath its transverse fibre . . .

Carefully we take them from the mouth of the mat, putting them carefully under the *ngainmara*, like younger siblings:

They are shining from the inner peak of the mat, from the opening of the shade . . .

Yes, yes indeed, *waridj*. I listen to your words: I follow you, for you speak as my great leader . . .   5

We cover them up, making them tabu, putting the clansfolk . . .

We are putting some clansfolk here: the others we shall put somewhere else!

We are putting people, making great numbers of people everywhere, going towards Milingimbi!

They play there, where the *djuda* stand: many *rangga* people, coming out from the Sisters . . .

These we put to one side, these clansfolk: for here, first, we are putting only a few: 10

These are only for Ngubarei, Dulabang and Galwia wells.

From them the water rises, rustling the wild banana plants . . .

Go, open the mouth of the mat, pulling aside its fringe . . .

It is done!

Yes, *waridj*. Go, clasp the *rangga*, the *djuda* that make the well . . . 15

Come, pull it strongly, so it emerges head first . . .

Come, let us put it aside . . .

We see her: what is that crying?
Go, put her back within the mat, beneath the transverse fibre:
     hide her, so no one may see . . .
What, another indeed? This is a male child!   20
Come, throw him into the rough grass: you may look after him,
     waridj Djanggawul.
What, another indeed? A tabu child crying?
Go, put her as sacred, covered up within the peak of the mat,
     shining, sacred, like a younger sibling . . .

Song 117

Here is another: come, put the *djuda* roots into that well, making
     it at Dulabang, at Ngubarei, at Galwia!   1
They see the water rising and roaring through the wild banana
     plants . . .
Foam splashing, water rising and pushing along the silt . . .
They stand with feathers shining, quietly and solemnly, from within
     the mouth of the sacred mat, within its peak . . .
Carefully, for these feathered strings have come from far away . . . 5
Carefully, for they have upon them the smell of the sea!
From far away, from Bralgu, the open sea: from the Place of the
     Sun, the Place of the Mauwulan . . .
The foam splashed upon them, staining . . .
Put them to dry: cover them up in the sacred well, like younger
     siblings, solemnly quiet . . .

Song 118

What is that crying, *waridj*? It is a nestling, crying softly from the
     sacred *djuda* tree . . .   1
For it saw the sun; the parakeets play in its rays, like the *djuda*
     roots:
Saw the red clouds reflecting the sunset, crying softly, with notes
     rising and falling . . .
Always clasping the limbs of the *djuda* tree . . .
It saw the red rays, the glow of the sunset spreading from the
     west, beyond Milingimbi . . .   5
The parakeets cry; they are drying their breast feathers: feathers
     like goanna fat, their nestlings . . .
They perch on the *djuda* tree, cocking their heads from side to side,
     red feathers reflecting the sunset!
Drying themselves, ruffling their feathers, in the warm glow of
     the sunset . . .

For they come from within the mouth of the mat, its transverse
    fibre . . .

Crying they saw the water rising up in the well: 10

Water roaring along, foaming and splashing . . .

Crying, they looked at the red sunset, the sinking sun: quietly,
    reverently, as if they were weary . . .

Watching the sun setting, waiting and calling, looking at the
    water:

It is gone. They dive into the well at Ngubarei, going deep within
    the well, out of sight.

Chapter Sixteen

COMMENTS ON PART SIX OF THE SONGS

IN this section of the Djanggawul epic, most of the songs refer symbolically to the removal of people from the Sisters' wombs, and to long feathered strings which are spread out, leading to various places associated with the Djanggawul. The significance of these strings, made from the breast down of the parakeet, or from goose feathers, has already been discussed in some detail. Here, however, the strings symbolize also umbilical cords—the directions in which they radiate indicate the places at which people will later be left. This hidden theme is pursued through most of the section, until towards the end (that is, in Songs 115 and 116) definite reference is made to the removal of the people. Although this removal of the first people has already received specific mention, at least symbolically, the emphasis has been on their *rangga* at the expense of their human quality. Here, however, the stress is on the latter. A few Aborigines go so far as to say that prior to Songs 115 and 116 only *rangga* were removed; but this is a literal, and not a comprehensive interpretation. These songs rely heavily on reiteration, and in this lies their peculiar charm and beauty. It is, moreover, quite impossible to reproduce here the play on words found in the original songs. We have tried to indicate this in the notes to the texts, but it really requires separate and detailed analysis. For example, special words are chosen because of their association with certain others and with the relevant theme; and a great number of words have alternate meanings, which vary subtly according to context.

In Song 89 the Djanggawul continue their journey, going towards Madi at Arnhem Bay, and 'making country' as they travel. On finally reaching this place, they build a sacred *nara* shade (line 7),

Comments on Part Six of the Songs

'. . . for there is something within that mat . . .' (line 8)—that is, within their uteri. The Sisters are '. . . weary, from . . . carrying all those *rangga* people, those clans, within . . .' (line 9), and soon they will give birth to them.

Song 90 refers to their putting sacred *djuda* roots into the well at Madi (line 1). This also refers symbolically to inserting the point of the *mauwulan*, for a threefold purpose: first, to make the well; secondly, for coitus; thirdly, to open the vulvae of the Sisters so that the people may flow out. In line 5, we read: '. . . straighten up the *rangga* . . .'; that is, the *mauwulan* is slanting sideways, and must be put in an erect position—symbolizing an erect penis (for example, coitus as a normal prelude to pregnancy). 'Carefully spread out the feathered strings, so they point towards . . .' (line 13): the sacred pendants are placed on the ground, and straightened out. The word used is *djarima*, which usually means 'shine' (that is, *djari*); the strings are like rays of light at sunset. In addition, however, they refer to the Sisters' clitorises, as *rangga* pendant manifestations, and to the umbilical cords of people who are removed from the wombs of the Sisters. This is a feature of considerable importance.

The places referred to in the song are listed in the sketch figure below.

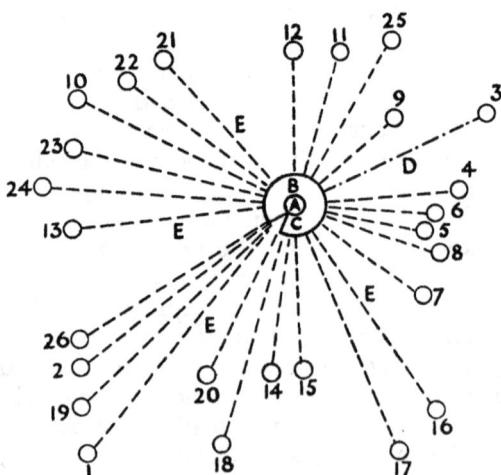

The Djanggawul have built a big shade at Madi, on the coast of Arnhem Bay. There they live, sending out their feathered strings to the various places which they know. To do this, they begin to sing, and at the same time open the *ngainmara* mat to 'let out' the feathered string for each place.

Comments on Part Six of the Songs

The rough sketch illustrated opposite shows the way in which they did this. It is taken from a native drawing to explain the significance of this song.

Key to Sketch on previous page:

A. is the sacred *ganbalaidj* arm-band, placed within the shade. The feathered strings or pendants are attached to it, and radiate out in different directions.

B. is the sacred shade of the Djanggawul.

C. is the mouth of the shade. The shade is so constructed as to represent a *ngainmara* mat; that is, it is circular and conical. Actually, the shade symbolizes the *ngainmara*, for it is said that the latter is opened to 'let out' the feathered strings.

D. is a feathered string inadequately made. The Djanggawul tried to make it; but tears formed in their eyes and impaired their vision so that they did not weave the feathers properly into the twine. Tears welled up in their eyes (*guburjudun* or *milwibwiwubdun*) and ran down their face.

E. shows the perfectly made feathered strings, the *barlga, ngadjaru* or *ngililwara*. These are sent out to the various places mentioned below. The Djanggawul 'straighten them out' (*dunabaijinga*), and spread them along 'like rays from the sun' (*djarijuma*); their ends point to the places to which they must go and they enter these in their spirit form.

1. Bralgu (or Bu'ralgu), the Spirit Country, from which the Djanggawul came to the mainland.

2. Jelangbara, Port Bradshaw: belonging to the Riradjingu linguistic group.

3. Gambuga or Wibiwoi, inland from Caledon Bay: Karlpu linguistic group. This feathered string was poorly made (D., above).

3. Dudeimiwi, north of Blue Mud Bay: Djapu linguistic group.

5. Wolijujumang, south of Blue Mud Bay: 'bottom' Djapu.

6. Wugaling, north of Blue Mud Bay: Djarlwak linguistic group.

7. Wulma, meaning 'Cloud', so named 'because clouds were standing there'; at Arnhem Bay, Ngeimil linguistic group.

8. Mudunganingil; between Arnhem Bay and Yirrkalla: Ngeimil.

9. Galwirligal (or Galwia), at Arnhem Bay, where the Djanggawul made a shade. While they were in the water there, the leech bit them, and so they gave the place this name: Ngeimil.

10. Nguwan(li), at Arnhem Bay: Ngeimil.

11. Ngainmaralji, the 'mat', at Arnhem Bay: Ngeimil.

12. Dulabang (Dulabam or Dulabei) or Ngubarei, at Arnhem Bay: Ngeimil.

13. Galbara, at Arnhem Bay: Ngeimil.
14. Djurimuwi (or Djurwarami), at Arnhem Bay: Ngeimil.
15. Wuwul, at Arnhem Bay: Ngeimil.
16. Marabai, north-west of Arnhem Bay: Djambatpingu.
17. Gunangi, inland from Milingimbi; in Gandjawulgi territory.
18. Galgidjboi, south-west of Arnhem Bay: Djambatpingu.
19. Buradbu: 'bottom' Djambatpingu.
20. Wagulwagul, the 'Uterus' or 'Mat', inland from Arnhem Bay: Dadawi.
21. Miliba, in between Port Bradshaw and Arnhem Bay: Ngeimil.
22. Buluboi, in between Port Bradshaw and Arnhem Bay: Ngeimil.
23. Ganjumingalei, a long way inland from Port Bradshaw: Ngeimil.
24. Buginja, near Port Bradshaw: Ngeimil.
25. Ngaladjeigandjeigin, between Caledon Bay and Port Bradshaw: Ngeimil.
26. Bilari, north of Port Bradshaw: Riradjingu.

The esoteric significance of this, however, is that the Djanggawul begin to sing, and at the same time the Sisters open their uteri to 'let out' the people, sending them to the various places; all have umbilical cords attached. Thus:—

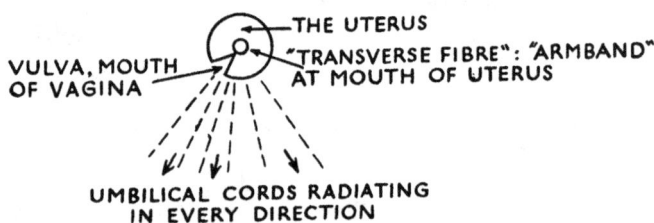

THE UTERUS
VULVA, MOUTH OF VAGINA
'TRANSVERSE FIBRE": 'ARMBAND" AT MOUTH OF UTERUS
UMBILICAL CORDS RADIATING IN EVERY DIRECTION

The arrangement of these places conforms to informants' descriptions, although their positions would appear differently on a map. In drawing this diagram the Aborigines take Madi, at Arnhem Bay, as the centre. All the places between 26 and 11 are situated in and around Arnhem Bay, and in the intermediate country between Arnhem Bay and Port Bradshaw (2). The latter is located, for this purpose, near Bralgu (1), for the Djanggawul landed there; (1) should obviously be extended much farther than this diagram permits.

Between 5 and 25 are a number of places extending from Blue Mud Bay in the south, up the coast to Caledon Bay and inland to the south of Arnhem Bay. Places 8 to 20 are scattered, with considerable variation in position; most, however, are in the bush country above Arnhem Bay, between Arnhem Bay and Yirrkalla, and westwards towards Milingimbi.

The following diagram, superimposed on a rough sketch of north-eastern Arnhem Land, reveals how the Aborigines viewed the position; it will also help to show the places mentioned above in their geographical setting.

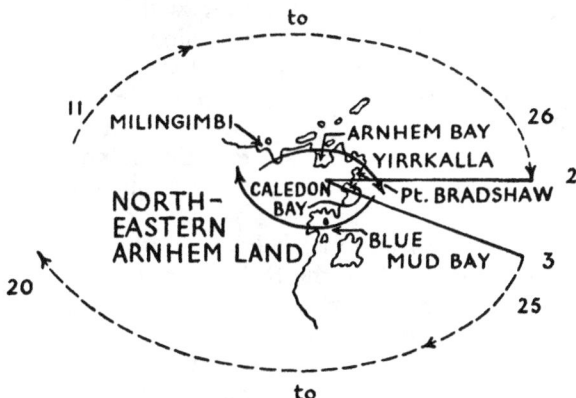

Note to the above sketch:

Not all these places lie on the lines forming the two arcs; they are located at various points within or without the arcs.

The following diagram shows the allocation of these places to the various linguistic groups; they are predominantly Ngeimil.

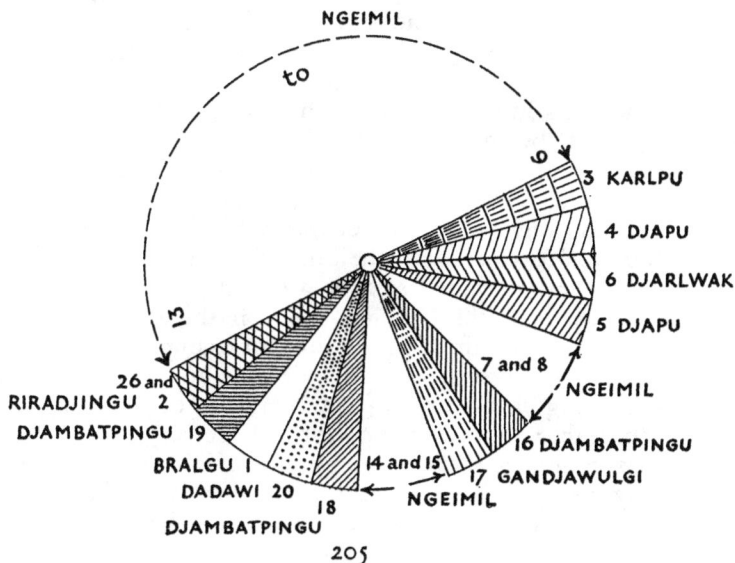

Comments on Part Six of the Songs

Song 91 continues the theme: '. . . put in the *djuda* roots, the *mauwulan* point, within the mouth of the shade . . .' (line 1) has the significance mentioned above. The terms used for shade are in some cases synonymous with mat and uterus. The feathered strings are spread out (line 2), and some are arranged on the mound of earth within the *nara* shade (line 3), representing the sacred sandhill at Port Bradshaw. As the Djanggawul look at the feathered strings, they think of the foam which stained them (line 5), symbolic of semen, or of afterbirth blood—that is, in reference to the umbilical cords. 'Feathered strings! Straighten them out, thus, reaching out to the water . . . spreading in all directions' (lines 10 and 11): this means that they are radiating from Madi. The two places mentioned in line 10 are situated at Arnhem Bay, in Ngeimil territory.

In Song 92, the *ngainmara* mat is bent and turned over so that it becomes conical (line 2), like the belly of a pregnant woman. One of the pregnant Sisters is turned over, and takes up her position ready for childbirth, within the *nara* shade (lines 2 and 3). The others carefully part her pubic hair, and peer into her vagina; they see the people within her (line 4). The *rangga* terms are used here, in addition to the collective terms for *rangga* and clans of people. The Djanggawul Brother is told to put his hand into his Sister's vagina, and so to pull them out (line 5). They are pulled from the mouth of the mat, *dalin*, that is, of the vagina; and they issue 'head first', one by one, from the 'mat' (line 8). In one instance, the Brother must 'loosen' a *rangga* which has become caught on the transverse fibre (line 11). The transverse fibre of the mat is said to be a 'bone' or muscle at the junction of the uterus and vagina—an 'arm-band', which constricts the top of the vaginal passage as a tight armlet cuts into the flesh of the arm (see Chapter 22). The *rangga*'s (child's) being caught on this, and subsequently loosened, refers to a difficult childbirth or to labour pains. Alternatively, and symbolically, the *mauwulan rangga*, which has two protruding ridges at the head, is caught on the inner transverse fibre of the mat. The same process is repeated with the other Sister (line 13).

The *rangga* and feathered strands are said to have been stained with foam, as were the original ones on the way from Bralgu (line 15); and they are dried in the sun (for example, line 17). *Djuda* roots are also put into the sacred well (line 26). The well is symbolically the vagina or uterus (that is, theme of returning to the womb); there they are covered up, 'for they are very sacred' (line 26). Aborigines comment that 'the *rangga* are living in the water, and no one may see through the water in which they rest.' The immersion of the *rangga* in the well causes the water to rise; that is, the wet

Comments on Part Six of the Songs

season has come, the tides flow in, and the wells surge up and flood. The invocations are Riradjingu, and refer to the *djuda* and to 'always putting one's hand into the uterus' (that is, as the Djanggawul Brother does to remove children).

Song 93 continues the theme, leading to a climax in Songs 115 and 116. The *djuda* are put into the well, together with other *rangga* (lines 3, 4 and 5), and the feathered strands spread out (line 7), while the well water rises (line 10). The invocations are Ngeimil, and refer to the *djuda* and to the goanna's vertebrae.

Song 94 repeats the flooding theme: the *rangga* stand quietly as the waters rise (line 7). The movement and sound of the water, like those of the sea tides, are enacted to-day in the Djanggawul *nara* ceremonies. Dancing representing the spring well water is accompanied by the sound a: a: !; this signifies not only the fresh water, but also the incoming waves at Port Bradshaw when the Djanggawul landed for the first time. The invocations are 'bottom' Ngeimil, and refer to the *djuda*. Songs 95 and 96 are very much the same; the *djuda bugali* in the former are Gwolamala, and in the latter, Dadawi.

In Song 97 the *djuda rangga* stand unperturbed (line 6), as the water continues to rise (line 8). The *bugali* referring to them are 'bottom' Karlpu. 'We are covering our spirit form, so no one may see . . .' (line 11): the word used for 'spirit' is *mali* (or, as it is sometimes pronounced, *maldi*); it means 'spirit form', but may be translated here (as it is elsewhere) as 'no one may see'. It refers to the *rangga*, which are the spirit form of the people, living or still unborn. There appears to be some confusion in the minds of mature male informants as to whether the Djanggawul Sisters gave birth to 'live' beings resembling human beings, or, on the other hand, brought forth spiritual representations in the form of *rangga* (containing the spirits of the human beings). The former seems to be the case when Songs 115 and 116 are considered; but the *rangga* were put into the sacred wells, and it is from these wells that people to-day (prior to their birth) receive their spirits. A person's spirit comes from a 'clan well'; it is found by a father or other close relative at what is translated as a 'spirit landing', and through this intermediary enters the mother and animates the foetus within her. The spirit, however, may not be found unless the mother is already pregnant.[1]

Song 98 continues with the surging water (line 6), and the invocations for the *djuda* are Djambatpingu. Song 99 tells of how more *djuda* are put into the well (line 3); the invocations are Karlpu and refer to the *djuda*, while one (*malangmalanga*) refers not only to the *djuda* trunk but to a species of shark.

[1]This subject will be dealt with later in detail.

Comments on Part Six of the Songs

Song 100 reverts to the parakeet, whose breast feathers are used in making the sacred feathered strings. The red sunset spreads its glowing reflections over the sky, and shines on these breast feathers (line 3). Its rays extend across the sky from the distant west, from the mainland beyond Milingimbi (line 8). The day is drawing to a close. The parakeets twitter on the *djuda* boughs, waiting until the last rays of the sun have disappeared; when it sinks beneath the horizon, they swoop down and enter the sacred *ngainmara* where they sleep (line 21). Djurabula and Wanbalala are on the mainland behind Milingimbi; Marabai is at Arnhem Bay, as are Jiganjindu, Dulabang and Bulbulmara, in Djambatpingu country.

Song 101 opens a new day; the Djanggawul continue on their journey (line 1), coming into Wulma, the Cloud Place (line 3). Shadows cast by passing clouds cool their bodies (line 7), but they go steadily along 'For within us are the sacred *rangga*, the people . . .' (line 11). Song 102 brings them to Wulma, where they sit down and construct a sacred shade (line 3). Miralaidj, the younger Sister, is not well: '. . . I am feeling ill . . . I feel tired, from carrying all those *rangga* people within . . .' (lines 6–7); the *rangga* objects or people are heavy within her. The Sisters have already let out small groups of people from time to time during the journey, but many are still in their wombs; they intend to continue giving birth to them all until they reach the western side of Milingimbi.

Song 106 refers to the opening of the mat (uterus), so that the *rangga* folk may be seen within (line 2). The Djanggawul Brother puts his hand in, and removes them from one Sister's womb (line 4); they issue forth head first, but the protruding ridges of the *rangga* are caught on the transverse fibre of the *ngainmara*. Their sacredness is stressed (line 6), for they have come from far away, from the island of Bralgu. Line 9 refers to the radiating feathered strings mentioned above.

Song 107 returns again to the parakeet, with the same content and symbolism as in Song 100; the birds finally disappear into the well, and the water rises (lines 10–13). Here the basket or mat is identified with the well. In line 9, for example, the parakeets dive into the well, while in line 14 they dive back into the sacred mat; in this case the words used refer to a sacred dilly bag, which is alternatively the mat, shade or uterus. Song 108 deals with the fertility theme, '. . . All of them—take them out, and put them aside' (line 3). The people, symbolically the *djuda rangga*, are removed and put into the well (line 10).

Song 109 concerns more *djuda* roots which are placed in the well (line 1), so that the water rises and covers them (line 8); but they 'stand with shining feathers, quietly, reverently, like younger

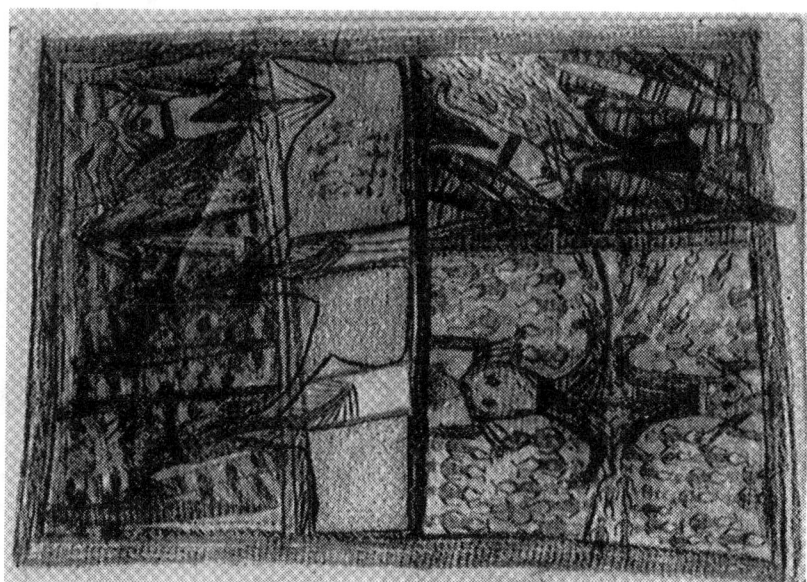

23. The Djanggawul Beings: the Brother removes *rangga* folk from his Sisters.

24. Scenes from the Djanggawul Cycle: the Sisters; Miralaidj in childbirth; sacred emblems, etc.

25. Postulants with Goanna Tail *rangga*.

26. Removal of *rangga* from the *jiritja* moiety shade.

siblings . . . ' (line 9). Although the significance of these words has already been discussed, we may mention briefly here the northeastern Arnhem Landers' concept of sacredness. The usual term for 'sacred' is *mareijin*, which has a much wider application than we have given it here. The word *mareijin*, then, is what is known as an 'outside' or an ordinary word, and may be used freely in the main camp. It is equivalent to the word *duju*, which is less frequently used. Although adults of both sexes may use the word *mareijin*, children of pre-initiation (that is, pre-*djunggawon* ritual or age-grading ceremonies) age may use only the term *gagi*. For example, if children see *mareijin* or tabu-ed food, their father will say, 'Look, this is *gagi*. You mustn't have this, for if you do, perhaps some one will kill you, or your mother will be killed by an "enemy" '. That is, the young child is warned not to eat *mareijin* food, for it is tabu; and if he does eat it he will be killed, or alternatively his mother must pay the penalty. Among fully initiated men, however, outside the hearing of the uninitiated, or on the sacred ceremonial ground, the following 'inside' terms are normally used: *rangga, dalbal, daria, mali, ngaungau* (or *ngaugngaug*), or *jugujugu*. The first is the most general, and may specifically refer to the sacred objects or emblems; the second may also mean 'cover up'; the third means 'tabu-ed'; the fourth, 'spirit form', or 'no one may see' (as in Songs 97 and 109); the fifth is also translated as 'no one may see', or 'tabu-ed'; while the last term is '(like) younger sibling(s)', the significance of which has already been noted.

Song 110 concerns another well, being made with the *djuda roots* (line 1) which are then put within it (line 3). The well water consequently rises (line 7), and is compared to the sea through which the Djanggawul came before landing at Port Bradshaw (lines 10–12). The invocations are Ngeimil, and refer to the *djuda*. Song 111 is much the same. More *djuda* are put in, and the well water rises about them (line 4). The *bugali* used are Dadawi, referring to the *djuda* and the clay-pan tree. The feathered strings (mentioned in line 5) are of red parakeet and goose feathers, the latter being described by the term *budjumi* (that is, *budjei*: *vide* Chapter 14, Comments to Part Five). Song 112 is similar to these. The *rangga* are dragged through the mud (line 5), and later covered and made *ngaungau, jugujugu* and *mali* (line 6). The invocations are Djarlwak, and refer to the *djuda*. Song 113 tells how the waters from the well are rising; the *bugali* are Gwolamala, and again refer to the *djuda*. In Song 114 the clouds are again mentioned (lines 2 and 4). The salt water foam still stains the Djanggawul's hair and foreheads (line 6), and they walk slowly along ' . . . for we carry the clans of *rangga*, the people . . . ' (line 7). They sit down (line 8) for they are weary (line 9). They construct a *nara* shade (line 10); one word used here for 'shade' is *gudijuma*, which suggests an incomplete structure. However, the shade is being made, for here the Sisters will give birth to many people. This song serves as a prelude to Songs 115 and 116. The scene is now set: 'Come, yes, our shade is finished!' (line 12).

Song 115 opens with the flattening out of the mat, which is put alongside one of the Sisters who is in labour. The mat is so arranged that people may be placed upon it as they are removed from the womb. The *mauwulan* point is inserted to open the vulva and facilitate delivery (line 2), and one *rangga* person is removed (line 3). 'Yes, undo the mouth of the mat, parting its fringe: from within the people, the men, come streaming out . . .' (line 8). 'Part or pull aside the fringe', *radarwarijundam*, may be translated in context as 'vagina'. Actually, however, the Djanggawul Brother pulls aside the fringe of the *ngainmara* mat; that is to say, he opens his Sister's vagina in order to extract the people; *radarwarijun* is used when a woman opens her legs for coitus or at childbirth, so that her vagina 'opens' at the same time. The fringe of the mat is the woman's pubic hair. The words *damulbandiwu* or *guramulgrulwul* ('singing inside' name) are used to refer to the people coming out: that is, the Sisters open their legs (vaginae), and out come people. They are said to describe male children (or men). *Damulbandi* is said, also, to be a special term used only in reference to people who have come directly from the Djanggawul Sisters' wombs; it is, Aborigines say, a 'very bottom inside' term. That is, it may be used only when alluding to the original people produced by the Sisters or, alternatively, to special fully initiated postulants performing the most sacred *nara* ritual.

In the same line (that is, 8), the word *muliliwul* is used. This is an 'inside' name for all the men, and is said to be synonymous with the term *galibingu* (which was subsequently changed to *mora*, *vide* Chapter 2) meaning a youth after circumcision. Thus circumcision novices to-day are identified with those who were originally removed from the Sisters' wombs. A boy who has just had his foreskin cut off is said to have 'emerged from his Mother'—that is, from one of the Djanggawul Sisters; for his whole initiation is symbolic of birth, while the culminating act of cutting his foreskin represents the severing of the umbilical cord at childbirth. At birth the male child is severed from his mother; later, when he is initiated, the further severing signifies that he has been removed from the world of females, and by virtue of his rebirth will become more obviously male. It is the importance of this connexion between the foreskin and the umbilical cord which throws into relief the real significance of circumcision as a ritual of symbolic rebirth, and makes it easier to understand the Djanggawul's association with circumcision as mentioned in the myth (*vide* Chapter 2). Line 10 refers to the Djanggawul's putting only 'half the people' at this place; others are to be left elsewhere.

Line 11, 'Come, shall we cut off their foreskins?' has the same significance as above; that is, the people are removed from the womb, and as soon as they are placed on the coarse grass their foreskins are cut by the Djanggawul Brother (symbolizing the severance of the umbilical cord). They are then called *galibingu* (see above). The word used for cutting off the foreskin is *dabi-gulgdun* (foreskin cut); the word *dabi* has (as mentioned in Chapter 14, Part Five of the Cycle, Song 77, in reference to line 16 *et seq.*) a variety of meanings, all of which are in some way associated. *Dabi* is not only the foreskin, but alternatively a basket or dilly bag, for the feathered pendants hanging from it are *dabi* and the term is extended to include the whole bag; the foreskin is, moreover, a 'bag' because of its physical resemblance to one. The feathered strings and pendants on the bag are *dabi*, not only because they are likened to rays of light from the setting sun (the rays are *dabi*, as in line 17), but because one pendant encloses the severed foreskin within a casing of wild honey wax. *Dabi*, then, being a foreskin, a bag, a feathered pendant and a ray of light, is also an umbilical cord, which in turn is symbolic of the foreskin etc. The *dabi* as a ray of light is a feathered string, symbolic of the umbilical cord; and, in addition, the feathered string (*dabi*) is a clitoris (for example, the elongated clitorises of the Sisters). The theme is elaborated so that the clitoris is symbolized by the fringe of the mat (the *ngainmara*); the fringe is then *dabi*, as is the fringe of a sacred dilly bag which is cut ritually by the sons of Djanggawul (*vide* Chapter 14, Part Five of the Cycle, Song 77). The fringe, however, symbolizes not only the clitoris but, more generally, the pubic hair of the Sisters (that is, the pubic hair is *dabi* like feathered strings). *Dabi* may also mean uterus (from its use in reference to a dilly bag), and a snake (that is, from the Sisters' elongated clitorises).

In this song (115) Bildjiwuraroiju, the elder Djanggawul Sister, first helps her younger Sister who is giving birth to children; then the rôles are reversed, and she in turn is assisted by Miralaidj. 'Yes, *waridj*, I take a clapping stick, singing as I tap it against the *mauwulan* pole' (line 12): that is, the Djanggawul Brother takes a *bilma* clapping stick and beats it rhythmically on the sacred pole, singing over the younger Sister who has just given birth to a number of people. Lines 13–15 refer to the male children removed from the womb, who are 'cut' (circumcised) immediately after birth. The Sisters tell the Brother to be careful (line 13); and when the foreskin is taken off it is ' . . . put . . . within the sacred basket' (line 14). As mentioned, the foreskin is moulded into one of the hard wild honey wax nodules which join the lengths of feathered strands hanging from the sacred dilly bag. The foreskin, itself symbolic of the umbilical cord, is put 'into' the feathered strand, which is also the umbilical cord; and it hangs from the bag (symbolic uterus) like an umbilical cord (symbolizing the initial birth of the people from the Sisters). Within the sacred dilly bag small *rangga* are carried, and these represent the people carried in the wombs of the Sisters.

Line 15, describing the people coming from the womb, includes the same words as those already discussed in regard to line 8, and also the word *budjei-warijun*, translated as 'foreskin pull'. This is an interesting word, which has as many alternate meanings as the word *dabi*, and is, moreover, closely related to it (*vide* Chapter 14, Comments to Part Five, Song 77; and above, Song 111). The male children are, after removal, placed within the sacred shade which has been built (*vide* Song 114), and 'They play there in the sacred shade . . .' (line 16); the word used for 'playing' is *gurlgai-jigalaran*, which alternatively means 'putting in *djuda* roots', or '*djuda* roots standing' (for example, Song 113, where *gurlgai-jibduma* is 'putting roots' into the well). It was, however, translated here as 'all the children play about round there'; it is used only for the male children playing, for *gurlga* (or *gulga*) means 'penis'. As they are playing there, 'They see the rays of the sun spreading from far away, beyond Milingimbi' (line 17); that is, the umbilical cords are symbolically spread out, representing glowing rays from the sunset (see above). Places mentioned by name in the original are on the mainland south of Milingimbi.

' . . . *rangga* people coming out as she sits with legs apart . . .' (line 20): the younger Sister sits down and opens her legs to let out the people. Line 21 refers to the waist-band which is put on a novice after circumcision; these bands are made of human hair twine and red parakeet feathers, and are similar to those worn by the Djanggawul and by the Sun Woman *vide* Chapters 1, 2 and 3, and Part One of this Cycle). The feathers in the waist-band are the glow of the sun, significantly associated with the *dabi* (above). Male children who have been circumcised are described by the term *galiboingumi*, and the waist bands are given to them when they return to the main camp after circumcision: 'They wear them, those who came from the sacred *ngainmara* . . .' (line 23).

Song 116 describes another side of this birth scene. Here female children are removed, and a distinction is made between the two sexes (*vide* Chapter 3). 'Go, sit down with thighs apart!' (line 1);

Comments on Part Six of the Songs

'. . . cover up the female children within the mat again, for they are tabu: put them well within the inner part of the mat, beneath its transverse fibre . . . ' (line 2): this is a general rendering of the line—'yes because go on put (it) back tabu covering up right inside inner part of mat's peak transverse fibre mat'. The word *didjuwaija*, translated as 'put (it) back (into)', refers to the Djanggawul's hearing the cries of the female children within the Sister's womb. The Brother partially removes one, but puts it back 'because women are sacred'. Actually, however, the Djanggawul Brother removes the female children and immediately places them under the sacred *ngainmara*, 'because they are women, and hence sacred'. The word for tabu, *ngaungau*, is here translated as '(women are) sacred', and so they are put 'right down at the bottom of the *ngainmara*'; that is, the Djanggawul hear the gentle cry of a girl-child, and put her back into the *ngainmara* (or uterus). Aborigines comment: 'We are not going to pull it out now,' says the Djanggawul. 'Carefully we take them from the mat, putting them carefully under the *ngainmara*, like younger siblings' (line 3). The female children are put into the mat: 'We cover them up . . . ' (line 6). Line 7, '. . . the others we shall put somewhere else', alludes to the girls which have been removed from the Sister, and are placed under the *ngainmara*: that is, 'we can put them somewhere, for we have not yet taken them out'. 'Yes, *waridj*. Go, clasp the *rangga*, the *djuda* that make the well . . . ' (line 15); the word used for *rangga* is *milngurma*, from *milngur* a well, referring to the *mauwulan rangga* which is responsible for making the wells. Lines 18 and 19 refer to a female who is put under the *ngainmara*, line 20 to a male child who is put in the rough grass (line 21). That is to say, the boys are put in the grass and later grow whiskers and hair on their bodies; but all the girls are kept secluded in the *ngainmara*, and being so protected do not grow body or facial hair. In line 21, the word for putting the boys into the rough grass is *dubduwan-ngana*, which means 'throw away'; that is, the men 'have to be away from the women, for when they grow up they will have whiskers and a beard, while the sacred women do not have facial hair. Aborigines, discussing this, added: 'That's why there is always trouble over women, for they are sacred; and that's why they can only have one husband at a time, for they are sacred. But we must have more than one wife, because we must look after what is sacred, just as we look after the sacred *rangga* now'. 'What, another indeed? A tabu child crying? Go, put her as sacred, covered up within the peak of the mat, shining, sacred, like a younger sibling . . . ' (lines 22 and 23). The concept of the sacredness of women has already been touched on briefly in earlier chapters.

Comments on Part Six of the Songs

Song 117 is virtually a continuation of Song 116, and *djuda* roots are put into the sacred well (line 1). The *mauwulan* stick is plunged into the ground and the well made, symbolizing coitus. The song indicates that, after the children have been removed, the *mauwulan rangga* is put into the well again; that is, the Sisters are again available for coitus. The well water rises (that is, ejaculation of semen) and floods the land (line 3), causing general fertility.

Song 118 concludes this section with the parakeets crying into the sunset. They are compared to the people removed from the Sisters, who are placed in the sacred shade (*vide* Song 115, lines 16–18), and play in the rays of the sunset (that is, '. . . the parakeets play in its rays, like the *djuda* roots'—line 2): for they, too, '. . . come from within the mouth of the mat, its transverse fibre . . .' (line 9). As the sun sinks behind the horizon (line 13) they cry once more, then suddenly dive into Ngubarei well '. . . going deep within the well, out of sight' (line 14). The well rises, and floods the land.

This part of the cycle is designed to serve as a kind of core for the whole epic: for here, after considerable development through the previous parts, the Sisters' function as Fertility Mothers is treated as a climax. The stress on the sacredness of women is manifested in the attitude towards and treatment of each sex immediately after birth, and this concept makes itself strongly felt throughout northeastern and north-central Arnhem Land society to-day.

Chapter Seventeen

THE DJANGGAWUL SONG CYCLE

PART SEVEN

The Djanggawul continue along the Arnhem Bay coast until they reach Duwalgidjboi.

Song 119

W E are walking along with the aid of the *mauwulan*, making
country: 1
We see the clouds rising up from Diriliwiri, stretching
into the sea near Gabumanmandu.
We walk quickly along with the *mauwulan*, poking the ground,
Bildjiwuraroiju inserting its point, and making country . . .
Carefully, *waridj*, with buttocks swaying, holding the *rangga*: for
within are the *rangga* clansfolk . . .
Yes indeed, *waridj*, I carry the *rangga*! We walk with swaying hips,
inserting the *mauwulan*, making country—plunging it in and out
at Duwalgidjboi . . .   5
Our heads are grey, as we walk, from the sea foam stains upon
us—grey like a father!
As we walk, our bodies are shadowed by passing clouds, rising
and spreading across the sky.
We walk quickly along, with hips swaying, inserting the *mauwulan*
point and making country . . .
Bildjiwuraroiju inserts the point of the *mauwulan*.

The Djanggawul Song Cycle

Song 120

Here let us sit and rest at Duwaljijalei . . .   1
Yes, yes indeed, *waridj* Miralaidj, I listen to your words, for you
    speak as my great leader: I always follow you . . .
I am sick, *waridj*, I am weary, from all those *rangga* people within . . .
Let us make our camp in here, building a shade . . .
Carefully heap up the mound of earth, like the sandhill, making
    it large: clear the ground, putting branches above the shade . . . 5
Putting the country there at Duwaljijalei, at Duwalgidjboi,
Standing within they may see the water, from the clearing, from the
    mouth of the shade . . .
Yes indeed, *waridj*, surely we shall put the mouth of the shade facing
    towards the sacred well.
They can see the well water rising, surging with foam, splashing
    and spraying:
Roaring water, slowly pushing the silt along . . .   10

Song 121

Go, put in the *djuda* roots, Bildjiwuraroiju,   1
Plunge in the *mauwulan* point, making a well . . .
They stand shining quietly, reverently.
Carefully spread out upon them the feathered strings, straighten
    them carefully . . .
For the splashing foam has stained them, far away on the sea, from
    the Spirit Country, from the place of the Sun and the Place of
    the Mauwulan . . .   5
Foam, splashing and roaring upon them . . .
From the smell of the sea, from the sound of the Baijini talking . . .
It is done, *waridj* Miralaidj! Yes indeed, we are straightening out
    the *rangga* . . .
They come from the transverse fibre of the mat, from the mouth
    of the sacred mat: tabu, hidden within the peak of the mat . . .
We cover them for they come from the mouth of the shade, the
    transverse fibre of the mat . . .   10
We make them always sacred, like younger siblings.

Song 122

Here is another: come, pull it out from the mat . . .   1
Go, part the fringe of the mat: we see the clansfolk within.
Yes indeed, *waridj* Miralaidj. I put my hand within the mouth of
    the mat, and grasp the *mauwulan rangga*.

216

Yes, pulling it out carefully: put the *djuda* within the transverse
fibre of the mat, spreading them out.
Yes, *waridj*, indeed I pull out another: yes, *waridj* Miralaidj, pulling
out another *djuda* . . .   5
Well, is it finished? Yes, go, put in the *djuda* roots and *rangga* . . .
They stand with shining feathers, quietly, reverently . . .
Carefully, dragging the mud, dragging the well-water *rangga* . . .
Go, make another well, put in the *djuda* roots, the *rangga* . . .
Carefully, straighten the feathered strings upon the *rangga*, for they
are sacred . . .   10
They see the well water at Duwalgidjboi, at Duwaljijalei:
Water roaring and splashing, foaming up as it flows strongly . . .
They stand quietly, reverently, with their shining feathers . . .

Song 123

Here is another feathered pendant for the *djuda*. Take it, carefully
pull it out . . .   1
We put in the *djuda* roots, the *rangga*, planting the *djuda* point to grow
into trees . . .
They stand quietly and solemnly:
Seeing the mouth of the sacred shade, and its clearing within . . .
Within is the mound, the sandhill, and above are the boughs of
the *nara* shade . . .   5
For we call the sacred invocations . . .
They stand within, seeing the well water rising, spray coming up . . .
For we call the sacred invocations . . .
Carefully straighten up the *djuda*, so they see the well at Duwalgi-
djboi, at Duwaljijalei:
They stand quietly, with shining feathers: 10
Grasp them, pulling them from the mud, pulling the *rangga* strongly,
making a well, and dragging the grass . . .
They come from within the mouth of the mat, from its transverse
fibre, its inner peak . . .
They are made tabu: they are sacred, like younger siblings.

Song 124

Take another *djuda*: pull it hard, and place it near by: 1
Carefully grasp the *rangga*, straighten its feathered pendants . . .
For they are splashed and stained with foam . . .
Foam that splashed them far away, out to sea, from the Spirit

217

Country, from the shine of the Morning Star, the sound of the
   Baijini . . .
From the smell of the sea, the Place of the Sun, the Place of the
   Mauwulan . . .   5
We dragged our paddles along, resting them: swaying our buttocks,
   coming from far away, from the Spirit Country, from Bralgu . . .
We cover them up, for they are tabu, their spirits like younger
   siblings: they are very sacred,
For they come from the transverse fibre of the mat, from the mouth
   of the mat, the sacred shade . . .
They stand there quietly, reverently . . .
Go, put in the *djuda* roots and the *rangga* . . .   10
They see the well water at Duwaljijalei, at Duwalgidjboi.
Straighten them up! They are very sacred. Covering them, for we
   have always covered them, from the Place of the Mauwulan!
They come from within the peak of the mat, from its mouth, from
   within the fringe of the sacred mat . . .

Song 125

Another! Come, put in the *djuda* roots, the *rangga* . . .   1
They stand with shining feathers, quietly, reverently.
They see the water at Duwalgidjboi, at Duwaljijalei, rising up in
   the well . . .
Go, put in the roots, calling the sacred *djuda* names . . .
Carefully make the well; grasp the *rangga*, dragging them through
   the mud, invoking the sacred names . . .   5
Carefully, straighten the feathered strings . . .
They have been covered up within the peak of the mat, within its
   transverse fibre; from the fringe, the mouth of the mat . . .
They stand with shining feathers, quietly, reverently.
They see the water at Duwalgidjboi, at Duwaljijalei, rising up in
   the well:
Rising and splashing, pushing along the silt, running strongly . . . 10
Well water rising, roaring and spraying . . .

Song 126

Take another: have we finished taking them out?   1
Come, pull it out!
Go, put in the *djuda* roots, the *rangga* . . .
Carefully straighten the *rangga*, putting them in:

Carefully, making the well, calling the sacred invocations . . .   5
Put in the roots, invoking the sacred names . . .
Carefully, pushing the mud and grass along as the well water flows.
Yes, *waridj* Miralaidj, indeed I straighten the feathered strings,
    the *rangga* pendants . . .
Feathers flutter down from the pendants: carefully, spread out the
    feathered strings . . .
They are very sacred: we cover them up within the mud: 10
They have been covered up within the transverse fibre of the mat,
    its inner peak . . .
Within the mouth of the mat, the transverse fibre, the fringe of
    the mat:
They come from far away, from the Spirit Country, from Bralgu,
    far out to sea, from the shine of the Morning Star . . .
The foam splashed up and stained them at the Place of the Mauwu-
    lan!

Song 127

Here is another, *waridj*: pull out that *djuda rangga* . . .   1
Let them see the water at Duwaljijalei, at Duwalgidjboi . . .
Come on, put in the *djuda* roots; making a well, calling the invoca-
    tions . . .
They stand with shining feathers, quietly, solemnly:
For they have been covered up within the peak of the mat, its
    transverse fibre, within the sacred shade: they are tabu, like
    younger siblings . . .   5
Carefully, for they are splashed and stained with foam . . .
Splashed from far away, from the Place of the Sun, from the sea
    near the Spirit Country, the shine of the Morning Star . . .
From the smell of the sea, and the sound of the Baijini . . .
We rested our paddles, dragging them through the sea, swaying
    our buttocks . . .
Yes, yes indeed, *waridj*. You are my great leader, and I always
    follow your desire . . .   10
They stand quietly, shining in sacred tabu-ness, like younger
    siblings . . .

Song 128

What is that crying, *waridj*? It is a parakeet nestling, with red breast
    feathers!   1
We saw it perched on the sacred *djuda* tree, on the *rangga* . . .
It saw the red glow of the sunset, crying softly . . .

The Djanggawul Song Cycle

Always quiet, watching the rays of the sun spreading from the west,
    beyond Milingimbi . . .
Crying softly, cocking its head from side to side, clasping that
    djuda tree . . .   5
Clasping the *djuda* limbs, watching the warm rays of the red sunset:
The glare of the glowing sun, and its warmth! Drying itself in the
    rays of the sun . . .
With steam rising from its wet breast feathers, its children, the
    sacred feathered pendants . . .
It saw the sun sinking away in the west, near Milingimbi . . .
Crying softly, watching the sinking sun . . .   10
Watching the sun over Milngurmuru and Maluwa, over Marabai,
    Jiganjindu, and Bulbulmara:
Quietly and solemnly, birds perched in sacred tabu-ness . . .
They looked at the mouth of the sacred basket. The sun has
    vanished!
They dive into the basket, so no one may see them:
Dive deep into the well, hiding themselves, for they are sacred:
    no one may see them there in the well.   15
They sleep quietly, solemnly, for they are very sacred, like younger
    siblings: no one may see them:
Within the peak of the mat, the sacred basket, diving down into the
    well at Duwalgidjboi, Duwaljijalei . . .
Diving right down with their nestlings, their children, their red
    breast feathers . . .
It is done!

Chapter Eighteen

COMMENTS ON PART SEVEN OF THE SONGS

THIS section of the Djanggawul Cycle is the smallest, and consists largely of repetition. The Djanggawul reach Duwalgidjboi, and proceed to make a well: most of the songs symbolize the removal of *rangga* folk from the *ngainmara*, the placing of *djuda* and *rangga* in the sacred well, and the rising flood waters which result. That is to say, the Djanggawul travel through the country, performing actions which are essentially the same as those they have performed elsewhere. They are making the country, creating sacred sites, erecting *nara* shades, and not only leaving human beings, but also putting into the wells sacred *rangga* objects which may be used to-day in *dua* moiety *nara* ritual. All their actions are associated with past events; their epic sea journey from Bralgu is recalled again and again. They themselves, by their presence and by their actions, are ensuring the general fertility of the land; they are simply fulfilling their major function as Creative Beings.

In Song 119 the Djanggawul pass through Ngeimil territory and eventually reach Duwalgidjboi, belonging to the Djambatpingu linguistic group (line 5). Djiriliwiri and Gabumanmandu (line 2) are 'inside' names of a place on the sea coast at Arnhem Bay. The *mauwulan rangga*, with its power to create springs of flowing water, is plunged into the ground at Duwalgidjboi and then withdrawn, so that a well comes into being (line 5). Clouds are spreading over the sky (line 7), and their 'head part' stretches down into the sea. Line 6 reads: 'Our heads are grey . . . from the sea foam stains upon us—grey, like a father!' The word used for 'like a father' is *bunjinang*, but this is not the normal word for father (that is, *baba*). It is classified as an 'inside' term, referring to the foam upon the heads of the Djanggawul, the salty encrustation which resembles the grey hair of an actual or classificatory father. (*Bunji* is the term for 'father' used by the Maung people of south Goulburn Island, in western Arnhem Land.) The Aborigines of north-eastern Arnhem Land frequently use kinship terms to illustrate their concrete or their more abstract ideas: for example, sacredness or tabu-ness 'like a younger sibling', breast feathers on the parakeet like *wagu*, children (or sister's children, man speaking), and so on. These kinship terms establish a sentimental bond between the object or idea and the people themselves, on a personal and intimate basis.

Song 120 tells how the Djanggawul sit down to rest, for the Sisters are again weary from carrying the *rangga* people (line 3). They construct a shade (line 4) at Duwalgidjboi, which has the outside names of Duwaljijalei or Djulngaijeri, and is situated among mud and mangroves on the Arnhem Bay coast. From the mouth of the shade, where they plan to take out the *rangga*, the Djanggawul can see the well water (line 7) splashing up and spraying (line 9). Song 121 concerns the plunging of *djuda* roots into the well; they are made to stand erect in sacred fashion line 3), and the feathered pendants are straightened out (line 4). The symbolism already discussed in previous chapters for example, Chapter 15) applies here. The song dwells on the origin of the strings, on their being stained with foam (line 5), and on the fact that they came from within the sacred mat, the *nara* shade (line 10).

Song 122 mentions the people who can be seen within the mat (line 2), that is, the uterus. The Brother puts his hand into the mouth (vulva) and removes the *rangga* (line 3); they are brought out carefully, and spread out one beside the other over a wide area. When this is done, the *rangga* are erected (line 6), and stand '. . . with shining feathers, quietly, reverently . . .' (line 7).

Song 123 continues this theme. 'We put in the *djuda* roots, the *rangga*, planting the *djuda* point to grow into trees . . .' (line 2): the Djanggawul put the point of the *djuda* (tree) *rangga* into the ground, and from each grows a living tree, developing roots, limbs and branches. In this way they planted many trees, and the feathered strings (normally attached to the head of the *rangga*) symbolized red parakeets. The *mauwulan rangga* made the wells, and the *djuda* placed in or around the well are nearly always trees; however, as we have noted elsewhere, this represents also symbolic coitus, as well as the opening of the Sisters' vulvae by inserting the sacred *rangga*. References to the Djanggawul's making country (for example, Song 119) include mention of this 'planting' of *djuda*, the making of wells, and of sacred places which have become ceremonial grounds. The dragging of *rangga* across the ground (in memory of the way the Djanggawul dragged their paddles through the sea on their way from Bralgu—*vide* Song 124 line 6 and Song 127, line 9) made grooves, which have to-day become hills and ridges. Moreover, each *nara* shade which the Djanggawul built from *djuda* boughs, the clearing within and before its mouth, and the symbolic sandhill, are now a dense jungle, a large clearing or plain, and a huge sandhill.

'Grasp them, pulling them from the mud, pulling the *rangga* strongly, making a well, and dragging the grass . . .' (line 11), refers to the *rangga* which have been put into the mud for future generations; these are removed, used ritually, and later returned to the mud. The invocations are 'bottom' Djambatpingu, referring to the *ba'ralgi* (*vide* Song 62), and to the *djuda*.

Song 124 is very much the same as those immediately preceding it. Emphasis is placed here, as elsewhere, on the foam that stained the *rangga* and feathered pendants (lines 3 and 4); this is important, for foam is symbolically a fertilizing element. Line 1 again symbolizes the removal of a child. Song 125 is similar in content. The *rangga* stand quietly and reverently (line 8), while the well at Duwalgidjboi rises and floods the country (lines 9–11). In Song 126 the removal of *rangga* continues (line 2), followed by their erection around and in the well. The invocations are Dadawi, referring to the *djuda*. The heavy waters from the rising well push along mud and grass and cause the *rangga* to shake. This in turn loosens the goose-feather down, used as bunched tassels on the parakeet feathered strings; it is later collected by the Djanggawul (line 9). This goose feather is called *budjei*—*vide* Chapter 16. The sacred *rangga* are hidden in the mud (line 10), which is approximated to the *ngainmara* mat; that is, the *rangga* are put into the mud and silt washed along by the well water and hidden (presumably to be left for 'new' generations), just as they were previously hidden within the mat. 'They have been covered up within the transverse fibre of the mat, its inner peak . . .' (line 11). This becomes clearer when one considers the symbolic significance of the well, which is frequently identified with the *ngainmara*. The *rangga* are covered up completely within the mud, or the mat, because they have come a long way, from Bralgu (line 13): they have returned to the uterus of their Mother.

Song 127 describes the removal from the *ngainmara* of more *djuda*, which are erected so they may see the water at Duwalgidjboi (line 2). The *bugali*, for the *djuda*, are 'bottom' Ngeimil.

The concluding song (128) of this section is that of the parakeet, sitting in the *djuda* tree awaiting the final sinking of the sun. The red rays of the sunset spread across from the mainland west of Milingimbi (line 4), and their warmth causes steam to rise from the red breast feathers of the parakeet (line 8). The birds continue to sit there, watching the sun setting over Djiriliwuramaiju (an 'inside' name for a place on the mainland beyond Milingimbi) and Manuwai (line 9). The latter place name means 'to stretch out one's legs, opening one's thighs'; it refers to the Djanggawul Sisters, opening their legs in order to 'empty out the people' from their uteri. Bilmingura (or Bilminngurai) and Magulmagul (or Magul-djaui) are other place names mentioned in the original. The former alludes to the leeches which went into the vaginae of the Two Sisters, and bit them internally. It will be recalled that in the myth (Chapter 2) the Sisters were collecting fish, using their legs as a fish trap, and as they squatted thus, with open legs, the leeches swam in. In the myth, however, it was said that the Sisters were collecting *ragai* bulrush roots in a billabong, and not fish, when the leeches bit them. The 'outside' names for this place were given as Djiralinguruma, Maluwa, Milngurmuru (line 11) or Magulmagul. Magulmagul means 'Vagina' (or, alternatively, uterus, *ngainmara*, or *nara* shade), because the leeches swam into the Sisters' vaginae. It is also called by that name because the Sisters opened their legs to remove people. Marabai (line 11) has already been mentioned, Jiganjindu and Bulbulmara being its 'inside' names.

As the sun at last disappears, the parakeets look at the mouth of the sacred basket (line 13). They dive within it, deep down so that no one may see them (line 14). This is then identified with the well, into which the parakeets dive (line 15). The mat reappears in line 17, correlated with the basket and the well. The final disappearance of the parakeet, is signified in the original by the exclamation *rid*; this refers only to the cry uttered by the male bird as it goes down into the water, the mat, or the basket; the female bird does not make this sound.

27. Dancing with the *jiritja* moiety *rangga*.

28. Neophytes await the showing of the Djanggawul emblems.

29. Meditation before the sacred Goanna Tail *rangga*.

Chapter Nineteen

THE DJANGGAWUL SONG CYCLE

PART EIGHT

The Djanggawul reach Marabai, where the Two Sisters lose their sacred emblems, the men taking over their rituals. The long penis of the Djanggawul Brother and the clitorises of the Sisters shortened. More people are born, and some are circumcised.

Song 129

WE are walking with the aid of the *mauwulan*, hips swaying, making country with the mauwulan point.   1
    Yes indeed, *waridj* Miralaidj, there we see clouds rising and spreading across Bulbulmara, across Jiganjindu, Marabai, Dambala.
Our bodies are shadowed by the spreading clouds, rising above our heads . . .
Carefully stepping along with buttocks swaying, for within are the *rangga* clansfolk . . .
Carefully we prod the *mauwulan* into the ground and drag it along, making country.   5
Our heads are grey, always stained with foam marks from Bralgu, from the sea near the Spirit Country . . .
We walk wearily, for we are very tired . . .
Carefully we are making country, inserting the *mauwulan* point . . .
Bildjiwuraroiju, are we coming close to our country?
Yes, we are drawing close: let us sit down here . . .   10
Yes, *waridj*, indeed, my body feels sick; I am weary from swaying my buttocks, from carrying all those *rangga* people . . .
We are making our camp, our sacred shade, arranging its mouth, and clearing it within . . .

From the mouth of the shade, thus, they can see the well water at
  Marabai, at Bulbulmara, at Jiganjindu, Dambala:
Water bubbling up, roaring, pushing along the mud . . .
Carefully we make the mound, the sandhill, in the clearing beneath
  the upper branches of the shade . . .   15
Go, *waridj*, carefully put in the *djuda* roots:
Straighten them, so they may see the well at Jiganjindu, at Bulbul-
  mara, at Marabai.
They stand with shining feathers, quietly sacred . . .
Go, put in more *djuda* roots: Bildjiwuraroiju plunges in the *mauwulan*
  point!
Straighten them, so they may see the well at Jiganjindu, at Bulbul-
  mara, at Dambala, Marabai.   20

Song 130

Turn over the mouth of that mat, straighten it, pull it towards me,
  towards the well . . .   1
Yes indeed, *waridj* Miralaidj. We open it, parting the fringe at the
  mouth of the mat: and we see the *rangga* people within the mouth,
  within the transverse fibre . . .
Open it right out: take them one by one from the mouth of the mat.
Grasp the head of the *mauwulan*, pulling hard; carefully, pull out
  the feathered strings . . .
Go, pull out another *rangga* stick, straightening it, from the inner
  peak of the mat.   5
Yes, *waridj*, spread out all the *rangga*: some are caught on the trans-
  verse fibre of the mat.
Yes, *waridj*, indeed. Go, open the mouth of the other mat, parting
  its fringe . . .
Yes, waridj, grasp the *djuda* carefully, pull it hard!
Yes, here is another: pull it hard, taking it out!
We see within the many *rangga* clansfolk . . .   10
Yes, *waridj*, here is another!
Surely, I listen to your words, for you are my great leader: I always
  follow you . . .
Go, pull out another, *waridj*, for we see the people within.
Yes indeed, *waridj* Miralaidj, we shall take out the *rangga*, the people!

Song 131

Go, put out another! Put it close to the mouth of the mat,
  straightening its peak . . .   1
Go, open the mouth, parting the long strands of its fringe . . .

The Djanggawul Song Cycle

Is it finished? Yes, we have finished straightening it out.

Go, put your hand within, grasping the *djuda*, pulling them carefully
out!

Yes, we are puting the *djuda* roots, at Jiganjindu, into the well: 5

Making the well, and calling the invocations . . .

They come from far away, from the Spirit Country, away across
the sea . . .

From the splashing foam that stained them, from the shine of the
Morning Star, the sound of the Baijini talking, the smell of the
sea . . .

Where the foam splashed up near the Place of the Sun, the Place
of the Mauwulan . . .

Carefully straighten the feathered strings, strings like the yam
creepers . . .   10

Let them dry in the warm rays of the rising sun:

The heat and glare of the sun drying them, so that sweat comes
out . . .

They see the steam rising up from their wetness:

The scorching sun looks down on the feathered strings . . .

They come from the inner peak of the mat, covered up, because
they are sacred . . .   15

Song 132

Put in these *djuda* roots, these *rangga*, making a well . . .   1

They stand with shining feathers, quietly, for we are calling the
sacred invocations . . .

Carefully, drag them through the mud and the grass, *waridj*,
straightening them up:

Yes, indeed, it is done. They are straightened.

They see the well waters rising at Bulbulmara, at Marabai, at
Jiganjindu, Dambala: 5

Roaring and splashing, water surging up . . .

Carefully, straighten out the feathered strings . . .

They are splashed with foam that stained them near the Place of
the Sun, the Place of the Mauwulan:

Splashing up as we rested our paddles, dragging them through the
sea, swaying our buttocks . . .

They stand with shining feathers, quietly, solemnly tabu: 10

For these feathered pendants come from the transverse fibre of
the mat, from its inner peak: covered up, tabu and sacred, like
younger siblings . . .

Let them dry in the warm rays of the sun, in its heat and glare . . .

They dry there, in the heat of the shining sun . . .

227

The Djanggawul Song Cycle

Song 133

Waridj, take these *djuda* roots. We put them into the well, making
    the well at Jiganjindu . . .   1
We are calling sacred *djuda* invocations . . .
Straighten out the sacred *djuda*, the *rangga* . . .
Carefully, drag along the mud and the grass . . .
They see the sacred well at Bulbulmara, at Jiganjindu, at Dambala,
    Marabai.   5
Carefully, *waridj*, spread out the feathered strings . . .
For they are splashed and stained with foam from far away, from
    the shine of the Morning Star, out at sea, from the Spirit Country,
    the Place of the Sun, the Place of the Mauwulan!
They stand with shining feathers, quietly, solemnly, drying in the
    warm rays of the glowing sun . . .
There they feel the rising heat of the shining sun, drawing the
    moisture from the feathered strings . . .
They see the scorching heat, and the haze . . .   10
For they come from the transverse fibre of the mat, from its inner
    peak, from the mouth of the sacred shade: covered up, tabu,
    so that no one may see . . .

Song 134

Put in more *djuda* roots, *rangga*, making a well . . .   1
They stand with shining feathers, quietly, solemnly, as we call the
    invocations . . .
Carefully, dragging along the mud and the grass!
Come, we put in these *djuda*, making a well:
Let them dry in the hot rays of the burning sun . . .   5
Drying their damp feathered strings in the heat, feathered strings
    like yam creepers . . .
The scorching sun looks down on them, its heat drawing out all
    the moisture from these feathered strings . . .
They are very quietly solemn, like younger siblings, watching the
    well water at Jiganjindu, at Marabai, at Dambala, Bulbulmara.
They come from the inner peak of the mat, from within the mouth
    of the mat, its transverse fibre: covered up, for they are very
    sacred . . .
From the sacred *nara* shade—covered up, tabu, so no one may
    see . . .   10

The Djanggawul Song Cycle

Song 135

There, *waridj* Djanggawul, put in the *djuda* roots, the *rangga*, making a well! 1

We call the sacred invocations . . .

Carefully drag along the mud and grass in the well, straightening them up, *waridj* Djanggawul.

They stand with shining feathers, quietly and solemnly, standing up in the ground . . .

They see the well water at Bulbulmara, rising and bubbling, splashing and foaming . . . 5

Pushing along the silt, flowing, with waves splashing together:

Waves, and rough water splashing, spraying up like the rising tide . . .

For they come from within the transverse fibre of the mat, from the mouth, the fringe of the mat, from its inner peak: covered up so no one may see, like younger siblings . . .

They are splashed with foam that stained them from far away on the deep sea, from the Spirit Country, the Place of the Sun, the Place of the Mauwulan . . .

From the sound of the Baijini talking, the smell of the sea . . . 10

Song 136

Put in more *djuda* roots, *waridj*, making a well . . . 1

They stand, the *djuda*, the *rangga*, with shining feathers, quietly, solemnly, watching the water at Jiganjindu, at Bulbulmara, at Marabai, Dambala.

We call the sacred invocations . . .

Straighten out the *djuda*, and the feathered strings upon them, invoking the sacred names . . .

Carefully drag along the mud and the grass in the well . . . 5

They come from far away, from Bralgu, the Spirit Country, from the shine of the Morning Star, out in the open sea . . .

Where the foam comes splashing up, staining them . . .

For we, *waridj*, rested our paddles there, dragging them through the sea, swaying our buttocks . . .

Yes indeed, *waridj*, I listen to your words, for I always follow you. You are my great leader, and I follow your desire . . .

Song 137

What is that crying, *waridj* Miralaidj? 1

It is a parakeet nestling, crying softly, for it saw the sinking sun.

Crying softly as it saw the rays of the sinking sun, the red glow
    of the sunset . . .
Calling gently, clasping the limbs of the *djuda*, moving down the
    branches . . .
It saw the rays of the sun sinking, away in the bush beyond Milin-
    gimbi: 5
Rays spreading over the sacred *nara* shades at Magulmagul, at
    Maguldjaui:
Sinking slowly behind Milngaidja, Milngurmuru, Bilminngura,
    and Maluwa:
The *djuda* trees stand there, shining, with the parakeets upon
    them . . .
Crying softly, cocking their heads from side to side . . .
They saw the warm glow of the sun, feeling its heat: 10
Twittering and crying, drying their red breast feathers, their
    children: 'Myself (said the bird) I am drying my feathers' . . .
They see the well water at Jiganjindu, at Dambala, at Bulbulmara,
    Djumbulwara, Marabai:
Waiting there in the sunset, they see the mouth of the sacred
    basket:
Crying out, they dive within it!

Song 138

We shall walk along, Sister, with the aid of the *mauwulan*, making
    country; inserting the point of the *mauwulan*, dragging it, Bildji-
    wuraroiju . . .   1
Our heads are grey: we sway our hips as we walk. Our bodies
    shadowed by clouds, rising and passing . . .
Carefully, we leave the sacred basket within the shade.
We sit twirling our firesticks, making fire.
Carefully, Sister, arrange the claypan wood, building the fire and
    spreading out the red glowing coals . . .   5
Yes, Sister, the fire is growing hot.
Let us hang this shining basket upon the tree . . .
Its feathered pendants shine in the sun, clasping the tree like a
    parakeet.
Yes, we are walking along with the aid of the *mauwulan*, making
    country . . .
With hips swaying, we plunge in the point of the *mauwulan*
    rangga . . .   10
What is that, Sister? Show me? I see a mangrove shell.
Come, pour them in here; put them as sacred, within the mat!

There I saw another of them!
Come, put them into the mouth of the sacred mat.
There is another mangrove shell!   15
Let us leave them within the peak of the mat, covering them up:
    they are sacred to us!
Here is another, Sister, a black periwinkle. Put it within, sacred to
    us!
Covered up in the basket, hanging up on the claypan tree . . .
It shines there quietly, solemnly, beside the water . . .
We are making that Dreaming, for us . . .   20
We are making it like a younger sibling, within the mouth of the
    mat, the sacred shade, covered up so no one may see . . .

Song 139

What is that, Sister, another?   1
Go, get it: I see a conical mangrove shell.
Come, put it in: it is sacred to us!
We take it from within the mud of the well of Jiganjindu, at
    Bulbulmara.
Shells lying there, quietly shining, solemnly tabu . . .   5
Come, let us cover them up like younger siblings; for they were
    made in the sacred well water, which covered them . . .
What is that? Where? There, Sister. Take it and put it in.
What is the name of this short mangrove shell? It is *nundu*.
Put it in, covering it up. Take it from within the mud of this well,
    the inner peak of the mat . . .
Cover it up, so no one may see, making it tabu, like a younger
    sibling . . .   10
Lift up the mat beneath your arm, putting the shells within it,
    pushing them into the peak of the mat . . .
Cover them up within the mat, parting the fringe at its mouth:
We stand here resting upon our *mauwulan*, for we have been moving
    fast, swaying our hips, and making country . . .
Yes indeed, Sister, true!
Oh! What is that crying, Sister?   15
It is a *djummal* bird, that has heard the incoming tide!
No, Sister, surely the fire has burnt our sacred basket! That is why
    the bird is crying!
Yes, yes, indeed, elder Sister!
We shall walk along, younger Sister, with the aid of the *mauwulan*:
    we shall see what has happened.

The Djanggawul Song Cycle

Song 140

We walk quickly along, with hips swaying, making country with
    the point of the *mauwulan* . . .   1
Carefully, swaying our buttocks, carrying the basket of shells . . .
We walk quickly, with the aid of the *mauwulan.*
We shall see what has happened to our basket. The long-drawn
    cry of the *djunmal* bird has warned us: perhaps the fire has burnt
    it . . .
Yes indeed, Sister, let us go now, and look!   5
Quickly, indeed, go and look!
There is nothing here, Sister! But we left the sacred basket hanging
    here!
Only the tree, the claypan tree, is standing alone!
Go quickly, with the aid of the *mauwulan*, hips swaying, making
    country. It must have fallen down, and been burnt in the fire.
Yes, Sister, indeed, it must have fallen somewhere!   10
Go quickly, run fast to look for the basket . . .
It must have been burnt in the fire.
There is nothing here, Sister!
We must ask the others: for here are the footprints of our Brother
    Djanggawul, and the *galibingu.* They may have taken it from us!
Go, pour the shells from our basket on to the glowing coals of
    the fire . . .   15
Why do they take the sacred basket from us, leaving only the shells?
We tip them upon the flames, the smouldering claypan wood . . .
We leave them, so we may look for that sacred basket . . .
Why do they take it from us in stealth, like children playing?
We walk fast with the aid of the *mauwulan*; we prod the ground,
    and drag it along . . .   20
Yes, Sister, indeed, we shall ask if those others have taken it. Why
    do they act like children, playing?
Why didn't they ask us? Why did they do it?
They came sneaking along and stole our basket, quietly, without
    asking!
Where is the sacred shade? There it is, Sister, hanging within the
    shade . . .
Let us go quickly, with the aid of the *mauwulan*. It is there, Sister,
    indeed!   25
Go quickly, young Sister!
Get the clapping sticks (says the Brother Djanggawul)! They are
    drawing close!
Rhythmically beating the sticks, clapping them carefully, so that
    the sound echoes from the mouth of the shade . . .

The Djanggawul Song Cycle

Singing, clapping the sticks, from the sandhill mound in the sacred shade . . .
They are drawing close! Go, start the *nara* ritual, making the sound of the sea, of waves breaking and splashing.   30
For those Two are drawing closer!
Clap the sticks fast, making the sound of the sea, of the waves breaking and spraying.
Carefully make the roaring sound of water, for the sacred *rangga* people who come from the transverse fibre of the mat . . .
Clap the sticks fast; rhythmically clap them!
They are drawing near! Let them hear the beating sticks, so that they slacken their pace . . .   35
Now they may grind the cycad nut for us, whitening their hands in its flour: it is better that way!
Ah, stop, Sister! What has happened?
Let us kneel down in the mud, crawling along!
We leave it for them, for our younger Brother.
We shall grind the cycad nut, preparing the bread for them, for our Brother!   40
We shall whiten our hands with flour, for it is better that way . . .
With our hands we shall hold the grinding stone; we shall hang from our foreheads our bags of 'coffee' tree fibre, collecting foods . . .
We leave that ritual for them, for they want it that way.
Yes indeed, Sister, surely we shall whiten our hands with cycad flour, grasping the transverse fibre of our mat, our sacred shade.

Song 141

Yes Sister, new people have been born here.   1
Go open the *ngainmara*, putting it within the sacred shade . . .
Sit carefully, turning it so that the peak of the mat is uppermost:
We see the clansfolk within.
Yes indeed, carefully we flatten the mat, with its transverse fibre: 5
We hear the clansfolk within.
The Brother shortens his long foreskin, cutting it, thus, at the first notch of the penis . . .
Then he opens the Sisters' legs to let people out from within; he shortens their clitorises . . .
For the clitoris is like the transverse fibre of a mat, covering the vagina so no one may see, making it sacred like a younger sibling.
Go, look at the clansfolk, the men emerging . . .   10

233

Many men, emerging after the cutting of the clitoris: all the first
 born, and the third born . . .
Go, here are more: the second lot has come out, and now the
 last . . .
People flowing out, in their different clans: all these half-people,
 these *rangga* clansfolk . . .
Others come out more slowly, those *rangga* people, some of the
 people, belonging to many clans . . .

Song 142

Come, shorten the penis again, grasping the foreskin and cutting
 another notch . . .   1
For the smell from the Sisters' vaginae rests upon it, and it has
 been dragging along . . .
Quietly pull the penis, the *rangga*, from the mouth of the mat,
 from its transverse fibre, its inner peak . . .
Put these *rangga* people like younger siblings, covering them up so
 no one may see, making them sacred . . .
For, quietly, blood is flowing from the transverse fibre of the mat,
 from its inner peak . . .   5
Part the fringe of the mat, let them rest on the fringe at the mouth
 of the mat, the basket, as we open it . . .
For they come from far away, across the sea near the Spirit Country,
 from Bralgu, covered up so no one may see . . .
Go, let us look at this clan of *djuda*, putting their roots into the
 sacred *nara* shade . . .
Into the mouth of the shade, into the clearing.
They stand shining, quietly, solemnly tabu, with the feathered
 pendants upon them . . .   10

Song 143

Go, hang up our basket in the sacred shade.   1
Its feathered pendants shine, looking at the mouth of the shade.
They hang there, those sacred baskets, quietly, in tabu-ness, like
 parakeets clasping the *djuda rangga* . . .
Thus, they see the rising well water, splashing and foaming . . .
Waves splashing together, well water rising, pushing along the
 silt . . .   5
Water running strongly, like the incoming tide, roaring and
 spraying . . .

Carefully straighten the feathered strings, like yam creepers . . .
They were covered up within the inner peak of the mat, for these
   rangga strings are sacred.
For the foam came splashing up, staining them, far out at sea near
   the Spirit Country, the Place of the Mauwulan, the Place of the
   Sun . . .
Where we rested our paddles, dragging them through the sea,
   with our buttocks swaying . . .   10
From the sound of the Baijini folk, the smell of the sea . . .

Song 144

What is that crying? It is a parakeet nestling, perched on the sacred
   djuda tree.   1
Clasping the tree, cocking its head from side to side, crying softly:
It saw the rays of the sun sinking beyond Milingimbi:
Crying, it saw the warm red sunset, the red reflections in the
   clouds . . .
Saw the glare of the sun's glow, crying softly . . .   5
Perched on the *djuda* tree, clasping the limbs with its claws, moving
   down the branches . . .
It saw the red sun sinking, the spreading sunset.
Saw the sun going down in the west, beyond Milingimbi . . .
Looking at the sun, playing there in its rays like the *djuda* roots,
   at Maluwa . . .
Crying softly, looking at the peak of the mat, and the *djuda*:   10
Drying its breast feathers, its babies, in the warm rays of the
   sun . . .
Birds quietly, solemnly, watching the sinking sun:
They look at the mouth of the sacred basket, hanging there . . .
Always clasping the limbs of the *djuda*, tree, moving their claws.
We hear them within the mouth of the mat!   15
Crying out, the parakeets vanish within the mat, going deep within
   it so no one may see them . . .
They are covered up, like younger siblings, tabu, covered up for
   sleep . . .
The sacred pendants, the feathered strings . . .

Chapter Twenty

COMMENTS ON PART EIGHT OF THE SONGS

THIS section of the epic is concerned primarily with the loss of the sacred basket and *rangga* emblems by the Two Sisters; the men (that is, the Djanggawul Brother himself and the *galibingu* circumcision novices who had been removed from the Sisters: *vide* Song 115) subsequently take over the sacred *nara* ritual, which is performed in the same way as its modern counterpart.

Songs 129–38 mainly describe the Sisters' giving birth to *rangga* people, making wells, and so on. They serve as a preface to the latter part of the section, indicating that the Sisters still retain absolute authority over the manipulation of their *ngainmara* mat, the *djuda* and the *rangga*. In these songs the Djanggawul Brother (like Bralbral) must defer to his Sisters: 'Surely, I listen to your words, for you are my great leader: I always follow you . . . ' (Song 130, line 12).

The Two Women, however, make the mistake of going out to collect mangrove shells—an activity which at that time should, in theory, have been carried out by the men (although it is difficult for modern Aborigines to imagine such a reversal of their normal division of labour). The Sisters have kindled a fire in their *nara* shade, and hung from a tree the dilly bag (or baskets) containing the *rangga* emblems. While they are away, the men decide to steal these sacred objects; but about the same time a certain bird warms the Two Sisters. They rush back at once to their camp, to find that their possessions have been taken. Guessing from the footprints on the ground that the men are to blame, they hurry towards their shade; but as they draw close, they are stopped by the men's clapping sticks, and their calling out during the *nara* dancing. It is impossible for the Sisters to recover their emblems without fighting; they therefore relinquish their right to them, and the original rôles of the sexes are transposed. The men are to play an active and executive part in the rituals, the women's part being complementary and relatively passive. The Two Sisters do not seem to mind surrendering their sacred rights (*vide* Song 140), for they have really lost nothing (*vide* Chapter 3); and they soon become resigned to grinding cycad nuts and making bread.

Immediately after the men have taken over the sacred ritual, more people are born, and as a symbol of emancipation the Djanggawul Brother shortens his penis. That is to say, he has now, in reality, become an adult: he has been circumcised, severed his symbolic umbilical cord. He also shortens the clitoris of each Sister, emphasizing symbolically the fact that the *rangga* have been taken from them. Moreover, the male children who have come from the Sisters are circumcised, symbolically severing their association with the women. The song of the *lindaridj* parakeet brings this section to a close; and as the sun disappears in the west beyond Milingimbi the birds dive down into the sacred basket, or *ngainmara* mat.

Let us return, then, to the detail of the songs. In Song 129, the Djanggawul continue to walk about in the immediate vicinity of Marabai. The place names have already been mentioned in Part Seven (Chapter 18), and it will be recalled that Marabai is in Djambatpingu territory: Bulbulmara, its 'inside' name, means the muddy stains or streaks in the water. (That is, the ebbing tide takes with it a certain amount of silt; and these streaks in the water are said to represent drawings, as in the case of sacred designs painted on stringy bark sheets). Jiganjindu is its 'singing-inside' name; and Dambala a 'very inside' term.

The theme of this song is carried over from previous sections. The Two Sisters are pregnant, and are walking wearily along (line 7). The younger Sister feels sick and exhausted from swaying her buttocks and dilated belly, for she carries so many *rangga* people (line 11); they sit down, therefore, and make a *nara* shade (line 12), with its mouth (or entrance) facing the well at Marabai (line 13). They clear the shade of dirt, and make a mound that symbolizes the sacred sandhill at Port Bradshaw (line 15); then they proceed to 'plant' *djuda* trees (line 17). The reference in line 5 to dragging the *mauwulan* along the ground is symbolic, here as elsewhere, and may represent the elongated clitorises of the Sisters dragging along the ground (*vide* Chapter 2): the clitorises approximate *rangga*, and hence the *mauwulan*. In the same way the Djanggawul

Comments on Part Eight of the Songs

Brother dragged his penis along, with similar symbolic significance. The references in Part One of this epic to the Djanggawul dragging their paddles through the sea on the way from Bralgu (*vide*, for example, Song 132, line 9) may have the same intent, although in that case one may only speculate.

In Song 130 the Sisters make ready to give birth to the people (line 1). The Brother looks into one Sister's vagina and sees the people, within the transverse fibre: that is, beyond the clitoris, or beyond the dividing wall between uterus and vagina (line 2). She opens her legs and the *rangga* folk are removed one by one (line 3). The Djanggawul Brother clasps the head of the *mauwulan* and, after pulling hard, removes it, together with its many feathered strings—some of which are likened to yam creeper runners (line 4). This symbolizes the removal of a child. Immediately afterwards, more are taken out in the same way, and spread in a row. 'Yes, here is another: pull it hard, taking it out! We see within the many *rangga* clansfolk . . .' (lines 9 and 10). 'Yes indeed, *waridj* Miralaidj, we shall take out the *rangga*, the people!' (line 14).

In Song 131 the theme is continued, as *rangga* people are removed from the *ngainmara*: 'Go, open the mouth, parting the long strands of its fringe . . .' (line 2). The Brother puts his hand into his Sisters' vaginae (line 4) and grasps the *djuda*, carefully pulling them out. These *djuda* are 'planted' at Jiganjindu, as the sacred Djam-batpingu invocations are intoned (line 6), and they grow to trees. The song then recalls their original journey across the sea, and the foam which splashed upon the feathered pendants (lines 7–9). These are spread in the sun to dry (line 11), symbolizing umbilical cords of the people removed from the Sisters.

Song 132 is similar to the last. *Djuda* roots and *rangga* are put into the well, 'making' it (line 1), and they stand shining quietly as the 'bottom' Ngeimil *bugali* to the *djuda* are invoked (line 2). The well water rises and spreads across the country, and this recalls the sea through which the Djanggawul paddled from Bralgu. The feathered pendants are again drying in the sun (line 13).

Songs 133 and 134 are also similar. In the latter, the invocations (line 2) are Gwolamala, and refer to various parts of the *djuda*: to the tree itself, to the roots and branches, to the bark, to its forked limbs, and to its 'very inside' name. It is emphasized that the feathered strings have come from within the mat, the *nara* shade '. . . covered up, tabu, so no one may see . . .' (line 10).

Song 135 describes the putting in of more *djuda* roots and *rangga* (line 1), and the *bugali* are Dadawi. The well water rises, flows and becomes rough (line 7), and is compared to the sea far way towards the Spirit Land (line 9). In Song 136, the 'preface' part of this section is drawing to a close; all the *rangga* and *djuda* are erected, shining quietly in the sun (line 2), and the *bugali* intoned are Djambatpingu, principally to the *djuda* (lines 3 and 4). In Song 137 the sun sinks and the *lindaridj* parakeet is softly crying. The sun's rays spread over various places which have already been mentioned in Chapter 17, Song 128. 'The *djuda* trees stand there, shining, with the parakeets upon them . . . ' (line 8), like *djuda rangga* decorated with feathered pendants. Finally, as the sun sinks, the birds suddenly disappear, diving down into the sacred dilly bag (or basket), line 14.

The climax of this section opens with Song 138. The Two Sisters are walking along with their *mauwulan*, in search of mangrove shells. They have left their sacred basket containing the *rangga* emblems in the *nara* shade. This is the dilly bag with feathered pendants, and the ritual objects are those which were carried across the sea from Bralgu and removed from the Sisters' *ngainmara*. However, the Sisters' *ngainmara* is (or are) still intact, and they are pregnant. Near the hanging basket they have made a fire by twirling two sticks together (line 4), and in the coals of this they intend later to roast their shells. As they leave the basket hanging on the tree, its feathered pendants shine in the sun, and the handle appears to represent a parakeet clasping the limb of a tree with its claws (line 8). The Sisters continue to collect mangrove shells, which they put into their *ngainmara* and make sacred (line 12). The younger Sister always defers to the elder: that is, the younger asks a question, and the elder replies (for example, line 11). They find a periwinkle (a black *dugarei* shell), and this too is placed into the mat as a sacred object (line 17). Line 18 reverts to the sacred bag hanging on the tree by the *nara* shade: 'Covered up in the basket, hanging up on the clay-pan tree . . . ' Aborigines translating the songs were uncertain as to whether this referred to the shells' being covered up in the sacred bag—for they had been declared sacred. However, we have been told that the Sisters left the sacred bag hanging near the fire, being themselves some distance away. In a traditional song of this type such misunderstandings do frequently occur, being rationalized by singers and audience alike: space, time and sequence are of secondary consideration. It is possible that the Sisters plan to put the shells, on their return, into the sacred basket. On the other hand, the basket mentioned in line 18 could be the *ngainmara* (sacred uterus) carried by each Sister, or the ordinary bag used for storing shells which are being collected. The first two assumptions, taken either separately or conjointly, seem to be more in keeping with the context.

The sacred basket 'shines there quietly, solemnly, beside the water' (line 19): that is, it is quiet, because it is near the well of

Comments on Part Eight of the Songs

Marabai. 'We are making that Dreaming, for us' (line 20): the word used for 'Dreaming' is *wongar*, a concept which has already been discussed in Chapter 3. Here it relates to the mangrove shells which, through their association with the Djanggawul Sisters and their being covered up within the *ngainmara* or sacred basket and made sacred, have here been declared totemic.

In Song 139, the Djanggawul Sisters continue to collect shells; they find a conically shaped *wau'lauwun* shell (line 2), and this too is put into their mat, as sacred. All these shells are gathered from the mud around the large well at Jiganjindu (line 4), where they have been lying '. . . quietly shining, solemnly tabu . . .' (line 5); in this respect they are compared to the sacred *rangga* which, after ritual use, are put back into the mud at the sacred well. The phrase, '. . . for they were made in the sacred well water, which covered them' (line 6) means that the shells have grown there, having sprung from within the sacred well itself.

Continuing, the Sisters find a *nundu* (line 8), a short conical shell with rounded end. This too they put into the peak of the mat (line 9) and made tabu (line 10). They now lift up the mat, and holding it under one arm, ram the shells down to make room for more (line 11). Now they rest wearily for a while, leaning on their *mauwulan* (line 13); but the cry of a *djunmal* 'message' bird warns them that something has happened to the sacred basket which they left hanging near the *nara* shade (line 17). The younger Sister suggests that the bird may be crying only because it sees the incoming tide (line 16); 'she is thinking that way', Aborigines explain. But the elder Sister is troubled. She knows the reputation of this bird, and fears that the glowing coals of the fire they left burning (*vide* Song 138, lines 4 and 5) may have flared up, and burnt their sacred basket (line 17). They decide to return to their shade to see what has happened (line 19). The elder Sister calls the younger *jugujugu*, for this word means either younger sister or younger brother, and may be used as an ordinary kinship term as well as in reference to the concept of sacredness (as we have treated it elsewhere).

Song 140 presents the picture of the Two Sisters hurrying along towards their *nara* shade, carrying under one arm their mat full of shells (line 2). They are anxious about their sacred basket, for the long warning cry of the *djunmal* bird has alarmed them (line 4). As they approach their camp, the young Sister runs ahead to look for the bag, but it is gone. 'There is nothing here, Sister!' (line 7) she calls back. They cannot understand it: '. . . But we left the sacred basket hanging here! Only the tree, the claypan tree, is standing alone!' (lines 7 and 8). In line 7 the Sisters use the word *ngug gwoijumum*, meaning 'bag (or basket) hanging up': they employ this for the basket or dilly bag, when they do not want to utter the sacred terms. Aborigines comment: 'You couldn't say the dilly bag's name, so you have to use this word. You couldn't call its name in front of anyone.' That is, the Sisters use this word because they think the men are listening to them. They are astonished to find only the tree standing there, with no basket hanging from it. They both rush down towards their sacred shade to look at the fire, for the basket may have fallen there (lines 9–12): but they can see nothing (line 13).

Then the Sisters, looking about, see the tracks of the Brother Djanggawul and the *galibingu* novices (line 14): 'We must ask the others . . . They may have taken it from us!' They pour out their shells on to the fire (line 15). The word *djulu'juwon*, used in this line, has been explained by Aborigines as meaning 'they (the Two Sisters) would like to ask the men for their basket—but they don't': this infers that the women already realize that their basket has been stolen. 'Why do they take the sacred basket from us, leaving only the shells?' the Sisters ask each other (line 16). They leave their shells roasting and go in search of the basket, walking towards the men's shade.

They are aware now, of what has happened: 'Why do they take it from us in stealth, like children playing?' (line 19): the word used here is *wagaljuwonngaidj*, 'playing with (it)'. The women regard the men as children, who are irresponsible, and have not yet learnt the real significance of ritual objects: children can hardly be blamed for doing something of which they do not understand the consequences, and which would normally be reprehensible in an adult! The Sisters, therefore, are not really angry, and are ready to be tolerant. They walk quickly towards the men, planning to recover the basket and its contents without argument. ' . . . Why do they act like children, playing? Why didn't they ask us? Why did they do it? They came sneaking along and stole our basket, quietly, without asking!' (lines 21–23). As the Sisters walk along their tolerance is turning to annoyance. They feel, Aborigines explain, that 'their Brother should have known better. If he had wanted it, why didn't he approach them, instead of stealing what was rightfully theirs'. Now they see the sacred bag hanging from the men's shade (line 24). 'It is there, Sister, indeed!' (line 25) they cry to each other, hurrying forward.

In the meantime, the Djanggawul Brother and his companions have aquired the sacred basket: they have stolen the sacred power from the women, and possession of this basket and its contents supplies them with the incentive to perform actively the *nara* rituals which were before solely controlled and organized by the Two Sisters. Seeing the women hurrying towards them, the Brother speaks to the *galibingu*: 'Get the clapping sticks!' (line 27). He hopes that by the rhythmic beating and singing, he will stop the Sisters; but they continue to draw closer, intent on recovering their sacred basket and its contents. The resonant sound of the men's beating '. . . echoes from the mouth of the shade . . .' (line 28), for they are singing from the symbolic sandhill within the clearing of the *nara* shade (line 29), prior to commencing the *nara*, re-enacting in ritual the great journey across the sea from Bralgu. The first is the *murijuwon*, 'making a roaring sound', which symbolizes the roar of the sea, and of the surf beating on the beach at Port Bradshaw when the Djanggawul disembarked from their bark canoe. (This is the opening ceremony of the *dua nara* to-day; the postulants move down the ground dragging spearthrowers or sticks, sometimes *rangga*, on the ground, making the sound *um! um!*—the noise of the sea.) The second is the *gwulawungan*, meaning the sound of waves breaking. (In the *nara* to-day, postulants stand still and exclaim *a! a!*) The third is the *gurlga-jigalarangan*, 'spray coming up from the water', or, more literally, 'spray like ejaculating penis'. This is a continuation of the preceding two, with the waves breaking and spraying. (In the *nara* ritual dancing, this is symbolized by postulants moving their arms upwards.)

The men continue to sing and clap their sticks; but the Sisters are still coming closer. The men beat the sticks faster and more loudly (line 32) and continue with their ritual. They 'take part for water' (that is, *jagarma-gwulawungan*), singing about the sea, and the rising spring water at the onset of the monsoonal period: *gwulawong* used here is a form of the word *gwulawungan* mentioned above. They dance the *jambarwongangia*, the 'sound of the sea spreading out', and end with the *gurlga-jigalarangan* (above). All the *rangga* people, the *galibingu*, are there, but they do not take the initiative; the Djanggawul Brother is leading them (line 27). 'They are drawing near! Let them hear the beating sticks, so that they slacken their pace . . .' (line 35): the word used here is *ngibalijuldun* or *rumbrumbdun*, that is, to 'walk along, closing one's knees so that one may not go too quickly'. The Sisters approach more slowly, and pause to listen.

Immediately, the song treats the Sisters as if they are definitely excluded from what is now the male part of the *nara* rituals. The men have the basket and its contents, and this is said to be all they require. Line 36 declares that it is much better for women to grind (or pound) the cycad palm nuts to make damper (for this is the staple food eaten by the men at *nara* ceremonies, and is now always prepared by women). The Two Sisters 'change': no longer are they the custodians of the sacred ritual. They comply with the wishes of the men, saying to themselves: 'It is better that we should do this; we shall let the men have our sacred basket, and the *rangga* within it'. Before, the men had no sacred emblems and no basket. It was they who ground the cycad nuts to make 'bread', and collected food for the women; they looked after the children, whom in one version they are said to have suckled. Now, the position has been reversed. Men have gained control of the executive powers, while women are to attend to the children and collect vegetable foods. However, the true sacred power of the women is unalterable, for it is fundamental, and biologically based; and it is that theme which pervades the *dua nara* religious cult. The women's hands will now be whitened as they grind the cycad nut to 'flour', for ' . . . it is better that way!' (line 36). In the same line the words *gadan gong* (grasp hand) is inserted. This could, literally, refer to the hand grasping the cycad nut and the grinding stone, to pound it up for flour, but it is explained by Aborigines to mean that the elder Sister, with her hand, restrains the younger: they will not go near the men, who are singing and dancing, but will remain some distance away. The Sisters comment, according to informants: 'It is better this way; it is better that our hands be whitened with flour' (*nga buga njina dugan*, 'stay back at the camp'—that is, not to come to the sacred shade).

Line 38 reads: 'Let us kneel down in the mud, crawling along!' (that is, *galgian dambal gauwul*, meaning, to come close, lower oneself, or to fall on to this ground). They have heard the men's beating sticks, and so they crawl, closing their eyes in reverence. It is important to repeat here that the Two Sisters are kneeling and crawling *not* because of the men, but *because of the sacred power now manipulated by* the men. This is a point made clearly by the Aborigines themselves. The women now ' . . . leave it for them, for our younger Brother' (line 39), which is a general rendering of 'leave it (or, let it remain) 'straight' for younger brother(s)'; *galag nguwarlgangmana* means more 'that it is "good" for them', rather than 'straight' for them (*dunabaijima*), as it was translated by informants. The Sisters say, in effect: 'We leave it to the men. They may now take the more active part in the *nara* rituals: for their dancing and singing cannot damage our prestige or our inherent power. (That is to say, our biological function, symbolically rendered in ritual, is not transferable to the male sex.)' Lines 41–3 emphasize the changed situation: the women must collect and grind cycad nuts, and find vegetable foods for the community. For this purpose each Sister suspends the cord of a net bag from her forehead, so that it falls at her back. Such net bags are made from the bark of the wild coffee tree, the fibre of which is teased and softened before being formed into twine. Symbolically, then, the Djanggawul Sisters decide to carry out the conventional activities of Aboriginal women in that area to-day. 'We leave that ritual for them (the men), for they want it that way' (line 43). The final line (44) indicates that although the men have taken the executive control into their own hands, women still have a vital share in the sacred life, even apart from the organized participation: '. . . we shall whiten our hands with cycad flour, grasping the transverse fibre of our mat, our sacred shade'; the *ngainmara*, the shade, is still the symbolic uterus, in spite of anything that the men may do.

Song 141 opens with 'new people' (line 1), the 'new generation', being born from the Sisters. These are 'Djambatpingu Djanggawul', born at Marabai, where the sacred bag was stolen from the Women. Although the Sisters have been deprived of their basket, their *ngainmara* mat is intact, and is put into the sacred shade (line 2). Moreover, although women have lost their power to control the performance of ritual, conditions (according to the Songs: for example, 141 *et seq.*) seem virtually unchanged. The Sisters' loss is indeed more symbolic than actual, and has specific relevance to contemporary society only when an explanation is sought of man's executive rôle on the ceremonial ground.

The Sisters take up their usual position (line 3), in readiness for giving birth; the Brother peers into their uteri, in which he can see (line 4) and hear (line 6) clansfolk. At this juncture, he decides to shorten his elongated penis (line 7), cutting it 'half-way' at the first notch (*vide* Chapter 2, in the Djanggawul Myth). His elongated penis is described in the original text, not merely by the more usual words, but also by the term *dabi* (foreskin), the significance of which has been discussed in Chapter 16. This symbolizes the Brother's abandonment of his former status and his assumption of ritual powers. It is equivalent to circumcision; the novice has his foreskin cut—he has severed his umbilical connexion with the mother, and is reborn. It is for this reason that the Djanggawul Brother's long penis is referred to by the term *dabi*.

In the following line (8) the Brother opens his Sisters' legs ' . . . to let people out from within; he shortens their clitorises . . .' This is done to signify their new status, and in imitation of his own cutting. The reason given in the song is 'For the clitoris is like the transverse fibre of a mat, covering the vagina so no one may see, making it sacred like a younger sibling . . .' (line 9). The clitoris is thus likened to the transverse fibre of the *ngainmara* mat; just as

Comments on Part Eight of the Songs

the transverse fibre 'blocks' or 'hides' the interior of the mat or basket (that is, a *rangga* object may be caught upon it, when being removed), the long clitoris always 'hides' (or covers) each Sister's vagina. (The 'arm-band' separating the vagina and uterus is also described as the 'transverse fibre of the mat', hiding the entrance to the uterus: *vide* Chapter 16.) So long are the clitorises of the Two Sisters (*vide* Chapter 2) that they conceal the entrance to the vagina; and in order to look within (line 4), to copulate, or to remove the *rangga* people, the Brother finds it necessary to hold the clitoris up and to one side. Aborigines declare that the clitorises were cut simply because they hid the vulvae. Men, they say, like to see a woman's vulva aperture; when they look at the vulva, fringed by the labia majora, they exclaim (as did the Djanggawul Brother): 'Ah, that's good! It's right for us to see this, and it's right for them!' 'For the long clitorises were just like penes.'

There are, however, two other reasons for this cutting. In the first place the women controlled all sacred ritual: they were like men to-day with penes: the penis symbolized the state of manhood, just as did the long clitoris. When this was cut they became correspondingly more feminine, according to the modern Aborigines' conception of the difference between 'maleness' and 'femaleness' as manifested in conventional behaviour. On the other hand, an interesting point is revealed by the words used in the latter part of line 9 (interlinear literal translation: 'because transverse fibre make (or made) covered up "so no one may see" make (or made) sacred make (or made) like younger sibling'). The Djanggawul Sisters have yielded their sacred emblems and dilly bag to the men (Song 140), and because they no longer take the dominant rôle in the rituals, they may be cut; before, this could not be done. That is to say, the elongated clitoris covered up the vulva, like the transverse fibre of the mat (or basket), and *rangga* were hidden within it (in the uterus). We may recall the many references to parting or pushing aside the fringe of the *ngainmara* mat (symbolizing the Sisters' pubic hair or clitorises). Having lost the basket and the *rangga*, the women have nothing to hide: the clitoris no longer needs to hide the vulva and hence the uterus (*ngainmara*), and may, therefore, be cut. Thus the women lose not only the penis symbol (the *rangga*), but the 'penis' (clitoris) as well.

Lines 10–14 tell of the emergence of men (male children) from the Sisters' wombs. People flow from the vulvae, no longer impeded by the obstructing clitorises; they come out singly or in groups, and are known by various special terms. The *mulalin* are those men who came out immediately after the clitoris cutting: the *balwaidjan* and *gundang-ngurun* are the first born; the *malei-jambarbarma* are the second born; the *jalwaidnga* are the third born and the *malaidjam* the last born. Many 'inside' and 'singing' terms are used in reference to them, and refer to the numbers of people removed; but all in this song are male (*vide* Song 115). In line 13 the compound word *gurlgai-jigalangarauwul* is translated as 'all coming out', that is, 'all flow out when the Sisters open their legs'. The word *gurlga* has been mentioned before, and has a variety of associated meanings depending on the context, and upon the words or particles attached to it: its significance of penis, *djuda* root, sun's ray, and so on, has already been noted.

In Song 142 the Djanggawul Brother shortens his penis by another notch (line 1); the significance is the same as in the preceding song, and penis is again referred to by the term used for foreskin. In line 2 however, a new theme is introduced, 'For the smell from the Sisters' vaginae rests upon it, and it has been dragging along.' The words used here are '*budjei-ngoija-ngarauwul budjei-warijundauwul*' (smell from vaginae lies on it, smell from vaginae drags along or pulls). The word *budjei* (or *budju*) has already been briefly discussed (*vide* Chapter 14, Comments to Part Five, Song 77, and Chapter 16, Comments to Part Six, Song 115). Here it means that the vaginal juices and semen adhere to the Djanggawul Brother's elongated penis, because he has had coitus with his Sisters; the severed part of the penis (or foreskin) retains this smell. The length of cut penis will become a *rangga* pole; and this 'smell' is symbolic of the salty sea smell left by the splashing foam on the way across from Bralgu. 'Smell from vaginae drags along' means that before his long penis was foreshortened the Djanggawul Brother used to drag it along, with this smell upon it (*vide* many references to *rangga* poles stained with foam that had splashed upon them, and the smell of the sea). In line 3 of the same song, 'Quietly pull the penis, the *rangga*, from the mouth of the mat, from its transverse fibre, from its inner peak . . .' means that after completing the sexual act, the Djanggawul Brother withdraws his penis from the mouth of the mat (the vulva), from the transverse fibre (from the obstruction of the long clitoris, or the juncture between vagina and uterus), from the inner peak of the mat (the uterus). The word used for 'pull out penis' is *budju-warijuwa* (*cf.* above) and means the pulling of the penis before it has been cut to remove the smell (*budju*).

Aborigines say that this line refers not only to coitus but also, symbolically, to the *galibingu* men who have come from the Sisters' uteri (*vide* Song 141, lines 10–14): they come from the mouth of the *ngainmara*, and they are cut immediately afterwards (*vide* Song 115). This theme is extended in the next line (4): 'Put these *rangga* people like younger siblings, covering them up . . . ' Line 5 reads: 'For, quietly, blood is flowing from the transverse fibre of the mat, from its inner peak'; that is, the 'blood flows from the Sisters, as from the 'little children' (people or males—the *galibingu*) removed from them'. When the boys' foreskins are cut the blood flows, and this is likened to afterbirth blood[1] (the umbilical cord of a newly born child is severed, as its mother's afterbirth blood flows). Conversely, the severed foreskin of the novice is identified with the severed (or foreshortened) clitoris of either Djanggawul Sister, and the flowing blood from the penis represents the blood emerging from the Sisters' genitalia. The people who have been circumcised are now put within the sacred *nara* shade (line 8): they are treated as *rangga*. There they ' . . . stand shining, quietly, solemnly tabu; with the feathered pendants upon them . . . ' (line 10). The song thus reverts to their *rangga* quality.

Song 143 relates to the sacred basket which has been seized by the Djanggawul Brother and the *galibingu*. It is hanging within the men's *nara* shade (line 1), its feathered pendants shining in the sun (line 2). It now appears that there are several of these baskets, which hang from the *rangga* like parakeets clasping a *djuda* tree (line 3). At the same time the well water is rising, and is compared to the incoming tide (line 6). The feathered pendants are straightened and likened to the yam creepers (line 7); and it is emphasized that they come from within the *ngainmara*: ' . . . for these *rangga* strings are sacred' (line 8).

Song 144 brings this important section to a close in the conventional way. A parakeet nestling, perched on the *djuda* tree, is crying (line 1); and this refers back to Song 143, line 3. These birds are watching the sun disappear over or behind various places already mentioned in (for example) Song 137. 'They look at the mouth of the sacred basket, hanging there' (line 13); that is, as it hangs in the *nara* shade (*vide* Song 143). Line 14, 'Always clasping the limbs of the *djuda* tree, moving their claws' also refers back to Song 143, line 3. 'We hear them within the mouth of the mat!' (line 15): the term mat has been substituted for basket, the one being virtually synonymous with the other, and both symbolizing the uterus (*cf.* Song 142, line 6). Then, suddenly, the parakeets disappear into the mat to sleep and can be seen no longer (lines 16–17); now, in their *rangga* sense, they are feathered strands (line 18), like those in Song 143, line 8.

[1] As mentioned elsewhere, the *nara* rituals do not to-day, even if they did in the past, sponsor circumcision. This is left to the *djunggawon* ceremonies, where there the blood flowing from newly cut novices symbolizes the menstrual and afterbirth flow of the Wauwalak Sisters (*vide* R. Berndt, *Kunapipi*, 1951).

Comments on Part Eight of the Songs

The underlying theme of the Cycle has been adhered to, and the various threads being woven into the developing pattern may be traced symbolically from the preceding song sections. It is this complex patterning of the symbolism which heightens the beauty of these songs, and with its subtle overtones and elaborations lends added significance to the simplicity of the basic theme.

Chapter Twenty-one

THE DJANGGAWUL SONG CYCLE

PART NINE

The Djanggawul reach Dulmulwondeinbi, where the clitoris of each Sister is again shortened. More children are born. The Brother has coitus with his young Sister, who has an arm-band within her; the breaking of this causes blood to flow. Dancing follows.

Song 145

WE walk along with the aid of the *mauwulan*, making country; Bildjiwuraroiju plunges in the *mauwulan* point . . .   1
Carefully part the fringe of the mat: lift up from within all the *rangga* clansfolk . . .
Carefully lifting our laden basket . . .
Have you finished, Sister? Yes, indeed, somewhere we shall make country.
With hips swaying, our bodies moving, we go along, Bildjiwura-roiju.   5
Our bodies are shadowed by spreading clouds, passing quickly across the sky:
Carefully, with hips swaying, we walk along with the aid of the *mauwulan*, plunging it in, and dragging it . . .
Our heads are grey, from the foam that splashed us on our way from Bralgu, from the shine of the Morning Star . . .
Foam splashing as we rested our paddles, dragging them through the sea, near the Spirit Country, the Place of the Sun, the Place of the Mauwulan . . .
Shall we put them in?   10

Yes, Sister, indeed. Go, put in the *djuda* roots, with the *mauwulan* point!
Yes, it is done. Now put in more *djuda*, straightening them . . .
We saw the well water rising, surging up.
Yes, go, hang up the sacred baskets, so their feathered pendants shine, quietly, sacredly like younger siblings . . .
Straighten up the pendants, the feathered strings . . .   15
Pendants hang from the sacred arm-bands, shining, like yam creepers . . .
Straighten the gleaming feathered strings, thus, so that they lead into the well at Dulmulwondeinbi . . .
Yes, straighten out others, thus, so they look back towards Jiganjindu, Bulbulmara, towards Dambala and Marabai.
Let them look back towards Damijaga well!
Covering them up, for they are very sacred, made by the water!   20
We cover them up within the mud, dragging the mud . . .
Hang up another basket on the boughs within the mouth of the sacred shade . . .
Carefully, shining as they hang, quietly, covered with foam from the Place of the Mauwulan . . .
Splashed with foam from far away, across the sea from the Spirit Country . . .
From far away, from the shine of the Morning Star, the sound of the Baijini, the smell of the sea . . .   25
From within the peak of the sacred mat, within its transverse fibre, within its mouth . . .
Here is another basket! Come, put in the *mauwulan* point!
They shine as they hang on the branches above the clearing, the *nara* shade . . .
Those are very sacred, like younger siblings, covered up so no one may see . . .
They come from the peak of the mat, from its transverse fibre, from within the fringe of the mat . . .   30
Carefully straighten them, dragging the mud, the well water . . .
They saw the well water rising, bubbling and splashing:
Water flowing strongly, roaring, with waves splashing together . . .
Yes, here is another, Sister, shining quietly here in the shade:
Hanging quietly, like a younger sibling.   35
These are tabu for us: they are very sacred. They come from within the inner peak of the mat . . .

Song 146

Hang up another basket! Let them shine quietly there, in tabuness: 1

Covering them up, for they are very sacred, shining quietly
there . . .
Plunge in the *mauwulan* point!
They see the water, shining there at the well:
Water rising up, splashing and roaring, flowing strongly . . .   5
Foam spraying up, pushing along the silt: waves splashing
together . . .
Carefully straighten the pendants, the feathered strings . . .
For they are stained with foam from Bralgu, the Spirit Country . . .
From our canoe, Birubira, travelling across the sea from the Spirit
Country, from the shine of the Morning Star . . .
Stained from the splashing foam . . .   10
Carefully, straighten the feathered pendants!
We rested our paddles, dragging them through the sea, near the
sound of the Baijini, the smell of the sea, at the Place of the
Mauwulan.

Song 147

Waridj, here is a *djuda rangga*!   1
Come, let us plant the *djuda* roots, making a well, calling the
invocations . . .
Put in the *djuda* roots, the *rangga*, invoking the sacred names . . .
They stand, shining quietly, solemnly tabu . . .
They see the water at Jiganjindu, at Marabai, at Bulbulmara,
Dambala, Dulmulwondeinbi.   5
Carefully drag the mud and grass, there at the well!
Yes, it is done, Sister: I am listening to your words. You are my
great leader, and I always follow you.
Carefully, let them see the water rising, roaring up with foam and
spraying, pushing along the silt . . .
Roaring like the high tide rising and spraying, mixed with mud . . .

Song 148

Pull out another, carefully, from the mouth of the mat, parting
its fringe.   1
Yes, it is done, Sister. Come, carefully pull out the feathered strings,
for they may be caught on the transverse fibre of the mat . . .
Yes, it is done: they are straightened!
Come, let us put the *djuda* roots there into the well, making a well.
Let them stand quietly there.
Yes, it is done: indeed, they are straightened! We call the invoca-
tions . . .   5

Carefully plunge the *djuda* into the well, dragging the mud.
Yes, it is done, Sister. You are my leader, I always follow you;
   I listen to your words . . .
For the foam splashed up and stained them, far out at sea near the
   Spirit Country . . .
Foam splashing up, as carefully we rested our paddles, dragging
   them through the sea, swaying our buttocks.

Song 149

Undo the mouth of the other mat, parting its fringe: 1
Go, put in your hand, grasping the sacred *djuda*, the *mauwulan*
   rangga.
Yes, I am grasping them now.
Come, pull out the feathered strings, carefully straighten them.
How is that: have you pulled them strongly? Yes go, put the *djuda*
   roots into the well, carefully, making the well . . .   5
They stand shining quietly, solemnly tabu, as we call the invoca-
   tions . . .
Put in the *djuda* roots, invoking the sacred names . . .
They see the water at Marabai, at Bulbulmara, at Jiganjindu, Dam-
   bala, Dulwondeinbi.
Carefully drag the mud, through the well, dragging the grass.
Yes, it is done: they are straightened!   10
For they come from within the transverse fibre of the sacred mat,
   covered up so no one may see.

Song 150

Pull out another *djuda*! We put the roots into the well, making the
   well: 1
Carefully straighten them. Yes, go, put in the *djuda* roots, the *rangga*,
   as we call the invocations . . .
Carefully drag the mud and the grass, invoking the sacred names . . .
They stand shining quietly, solemnly . . .
For they come from the transverse fibre of the mat, from its mouth,
   from its inner peak . . .   5
Covered up, for they are very sacred, tabu: from within the transverse fibre, the mouth of the mat.
Seeing the water from the mat, the sacred shade: foam splashing
   up at Jiganjindu, at Bulbulmara, at Marabai, Dambala, Djumbulwara.

Splashed by the surging water, roaring up . . .
Rough water spraying, waves splashing together, pushing along
the silt and flowing strongly . . .

Song 151

Pulling out another *djuda* from the inner peak of the mat, pulling
it carefully.   1
What, are the feathered strings caught up? We call the invocations . . .
They stand, shining quietly, as we invoke the sacred names . . .
Carefully, straighten out the feathered strings:
For the foam has stained them, splashing up from the sea away
near the Spirit Country, the Place of the Mauwulan, the Place
of the Sun . . .   5
Carefully, let them see the well water rising and spraying, with waves
splashing together . . .
Pushing along the silt, flowing strongly, rising and roaring in like
the high tide . . .
Fresh and salt water mingling, as the feathered pendants stand
quietly shining . . .

Song 152

Pull out another *djuda*, carefully, turning over the feathered arm-band
pendants: 1
Go, put the *rangga* point, the *djuda* roots, into the well, making the
well, as we call the invocations . . .
They stand shining quietly, from within the peak, the mouth of
the mat, the sacred shade . . .
Carefully, arrange the pendants, the feathered strings . . .
They stand quietly, solemnly tabu . . .   5
For the splashing foam has stained them, away at sea near the
Place of the Sun, the Place of the Mauwulan: near the sound of
the Baijini, the smell of the sea . . .
Straighten the great *djuda*, with the sacred *djanda* goanna-fat name:
Covered up, from within the mouth of the mat, its inner peak:
from the transverse fibre, from the parted fringe of the mat;
for it is tabu.

Song 153

Pull out another, strongly, putting it here, towards us: 1
Come, pull it out! We put in the *rangga* point, the *djuda*, straightening
it in the well, looking towards Jiganjindu, and Bulbulmara.

Go, put in the *rangga* point, the *djuda* roots! Is it done?
Yes, straighten the *djuda*, dragging the mud: well water rises,
     pushing aside the grass, as we call the invocations . . .
They stand shining quietly, as we invoke the sacred names . . .   5
They see the well water rising and roaring, waves splashing to-
     gether . . .
Surging up, splashing, as water flows in at high tide, pushing the
     silt along . . .
Yes, carefully, for they are stained with foam that splashed them as,
     with swaying buttocks, we dragged our paddles: out at sea near
     the Spirit Land, the Place of the Sun, the Place of the Mauwu-
     lan . . .

Song 154

Pull out another *djuda*, grasping the *mauwulan*, and the arm-band
     pendants!   1
Come, put in the point, put in the *djuda* roots, making a well . . .
The *djuda* stand quietly shining, as we call the invocations . . .
Carefully drag them through the mud, invoking their sacred names.
They see the well water rising at Dulmulwondeinbi, at Marabai, at
     Dambala, Bulbulmara: 5
Carefully arrange the pendants, the feathered strands . . .
Straighten out another, so that it leads to Bunjinang.
How is that? Yes, it is done. Carefully, we arrange the strings . . .
Carefully, they were covered up like younger siblings, sacred in
     their tabu-ness, within the transverse fibre of the mat, the sacred
     shade . . '

Song 155

Pull out another, grasping firmly the sacred *rangga*:   1
Yes, go, turn it over and straighten it.
Go, put the *djuda* roots into the well, making the well:
Carefully straighten it, so that it stands erect, thus, *djuda* from
     Bunjinang!
Yes, for we call the sacred invocations . . .   5
Yes, Sister, thus: let them see the water at Marabai, at Dulmul-
     wondeinbi, Jiganjindu, at Dambala, Bulbulmara, Gwoijaring:
Rising and surging up, foam splashing up like the high tide . . .
Hearing the roar of the water, for they come from the mouth of the
     sacred mat, from its inner peak, covered up in there like younger
     siblings . . .

The Djanggawul Song Cycle
Song 156

Pull out another *rangga*, another *djuda* . . .   1
Is it done? Yes, come, turn it over and straighten it there, so it
    may see the well.
Go, put in the *djuda* roots: carefully straighten them!
Is it done? Yes, we call the sacred *djuda* invocations . . .
They stand quietly shining, solemnly tabu; straighten them up!   5
Carefully drag the mud; yes, carefully drag the grass along, in the
    well . . .
They see the water, rising and roaring . . .
Foam spraying as the water surges, roaring, pushing along the
    silt . . .
For they come from the transverse fibre of the mat, from its inner
    peak, from parting the fringe at the mouth of the sacred mat,
    the sacred shade . . .

Song 157

What is that crying? It is a parakeet nestling crying softly, upon the
    djuda: 1
Crying softly, as it saw the warm rays of the sun in the west, at
    Djurabula.
Crying as it saw the sun, the long cry of the parakeet:
Drying its feathers in the rising heat of the sun . . .
Drying its red breast feathers, its nestlings. 'Ah, my children!
    (says the parakeet). My downy feathers!'   5
It clasps the tree, as feathered strings cling to the sacred *rangga* . . .
Clasping the *djuda* with its claws, moving along . . .
It saw the sun's rays and the red glow of the sunset:
'You, red clouds! You I saw reflected in the sacred *nara* shade,
    spreading from Milngurmuru, from Milngaidja.'
Crying, the birds vanish within the peak of the mat, and are covered
    up . . .   10

Song 158

Go, carefully flatten the mat and its transverse fibre; spread it firmly
    out on the ground, opening it wide . . .   1
Yes, go quickly, get a stone knife.
Where is the transverse fibre of the mat?
Lie down carefully, quietly, in the *nara* shade, resting your head
    as if in sleep on the *rangga* emblems:
In the sacred shade where we have made country, building the
    sandhill mound: 5

Go, carefully lie there with legs apart!
I shall cut the clitoris, and put more *rangga* people:
Is it done? Yes, come close to me for coitus!
What is that there, blocking me? There is something within the
    vagina; I must go carefully!
Yes, go, cut the clitoris . . .   10
Ah, go carefully! Be gentle!
The sound of my cry flies over to Dulmulwondeinbi. Be gentle!
Shall this one sound go over to Dambala?
Carefully they are dancing towards the sacred well, at Jiganjindu,
    Bulbulmara, Marabai:
For within the well we shall cover up the sacred severed clitoris,
    within the well at Jiganjindu.   15
Covered up, from within the mat, its transverse fibre, its inner peak . . .
Thus, turn over, into the warm caressing rays of the sun . . .
Open your legs to the healing warmth of the sun, labia minora
    glowing with redness, with blood, like the breast feathers of the
    parakeet!
We take hot coals from the wood of the claypan tree, heating a
    stone to dry the blood from the cut clitoris.
Covering up that clitoris within the mat, with its transverse fibre,
    making it like a younger sibling: 20
Reverently put it within the *ngainmara*, covering it up for sleeping.
For the *mauwulan* has been plunged in, all the way, dragging along;
    so carefully, dry the smell . . .

Song 159

Go, take that hot stone, and heat it near her clitoris: 1
For the severed part is a sacred *djuda rangga*. Covering up the clitoris
    within the mat, within its transverse fibre, within its mouth,
    its inner peak . . .
Go, the people are dancing there, like *djuda* roots, like spray, moving
    their bodies, shaking their hair!
Carefully they beat their clapping sticks on the *mauwulan* point . . .
Go, stand up! See the clansfolk beyond the transverse fibre of the
    mat!   5
They come from the Sister's womb, lifting aside the clitoris, coming
    out like *djuda* roots . . .
Into the sacred shade, the *rangga* folk come dancing from the inner
    peak of the mat . . .
Only a few people will be left here: some we shall put into the
    coarse grass.
We are putting the *rangga* clansfolk . . .

The Djanggawul Song Cycle
Song 160

Go, put out the *rangga*, making it big: open your legs, for you look
    nice!   1
Yes, take Miralaidj, my Sister. Yes, the mouth of the mat is closed.
Yes, go, rest there quietly, for the vagina is sacred, and the *rangga*
    are hidden there, like younger siblings, covered up so no one
    may see.
Thus, climb up, put it into the mouth of the mat!
What is this, blocking my penis? I rest above her, chest on her
    breasts!   5
Do not push hard! The sound of her cry echoes.
Covered up, so no one may see, like a younger sibling . . .
Do not move what is within, for it is sacred!
For it rests there within, like the transverse fibre of the mat.
Blood running, sacredly running!   10
Yes, they, the *rangga* clansfolk, are coming out like *djuda* roots, like
    spray . . .
Go, digging within, causing the blood to flow, sacred blood from
    the red vagina, that no one may see!
Very sacred stands the *rangga* penis!

Song 161

Hit your loins, so that blood flows into the mouth of the sacred
    shade: 1
Yes, go, cover up the blood which has fallen!
For yes, go, let the *rangga* people come out . . .
Put your foot on the navel, releasing the blood, pushing strongly
    and breaking up the clot, to let it flow . . .
Go, put your foot on the navel, carefully, so that the sacred blood
    may flow . . .   5
It is done. Yes, go, cover the fallen blood in here, dragging the
    mud in the well to cover it up . . .
Is it done? Yes, put her into the mouth of the shade, beneath the
    transverse fibre of the mat: she is tabu, like a younger sibling.
    Let her sleep there within, quietly, shining, like a younger
    sibling . . .
The sound of clapping sticks, tapping against the *rangga*!
She lies there quietly, moving her shoulders to the rhythm, lying
    in sacred tabu-ness . . .
The sound of the clapping sticks echoes within, the sound of
    singing . . .   10
For she is within the inner peak of the mat, the sacred shade!

The Djanggawul Song Cycle
Song 162

Go, stand up there in the sacred *nara* shade, in the sacred clear-
ing . . .   1
Go, stand up within, looking at the *rangga* clansfolk . . .
They come from the younger Sister, like *djuda* roots, like spray—
only a few of the people . . .
We put them aside, these *rangga* clansfolk . . .
Go, let the sacred children dance, swaying their hair from side to
side, gently swaying their bodies . . .   5
Here we have put only a few of the *rangga* people . . .
Some, presently, we shall put elsewhere, at Djiriliwuramaiju, at
Maluwa, at the Place of the Clapping Sticks . . .
We shall let out many people there in the west, at Magulmagul,
at Milngurmuru, Milngaidja . . .
There we shall put aside large numbers of *rangga* clansfolk . . .

Song 163

Go, put out the clansfolk, so that they see the well.   1
Let them come, thus, close to it. We are putting the different clans
into different places . . .
It is done! Yes, it is done!
Go, let them stand together, coming from within the transverse
fibre, the mouth of the mat . . .
Go, let them stand together, like fighting men from the west . . . 5
Stand in rows, like clouds blown up by the south wind, like fighting
men . . .
Yes, it is done. They move into the wells that they saw at Dulmul-
wondeinbi, Marabai, Gwoijaring, Jiganjindu, Bulbulmara, and
Dambala.
They stand there, for we have put out the *rangga* clansfolk, arranged
like fighting men . . .
They come from the transverse fibre of the mat, from the mouth of
the mat!
For the long clitoris has dragged on the ground, the protruding
clitoris . . .   10
Thus the people have come out from the parted labia majora . . .

Song 164

Go, let us put out more, standing with knees together, watching
the well water rising . . .   1

258

They stand like fighting men from the west, like clouds blown up
    by the south wind, standing together . . .
From within the sacred mat, from its transverse fibre, its parted
    fringe . . .
People coming out from within the parted labia majora, pushing
    aside the long clitoris . . .
From resting within the womb: pulling them out from the womb! 5
The long clitoris is cut, the clitoris smell removed, after dragging
    along . . .
Lying within the uterus!
Yes, it is done. What shall we do?
Let us go to the *nara* shade. Carefully rest our paddles, dragging them
    through the sea; dancing like the spray, the roar of the sea!
Dancing within the sacred clearing, beneath the upper branches,
    urged on by the leader facing the dancers . . .   10
Go, roar like the sea—from far away, from Bralgu; sound echoing
    through the shine of the Morning Star, away out to sea near the
    Spirit Country, where the rough waves play: all this we dance!

Song 165

Carefully we rest our paddles, dragging them through the sea; and
    we make the sandhills—the leader dancing in front!   1
Those from the mat move carefully from side to side, dancing the
    sound of the waves, the splashing surf:
Knees moving like waves splashing together, like surging waters!
The clansfolk, the sacred *rangga*, who came from within!
Carefully, dancing backwards and forwards like *djuda* roots, like
    spray, in the sacred shade . . .   5
Roar like the water, far out at sea near Bralgu!
Water rising and splashing—our spearthrowers shaking . . .
Water flowing strongly—we dance from side to side!
Roar, like the rising waves splashing together, foam coming up
    into the mouth of the mat.
Rangga clansfolk dancing, the *djanda* Goanna Tail *rangga*! Plunging in
    the *djuda*, the leader dancing in front: calling the invocations! 10
From within, the *rangga* clansfolk . . .

Song 166

Go, roar like the water!   1
Sister, we call out the sacred names for the water, roaring loudly!
Go, call out, roaring like the water from far away, from Bralgu,
    out at sea near the Spirit Country . . .

The Djanggawul Song Cycle

From the wide sea beyond Port Bradshaw, waves splashing to-
gether out at sea, near Bralgu . . .
Roaring and surging, foam rising and waves splashing together . . . 5
Carefully, roar like the sea, putting in the *djuda rangga* . . .
Put the *djuda* roots into the well, calling the invocations . . .
We put them into the well, making the well, at Djumbulwara, at
Marabai, at Bulbulmara, Jiganjindu, Gwoijaring, Dambala!
Carefully, led by the leader, putting the *djuda* into the mud, dragging
the mud . . .
Quietly they shine, covered up, for they are sacred . . .   10

Song 167

Go, roar again like the water, in dancing!   1
Water from far away, from the shine of the Morning Star, from the
Spirit Country, the Place of the Sun . . .
Carefully, roar from the sacred arm-band pendants, from the
growing *djuda*—shaking the spearthrowers!
Water flowing strongly, foam rising and splashing!
Go, put the *djuda* roots into the well, making the well at Bulbul-
mara: 5
Carefully put them into the mud, dragging the mud, covering them
up in the well at Djumbulwara.
Yes, it is done. They stand and grow, for we call the invoca-
tions . . .
Carefully straighten the pendants, the feathered strings, invoking
the sacred names . . .
Carefully, arrange the *djanda* Goanna Fat strings: they stand,
quietly shining . . .

Song 168

For the foam splashed up on them, staining them: 1
From far away near the Place of the Mauwulan, from the sea, near
the Spirit Country, the shine of the Morning Star . . .
From the sound of the Baijini, the smell of the sea . . .
Foam splashing up on them, staining them!
Carefully we rest our paddles, dragging them through the sea,
swaying our buttocks . . .   5
Thus, they see the well water at Marabai, Gwoijaring, Djumbulwara,
at Jiganjindu, Dambala, Bulbulmara!
Water rising and splashing, flowing strongly, spraying and roaring
up like the high tide . . .
The *djuda* are standing, quietly . . .

The Djanggawul Song Cycle

Song 169

Go, roar like the sea: carefully beat the clapping sticks . . .   1
Let them rest carefully on the *mauwulan rangga*: now seize them,
    clapping them hard!
Go, roar like the sea, putting the *djuda* roots into the ground . . .
Planting the *djuda* roots, firmly, calling the invocations . . .
Carefully put in the *djuda* roots, making the well at Jiganjindu, at
    Marabai, invoking the sacred names . . .   5
Carefully arrange the pendants, the feathered strings—goose and
    parakeet feathers, strings like yam creepers . . .
They are sacred, from within the peak of the mat, like younger
    siblings: covered up so no one may see, for they are tabu.

Song 170

Roar strongly again, like the water, splashing far out at sea, near
    Bralgu, the Spirit Country . . .   1
The wide sea near the Spirit Country . . .
Go, put the *djuda* roots, with the arm-band pendants, firmly into
    the well, making a well . . .
Yes, carefully put them into the mud, dragging and smoothing the
    mud in the well . . .
Yes, it is done. Go, put in the *djuda*, straighten them, calling the
    invocations . . .   5
They stand quietly, shining, as we call the invocations . . .
Carefully straighten the feathered strings, let them look back-
    wards . . .
They come from the transverse fibre of the mat, like younger
    siblings, covered up so no one may see: for they are sacred!

Song 171

Go, roar like the sea! Again we call from the sacred shade, where
    the *rangga* clansfolk are dancing . . .   1
Carefully paddle, with swaying buttocks, resting the paddles and
    dragging them . . .
Water coming up, from far away at the Place of the Sun, from the
    sea near the Spirit Country, the Place of the Mauwulan . . .
Go, put the *djuda* roots into the well, making a well, for we invoke
    their sacred names.
Carefully straighten them, as we call the invocations . . .   5

Carefully drag the mud around them, covering up the *rangga* heads
   in the well . . .
Carefully arrange the feathered strings, the feathered headdresses . . .
Carefully, from the transverse fibre of the mat, covered up like
   younger siblings, so no one may see.

Song 172

Go, roar again like the sea, carefully inserting the *djuda*:   1
Dance like the water, far away at Bralgu!
Gently paddle along, resting the paddles, dragging them through
   the sea . . .
Go, put in the *djuda*, and the *rangga* from within the peak of the
   mat . . .
Carefully roar like the sea from far away, at the shine of the Morning
   Star, away near the Spirit Country . . .   5
The leader holding the sacred mat, dancing within the shade, calling
   the invocations . . .
Carefully straighten the pendants, the feathered strings, covered
   up like younger siblings, so no one may see, in sacred tabu-
   ness . . .

Song 173

Go, roar again like the sea, like the splashing water . . .   1
The sea, far away at the Place of the Sun, near the Spirit Country,
   near the place of the Mauwulan . . .
Go, put in the *djuda* roots, with the arm-band pendants upon them . . .
They stand quietly as we invoke the sacred names, putting them in
   and making a well at Marabai . . .
Carefully, we call the sacred invocations . . .   5
Carefully, insert the *mauwulan rangga*, planting the *djuda*, calling the
   invocations . . .
Turn them, thus, so they see the water at Marabai, at Bulbulmara.
Straighten them up, the *djanda* Goanna *rangga* . . .
They come from the transverse fibre of the mat, from its inner peak,
   from its mouth, parting its fringe . . .

Song 174

What is that crying? It is a nestling, crying softly, as it saw the sun. 1
It is perched on the sacred *djuda* tree, clasping the *rangga* tree with
   its claws . . .

From the tree it looked at the rays of the sun, in the west beyond
   Milingimbi:
Saw the warm rays of the sun, the shining sun!
Drying itself, ruffling its feathers, its nestlings. 'Myself (says the
   bird), I am drying my red breast feathers, my babies!'   5
Parakeets, perched in a row on that *djuda* limb . . .
Crying softly, cocking their heads from side to side . . .
They saw the rays of the sun, and felt its heat . . .
Crying softly, they saw the mouth of the sacred basket . . .
Saw the sun, as they sat quietly, and solemnly: 10
Crying, they fly deep down within it, covered up like younger sib-
   lings, so no one may see.
'Myself (says the bird), I have red breast feathers, my nest-
   lings . . .'
It is done: they are asleep.

Chapter Twenty-two

COMMENTS ON PART NINE OF THE SONGS

W E are nearing the end of the Djanggawul epic. The sacred basket and the *rangga* emblems have been stolen from the Two Sisters, and the men now have their own *nara* shade. The Djanggawul continue to walk along, making country, until they reach Dulmulwondeinbi, at the other side of Marabai. The Sisters are still pregnant, and although they appear to manipulate the *rangga* emblems this is not really the case. As they go, the Djanggawul see the sacred basket hanging from the shade, and also insert *djuda rangga* into the wells.

Much of the first half of this section is a continuation and repetition of previous parts, particularly of Part Eight. It consolidates and emphasizes the basic theme of the epic, and serves as a preface to Songs 158–64, which concern the cutting of the younger Sister's clitoris and the emergence of the *rangga* folk. These songs indicate the meaning of the symbolism found in the preceding Parts, and reaffirm the origin of the people who were the ancestors of the present-day Aborigines. In Song 160 the Djanggawul Brother has coitus with his younger Sister. In the process he breaks an armband lodged within her, causing a flow of blood, which is declared sacred. There is some resemblance here to an important feature of the Wauwulak mythology.[1]

The *rangga* clansfolk have danced from the womb of the younger Sister, and stand in groups before entering the sacred *nara* shade. The final section of this Part (that is, Songs 165–74) indicates the

---

[1] *Vide* R. Berndt, *Kunapipi*; this element is treated also in a love song cycle known as the 'Goulburn Island Love Cycle'—*vide Love Songs of Arnhem Land,* a volume in preparation.

ritual significance of the preceding songs, and deals with their *nara* dancing, which symbolizes the Djanggawul's journey across the sea from Bralgu. It is performed under the direction of a leader— the Djanggawul Brother himself. These *rangga* people are the 'Sons of Djanggawul', just as male postulants to-day are the 'Sons of Djanggawul', and the ritual they observe is said to be the same in all details.

In Song 145, the Djanggawul continue their journey. The Sisters carry under one arm their *ngainmara* mat, full of *rangga* people (lines 2 and 3); that is to say, they are again pregnant. In line 4 we see that although the men have taken over the sacred rituals and the *rangga* emblems, they still defer to the Sisters. As the Djanggawul go on towards Dulmulwondeinbi they plant *djuda* trees (line 11), and plunge the point of their *mauwulan* into the ground so that water gushes forth (line 13). The sacred basket is hung up, its feathered pendants shining (line 14); within it arm-bands are hidden, but the pendants attached to them protrude and shine (line 16). The symbolic significance of these is seen in Song 160. The basket is the uterus (or vagina) of Miralaidj, and the arm-band hidden within is the sacred 'arm-band' which is broken by the Djanggawul Brother during coitus; the protruding feathered pendants represent alternatively flowing blood, or her clitoris. The treatment in this song suggests what will happen later. The feathered strings are so arranged that they lead towards various places, and in this context symbolize umbilical cords of the *rangga* folk who are presently to emerge. They are then covered up in the mud of the wells (line 21); that is, like *rangga* put into the water or mud after ritual use or, alternatively, covered within the uterus. In lines 28 and 34, baskets hang from the sacred shade; these, too, are associated with the Two Sisters, but are now in the possession of the men. Their feathers shine, but they still bear foam stains from their journey over the sea from Bralgu (line 24). They are very sacred.

Song 146 repeats this theme. The sacred basket hangs from the *nara* shade (line 1); the *mauwulan* is plunged into the ground, and a well is formed (line 3); the well waters rise (line 5), and are likened to the sea out from Bralgu (line 8). In line 9 we find the name of the canoe in which the Djanggawul came to the Arnhem Land mainland—Birubira. It was made of bark, sharply pointed at each end, unlike the bark canoes made in this area to-day, but resembling those at Goulburn Islands. The concluding part of the song (lines 8–12) again recalls their long journey from Bralgu, and serves as an introduction to the *nara* dancing of the *rangga* folk, mentioned in Songs 165–74.

Comments on Part Nine of the Songs

Song 147 concerns the planting of *djuda* and the making of a well (lines 1 and 2); the accompanying invocations are Djambatpingu, referring to the *djuda*. Line 7 is interpreted as the younger Sister speaking to the elder, deferring to her judgment. Again, when the *djuda* are inserted the well water rises, like the high tide (lines 8 and 9).

Song 148 describes the feathered pendants and strings being removed from the *ngainmara*. They are taken out carefully '. . . for they may be caught on the transverse fibre of the mat . . . ' (line 2); this refers to the arm-band as well as to the clitoris, both symbolized by the cross or transverse fibre. The *bugali* intoned are Djambatpingu, for the *djuda* and *ba'ralgi*. Again (line 7; as in Song 147, line 7) Bildjiwuraroiju is deferred to as the leader, although she and Miralaidj have lost their basket and *rangga*.

In Song 149 the *ngainmara* is opened, and the Brother inserts his hand to pull out the sacred *djuda* and *mauwulan* (line 2): he is removing *rangga* folk from his Sister's womb. The *djuda* are then put into the ground, forming a well (line 5). 'They stand shining quietly, solemnly tabu, as we call the invocations . . . ' (line 6); these are Dadawi, referring to the *djuda*.

Song 150 is much the same as this. Another *djuda* is removed, and its roots put into the well while the Djanggawul call various *bugali* associated with the 'bottom' Ngeimil. The sacred *rangga* shine, as the well water rises and splashes. Song 151 continues this theme, the invocations being Gwolamala for the *djuda* and feathered pendants. The feathered strings are arranged (line 4), and attention is drawn to the foam which stained them on the way from Bralgu (line 5). The well water rises, and so does the high tide from the sea; the two mingle together (*ngadaijunda*; line 8).

Song 152 too is largely the same: another *djuda* is pulled out (line 1); the *rangga* point is plunged into a well, and water gushes forth (line 2). The invocations are Riradjingu, for various parts of the *djuda*. The feathered pendants are arranged, and *rangga* are erected, with emphasis on the large Goanna Fat *rangga* (line 7). In Song 153 more *rangga* are removed and put upright in the well; the invocations are Ngeimil and Riradjingu, for the *djuda*, and the *djanda* goanna's vertebrae. More repetition occurs in Song 154, where the *bugali* are 'bottom' Karlpu, for various parts of the *djuda*. Bunjinang in line 7 is situated between Port Bradshaw and Caledon Bay, in Karlpu territory. In Song 155 another *djuda* is pulled out, and stood upright in the well (line 3); it is placed slightly aslant, but the Two Sisters say, 'You are not to put it sideways!' (line 4). The invocations are Karlpu, associated with the shark and *djuda*. Song 156 concerns sacred *rangga* and *djuda*, the last to be removed in this section. Djambatpingu *bugali* are intoned for the *djuda*; the *rangga* are erected, and stand shining; the water rises and the foam splashes: for all have come from within the sacred *ngainmara*. Then comes the conventional parakeet song (Song 157), which closes this section. The male birds call out as they finally enter the peak of the mat and are covered up within it.

Song 158 introduces the main features of this part. The first line refers symbolically to one of the Sisters, who is being arranged by her Brother in the sacred shade. A stone knife is obtained (line 2); and the Brother asks, referring to her clitoris, 'Where is the transverse fibre of the mat?' (line 3); the significance of this has already been mentioned in Part Eight, Chapter 20. The clitoris of each Sister had already been cut; but they were still much longer than those of women to-day. In this part, it is said, Miralaidj alone submits to this second operation. '. . . Lie down carefully, quietly, in the *nara* shade, resting your head as if in sleep on the *rangga* emblems:' (line 4)—the *rangga* stored in the shade serve as a pillow for her head. 'In the sacred shade where we have made country, building the sandhill mound,' (line 5) suggests that the Sisters have returned to their own shade from which they had been ousted by the men. It refers to all the country they have made, to the shade itself and its clearing, and to the symbolic sandhill at one side of the shade—the mound of earth, still seen on the *nara* ground, representing the sacred sandhill at Port Bradshaw. The younger Sister is told to '. . . lie there with legs apart' (line 6): the word used here is *bilnggduwa*, 'with open thighs', her legs having been parted by her Brother. 'I shall cut the clitoris, and put more *rangga* people . . .' (line 7), he says. He intended to make her clitoris slightly shorter, but not yet as small as a woman's clitoris is to-day. The severed piece would be 'soaked' or put into water, and 'made' a *rangga*: not an ordinary *rangga*, but a special clitoris emblem. On account of the cutting, the Djanggawul desire to put at this place more people (line 7), to be custodians of the sacred clitoris *rangga*.

The Djanggawul Brother then asks his Sister to move closer to him for coitus (line 8), but soon finds that something is wrong. 'What is that there, blocking me? There is something within the vagina; I must go carefully' (line 9) says the Brother. He has inserted his penis, but now discovers that an arm-band (*vide* Song 160) is blocking her vaginal passage.[1] This obstruction is further likened to the transverse fibre of the *ngainmara* mat, upon which *rangga* catch as they are pulled out.

[1] The reason why this armband is 'blocking' the younger Sister, as it did other Ancestral Women, is not discussed here. It has been treated in *Love Songs of Arnhem Land*.

Comments on Part Nine of the Songs

This theme, treated so briefly in line 9, is not developed further; and line 10 returns to the shortening of the clitoris. The cutting has not yet been completed, as line 8 would lead one to suppose. While the clitoris is being cut, the Sister exclaims 'Ah, go carefully! Be gentle!' (line 11). The sound of her cry drifts over (line 12) to Dulmulwondeinbi (also called Djumbulwara, etc.) and to Dambala (line 13). As the Brother cuts her clitoris at the *nara* shade, all the *galibingu* men (who had originally come from the Two Sisters) dance outside near the sacred well (line 14). The severed part of the clitoris is then put into the well water, as a *rangga* (line 15). The rest of the clitoris, still attached to Miralaidj, is covered up within the mat (line 20): for the *ngainmara* mat is equivalent to the uterus (or vagina), and the clitoris was cut from the vagina. The remaining end of the clitoris is termed 'nut' or 'knob', and likened to the transverse fibre of the mat (although, as in line 9, the transverse fibre may also be the arm-band blocking the vagina: see Chapter 19, Comments to Part Eight, Song 141). The peak of the mat is the *mons veneris*, and the inner peak the vagina or the uterus.

Miralaidj turns on her side, warming herself in the sun (lines 17 and 18). She is sore from the cutting of her clitoris, and opens her legs wide to the healing heat of the sun. This reveals her labia minora, glowing redly 'because the sun makes them hot'; the redness symbolizes the red breast feathers of the parakeet. Thus this incident is linked with the main theme of the epic. (In the Miligimbi version of the Djanggawul cycle the rays of the sun come from the vaginae of the Sisters, from within the red labia minora or the red walls of the vagina; and they too are associated with the red breast feathers of the *lindaridj* parakeet.) Line 18 reads: '. . . labia minora glowing with redness, with blood, like the breast feathers of the parakeet!' The glowing redness is considerably accentuated by the flow of blood from the severed clitoris. To ease this, a stone is heated in the fire and placed immediately beneath the foreshortened clitoris (line 19); much the same method is used in the case of menstruating girls, and of boys who have been circumcised.

The blood which has fallen is covered up, while the severed end of the clitoris is declared sacred and placed in the *ngainmara*, and treated as a *rangga* (line 20). In line 21 the *rangga* and the young Sister are put into the mat to sleep; this is interpreted also as the placing of the clitoris *rangga* within the mat, or symbolically, as the Djanggawul Brother inserting his penis into his Sister's vulva. The last line (22) of this song, 'For the *mauwulan* has been plunged in, all the way, dragging along; so carefully, dry the smell . . .' refers to the coitus the Brother and Sisters have had. The *mauwulan* is the Brother's *rangga* penis, and the latter part of the line relates to the smell of seminal and vaginal juices adhering to the penis or to the clitoris. The word for 'dry the smell' is *budjei-raidjurma* (smell dry); the significance of *budjei* has already been discussed (*vide* Chapter 14, Comments to Part Five, Song 77; Chapter 16, Comments to Part Six, Song 115, and particularly Chapter 20, Comments to Part Eight, Song 142). Aborigines explain that this line (22) refers specifically to the smell of the Sister's clitoris, or to the 'drying up' of the woman's smell.

Song 159 begins with the heated stone being placed below the shortened clitoris of the Sister (line 1), while the severed end is now regarded as a sacred *djuda rangga* (line 2), called a *darlba*, or tree, and placed within the *ngainmara*. The *galibingu* people who were removed from the Sisters' wombs continue to dance '. . . moving their bodies, shaking their hair!' (line 3), and the clapping sticks are beaten upon the *rangga* poles (line 4). Other clansfolk may be seen within the *ngainmara* uterus of the younger Sister (line 5): 'They come from the Sister's womb, lifting aside the clitoris, coming out like *djuda* roots . . .' (line 6). It is said that as the people issue from Miralaidj's vulva they lift aside her clitoris, which obstructs their way—just as *rangga* are caught on the transverse fibre of the *ngainmara* (*vide* Song 158). In other songs referring to people emerging from the Sisters, the Brother inserts his hand, first lifting back the clitoris, and pulls them out one by one. Here, however, '. . . the *rangga* folk come dancing from the inner peak of the mat . . .' (line 7) into the sacred shade. These are the men who perform the ceremonies mentioned in Songs 165–73. Line 8 tells of the men (or male children) being put into the coarse grass; they are 'thrown away', *malei-jalgdun* (clan thrown away), but the female children are covered carefully with the *ngainmara*.

Song 160 describes the Djanggawul Brother's having coitus with his Sister Miralaidj. Line 1 refers back to the incident mentioned briefly in Song 158, line 9. 'Go, put out the *rangga*, making it big: open your legs . . .' The first part of the line refers to the Djanggawul Brother erecting his penis (*jindigong*, big making); it is treated as a sacred *rangga*. The latter part refers to the young Sister's legs being opened. The Brother is attracted to her and this heightens his desire: '. . . you look nice!' (line 1). The word used here is explained as 'getting to look nice or pretty', or 'she looks nice with her legs apart'; this refers more to her vulva than to her general appearance. The Brother then embraces his Sister (line 2); but '. . . the mouth of the mat is closed' (that is, *dam-daljuwon-ngainmara*, mouth shut mat). Again, as in Song 158, Miralaidj's vagina is 'shut' or blocked by the 'arm-band'.

Comments on Part Nine of the Songs

Line 3 reverts to the sacredness of the vagina; it is *ngaungau* (tabu), because it normally hides the *rangga* people. On the other hand, it is also explained as meaning that the young Sister herself goes into the *ngainmara* mat, and is covered up or hidden on account of her sacredness. Line 2, '. . . take Miralaidj . . . ' would then mean that the Brother is removing her. Further, the sacred terms *mareijingu dalbaljumandalwul juguljuguljumandalwul ngaungaujumandalwul*, can refer to the Brother's penis, being 'covered up' within his Sister, or to the assumption that there is its proper place; that is, it should be hidden within the vagina, as a *rangga* pole is hidden within the *ngainmara*. 'Thus, climb up, put it into the mouth of the mat!' (line 4). The first word of this line (*vide* interlinear text) is *ngalduwan*, meaning 'climb up (or on) to', and explained as 'ready for coitus', or 'to put one's chest against the woman's breasts and rest upon her'. The Brother inserts his penis, but discovers that something is still hindering him. 'What is this, blocking my penis?' he cries (line 5). Once again, the arm-band is responsible. The Brother rests upon his Sister's breasts and continues to have intercourse; however, she asks him not to push strongly with his penis, in case he should hurt her (line 6).

Apart from the fear of hurting his Sister, the Brother is careful not to copulate roughly lest all the people should be released. He puts his penis in gently, for 'he wants to save those people in the Sister's womb. He doesn't want them all to come out in one place: that's why he does this carefully.' The Brother 'hides' his penis in her vagina (line 7), like a *rangga* in the *ngainmara*. He is anxious not to move that which is within (line 8), because it is sacred; he does not want to move the arm-band separating the vaginal duct from the uterus, which contains blood, and above that the *rangga* emblems and *rangga* folk (*vide* accompanying sketch). The next line (9) refers to the arm-band 'resting' or 'sleeping' in there like the transverse fibre of the mat. With all his care, however, the Djanggawul Brother's penis 'breaks' part of the arm-band, and causes blood to flow.[1] 'Blood running, sacredly running!' (line 10); 'Yes, they, the *rangga* clansfolk, are coming out . . . ' (line 11): the action of his penis, having partially broken the arm-band and caused Miralaidj's blood to flow, releases some of the *rangga* people from within her womb; but since he copulates gently, only a few come out. The next line (12), 'Go, digging within, causing the blood to flow, sacred blood . . . ' includes the word *belang* which means 'dig', and is explained as 'digging out of woman': the penis causes the blood to flow. The blood comes from the red walls of the vagina (line 12: see Song 158, line 18); and just as this is sacred,

---

[1] This is the menstrual flow: *vide Love Songs of Arnhem Land.*

so is the erect penis of the Djanggawul Brother—for his *rangga* penis stands erect and sacred as a symbol of fertility and fructification (line 13).

The following rough sketch is from a native drawing.

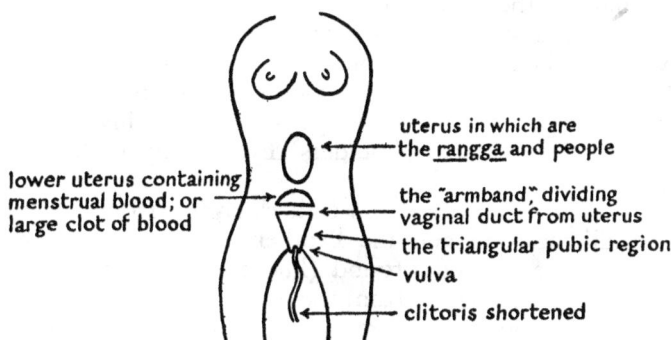

uterus in which are
the <u>rangga</u> and people

lower uterus containing
menstrual blood; or
large clot of blood

the "armband" dividing
vaginal duct from uterus

the triangular pubic region

vulva

clitoris shortened

THE YOUNGER DJANGGAWUL SISTER, MIRALAIDJ.
(from an Aboriginal drawing)

Song 161 opens with the younger Sister, Miralaidj, hitting her thighs and loins in order to 'drop' the blood, so that it is all released at once. The blood which has fallen is covered up by scraping earth over it (line 2). At the same time, rangga folk are coming out (line 3). Line 4 is interesting: 'Put your foot on the navel, releasing the blood, pushing strongly and breaking up the clot, to let it flow . . .' When the Brother had coitus with Miralaidj, his penis broke through the obstructing arm-band (*vide* Song 160). This caused the blood to flow internally, much of it being forced upwards to the lower part of the uterus (see Sketch Figure above), to form a large clot. To release the clot, Bildjiwuraroiju places her foot on her Sister's belly, at her navel, for she is lying down, and feels pain in that region. (This pain corresponds to normal menstrual 'pains', where the blood gathers in the 'lower uterus', and each month (or 'moon') is automatically released. In the case of the younger Sister, this process did not take place naturally, but had to be forced.)[1] By this pressure the elder Sister endeavours to 'break

[1] The significance of this clot of blood has been noted in the volume *Love Songs of Arnhem Land*, but will be discussed in greater detail later when the Wauwalak Myth Cycle is analysed. The blood clot goes to form the foetus, the bones of which grow from semen. The clot of blood is normally released at menstruation from women who have not conceived. In the case of Miralaidj, however, some contradictory elements appear. The pressure exerted on her navel implies that she has conceived, and that consequently the clot of blood will not dissolve and flow naturally. Bildjiwuraroiju's

up' the clot of blood so that it will liquefy and flow, for it blocks the mouth of the uterus which contains the people. She is successful: '. . . carefully, so that the sacred blood may flow . . . It is done . . .' (lines 5–6). The blood is then (line 6) covered up with mud in the well (like the *rangga*). The young Sister is put within the *ngainmara*, for she is sacred (line 7), and there she shines quietly '. . . like a younger sibling . . .' (or, in context, 'younger sister'). This is done to the '. . . sound of clapping sticks, tapping against the *rangga*' (line 8): the *rangga* folk are dancing and singing, and the Sister moves her shoulders rhythmically to the clapping (line 9).

Song 162 concerns the *rangga* folk emerging from the younger Sister. Bildjiwuraroiju and the Brother stand in the sacred *nara* shade, upon the cleared ground (line 1), and watch the *rangga* people as they '. . . come from the younger Sister . . .' (line 3); but at this place only a few are to be left. One of the words used here is *gurlgai-jigalaran*, the significance of which has already been discussed, derived as it is from *gurlga*, penis, and having associations with the *djuda* roots and the rays of the sun. After they have come out, '. . . the sacred children dance, swaying their hair from side to side, gently swaying their bodies . . .' (line 5). Other *rangga* folk are to be let out at Djiriliwuramai, situated at the back of Milingimbi, at Bilmingura, the Place of the Clapping Sticks (for 'the Djanggawul beat their clapping sticks very hard at this place'), at Milingurmuru and at Milngaidja: both the latter are 'inside' names for places beyond Milingimbi, where the last of the people are to be removed (lines 7 and 8).

Song 163 continues the theme, with more *rangga* folk being '. . . put out . . . so that they see the well' (line 1). They draw closer to this well, as the Djanggawul place people correctly according to their different clans. Now they are standing about in strict formation (line 5), with knees close together, 'like fighting men'. This particular formation is used by an 'enemy' when going through the Bush either to engage in sorcery, or to attack or ambush a person or camp. An 'enemy' means one or more individuals who

pressure therefore, suggests that conception is not desired; but this appears to be out of keeping with the basic intention of the Cycle. It is more likely that the intention is to attribute to the young Sister not merely one peculiarly female function (child bearing), but also another (menstruation) which has received considerable attention in north-eastern Arnhem Land.

This feature, menstruation, is thus given supernatural sanction and importance. At the same time, the north-eastern Arnhem Landers' emphasis on menstruation (as expressed in, for example, the Wauwalak Cycle) has perhaps been responsible for its inclusion here.

are to participate actively in a feud, or engage in armed combat for various reasons. It is used here only figuratively, indicating the position taken by the *rangga* people as they emerge from the womb. In line 5 we read '. . . like fighting men from the west . . .' (*wulbaria bandi'ia* (like an) 'enemy' (of) Milingimbi people); the Yirrkalla Aborigines look upon those from the west, in the Milingimbi region, as being 'warlike', for there are and have been a number of feuds among these people belonging to the one cultural bloc. The *rangga* folk stand in rows, side by side, and thus they are likened to the south wind, which brings many clouds in its wake (line 6).

In line 7, the *rangga* people move into the wells at the various places mentioned. This symbolizes their spiritual immersion in the well water: for just as *rangga* emblems are put into a well, so the *rangga* folk enter the well that their spirits may live eternally.[1] Line 9 reads: 'They come from the transverse fibre of the mat, from the mouth of the mat!': the 'mat' here is the uterus, and its 'mouth' the vulva. 'For the long clitoris has dragged on the ground, the protruding clitoris' (line 10); this refers to the long clitoris which dragged along during the Djanggawul's travels, and which the *rangga* folk pushed aside as they came from the womb (*vide* Song 159, line 6), and to the way in which it protrudes from the vulva. The last line of this song, 'Thus the people have come out from the parted labia majora . . .' serves to stress their origin.

Song 164 again describes the special formation adopted by the *rangga* folk when they are removed; and lines 1–4 consist largely of repetition. In line 5 their original association with their Mothers, the Two Sisters, is again stressed, for they came 'From resting within the womb. pulling them out from the womb!' (*walg-ngoi-jangara walg-warijunda*); the ordinary everyday term for uterus is used here, and not the symbolic words, *ngainmara*, *wagulwagul*, and so on.

The word *walg* is particularly significant, for it is used to mean 'afterbirth', or (in context) navel cord, although here it is synonymous with 'uterus'. It is derived from the sacred term *wagulwagul*, which has been generally used here in this cycle for uterus, vagina, mat, sacred shade, whale and so on. Another important derivative of this word is *wagu*, which means 'son' or 'daughter' (woman speaking; sister's son or daughter, man speaking), and is used as an ordinary kinship term. *Wagu*, directly derived from *wagulwagul*, is thus closely related to *walg*, since it is felt that the 'child', the

---

[1] This aspect will be dealt with in a later work, for in this context it involves many problems which are, in the north-eastern Arnhem Land region, somewhat complex, and need to be discussed in some detail.

'womb' of its mother, and the 'afterbirth' are inescapably associated. The word *wagu*, 'child', thus provides us with an additional reference to the physiological origin of children, and exemplifies the stress placed on this aspect by local Aborigines. The terms *judu* (singular: 'semen') and *djamarguli* (plural: from coitus, or 'as a result of working in copulation') have already been mentioned in reference to their everyday meaning of 'child' and 'children'. As a corollary of this emphasis on physiological features, a man may be called *gurlgamiri* (*gurlga or gulga*, a penis, *miri*, having or with), and a woman, *dagumiri* (*dagu*, a vulva or vagina, having or with).[1]

Line 6 reads: 'The long clitoris is cut, the clitoris smell removed, after dragging along . . .' The word used here for the clitoris is *dabi*, associated with the umbilical cord, foreskin, sun's rays and so on; it suggests the *rangga* folk's severence from the Mother at birth through the cutting of the umbilical cord. The word *budjei* refers to the 'smell' of the clitoris (*vide* above, Song 158): that is, the smell of the vaginal and seminal juices adhering to it. These juices have stained the clitoris, leaving on it an 'encrustation' of white substance which is likened to (or is symbolic of) the foam stain or sea marks left on the *rangga* that were brought across the sea from Bralgu (see previous references in songs to foam splashing). On the other hand, Aborigines comment that only the Brother's penis could have become stained with vaginal and seminal juices, and that the clitoris could not really have become marked in this way, since it was not used actively in coitus: this staining took place while it lay in the bottom of the bark canoe during the sea journey. From that point of view, the clitoris was a *rangga*, and the splashing foam which dried upon it had a distinctive smell (that is, on the assumption that foam = semen, and hence has a similar smell). As the *rangga* people issue from the womb the Djanggawul Brother cuts the clitoris, and the smell goes away.

Line 7 is much the same as line 5, but a different word is used for uterus: *wulba*, an 'inside' term, which is also explained as 'blood always lying in that hole (*wulba-ngoijangara*), and they cover it up all the way'; this is regarded as being equivalent to *walg* (in line 5: above) in the sense that it means 'afterbirth' and thus 'afterbirth blood'. That is, the afterbirth and afterbirth blood, when the *rangga* people emerge from the Sisters' wombs, are covered up within a hole in the ground, as is the practice to-day ('for this is the law for these people, and they do it now'). It may also refer to the blood which is still within the Sisters' wombs waiting to flow out after

---

[1] We have already seen the use of the term *gurlga* or *gulga* in these songs, while *dagu* is derived from *da*, a 'mouth' or lip (e.g. labia majora) of the *ngainmara* (vagina or uterus), and suffix *gu*, 'belonging to'.

Comments on Part Nine of the Songs

childbirth.[1] When this is finished, the *rangga* people led by the Djanggawul Brother return to the *nara* shade (line 10). There is, however, no indication that they have been away from it altogether, and the inference is rather that they now re-enter the shade itself from the outside clearing. It will be recalled (*vide* Song 158, e.g. lines 4 and 5) that the younger Sister was 'cut' and had intercourse with her Brother within the *nara* shade, in the company of her Sister, while the *galibingu* people danced outside on the cleared ground (line 14). Now they all enter it; and, although the Song makes no reference to this, Aborigines say that the Sisters still remain within the sacred precincts, for they direct and instruct the postulants in their dancing.

Once in the shade, they begin to perform *nara* ritual (lines 9–11), re-enacting in their dancing the momentous trip by bark canoe from Bralgu, and making the sound of the sea. In line 10, '. . . urged on by the leader facing the dancers . . .' is a general rendering of *gada(n)-gumur-wonjagong*, grasp chest give 'rough' word. The phrase 'grab or clasp one's chest' refers to a leader of ceremonies: he stands before the dancing *rangga* folk, in front of their chests *gumur*) as if clasping them, urging them to dance better 'by using strong or rough words', and by his own example. The final line (11) of this song tells of the ritual which is being danced.

In Song 165 the *nara* ritual continues, while the *rangga* folk are urged on by their leader—the Djanggawul Brother himself. 'Those from the mat move carefully from side to side, dancing the sound of the waves, the splashing surf' (line 2). They drag a stick along the ground, symbolizing dragging of the paddles through the sea (line 1); they lift their knees up and down, and this represents the splashing of the rough sea, and its surging waters (line 3); again the stick is dragged up and down the ground, and this is the rise and fall of the tide. They themselves are the *rangga*, but at the same time they dance with various *rangga* emblems (lines 4 and 10): for example, the goanna tail *rangga*, which relates to the *djanda* goanna at the sacred sandhill at the Place of the Mauwulan (Mauwulanggalngu, Port Bradshaw), already symbolized by the low mound at one side of the *nara* clearing. They dance backwards and forwards in the sacred shade, '. . . like *djuda* roots, like spray . . .' (line 5); they make the roaring sound of the sea—*a! a!* (line 6); they shake their spearthrowers to symbolize the rising sea, waves splashing and spraying (line 7); and again the sticks are dragged along, the water running strongly (line 8). In line 10 they continue to manipulate the *rangga*, calling out Djambatpingu invocations as

[1] See Song 161, in reference to the coagulated blood within the younger Sister: this is identified with the blood emitted after childbirth.

they do so. They posture with the Goanna Tail, writhing with it on the ground, and shuffling along on their backs with it clasped to their chests; they plunge into the ground the sacred *djuda*, symbol of the sacred tree, and of the *rangga* penis of the Brother (*vide* Song 160, line 13). Finally, their origin is emphasized again, for they come 'from within' (line 11).

Song 166 again is largely repetition. The *nara* dancing continues; in line 2 the presence of the younger Sister, Miralaidj, is mentioned, and sacred invocations are called. In line 9, although *gumur-gada(n)* is used in reference to the ceremonial leader (for example, Song 164, line 10), it has a different meaning in this particular context, and *gumur* here means 'front'; the Djanggawul ram the *djuda* into the ground, heaping up and hardening the mud around it with their hands.

Song 167 reiterates this theme. The *rangga* folk are carrying out the water dancing (line 1), inserting *djuda* so that they grow into trees (line 3), shaking the spearthrower to symbolize the waves splashing together, ramming their *djuda* into the mud (line 6), arranging the feathered strings (line 8), and posturing with the *rangga*. The invocations are 'bottom' Ngeimil. The next song (168) is much the same, most of it being concerned with dancing at the wells mentioned in line 6. In Song 169 the measured beating of clapping sticks continues, some being tapped against the *mauwulan rangga* poles (lines 1 and 2). More *djuda* roots are 'planted' (lines 3 and 5), and feathered strings arranged, like yam creepers. All are sacred, for they come from the sacred *ngainmara* (line 7). The *bugali* in this case are Djambatpingu.

Song 170 continues the *nara* dancing, the placing of *djuda* roots, *rangga* and arm-bands within the well, and the smoothing over of mud to cover them so that no trace may be seen (line 4). The invocations here are Gwolamala, relating to the *djuda*.

Song 171 too repeats the same theme. The *rangga* folk dance, re-enacting the Djanggawul's original journey across the sea, and move their sticks as if paddling (line 2). The invocations here are Djambatpingu, referring to the *djuda* and to the *ba'ralgi*. In line 6 the *rangga* are pushed into the mud '. . . covering up the *rangga* heads in the well . . .' The feathered headdresses mentioned in line 7 are feathered bands of 'halo' shape, with hanging pendants, worn by the Two Djanggawul Sisters. They are usually worn by women during sacred dancing in the main camp,[1] and may be the same feathered strings used to decorate the *rangga* emblems; symbolically they refer to the elongated clitoris, to the umbilical cord,

---

[1] They have also some significance in regard to marriage, love-making and divorce: *vide* A. P. Elkin, R. and C. Berndt, *Art in Arnhem Land*, and R. Berndt, *Love Songs of Arnhem Land*.

276

or to the rays of the sun. These feathered strings are all sacred, and all come from within the *ngainmara* (line 8).

In Song 172 the ritual leader dances with the sacred *ngainmara* (line 6), as men to-day dance with the feather-decorated dilly bags; and 'top' Djambatpingu *bugali* are called. In Song 173 the dancing continues until the last *djuda* have been inserted into the well, and the Ngeimil invocations called. The *djanda* goanna *rangga* are erected (line 8), so that they see the water at Marabai and Bulbulmara; again, we are told that they come from within the sacred mat (line 9). Now the *nara* has drawn to a close. In Song 174, the conventional ending is presented. The parakeet nestlings cry as they watch the setting sun, and suddenly fly down to disappear within the mouth of the sacred basket, where they are covered up in sacred tabu-ness: '. . . covered up like younger siblings, so no one may see . . .' (line 11). 'Myself (says the bird), I have red breast feathers, my nestlings . . . It is done. They are asleep' (lines 12 and 13).

The concluding section of this part, then, presents us with a glimpse of the first re-enactment of the Djanggawul's journey, and not only reveals elements of *nara* procedure, but also gives reasons for its performance. The real intention of this section is, apparently, to show how closely allied this re-enactment is to the original adventures and behaviour of the Djanggawul. The presence of the First Mothers at the sacred shade, the fact that the ritual itself is under the leadership of the Djanggawul Brother, and is performed by the *rangga* folk, all serve to accentuate its sacred quality. Even if, to-day, these Ancestral Beings are no longer seen at the *nara* in their material form, their spirits are present. The neophytes are still the *rangga* folk; the dancing, singing, posturing, and invocations have remained essentially unchanged, while the *rangga* emblems and feathered strings are all possessed of the same 'eternal' sacred essence with which they were originally endowed.

Chapter Twenty-three

THE DJANGGAWUL SONG CYCLE

PART TEN

The Yirrkalla version of the Djanggawul epic is drawing to a close. More people, both male and female, are taken from the Sisters, and the sacred quality of woman is emphasized. Rangga and feathered strings are removed from the ngainmara and baskets; the nara ritual continues, and the fringe of the basket is cut.

Song 175

Go, flatten the mat out widely, stretching its mouth and its
    transverse fibre . . .   1
    Yes, that is right Sister; indeed, it is done!
Go, take another from within it, parting the fringe of the trans-
    verse fibre . . .
It is done. Yes, carefully we straighten it . . .
Go, there is another within: take it out . . .   5
Go, undo the mouth, parting the fringe!
Go, put your hand in, firmly, and pull out a man: place him among
    the grass . . .
Go, put your hand in firmly, pull out another man, placing him in
    the grass . . .
Go, again put your hand firmly within. Pull out a man from the
    transverse fibre of the mat, throw him aside into the coarse
    grass!
There they lie in the grass, men, crying together . . .   10
For theirs is a strong cry!
Go, again put your hand within, for there, too, they are crying
    hard . . .

How is that? Thus we are treating the men.
Come, pull them out strongly, and throw them aside . . .
Yes, we put them into the grass, for they are men.   15
Go, again put your hand within, for many of them are crying . . .
How is that? Thus we are treating these men!
Come, throw them aside, one by one, in a group, into the grass . . .
We shall leave here only a few clansfolk . . .

Song 176

Go, put your hand again within the mouth of the mat, for indeed
    they are crying . . .   1
How is that? Come, pull out two together.
What is this? It is a man.
Go, throw them one by one in a heap among the grass; let them
    cry there together . . .
Here we are putting only a few of the clansfolk . . .   5
Elsewhere we shall leave the rest of the people . . .
They stand there, scattered, like clouds rising up from the west
    beyond Milingimbi, from Djiriliwuramai, from Maluwa, from
    the Place of the Clapping Sticks.
Yes, Sister, thus we shall put out the clansfolk . . .
For thus you speak to me, and you are my leader . . .
We shall throw out only a few, into the wells at Jiganjindu, Bulbul-
    mara, Djumbulwara, at Gwoijaring, Marabai.   10

Song 177

Here we are putting only a few of the *rangga* people . . .   1
That they may grow and follow the law of the Djanggawul, putting
    the law for the new generation.
Yes, that is why we undo the other mat. Indeed, that is so!
Go, part the fringe of the mat, opening wide its mouth . . .
It is done? Yes it is done. Go, put your hand firmly within . . .   5
Have you grasped them? Yes, I have grasped them. Come, let us
    pull them out.
We look within; ah, these are women!
Go, put them back, like younger siblings, covering them up within
    the mat so no one may see . . .
Yes, that we must do! I pulled them out in ignorance: for you
    should have told me Sister . . .
We put them back, covered up within the peak of the mat, the
    transverse fibre, making them·sacred . . .   10

Go, again put your hand within!
It is done? Yes, I have grasped them. Come, let us pull them out!
What is that? It is a tabu-ed woman!
Go, hide her there, within the transverse fibre of the mat.
Go, quietly put out the people, all over this place.   15
We see the group of young women, there together . . .
Go, again put your hand within!
Have you grasped them? Yes, come, let us pull them out!
What is this? It is a woman, tabu, like a younger sibling. Let us
    cover her up within the transverse fibre, parting the fringe, of
    the mat . . .
Covered up, hidden, for she is sacred, tabu, like a younger sib-
    ling . . .   20
Yes indeed, Sister, we cover her up completely within the mat,
    within its transverse fibre, so no one may see . . .

Song 178

What is that, indeed, crying, softly crying?   1
Yes, Sister: go quietly grasp the mouth of the mat, tabu, like a
    younger sibling . . .
Go, carefully put her back within the mat, covering her up within
    its transverse fibre . . .
Put her firmly within the peak of the mat, covering her up within . . .
Go, put in another, quietly, like a younger sibling: 5
Put her in firmly, quietly, that first born: cover her up, tabu, so no
    one may see . . .
Yes, Sister, indeed; it is done!
What shall we do with these? Shall we put the others outside, with
    the men?
No! Let us put them within the mat, covering them up as sacred,
    tabu—quietly, reverently, like younger siblings . . .
For they are sacred, they are tabu, we put them within the trans-
    verse fibre of the mat!   10
We put them within the mouth of the mat, parting its fringe,
    covering them up deeply within the mat!

Song 179

Go, seize the fringe of the mat, carefully pull it shut . . .   1
Go, seize its mouth and carefully fasten it up, covering it. Fasten
    it, drawing it nearer . . .

No, keep on sewing it carefully, covering them up within the sacred uterus.
You have grasped the mouth of the mat? It is done.
We grasp the fringe of the mat, dragging along the clitoris. We have covered them up and made them sacred, so no one may see, made them like younger siblings . . .   5
For women are inside the womb, and quietly we cover them up with the mat . . .
They come from far away, from Bralgu, from the deep sea near the Spirit Country . . .
From the shine of the Morning Star, from the sound of the Baijini folk: from the splashing foam, and the smell of the sea . . .
Quietly we rested our paddles, dragging them through the sea, swaying our buttocks, at the Place of the Mauwulan.

Song 180

Come, we see the clansfolk! Take the sacred basket, and put it within . . .   1
They come from the Place of the Mauwulan, from the sea near the Spirit Country . . .
That is true, Sister, indeed.
Go, here is another, stained with foam; salt water splashing up near the Place of the Mauwulan! It comes from the Place of the Sun, from the open sea . . .
Yes, go, pull out another from the mouth of the mat.   5
Go, put this sacred basket at Ngubarei, Galwia, Dulabei . . .
Go, put another within the transverse fibre of the mat . . .
Put another! Yes, it is done. Go put in your hand, hiding it there . . .
Come, pull it out, drying it near the transverse fibre of the mat . . .
Drying these goanna-fat feathers, the *djanda* goanna *rangga* . . . 10
For they are stained with splashing foam from the Place of the Mauwulan, from far away . . .
Feathered strings, covered up in the water so no one may see, for they are very sacred . . .
Dry another, stained with the splashing foam . . .
Carefully straighten the arm-band pendants, the feathered strings, at Djumbulwara, at Jiganjindu.
Straighten the feathered pendants, goanna-fat strings, so they see the wells at Marabai, Bulbulmara, Dambala.   15
Dry another in the caressing rays of the sun, in its glowing heat, so the sweat comes out as they see the scorching haze . . .

The Djanggawul Song Cycle
Song 181

What is that crying? Is it a parakeet nestling?   1
Yes, the nestling! For it saw the red glow of sunset, as it perched
  on the sacred *djuda* tree . . .
Always perched there, crying softly, clasping the *djuda* with its
  claws as it moves down the limb . . .
Drying its red breast feathers, its children . . .
Crying, it saw the warm rays of the glowing sun . . .   5
Drying itself in the warm glow of the sunset, softly crying . . .
It saw the mouth of the mat, as it perched on the *djuda* tree:
Clasping the tree with its claws, in quiet tabu-ness.
Crying, it dives down into the peak of the mat . . .
Dives down from the *djuda*! 'I (says the bird), with my breast
  feathers, my children . . .'   10
It is done! They sleep, in solemn tabu-ness.

Song 182

Go, take another mat and put it within, carefully turning over its
  mouth . . .   1
Go, undo it: carefully part its fringe, then put in your hand . . .
Come, carefully pull them out, shining, from the transverse fibre
  of the mat . . .
It is done. Yes, pull out another basket.
It is done? Yes, come, put them upon the flattened part of the
  mat,   5
Carefully dry them, in the warm rays of the sun.
Here is another basket. Have you grasped it?
Yes, come, pull it out, into the transverse fibre of the mat.
Go, grasp another basket. You have it? Yes, let us pull it out!
Go, pull out two more baskets and put them within . . .   10
Let the hot sun dry them, for they are splashed with foam . . .
Splashed with foam from far away on the wide sea, near the Spirit
  Country . . .

Song 183

Here is yet another; yes, let us take them out . . .   1
Come pull them out, and lay them on the transverse fibre of the
  mat.
Let them dry in the warm rays of the glowing sun . . .
They see the pendants, the feathered strings, splashed and stained
  from the Place of the Mauwulan . . .

It is done, Sister. Yes, go, take another basket, pulling it out . . . 5
Come, let it dry within the transverse fibre of the mat.
The warm rays of the shining sun look down on them, with rising
 heat . . .
For they are stained with foam, soaked with the smell of the
 sea . . .
Carefully put all the feathered strings, the *djanda* goanna *rangga* . . .
For they are tabu, covered up at Ngubarei, Galwia, Dulabei.   10
Is it done? Yes, come, take another basket.
Is it done? We pull them out, laying them within the mouth of the
 sacred shade . . .

Song 184

Go hang those baskets upon the *djuda* tree . . .   1
They stand shining quietly, drying their dampness . . .
Carefully, cover the feathered goanna-fat strings, arranged, spread-
 ing them in the warm rays of the glowing sun . . .
Carefully straighten the feathered strings, thus, so they see the wells
 at Jiganjindu, Marabai and Bulbulmara.
Here is another basket, always hanging upon the *djuda* tree . . . 5
They clasp the *rangga*, shining quietly in tabuness:
For they are splashed with foam, hanging among the branches of
 the shade . . .
Straighten the pendants, the feathered strings, covered up in the
 water, so no one may see.

Song 185

Here is another basket; hang it within the mouth of the *nara* shade,
 near the sacred sandhill . . .   1
Carefully they hang there, shining quietly; we saw them on the
 djuda tree . . .
We cover them up inside the mouth of the mat, its inner peak . . .
Carefully dry the pendants, straightening the feathered strings . . .
Carefully dry them, for they are splashed with foam from far away,
 out at sea near Bralgu, the Spirit Country, the shine of the
 Morning Star . . .   5
Carefully, so that they see the water at Gwoijaring, at Dambala,
 Marabai, Djumbulwara, Jiganjindu:
They see the water splashing up in the well.
Carefully, so no one may see them, for they are very sacred . . .

The Djanggawul Song Cycle
Song 186

Go, undo the mat; put them back in there, laying them down on
the transverse fibre, carefully straightened . . .   1
Undo the mouth of another, parting its fringe, and lay them down
on the transverse fibre . . .
Undo another, and lay them down on the flattened mat, straightening
its mouth . . .
Yes indeed, Sister. I listen to your words, for you are my great
leader: I follow your desire . . .
Carefully, dry them in the warm rays of the glowing sun . . .   5
Let them dry their moisture, these pendants, these feathered strings
shining as they lie quietly there . . .
For they have been covered up like younger siblings within the
peak of the mat, its parted fringe . . .

Song 187

Go, roar like the water!   1
Carefully, beat the clapping sticks on the *mauwulan* point . . .
Above the sacred covered basket . . .
We cut the fringe of the basket, calling the invocations . . .
Carefully we cut the fringe from another basket, invoking the
sacred names . . .   5
Go, cut the fringe at the mouth of the basket, within the *nara*
shade, carefully, calling the invocations . . .
They stand within, seeing the wells at Bulbulmara, Jiganjindu, at
Dambala, Marabai, Djumbulwara.
Carefully cut the fringe at the mouth of the basket, attaching the
feathered pendants . . .

Song 188

Ah! Go, roar like the sea upon the basket!   1
It is done. Yes, go, cut the fringe at its mouth, carefully calling the
invocations . . .
Carefully attach the feathered strings to the *djanda* goanna *rangga* . . .
Carefully cut the fringe at the mouth of another basket, invoking
its sacred names . . .
Carefully cut the fringe at its mouth, calling the invocations . . . 5
Carefully attach the feathered strings to the *djanda* goanna *rangga* . . .
They see the water at Marabai, Gwoijaring, Jiganjindu, Dambala,
Djumbulwara.

(End of the Yirrkalla Version of the Djanggawul Epic.)

Chapter Twenty-four

COMMENTS ON PART TEN OF THE SONGS

THIS concludes the Yirrkalla version of the Djanggawul epic.
It differs from other cycles in the abruptness of its ending,
which fails to draw all the associated threads together in
relation to the common theme. The reason put forward for this is
that the story is only half completed: the Milingimbi version picks
up the threads and carries them on, bringing the adventures of the
Djanggawul to a more or less gradual conclusion. Here, however,
for reasons mentioned in the *Foreword*, the Milingimbi version cannot
be presented. It requires detailed treatment in a separate volume,
for it not only continues on from this juncture, but also repeats
the whole epic from the local point of view, revealing many other
aspects not brought forward here.

This concluding part reverts to the removal of more *rangga*
folk from the Sisters, with emphasis upon the difference between
the sexes. The male children are 'thrown away' into the coarse
grass, while the female children are protected and hidden within
the sacred *ngainmara* mat. This procedure has already been considered in Part Six, Chapter 16, and we need not dwell at length
upon its significance. It accentuates the biological differences between
the sexes; and the special care taken with female children is said to
have stemmed from the importance attributed to women in the
Djanggawul cult. That is to say, female children reflect the divine
sacredness of the Two Djanggawul Sisters; they are themselves
sacred, in a way to which men as *rangga* beings or as neophytes
may never attain. Even to-day women, merely through being
females and possessing physical features which are natural to their

285

Comments on Part Ten of the Songs

sex, are automatically sacred through no conscious effort of their own.

This does not mean, of course, that men possess no inherent element of sacredness: Aborigines of both sexes, by reason of their original birth or 'creation', have what may be described as a certain indestructible sacred essence. This sacred *rangga* quality cannot be destroyed by death. It is the spiritual link between a person and his ancestors; the concept of the spiritual immutability of man, which is thus assumed, finds one means of expression in the idea of 'Dreaming'. All the Aborigines of this area came initially from the Two Mothers, Bildjiwuraroiju and Miralaidj; their original sojourn within the wombs of these Two Sisters endowed them with the sacredness that is theirs to-day. In female children, however, this common sacred element is enhanced; woman is sacred, and no matter what she may do throughout her lifetime she must remain so. For this reason, and because they are physically different from men, women remain apart, confident of their importance and assured of their ritual status.

Without elaborating this theme, we may draw attention to its sociological significance. Women are honoured in Yirrkalla and Milingimbi society because they are the mothers of the race: it is through them that children are produced, thus ensuring the continuity of the group and its culture. This is a basic element of local thought, and it is basic too in the ideology of the Djanggawul Cycle. Aboriginal religion, as manifested in this cult, thus centres about one fundamental theme: the survival of man is assured through the fertility of woman, and this fertility is transferable to all other animate features of man's environment. Whether this assumption remains valid depends in the last resort on the divine Beings themselves, for it was through their personal efforts that the state of life known to-day came into being and continues to function. Furthermore, this state of affairs cannot continue unless the ritual which they instituted is carried out; in this lies man's vital essential contribution, in the divine scheme which has been created for him and for all around him.

The importance of the performance of *nara* ritual is mentioned in Song 177: *rangga* folk are born, in the expectation that they will grow up to follow the 'law of the Djanggawul' (line 2). Song 181 terminates the first section of this Part; the concluding songs concern the sacred baskets, with the cutting of the fringe as is done to-day in the *nara*.

Let us consider now some of the details noted in these songs.

Song 175 finds the Djanggawul still at Dulmulwondeinbi, in Djambatpingu linguistic group territory. The sacred *ngainmara*

286

is stretched out and flattened to receive *rangga* people who will be removed from the Sisters. In line 1, '. . . stretching its mouth . . .' —the word *bilnggduma* is used, and means 'opening the vulva' (line 1). The long fringe (symbolic clitoris or pubic hair) is pushed aside, and the people removed (lines 3, 5 and 6) by the Djanggawul Brother, who inserts his hand into his Sister's vagina (lines 7-9, 12 and 16). The *rangga* folk taken out are male, and are put in the coarse grass: 'Go, again put your hand firmly within. Pull out a man from the transverse fibre of the mat, throw him aside into the coarse grass . . .' (line 9); the transverse fibre refers to the arm-band blockage mentioned in Part Nine. In line 10, 'There they lie in the grass, men, crying together,' the word used for 'all crying all around' is *gurlgai-jigalarang*, which has been variously translated elsewhere, and the meaning of which (within a certain range) alters according to context. The 'strong cry' of the *rangga* men (line 11) is imitated to-day in ritual cries during the *nara*. Again and again the Djanggawul bring forth men. In line 13 the elder Sister, pausing, discusses the matter with the younger, who continues to give birth to people. Bildjiwuraroiju is making sure that their Brother handles only the men; each one as he emerges, is taken by the Brother and thrown to one side in the grass. 'What is that one?' she asks. 'Like that you may throw those men; but if you find women you must let me know, for women are sacred and must be hidden within the *ngainmara* again.'

Song 176 repeats this theme, as more men are removed from the Sisters. As they emerge, the elder Sister inquires into their sex (line 3); she is still looking for women. Comparatively few people are left at this place (line 5), for the Djanggawul intend to leave a large group somewhere else (line 6)—possibly on the mainland beyond Milingimbi (this is treated in the Milingimbi version).

In Song 177, more *rangga* people are being born. They must 'grow and follow the "law" of the Djanggawul, putting the law for the new generation' (line 2). This is a general rendering of: 'for just (put) law for the people (Aborigines) for the new time'. That is, the Djanggawul put there a small group of people, who will grow up to adulthood and follow their law (*damingga*). Not only the *rangga* folk, however, but the 'new' generation as well (*durbudur-bulnguwul*)—that is, all those people of the generations to come— are obliged to do so too, for, '. . . that is why we undo the other mat' (line 3). Thus, the Djanggawul give birth to people so that their cult will live.

In line 7, they '. . . look within; ah, these are women!' (that is, female children within the uterus). The Brother pulls one out; but at once the elder Sister takes her and covers her up with the *ngainmara*, making her tabu. 'Yes, that we must do,' she says. 'I pulled them out in ignorance: for you should have told me, Sister . . .' (line 9). (The interlinear text translation is, Yes all right just I ignorant pull out because you me information (or 'word') talk Sister.) Aborigines explain that 'if the elder Sister had known a girl-child would emerge, if she had been told immediately by the younger Sister (from whose uterus the child came), she would not have allowed the Brother to pull it out; instead, it would have been left in the womb'. This being now impossible, Bildji-wuraroiju does the next best thing; she places the female child under the *ngainmara* (line 10), for 'all women are sacred'. Again the Brother pulls out a girl. 'What is that?' asks Bildjiwuraroiju, and seeing the child she exclaims, 'It is a tabu-ed woman!' (line 13) —*ngaungau daiga*! They hide her within the mat (line 14). Others are treated in this way, until there is a small group of young women (line 16). Still more are pulled out, declared tabu and covered with the *ngainmara* (line 19): 'Covered up, hidden, for she is sacred, tabu, like a younger sibling . . .' (line 20). The sacredness of the female child is treated in some detail, the same words being used for her as for the Djanggawul Sisters themselves, and their *rangga* and feathered pendants.

Song 178 mentions the female children crying, as Song 175 has referred to the male children's cry. In contrast to the strong, some-what harsh, sound of the boys, the girls are ' . . . crying, softly' (line 1); the term describing this is the same as that used for the cry of the parakeets. More girls are removed and placed within the shelter of the *ngainmara*. Line 6 reverts to the 'first born' girl. As an increasing number emerges, the question arises as to whether they should be placed with the boys (line 8). However, the Djangga-wul continue to place them all beneath the *ngainmara* (line 9), for they are sacred.

Song 179 continues to stress the female children. Once these have been put in the *ngainmara*, the Two Sisters take hold of the opening (that is, mouth) of the mat and fringe and draw it closed (line 1). Symbolically, this refers to the fact that the Sisters have now temporarily finished giving birth to people: for the mouth is the vulva, the fringe the pubic hair or clitoris. Because the mat is full of girls, it is drawn shut and 'sewn up'; the sewing means stitching with a quill to which fibre has been attached or with a pointed bone to which fibre has been waxed or, alternatively, the closing of the mat's 'mouth' by interweaving the two fringe edgings. At the end of line 2, ' . . . drawing it nearer' refers to an attempt to reopen the mat, but this is discouraged: 'No, keep on sewing it carefully, covering them up within the sacred uterus' (line 3). That is, the girls 'return to the womb' (and a comparison may be drawn here with the novices' return to their Mothers' wombs at initiation): the word used is the 'inside' term, *burbaljuma*, which ordinarily means 'uterus'. It has, however, additional significance; Aborigines explain it as 'the inside name for the sacredness within women, the sacred womb', inferring that by reason of their possessing a womb, like the Djanggawul Sisters, women are sacred. The same term is employed to mean 'the movement of the foetus in a woman's uterus', or the movement of the *rangga* children in the uteri of the Sisters. Aborigines comment: 'it means that the pregnant Sisters move their bodies, for they feel the movement of children in their bellies'. It may be used, too, to describe a woman moving in her sleep.

Line 5 refers to ' . . . dragging along the clitoris . . . ' In the same line the fringe ('We grasp the fringe of the mat . . . ') is for the first time in this part referred to by the term *dabi*, the significance of which has already been noted. The use of *dabi* in association with *manbal-warijunda*, 'clitoris dragging along', suggests that the 'fringe' is not pubic hair but really a clitoris; and it is this which is drawn shut and sewn. In line 6, the allusion to the women's being within the uterus (or uteri) is repeated: and the following lines dwell on their origin and journey (lines 7–9).

Song 180 reverts to the sacred basket, which is usually identified with the *ngainmara* mat. The basket, with its feathered pendants, has come from far away across the sea, from Bralgu (line 2); and it is stained with foam (line 4). From it *rangga* folk are removed; the Djanggawul Brother puts in his hand and withdraws the sacred *rangga* (lines 8–10). He removes the *djanda* goanna *rangga* and goanna-fat feathered strings, symbolic of the *rangga* people; some are hidden in the well water (line 12), while other strings are spread in the sun to dry (line 16). The meaning of this Song is that the women have been hidden in the *ngainmara* (*vide* Song 179). The *ngainmara* becomes the basket in Song 180 (this is the basket which was stolen from the Two Sisters by the Djanggawul Brother and his companions, and which hangs on the *nara* shade), and the female children are again removed; but now they have assumed their *rangga* quality, and are brought out as emblems and feathered strings. Song 181 concludes the first section of this Part, in the conventional way. The parakeet nestlings perch on the *djuda rangga* trees, warming themselves in the glowing rays of the sinking sun. They look at the mouth of the mat (or basket) and suddenly dive within it; 'It is done! They sleep, in solemn tabu-ness' (line 11).

In Song 182, the mouth of the mat is undone and its fringe pushed carefully aside (line 2); *rangga* emblems (esoterically, people) are to be removed. The words mat and basket are used alternatively here. The *rangga* emblems are laid out on the flattened part of the mat (line 5), where they dry in the sun (line 6). Other baskets are opened, and their contents laid out to dry. Song 183 continues the pulling out of *rangga* from the baskets (line 1), and the feathered strings are spread out to dry. In line 8, 'For they are stained with foam, soaked with the smell of the sea . . .' the word *budjei-jurjunda* is used (*vide* Song 164, etc.). The sun is drying up this sea-smell; alternatively, the smell refers to the Sisters' vaginae or clitorises. In line 9, the feathered strings symbolize goanna fat, and the *rangga* are *djanda* goanna emblems. Some are covered up in the sacred wells mentioned in line 10, and others are placed in a row within the *nara* shade (line 12).

Song 184 brings us to the sacred shade (mentioned in the last line of the preceding song), where the baskets are hung on the *djuda* tree. Their feathered pendants gleam in the sun (line 2), and they clasp the *rangga* like parakeets clasping the limbs of the tree (line 6). Finally they are hidden within the well water.

The next song (185) deals with another basket which is hung at the mouth of the *nara* shade, beside the clearing which is used for dancing, and the sacred mound which represents the sandhill at Port Bradshaw (line 1). It too, is drying in the sun, for it has been splashed with foam during the long sea journey from Bralgu (line 5). Water surges up in the well (line 7), and the feathered strings are covered up because they are sacred and tabu (line 8). Another mat is opened in Song 186, and the pendants spread out to dry in the sun (line 5): two other mats (or baskets) are opened out. The *rangga* and pendants are sacred, for they come from within the peak of the sacred mat.

In Song 187 the *nara* ritual is in progress; the *rangga* folk dance like the incoming tide, making the roaring sound of the sea (line 1). The clapping sticks are beaten over the sacred unfinished dilly bag (line 3), just as is done in the *nara* to-day. The 'sons of the Djangga-wul' are assembled on the ground, and before them is the uncompleted bag with hanging fringe. (The significance of this ritual has already been discussed in Chapter 14, Part Five, Song 77.) They commence to cut the fringe, each man cutting a few strands and passing it on to the next as the sacred invocations are called. In line 4 the cutting is referred to by the following words: '. . . *manba-gulgdun dabigulgdun*.' The first of these words means clitoris, and refers to the cutting of the Sisters' clitorises, symbolized in the ritual cutting of the fringe; the second word may mean 'foreskin', 'clitoris', basket, 'pendant', 'ray of sun', and so on, and represents not only the shortening of the clitoris but the severance of the umbilical cord. This cutting is always accompanied by the calling of invocations; those used here are Djambatpingu, and all refer specifically to the sacred basket. Great attention is paid to the cutting of this fringe, for the feathered pendants are attached to its topmost ridge (line 8), and a final plaiting is added to give the bag a firm edging.

Song 188 concerns the special dancing which is held for the basket (line 1). The cutting of the fringe is continued until all has been removed; invocations are called, the feathered pendants are attached, and *djanda* goanna *rangga* are arranged on the *nara* ground. Not only one basket is cut, but many, each being given a special sacred name. When finished, they are all hung from the *rangga,* which are stood upright in the ground so that they see the sacred water at the places mentioned in line 7; and at this point the cycle abruptly concludes.

Chapter Twenty-five

EPILOGUE

W E are now in a position to summarize and discuss the contents of the Djanggawul epic, as described in the Yirrkalla version. To facilitate this, a chapter of detailed comments has been added to each part, or group of songs. These separate chapters have reviewed briefly the significance and symbolic intent of each song; they have indicated, too, the various threads running through all the parts, and their interrelated themes. We have thus already glimpsed the cycle as an integrated whole, and noted the fundamental elements which have emerged. It remains, now, for us to draw broad conclusions on this basis. Final conclusions must, however, rest on our analysis of the Milingimbi version of this same cycle. That version is complementary to the one reviewed here, and although its basic themes are similar, and its fundamental intent is the same, it does contain a number of additional features. These differences, insignificant as they may seem, must be taken into account in making our final summary of the Djanggawul cult in north-central and north-eastern Arnhem Land.

Reading through the mythology and songs of the Djanggawul cult, we can perhaps begin to appreciate something of the care and thought which have gone into their construction, in the form in which we see them to-day. Through them it is possible for aliens such as ourselves to understand in some degree the fundamental issues involved in one Aboriginal religious cult. Moreover, it is only through the medium of such material, particularly in the form of interlinear translations, that we may attain more than a superficial understanding of Aboriginal thought and behaviour. These

Epilogue

songs express what may be described as the spiritual quality of this particular Aboriginal society. They are essentially traditional, and have developed within the society as the result of group rather than of conscious or acknowledged individual effort. The individual is thus subordinated to the social conscience, in that he becomes the instrument through which they are transmitted, and through which they continue to live. The fact that he may add something to them in the course of transmission is not, here, a significant factor in this process: for if their inherent 'power', or their sacred aura, is to remain, they must retain what is felt to be their original structure in recognizable form. In this lies their essential value as documents of social thought and religious belief. Being predominantly traditional, they stem from the past; and because the concept of the 'Eternal Dreaming' is a living reality in Aboriginal life, these songs continue to retain at least the main ingredients (or what people themselves regard as the main ingredients) of their original content. Moreover, their oral transmission has been associated with special rhythms and ritual postures, and with accompanying dances, providing means of expression for the sacred thought and emotion not merely of one but indeed of many generations of Aborigines.

The Djanggawul songs and mythology comprise a body of knowledge which is not restricted, in the sense of being available to only one section of the community, but is shared by all adults and (to a much lesser extent) children. For practical purposes, a distinction is made between, on the one hand, the executive authority wielded by the men, and on the other, the more submissive participation of the women. Women know the content and rhythms of the songs, but 'officially' they are not supposed to know the ritual or the sacred invocations, or to see the *rangga* emblems. Generally speaking, however, they do know more about these than would be suspected from conversations with men alone. A number of women have described to my wife, in confidence, various features of the rituals performed exclusively and 'secretly' by men. They have described the *rangga* emblems, and told her many of the sacred terms used in invoking. An explanation of this lies in the Aborigines' concept of sacredness, which is not restricted to the confines of the ceremonial ground. It is, on the contrary, widely diffused throughout the society, and appears to permeate every institution and activity of the people. Women, as we have seen, by virtue of their childbearing ability as symbolized by the womb, possess a special sacred quality peculiar to themselves, in which men may not share. However important man may be—and the indispensable part he plays in conception receives much attention in the Djanggawul epic—woman has the more spectacular

293

Epilogue

rôle, and the miracle of childbirth is hers alone. Upon that simple but fundamental thesis much of this traditional epic is based.

Woman's participation in the *dua nara* is thus both logical and necessary. Each sex, however, has its own part to play; and the Djanggawul cycle has indicated not only the physical but also the culturally defined ritual differences between men and women.

In this volume, when describing the beliefs and practices associated with the Djanggawul cycle and the performance of *nara* ritual, we have purposely employed the term cult. This does not mean, however, that it is controlled or shared by a select group, the acceptance of members within the order being determined by totemic, clan or linguistic group affinities, by status, prestige or economic position. This is not so. The Djanggawul cult is one of a number existing contemporaneously in this region, each having its own mythology and associated ceremonies. All these cults are in some degree interrelated, and all male members of the society are eligible as active participants. Boys and young men pass automatically through the age-grading ceremonies of the *djunggawon*, *kunapipi* and *ngurlmag*. In addition to these, there are certain revelatory rituals, which are not initiatory. The extent of a man's active participation in the latter, and his eligibility for leadership, depend upon several factors—for example, on his moiety and kinship affiliations, and on whether or not the cult's mythology and ritual belong to his particular linguistic group or clan, and to his father's family. Such factors, however, never operate to debar him altogether, and in many cases his relationship to the cult through his mother's family may have a compensatory effect. The same conditions apply in the case of the major religious cults, the *dua* and *jiritja* moiety *nara*. All men may be accepted as initiands to the *nara* ceremonies, and all may subsequently become neophytes; but the measure of their active participation and leadership depends on the factors mentioned above. Only a *dua* moiety man, belonging to the most powerful *dua* linguistic group and clan, can rise to ceremonial headmanship in the *dua nara*; and here, too, the principle of descent may operate. The writer's main informants in recording and discussing the Djanggawul songs, mythology and so on were *dua* headmen, assisted by other men who were correspondingly 'graded' in the ritual sphere.

Comparison of the myth (Chapter 2) with the Songs reveals certain inconsistencies. These may perhaps stem from the fact that the myth is an over-all sketch of the Djanggawul's journey and adventures; it allows rather more latitude and scope to individual narrators, and does not purport to describe various incidents in any great detail. On the whole, it does agree basically with the Songs; but

294

Epilogue

whereas the latter terminate abruptly at Arnhem Bay, the myth draws to its anticipated conclusion somewhere beyond Milingimbi. Presentation of the Milingimbi version will throw some light on this question of the myth in its relation to the songs: for, as mentioned earlier, it not only repeats much of what has been set out here, but continues on to the Balbanara district, on the mainland south-west of Milingimbi. Even so, some of the place names mentioned in the myth are omitted from the Songs, and some of the incidents said to have taken place are not correlated. For example, we are told in the myth that the Sisters' clitorises were first cut at Dambala(nguru), whereas in the Songs this is done at Marabai. The two places are, however, close together; the most important point is that in both instances the cutting occurs after the Sisters have lost their sacred basket and *rangga*. Several other details, such as the piercing of the Sisters' hands by the *gabila* mangrove 'nail' fish, are not treated in the Songs; the latter incident, however, took place when the *rangga* fish traps were being erected (Part Four), so that this seems to be a matter of omission rather than of contradiction. Other features, like the *jiritja* moiety water blocking the Djanggawul at Waruwi, the flying foxes at Maiilwi, the meeting with Buralindjingu, and the Djanggawul's sojourn on Galiwinggo Island, are contained in the Milingimbi version. In the Songs, no mention is made of the killing of Miralaidj by sorcery, and of her miraculous reappearance; possibly this was not a traditional element, and was inserted without sacred sanction.

Where actual discrepancies are found between myth and Songs, it is difficult to find a satisfactory explanation. It is perhaps reasonable to suggest, as above, that the traditional songs are less subject to apparent alteration, while the myth depends on individual telling without the operation of the same social controls, and the story-teller is not bound to adhere rigidly to the main theme. Nevertheless, the myth provides a 'setting' for the Songs, and helps us to glimpse the whole in perspective even if not in considerable detail; on the other hand, it does not reveal the symbolic significance of the cycle in the same clear fashion as the Songs.

The Songs are presented here in the way in which they are sung The original sequence, word order, and structure are retained (except that when sung rapidly there is some slurring and abbreviation of words, not manifested in slower singing). The only thing lacking is the accompanying music; for they are, as mentioned, sung in conjunction with ritual and dancing. When the anthropologist has knowledgeable and competent informants, is acquainted with the language and with the ritual, and records the words as they are sung, the margin of possible error is considerably

295

minimized. Moreover, the constant repetition, which serves to impress on listeners the main features of the Songs, has a similar effect upon the singers themselves. An important device where transmission is entirely oral, with no visual aids except the sacred objects employed in the rituals, it also helps to ensure that the essential outline of the Songs is handed on from one generation to another. With the myth, however, it is rather a different matter. The myth is never narrated consecutively as a story, and there is no accompanying check of song and ritual. It is told in fragments, so to speak, to explain certain physiographical features, elements of social behaviour, or ritual activities; or brief extracts from it may be cited in the course of relevant discussion. The myth as related in this volume is composite, and represents a synthesis of several versions.

In some points, the myth as told by women does not conform to that told by men. Essentially, however, all the versions are in agreement. Women, too, stress the long penis of the Brother and clitorises of the Sisters; the stealing of the basket and *rangga*, and leadership of the *nara* rituals; the association with the sun and with the *lindaridj* parakeet; and the sacredness of menstrual and after-birth blood. They are inclined to emphasize the powers of the Two Sisters at the expense of the Brother, and to credit them with creating and leaving the most important animal and vegetable foods for the benefit of the Aborigines who were to follow them. The important childbearing rôle of the Djanggawul Sisters, setting the pattern which women follow to-day, is said to have been introduced by themselves. Before this, among the spirit people inhabiting the land, women would select babies from the many to be found sitting among the foliage of the cycad palms, and take them back to camp to be breast-fed by the men. Women, it is said (with a certain amount of rationalization), were too busy with sacred ritual to attend to the bearing and rearing of children. The Djanggawul, however, started the practice of child-bearing as it is now known, and were the True Mothers of the Aboriginal race in this region.

Let us turn now to a review of the Song Cycle as it is presented here.

In Part One the Djanggawul leave Bralgu, the island of Spirits, to which they had come from somewhere farther across the sea. The Songs emphasize the fact that this was the place from which they voyaged to the Australian mainland. The Morning Star, too, was sent from Bralgu, and from there rose the sun, the influence of which is felt throughout the cycle: for, as mentioned in Chapters 1 to 3, the Djanggawul Sisters

Epilogue

are associated with the sun, and the rays of sunlight in concrete and tangible form are the red breast feathers of the parakeet, and the feathered *rangga* strings.

The main theme of this part (One) is the Djanggawul's journey through the rough sea, guided by the rays from the Morning Star which shine upon the water. On the journey they see many fish, and marine animals; the movement of these, together with the Djanggawul's paddling, creates waves and causes the sea to grow rough. Foam sprays over the canoe, staining their bodies and hair, and the *rangga* emblems stored away in the *ngainmara*. A whale appears and is likened to the *ngainmara* mat; and, later, *rangga* emblems and *ngainmara*, thought to have been irrevocably damaged by moisture, are tossed overboard. The Morning Star gives way to the glow of early morning as the Djanggawul near the mainland. Various birds herald the coming dawn; the warming rays of the sun appear, and the Djanggawul enter Port Bradshaw harbour.

This part sets the pattern for the rest of the cycle, by introducing different elements which are developed and co-ordinated as the Songs proceed. The movement of the sea, with the incoming and the ebbing tides, is an integral feature, and is associated with the rising and flooding of fresh-water wells. The foam caused by such movements is also symbolically important, and is constantly mentioned in connexion with the *rangga* and feathered strings. In fact, the fluctuations of the tides, and the rising well-waters flooding the land, come to serve as a dominant theme. It is this section of the cycle which sponsors much of the basic *nara* ritual, as set out in Parts Eight, Nine and Ten.

In Part Two the Djanggawul arrive at Jelangbara, Port Bradshaw, and make wells by plunging into the ground the point of their sacred *mauwulan* pole. They also 'plant' trees, which spring from their *djuda rangga*; and various birds and reptiles become totemic through association with them. Here, too, the parakeet is mentioned for the first time. Its red (or deep orange) breast feathers reflect the rays of the setting sun, and are looked upon as being part of the sun itself; this attitude is particularly important, in view of the significance of the parakeet-feathered strings used on the *rangga* and sacred baskets or dilly bags. As these birds sit in the trees which have grown from the *djuda*, they ruffle and dry their feathers in the warmth and glow of the sun, just as the Djanggawul dry the feathered strings which were moistened by sea spray and foam.

The Djanggawul construct a *nara* shade, hanging from it sacred baskets, and make a mound at one side of the clearing used as a dancing ground. This represents the sacred sandhill at the Place of the Mauwulan, where the *djanda rangga* goanna appeared, and left his tracks. (In memory of this occasion, and because that sandhill was particularly sacred, a small symbolic 'sandhill' of earth is always made at the *nara* ground.) The goanna then jumps into the fresh-water well, and the water rises

Epilogue

(just as the various sea creatures brought about the movement of the sea and its tides). An alien element is superimposed here, as the Djanggawul come in contact with the Baijini folk. This element, although important in many ways, is not co-ordinated with the rest of the cycle, and can thus be accorded only passing reference. The Baijini cycle itself will be presented and discussed later; it is associated with the Macassan cycle, since the Aborigines regard the Baijini folk as aliens, physically and culturally distinct from themselves.

In Part Three the Djanggawul leave Port Bradshaw, and search for a place at which to construct a *nara* shade. As they travel along they 'make country', plant *djuda* trees, plunge their *mauwulan* into the ground so that wells gush forth, and arrange feathered strings which grow into yam creepers and foliage. Billowing white clouds beckon the Djanggawul onwards. Geese, which are in reality *rangga*, are placed in the well, and the water bubbles up; these geese symbolize the *rangga* children who will later emerge from the Sisters. Various fish are caught and declared sacred, and come into 'Dreaming'. Water goanna, too, are put into the well. In consequence of all this the water surges up and overflows, flooding the countryside. At last the *nara* shade is erected, and the foam-splashed *rangga* emblems are removed from the *ngainmara* and dried in the sun.

Part Four sees the Djanggawul reaching Arnhem Bay. Here more *djuda* are planted, and upon them parakeets perch crying. One of the Sisters feels unwell, and cannot walk quickly. She is pregnant; her uterus is full of people. A place is prepared, and the people are removed from her. Fish traps, with *rangga* posts, are arranged at Wagulwagul, the Place of the Mat. The well water continues to rise and spreads across the country, bringing fish which are caught in the trap. Later, the Djanggawul sit in their shade and decorate the *rangga*.

Part Five refers, symbolically, to the removal of the *rangga* folk from the Sisters. As the Djanggawul walk along, they reach a tidal creek in which a whale is stranded; this is the *ngainmara* mat, and refers back to the whale mentioned in Part One. Later on a shade is constructed, and a fire kindled to provide warmth for the Sisters during the process of childbirth. Mangrove shells and *rangga* are removed from the *ngainmara*, and the fringe of the mat or basket is cut (an act of *nara* ritual significance). The ground at the sacred shade is specially laid out, with the symbolic sandhill of the Place of the Mauwulan to one side (*vide* Part Two). More *djuda* are placed in the well, and the water rises; the parakeets, perched on the *djuda*, dry their feathers in the glow of the setting sun and finally disappear.

Part Six continues the theme which made its appearance in the preceding part. Most of the Songs here relate symbolically to the removal of the people from the *ngainmara*-womb. Feathered strings are spread out on the ground, leading or pointing to various places associated with the Djanggawul, and representing umbilical cords. More people are removed from the Sisters, and the male children are likened to circumcision novices. The cutting of the umbilical cord signifies the cutting of the foreskin. In both cases there is a severance from the Mother, and the significant point made here is that circumcision is ritually a rebirth. Children are placed in the sacred shade to play in the sun's rays, and a comparison is drawn here with the parakeets drying themselves in the sun. In this part, too, a division between the sexes is noted for the first time (a theme elaborated in Part Ten); male children are removed first, and left unprotected in the coarse grass, while female children are taken out later and are protected by the *ngainmara* mat.

Part Seven continues with the removal of *rangga* folk. More *djuda* and other *rangga* are put into the sacred well, and the water rises and floods. A *nara* shade is built; and more *rangga* are hidden in the well, which is equated with the *ngainmara* or womb.

Part Eight is principally concerned with the Djanggawul Sisters' loss of the sacred basket and *rangga* emblems. They are stolen by the Brother and his *galibingu* companions (circumcision novices: *vide* Part Six), who take over the *nara* ritual. The Two Sisters have hung their basket, or dilly bag, from a tree in their shade above a fire which they have prepared, and have gone out to collect mussels. *Rangga* folk are again removed, and *djuda* planted. Warned by a bird, the Sisters return to find their basket and *rangga* gone. They discover that the men have taken it, and hear the ritual in progress. In this way, the women come to lose their active control of the *nara*. Nevertheless, although deprived of this function, they retain absolute authority over the *ngainmara*, the *djuda* and other *rangga*. They do not mind surrendering their sacred objects to the men, for they have really lost nothing.

This section is probably the most spectacular in the whole cycle and, to the Aborigines, the most important: for it not only explains the monopoly which the men hold to-day in so far as executive control of the *nara* is concerned, but also emphasizes the economic division of labour between the sexes (that is, the Sisters are now to grind cycad nuts for 'bread').

Immediately after this, the Djanggawul Brother shortens his penis, a sign of 'emancipation', representing symbolically the severance of the umbilical cord, this in turn being identified with circumcision (*vide* Part Six). Then comes the cutting of each Sister's elongated clitoris; this action symbolizes the severing of the umbilical cord which links the *rangga* children with the mother, the loss of their *rangga* and basket and of their symbolic penes, and their acceptance of their new status (upon losing their former executive powers for controlling the *nara* ritual). When the cutting is completed, more *rangga* folk are taken from the

Epilogue

ngainmara; and this part concludes with the stolen sacred basket hanging from the men's *nara* shade.

As Part Nine opens, the Djanggawul are again continuing on their way, 'making country'. The Sisters are still pregnant. One lies in the sacred *nara* shade (although they have lost their basket and *rangga* they have not, apparently, been debarred from the *nara* shade or ground); her clitoris is again shortened, and more people are put out. The Djanggawul Brother attempts to have coitus with the younger Sister, Miralaidj, but his penis is 'blocked' by an arm-band lodged in her vagina. The cut clitoris is healed in the warmth of the sun; the blood which flows from it, and the red walls beyond the labia majora, are symbolic of the red rays of the setting sun, and of the red breast feathers of the parakeet. Miralaidj is then covered by the *ngainmara*, to signify her sacredness. *Rangga* folk dance from the Sisters' wombs into the *nara* shade. Again the Brother attempts to have coitus with Miralaidj; his *rangga* penis is erected, and in copulating he breaks the arm-band inside her vagina. Blood flows, and numbers of *rangga* people emerge. Bildjiwuraroiju aids her younger Sister by releasing, through abdominal pressure, a clot of blood which eventually liquefies and flows. Again Miralaidj is placed beneath the *ngainmara*, in sacredness. *Rangga* folk stand in the shade with the Brother and the elder Sister, and the first *nara* dancing begins in earnest. They stand in strict formation, like rising clouds, like 'fighting men'.

At this juncture, there is much stress on the *rangga* folk's having come from the Sisters: 'From resting within the womb: pulling them out from the womb! . . . Lying within the uterus!' This is a reference to their initial journey across the sea from Bralgu, and to their sojourn in the *ngainmara* and later in the sacred shade. The *nara* ritual continues, the *rangga* folk being guided by their leader, the Brother himself under the direction of Bildjiwuraroiju. Most of the ritual is related to incidents mentioned in Part One, for it is a re-enactment of the journey of the Djanggawul.

In the final Part (Ten), more *rangga* are removed; and the distinction between the sexes, originally noted in Part Six, is elaborated. The female *rangga* children are separated from the male children and declared sacred for they are like the Djanggawul Sisters—the source of all sacredness and ritual power. It is said that the *rangga* folk are born so that they may grow up to follow the Djanggawul law. The girls are 'sewn up' in the *ngainmara*; but they are later removed, having assumed or intensified their *rangga* quality. Many sacred baskets or dilly bags are hung from *djuda* and from the *nara* shade; from them *rangga* are removed, and with their feathered strings are placed to dry in the sun. The *nara* ritual proceeds, and the epic concludes suddenly with the cutting of the fringe of the basket.

Epilogue

This brief summary has mentioned only sparingly the symbolism manifested in the cycle, being confined chiefly to a description of the main incidents dealt with in the Songs. We may now indicate something of their symbolic significance, and the basic trends which emerge.

The most important theme, which extends throughout the whole cycle, centres about the sacred *ngainmara* mat. This is the symbolic uterus, which makes its appearance in the early stages of the epic. The *ngainmara* conical mat, while always retaining this essential significance, is also expressed in other terms; it may be a whale, a basket or dilly bag, a well, or a *nara* shade, and all these come to be associated with its particular function. Although the Songs may mention only one uterus, usually the reference is to both Sisters, so that when one *ngainmara* is described, the context may suggest two. (Nouns, in dialects of this language group, retain the same form for singular and plural.)

Incorporated in this theme, and an important adjunct to the *ngainmara*, are the sacred *rangga* emblems with their feathered strings, made chiefly from parakeet breast feathers. These *rangga* are always referred to in conjunction with the *ngainmara*; fundamentally, they symbolize the male, the *ngainmara* the female. The *rangga* are manifested in various forms, each with its separately defined function: the *djanda* goanna and goanna tail with the *mauwulan*, have the power to bring forth water when plunged into the ground, while the *djuda* when 'planted' grow into green trees, and the feathered pendants attached to them become live parakeets. These are the primary *rangga* (although secondary *rangga* do exist, and are used on the *nara* ground), and they symbolize the penis. Once the basic significance of the *ngainmara* and the *rangga* is realized, and their importance as a twofold combination, many of the situations in the Songs become clear. Understanding of this simple but fundamental framework of the Djanggawul cult helps us to understand its more complex manifestations, and its wider implications. The symbolism of the *rangga* is also extended further, like the *ngainmara*, to include certain trees, the elongated penis of the Djanggawul Brother, and the people who emerge from the Sisters.

Although the *rangga* does not invariably represent the male (for example, it is frequently used to signify both male and female children emerging from the 'mat'), as the *ngainmara* does the female, this is its more usual significance. The testes, however, are absent from this constellation. It is possible that the hanging of sacred baskets from the *rangga* may have some relevance here, but since this is not the Aboriginal interpretation we shall not speculate further along those lines.

Epilogue

The two elements, the *ngainmara* and *rangga*, in their various forms, serve as a combination through which two basic situations find expression. The symbolism relates in the first place to sexual intercourse, in the second to pregnancy and eventual childbirth. Apart from such symbolic representations (although these are more numerous), direct references to coitus and childbirth are made, and help to explain the others.

Let us consider the first situation. *Rangga* emblems are kept within the *ngainmara* mat, being from time to time withdrawn and inserted into the ground; they are put away in the *ngainmara* and covered up, in sacredness; they are plunged into the ground to make wells, so that water gushes forth; *djuda rangga* are 'planted', so that trees grow from them; totemic objects and animals (birds or reptiles) are put into a sacred well, so that the water rises and overflows; *rangga* are put in the shelter of a *nara* shade, or returned to a sacred basket or dilly bag; parakeets fly into the *ngainmara*, basket, or well and are hidden within it out of sight; and the Djanggawul Brother erects his *rangga* to place it within the *ngainmara*. All these situations, and many more, symbolize the insertion of the Djanggawul Brother's penis in the *ngainmara*, which although really the uterus, may also signify vagina or vulva. The most complete symbolic representation of coitus is the plunging into the ground of the *mauwulan rangga* forming a well, with gushing water (that is, penis insertion/vagina/ejaculation/withdrawal). The rising water flooding the countryside signifies fertilization.

In the second case, the same elements are employed, but their significance is altered: the *ngainmara* (like its various associated forms) is solely the uterus, and the *rangga* and feathered strings are children (people or *rangga* folk). This seems, indeed, to be their most important manifestation. It is expressed in a number of obvious situations which have been indicated throughout this work. For example, *rangga* emblems and feathered strings are removed from the mouth of the *ngainmara* mat (shade, basket or well); the *ngainmara* is heavy, being full of *rangga* people; fish, which are declared totemic, are caught in fish traps (constructed from *rangga* poles); and fish escape from the mouth of the whale, or are swallowed when brought in by the rising tide. The ideal symbolic representation is the *ngainmara* mat full of *rangga*, which are later removed (that is, uterus/pregnancy/delivery of *rangga* folk).

These two correlated themes, then, are basic to the cycle; together, they centre about one of the fundamental drives of mankind. The need for sexual satisfaction is simply and symbolically expressed, with a complete absence of consciously erotic manifestations; following this come pregnancy and, eventually, childbirth. The

Epilogue

importance of physiological paternity has not, moreover, been left a vague issue. The complementary rôles of male and female are established traditionally, both symbolically and (to a lesser degree) directly.

In addition to these, and in varying degrees linked with them, there are a number of subsidiary threads. There are four predominating themes, all in some degree interrelated, and almost invariably used in conjunction with the *ngainmara-rangga* concept. The first is crystallized in the umbilical cord, which is symbolically manifested in a variety of forms, the most important being the elongated clitorises of the Two Djanggawul Sisters, the long penis of the Brother, the prepuce, rays from the Morning Star, rays from the setting sun, feathered strings, and so on. Various examples are found in the Songs: the Djanggawul Brother cuts his long penis, after he and his companions have stolen the sacred basket and *rangga* from the Sisters; he shortens his Sisters' clitorises after the theft, when he and his companions have taken over control of the *nara*; and feathered strings removed from the *ngainmara* are arranged on the surface of the ground. The ideal illustration of the theme is as follows: *rangga* folk have their foreskins cut immediately after they have issued from the *ngainmara*-uterus, the foreskin symbolizing the umbilical cord, and its cutting their severance from the Mother; this is the intent of circumcisional initiation, with its subsequent 'rebirth'.

The second theme is connected with the sun. This element is symbolically manifested in several ways, the most obvious being: rays of light from the setting sun; the red reflections from the sunset, caught on the breast feathers of the *lindaridj* parakeet; the feathered *rangga* strings, the sacred basket pendants and the hair string waistband intertwined with red feathers; the parakeet itself, with breast and throat feathers; fire; blood (flowing after birth, at menstruation, or as a result of the Djanggawul Brother's breaking the arm-band blockage in the younger Sister's vagina); red ochre; and the red walls of the vagina or labia majora. One of the most strongly emphasized of these is the parakeet, with its red breast feathers, constantly appearing throughout the cycle.

The third theme relates to water, in its fresh or salt manifestations. The pattern is set during the initial stage of the Djanggawul's journey to the north Australian mainland. The movement of the sea is brought about (or intensified) through their paddling, and the presence of fish and marine creatures. This causes the ebb and flow of the tides. When the Djanggawul leave the sea to travel inland, and later along the coast, this theme is continued in the well waters rising and overflowing in conjunction with the tidal fluctuations. Even when the wells predominate, however, the sea is not forgotten; the original theme is recalled again and again throughout the cycle. It is the sea, too, which receives much attention in the *nara* rituals (for example, in those performed by *rangga* folk, mentioned in the cycle). Nevertheless, the importance of the well waters must not be underestimated. Apart from their association with the sea and its tides, they are in their own right spirit centres; and these are sacred, for the *rangga* emblems have been put within them or within their mud, and *djuda* have been planted around them. Moreover, the well is identified with the uterus, with the *ngainmara*, and with the sacred *nara* shade.

The fourth theme is concerned with seminal fluid, which is symbolized by the foam of the sea, or by rough water surging from an overflowing well. It is this foam which splashes on to the *rangga* emblems and *ngainmara* mat during the Djanggawul's journey from Bralgu, staining not only these objects and the feathered strings, but also the long clitorises and penis, and leaving on them a distinctive 'sea smell'. References are made throughout the cycle to the drying of the feathered strings of the *rangga*, and of the baskets.

These elements then, with the *ngainmara* and *rangga*, provide the skeletal structure or framework of the cycle, upon which the various situations have been constructed and elaborated.

Apart from the purely human element, reflected in the removal of *rangga* folk who serve as a nucleus from which has grown the present Aboriginal population, the cycle is concerned, in its wider implication, with the universe about them. The Djanggawul are said to 'make country' as they travel. We have seen however, from both the Myth and the Songs, that the country as such was already there on their arrival. Where the Songs describe their 'making country', therefore, we must assume that they merely put additional physiographical features. They made the sacred sandhill at the Place of the Mauwulan, which is symbolically represented in every *nara* to-day; they made innumerable wells, both sacred and secular, and planted multitudes of trees; and from their *rangga* and feathered strings birds, reptiles, animals and vegetables (yams) came into being, or became totemic. The Morning Star was sent for them by the Spirit people at Bralgu, to guide them through the sea to Port Bradshaw. And the sun came up for them, driving away the darkness and lighting up the land, sending its glowing rays in every direction, and warming all it touched.

Apart too from the matter of human fetility, the cycle concerns the fructification of the land, symbolized in the fluctuating tides of the sea, and the rising well waters. The plunging into the ground of the *mauwulan rangga*, with water gushing forth at its withdrawal, does not represent human sexual intercourse alone; symbolic coitus is taking place with the earth, so that it will be fertilized. The well water overflows and spreads across the land; the incoming tides push up the shallow tidal creeks and cover the low coastal plains: all symbolize the fertilization of the land. New vegetation will grow; the dormant grass and plants will send out their shoots; trees will bear leaves, blossoms and fruit; and the natural species will increase. The *djuda rangga* carried by the Djanggawul are always 'planted' near well waters, and their roots are said to be like penes that fertilize the earth. Billowing clouds from the north-west beckon the Djanggawul onwards, as they move from place to place; and the intensity of the sun's heat scorches the grass, making the shadows of the clouds welcome and desirable, and drying the moistened *rangga*. All this symbolizes the coming monsoonal rains, which will replenish the earth, renew all plant and vegetable matter and the natural species. Further, it indicates man's place in the universe, emphasizing the fundamental similarity between himself and his environment. The sexual drive in man results in the increase of his own species, just as he sees to be the case among the living creatures around him: and that basic theme is extended and elaborated to include his whole physical environment. According to this point of view, the earth itself must, therefore, be fertilized in much the same way as man—through symbolic coitus, the plunging *mauwulan*, the piercing *djuda* roots, the flooding well, and the spreading incoming tide. All this to the Aborigine of north-eastern and north-central Arnhem Land, living as he does in close proximity to his environment, is real and vital. It constitutes for him a faith which is based essentially on his own experience, on a fundamental human and animal drive, projected on to his non-human and (as *we* see it) inanimate environment.

The Djanggawul myth and its songs, then, may be regarded as centring on the two primary drives of man: the first, sex, with its natural consequences, the second, food, which enables him to survive. Both are of equal importance, and both receive considera-tion in this cycle. The dominating interest however is that of sex, in a broader sense than this is usually understood in our own society; the Aboriginal thesis is that through the operation of this drive seasonal fluctuations will occur, and will automatically ensure the provision of food. From the Aboriginal standpoint, then, man's survival is essentially dependant on the success of the sexual drive: for food cannot become available unless the natural species copulate and increase, unless the rains fall, the wells overflow and the tides spread and fertilize the land. This attitude to them is fundamental, and for that reason it has become an outstanding theme in the sacred Djanggawul cycle.

Epilogue

These factors obviously centre about the survival of the Aboriginal social group, and in that respect they suggest an important sociological attitude. The Djanggawul Sisters, through their perpetual pregnancy, and their ability to produce great numbers of *rangga* folk, the ancestors of the present-day Aborigines, express their true function as Fertility Mothers. They define the physical differences between males and females, between the *rangga* and the mat; expressing this symbolically, they put the *rangga* boys who emerge from their wombs into the coarse grass, the *rangga* girls into the shelter of the *ngainmara*-uterus mat. By stressing the sacredness of womankind, this Aboriginal culture has enshrined motherhood, for it is realized that the continuity of the group is dependent primarily, and in a more spectacular way, on the female. To ensure this fertility, however, 'that the *rangga* within the *ngainmara* may remain plentiful', the contribution of the virile male is essential. The myth, therefore, acknowledges both physiological paternity and maternity. The *rangga* is as sacred as the *ngainmara*; and insemination (symbolically expressed in a variety of forms) is a biological necessity in the fertility sequence of coitus, conception, pregnancy and childbirth.

Two other important features receive attention in this cycle. The first, and perhaps the more important from a sociological point of view, is the division of labour between the sexes. The Djanggawul Sisters lose their sacred basket or dilly bag and *rangga* emblems, and the men take over control of the *nara* ritual. Now the Sisters must grind the cycad nut to make 'bread'; their 'hands must be whitened with its flour'. This mythological incident indicates, symbolically, the present division of activities between the sexes. It is not a question of any alteration in woman's status: she is not subordinated, or relegated to an 'inferior' position. On the contrary, stress is placed on the complementary nature of their activities. Woman must not resemble man, any more than man may resemble woman, the essential nature and implications of each (apart from biological factors) being culturally determined; hence the clitoris of each Sister is cut, so that it may not resemble a man's penis. Man may not be idle, merely collecting and preparing food while woman performs all sacred ritual, possesses all the *rangga* emblems and in addition carries out her important task of producing children. If women are to ensure the continuity of the group through childbearing, then men must perform the sacred ritual and do the more strenuous work; for this reason, so we are told, the men stole from the Sisters the sacred basket and *rangga* and took charge of the *nara* ritual.

The second feature is the institution of the sacred *nara* ritual,

306

which is created by the Djanggawul themselves. The *rangga* folk dance from the wombs of their Mothers into the *nara* shade; the sacred clapping sticks are beaten, the songs rhymically sung, and they sway their bodies in the dance. The first *nara* is being performed, re-enacting the travels of the divine Beings; and the *rangga* folk have been produced 'so that they may follow the law'. The people, that is to say, by performing the *nara*, by re-enacting the travels of the Djanggawul and manipulating the *rangga* emblems, ensure the continuation of the life they know and love. The *nara* performed by the *rangga* folk under the direction of the Djanggawul is described as being exactly the same as that carried out by present-day Aborigines. It expresses the faith which they have in their social group, in their culture, and in their environment; it ensures the continuance of all the elements expressed directly and symbolically in the myth and in the Songs. Women will continue to bear children, the seasons will continue to come and go in ordered sequence, and the land will continue to produce food in abundance. All this will come about only if the *nara* is enacted, if the power of the Sacred Beings is made available, and if the faith of the people themselves—both men and women—retains the intensity and depth originally inspired by the Djanggawul.

The implications of the Djanggawul cult are numerous, and should be the subject of detailed and comprehensive treatment. Here, however, we can touch on them only briefly.

There is, for instance, the assumption that these Beings came from another country, somewhere to the east or north-east, bringing with them their sacred objects and ritual, and the essentials of their cult. That is, they were originally aliens, who presumably introduced their ideology to the indigenous inhabitants. The latter are here referred to vaguely as spirits, and not as human beings; this is, possibly, a form of rationalization, to the effect that the first 'real' people were those who adopted the Djanggawul cult.

Then there are what may be termed the various psycho-analytic points of view. Followers of Géza Roheim, for example, may see in the stress on the Mother, and (for instance) the identification of circumcision with the severing of the umbilical cord, a manifestation of the universal Oedipus Complex. Abram Kardiner and his school may find in the Djanggawul a projection of the emotions arising from the Aborigines' response towards their own parents during their early formative years. Moreover, the myth and songs may perhaps be regarded as, primarily, an expression of the fundamental motivations of the people, the narrative itself serving merely as a connecting thread, which provides a semblance of coherence.

Epilogue

Certainly we may assume that the elements which have been transmitted from one generation to another bear some relation to the cultural emphasis of the people, the emphases during the process being on those which were (consciously or otherwise) felt to be congenial. However, this question obviously raises many issues which cannot be dealt with here.

Finally, what is the future of the ʾcult in the contact situation? The theme of fertility is obviously important in this respect, affecting as it does the continuance of the local Aboriginal group. Elsewhere in Australia, with few exceptions, the Aborigines have declined in numbers under the disrupting influence of the alien culture. In north-central and north-eastern Arnhem Land, the emphasis on reproduction, among both human and animal species, appears to have served, so far, as a potent factor in combating this trend. The Djanggawul cult, therefore, may well be significant in helping to ensure that the Aborigines of this region continue to survive. Perhaps because of its basic associations, it is still a vital force in the society, with (in so far as such comparisons are possible) an even greater emotional hold on the people than other local cults which flourish contemporaneously with it.

This subject, too, needs careful consideration. Nevertheless, if something at least of the faith and the beliefs of the Djanggawul cult can be carried on into the changing society which is developing as a result of alien contact, it may help to ensure the north-central and north-eastern Arnhem Landers' physical survival. Moreover, the blending of such essential features of their traditional life with the new elements which they inevitably absorb from the alien culture will provide them with a situation which is in some degree congenial to them; and the psychological effects of this will have, also, an important bearing on their survival.

The themes which we have noted in this work are not limited in their application to one human group in one specific area. Although phrased in the terms of this particular culture, they have, so to speak, a universal validity. This being so, there is no reason why the Djanggawul cult, adapted perhaps to meet the demands of the present crisis in Aboriginal life, should not endure as a living faith, to play its part in ensuring the continuity of the Aboriginal group, as a people adjusted to meet, in their own way, the changing world which confronts them.

GLOSSARY

Ancestral Times, see *wongar*.

baba, father.

babaru, father's clan; a concept of moiety unity with descent through the father.

Baijini, pre-Macassan visitors to the north-eastern Arnhem Land coast: now considered to be virtually contemporaneous with the Djanggawul.

baima, 'let (them) stay there'; 'always there'; or 'stay(ing) behind'.

Banaitja, son of Laintjung, an Ancestral Being, of the *jiritja* moiety: represented totemically as a barramundi fish.

Bildjiwuraroiju, the elder Djanggawul Sister: see *gungman*.

billabong, usually a lake fed by a main stream, or a branch of a river that, instead of returning to the main stream, comes to a dead end. Billabongs are formed, too, during the monsoonal season in low-lying parts of the country, and may remain for the greater part of the year.

bilma, see clapping sticks.

Bralbral, the companion of the two Djanggawul Sisters and their Brother. He also came from Bralgu, and journeyed with them for some little time.

Bralgu, the mythical island(s) of the dead for members of the *dua* moiety, from which the Djanggawul set out on the last stage of their journey to the Australian mainland.

Brother, the Djanggawul Brother, who came with the Two Sisters.

budjei, smell; salty 'sea' smell; smell of vagina.

bugali, invocation; invoking the presence of (in this case) the Djanggawul.

'bush' foods, those of indigenous growth (uncultivated).

Glossary

clan, see *mala*.

clapping sticks, sometimes called *bilma*: two sticks of resonant wood clapped together by a singing man, while another man blows on the drone pipe.

conical mat, see *ngainmara*.

Creative Beings, that is, the Djanggawul Sisters and Brother. (Also certain other Ancestral Beings connected only indirectly with the theme considered here.)

cycad palm nut, 'bread': cycad nuts are specially prepared and made into 'dampers' like bread, wrapped in fine paperbark, and stored for ceremonial times. In this context it is usually employed sacramentally.

dabi, foreskin, umbilical cord, clitoris, sun's rays (as well as other symbolic references).

dagu, vagina, vulva, sun's disc (and other symbolic references).

dal, see 'power'.

dalwuldalwul, mouth of the *ngainmara* conical mat; symbolic of vulva, etc.

deimiri, species of sawfish.

dilly-bag, general term for certain indigenous twined baskets used by both men and women. There are many shapes and sizes, some painted with coloured ochres, others hung with feathered pendants: in the context of this study, usually the latter. (In all cases, symbolic of the uterus.)

djalga, water goanna; also sacred emblem.

djanda, sacred emblem; goanna; goanna tail; phallic symbol; same function as the *mauwulan rangga*.

djawuldjawul, a mangrove bird.

djuda, tree *rangga* emblem, from which trees sprang up when plunged into the ground by the Djanggawul.

djunggawon, age-grading circumcisional ceremonies associated with the Wauwalak Cycle, which is connected only incidentally with the Djanggawul.

djummal, a mangrove bird (unidentified); also called a 'message' bird.

Dreaming, see *wongar*.

drone pipe, didgeridoo; hollow wooden musical instrument into which a man blows to provide an accompaniment to singing and dancing.

dua, one of the two moieties in the dual organization: the moiety to which belong the Djanggawul and the totems associated with them.

dua nara, the ceremonies instituted by the Djanggawul; the ritual expressions of the songs and mythology of these Beings, controlled by members of the *dua* moiety.

dugarei, a periwinkle or black shell, collected by the Djanggawul Sisters while their sacred bags and *rangga* emblems were being stolen by the men.

duldjiduldji, point of the sacred *mauwulan rangga* emblem.

Glossary

'Eternal stream', see *wongar*.

'feathered ball', disc of the Morning Star. These 'balls' are made by the Spirits of Bralgu, attached to long strings and poles and sent into the sky as they dance.

gadin, clitoris (referring to those of the two Djanggawul Sisters).

gadu, daughter or son (man speaking); brother's children (woman speaking).

galibingu, a circumcision novice.

ganinjari, sacred 'yam' stick or 'walking stick' emblem possessed of life-giving properties (used by the Djanggawul to obtain water).

Goanna Tail *rangga*, see *djanda*.

ground, sacred, used for sacred dancing, for example, of the *nara*; in this context it is symbolic of the uterus of either Djanggawul Sister.

gudara, sister's daughter's son or daughter, son's son or daughter (man speaking). See *mari* (*gudara* is the reciprocal of *mari*).

gumur, chest, front, barrier, etc.

gungman, referring to the elder Djanggawul Sister; a general word meaning a mature woman of child-bearing age, with children.

gurlga, penis; roots of tree (and many associated symbolic references).

jelagandja, a spirit bag; dilly bag; symbolic uterus.

Jelangbara, Port Bradshaw; sacred site on which the Djanggawul landed, of great significance in this cycle.

jiritja, one of the two moieties in the dual organization: associated with certain Spirits, Ancestral Beings and so on with which the Djanggawul came into association.

jiritja nara, the ceremonies associated with this moiety: connected only indirectly with the Djanggawul.

judu, child; semen.

jugujugu, younger sibling.

Julunggul, Rock Python snake, Rainbow, phallic symbol; used in association with the Wauwalak Sisters, a separate *dua* moiety cycle.

kunapipi, ceremonies related to the Wauwalak Sisters, and to a Fertility Mother concept introduced into northern Arnhem Land from the south; of higher ritual value than the *djunggawon*.

Laintjung, a *jiritja* moiety Ancestral Being who, with his son Banaitja, is the sponsor and instigator of the *jiritja nara* ceremonies.

ligan, jutting limb of a tree; elbow (of the Djanggawul Brother); sacred emblem; part of the *djuda rangga*, etc.

lindaridj, parakeet; feathers; redbreast feathers; feathered string and pendants. Of great importance in this cycle, with many symbolic references.

linguistic group, see *mata*.

maidjara, all the sacred emblems together.

Glossary

mala, in general speech, a crowd; specifically, a clan, with which one or more linguistic groups (*mata*) are associated; exogamous, and of patrilineal descent.

malara, group of clans; crowd; flock (of birds).

mali, human spirit, living or dead; used also in reference to *rangga*; a likeness, shadow, or reflection.

mandiela, circumcision ceremony associated with the Wauwalak Cycle: introduced into north-central Arnhem Land, but not into the north-east.

marabinjin, a species of sawfish.

mareiin (or *mareijin*), meaning sacred: also, a *nara* ceremony. Used in reference to men and women under certain conditions, to ceremonies, emblems, etc.

mari, mother's mother, mother's mother's brother, mother's brother's son's wife, mother's mother's brother's son's son or daughter, wife's brother's wife. See *waridj* and *gudara*.

mata, a linguistic group: one or more may belong to a clan or *mala*: exogamous, and of patrilineal descent. The *mata* is one of the most important units in eastern Arnhem Land social organization.

mauwulan, sacred emblem (*rangga*); stick used by the Djanggawul as a 'walking stick'; of life-saving properties (used to obtain water and make wells).

milngur, 'well', gushing spring; of symbolic significance.

Miralaidj, the younger Djanggawul Sister. See *wirlgul*.

moiety, see *dua*; *jiritja*; patrilineal in descent, and exogamous.

mugul rumarang, actual wife's mother (tabu).

munji, red berries of an unidentified bush.

nara, ceremony, see *dua nara*; *jiritja nara*.

native companion, the brolga bird.

ngadiba, waist-band of human hair.

ngadili, black cockatoo.

ngainmara mat, conically shaped. Of major significance in this cycle, belonging to the Djanggawul Sisters; a uterus symbol, a whale, etc.

ngandi, mother.

ngaungau, tabu.

ngurlmag, ceremonies of the Wauwalak cycle, of higher ritual status than the *kunapipi* or *djunggawon*.

nundu, a short conical mangrove shell (collected by the Djanggawul Sisters when their sacred emblems and bags were stolen by the men).

'power', sacred and ritual power, *dal*. A quality possessed by the Creative Beings, including the Djanggawul.

ragai, bulrush roots.

rangga, sacred emblem: used throughout this Djanggawul cycle.

rangga folk, *rangga* clansfolk, 'Sons and Daughters of the Djanggawul', those who initially emerged from the Djanggawul Sisters; ancestors of the present-day eastern Arnhem Landers; various symbolic references.

sacred hut, see shade, sacred.

sacred poles, emblems with life-giving properties (that is, *rangga*).

shade, sacred; hut or shelter placed (in this context) on the *nara* cere- monial ground from which dancers emerge; in it the *rangga* emblems are stored. Symbolic of the uterus, etc.

spearthrower, wooden object used to propel a spear.

spring water, which gushes forth when a *rangga* emblem is plunged into the ground; water bubbling up from the ground; well or waterhole overflowing. Symbolically significant.

'sugarbag', bee, wild honey (deposited in the ground or tree).

totemic, natural species and inanimate objects etc, which through their divine association with the Djanggawul Sisters and Brother (or other Creative Beings) become totemic. The Djanggawul them- selves were not totemic.

trepang, bêche-de-mer, sea slug: collected in historic times by the Baijini (pre-Maccassans) and Macassan traders.

Two Sisters, in this context the Djanggawul Sisters; the Fertility Mothers.

wagu, sister's son or daughter (man speaking); own son or daughter (woman speaking).

waridj, mother's mother's brother's son's son; or *mari*; a non-tabu-ed 'mother-in-law' (mother's brother's wife).

waterhole, see well.

Wauwalak, Two Sisters of the *dua* moiety, who sponsored the *djunggawon*, *kunapipi*, *ngurlmag* and *mandiela* ceremonies.

well, a waterhole, made by the Creative Beings: in this area, either rock- holes, soaks or deep wells of a permanent nature, in low-lying coastal regions subject to tidal fluctuations and monsoonal flooding. Many symbolic references.

wet season, monsoonal period, commencing in approximately November– December, and ending in approximately April–May.

wirlgul, referring to the younger Djanggawul Sister: an adolescent or pre-adolescent girl.

wongar, Dreaming, (belonging to the) 'Eternal' Dreamtime or 'Eternal Stream', Ancestral Times; Mythological period. Some Ancestral Beings and Spirits are *wongar*, but not the Djanggawul. Mainly a totemic concept.

wulma, cloud.

yam stick, woman's digging stick; in this context, used by the Djanggawul, a sacred emblem. See *ganinjari*.

GENERAL INDEX

Aboriginal Women, Sacred and Profane (Kaberry), 57
Africa, xxii
age-grading in rituals, 14, 52, 209, 294
alien contact on Arnhem Land coast, xxiii, 28, 53, 55, 58, 89, 180, 298, 308 (see also: Baijini)
American Anthropologist, The, xviii, 53, 54
Américana Indígena, xxiii
anthropologist, attitude towards material, xx, xxii
Aranda Traditions (Strehlow), xxi
armband, blocking younger Sister, 204, 206, 245, 264, 265, 266, 267, 268, 269, 270, 271, 287, 300
Arnhem Land, its History and its People (Berndt), xviii, xxiii, 5, 28, 53, 54
Art in Arnhem Land (Elkin, Berndt), xviii, 32, 54, 57, 276
Australian National Research Council, xix, xx

Baijini Folk, as contemporaries of Djanggawul, 28, 34, 54, 55, 78, 85, 86, 101, 102, 108, 109, 116, 117
— —, light skin of, 101,102, 116
Banaitja, xvii, xviii, 14, 36, 47, 51, 54
Bara clan, 82
B(a)ra(l) b(a)ra(l), 2, 24, 26, 31, 45, 63, 65, 66, 67, 68, 69, 70, 71, 72, 73, 74, 76, 77, 79, 80, 84, 91, 93, 94, 96, 98, 99, 100, 101, 102, 105, 106, 110, 115, 118, 119, 121, 124, 125, 131, 132, 133, 136, 153, 164, 236
Bara(l) bara(l) clan, 84
ba'ralginvu(l) as invocation, 155, 181, 223, 266, 276

Barara linguistic group, 78, 82
basket, sacred, symbolism of, 4, 64, 66, 87, 91, 117, 140, 148, 149, 150, 165, 170, 177, 178, 185, 189, 195, 208, 211, 224, 234, 247, 265, 277, 281, 289, 290, 300, 301 (see also: *ngainmara*)
Berndt, R. M. and/or C. H., xvii, xviii, xix, xxiii, 5, 6, 10, 11, 12, 27, 28, 32, 52, 53, 54, 57, 58, 60, 247, 264, 276
Bildjiwuraroiju, deferred to as leader, 266, 300
birth, treated in mythology and songs, 4, 5, 6, 7, 10, 11, 17, 18, 19, 22, 23, 30–1, 32, 33, 34, 36, 37, 38, 41, 42, 43, 47, 50, 56, 57, 82, 83, 86, 87, 111, 115, 118, 136, 140, 151, 152–3, 154, 156, 170–1, 174, 176, 177, 178, 179, 181, 185, 193, 195, 197, 198–9, 201, 202, 204, 206, 207, 208, 210, 211, 212, 214, 221, 222, 223, 233, 234, 237, 238, 244, 247, 249, 256, 257, 258, 259, 266, 267, 269, 270, 271, 272, 273, 274–5, 278, 279, 280, 281, 285, 286, 287, 288, 289, 293, 296, 298, 299, 302, 306, 307
Black Civilization, A. (Warner), xvii, xxi, 11, 49
blood, symbolic associations of, 5, 17, 45, 247, 256, 265, 268, 270–1, 274, 300, 303
bones, likened to *rangga* emblems, 7, 114
budjei, use of term, 178, 209, 212, 223, 246, 269, 274, 290
Buralidjingu, 22, 43, 44, 295

Capell, A, xxi
child, significance of terms for, 111, 117, 274

circumcision, novices, 44, 45, 52, 116, 210, 211, 212, 236, 244, 247, 299, 303
—, of *rangga* folk, 51, 197–8, 210, 211, 212, 225, 236, 237, 246, 247, 303
—, reasons given for, 45, 48, 51, 237, 299
—, significance of, 210, 211, 212, 237, 244, 247, 299, 303, 307
clan patterns, given by Djanggawul, 5, 17, 26, 87, 88
clans, origin of, 10, 47, 48, 234, 258, 272
clay, white, associated with Djanggawul, 96–7, 113, 122, 123, 141, 158
clitoris, interpretation of as *rangga*, 10–11, 26, 110, 132, 178, 202, 210, 237, 256, 267, 268, 269, 274
—, symbolism of, 4, 10, 11, 22, 26, 42, 52, 55, 133, 176, 178, 211, 233, 244, 245, 246, 247, 256, 258, 259, 265, 266, 267, 268, 269, 274, 276, 281, 287, 288, 289, 290, 299, 303, 306
cloth, wearing of on Arnhem Land coast, 28
clouds, symbolism of, 88, 108, 131, 135, 144, 148, 152, 155, 156, 158, 258, 259, 273, 279, 300, 305
coitus, emphasized as factor in natural fertility, 6, 7, 17, 115, 133, 154, 214, 304–5, 306,
—, treated in mythology, ritual and songs, 6, 17, 18, 21, 39, 43, 87, 110, 113–14, 115, 132–3, 134, 135, 136, 154, 158, 175, 177, 202, 214, 222, 246, 257, 265, 267, 268–9, 270, 271, 304–5, 306
conception, Aborigines' theory of, 6, 18, 133, 207, 271, 274
continuity, as feature of Djanggawul ideology, 6, 13, 23, 62, 111, 286, 306, 307, 308
cult, use of term in this study, 294
cycad palm 'bread', as symbol of food resources, 22
— — —, ritual eating of, 22, 44

dabi(n), use of term, 178, 211, 212, 244, 274, 289, 290
Dadawi linguistic group, 30, 32, 38, 48, 114, 134, 135, 155, 157, 177, 181, 204, 205, 207, 223, 238, 266
Dalwongu linguistic group, 34, 76, 90
dancing, of *rangga* folk, 39, 40, 41, 233, 236, 242, 243, 249, 256, 259, 260, 261, 262, 264, 265, 268, 269, 272, 275, 276, 277, 284, 290, 291, 300, 304, 307
—, symbolic, in *nara* rituals, 5, 14, 16, 17, 18, 19, 20, 21, 23, 85, 158, 177–8, 179–80, 207, 223, 242, 259, 260, 261, 262, 265, 275, 276, 277, 284, 290, 191, 300, 304, 307
—, totemic, 14, 17, 18, 19, 20, 21, 23
Daughters of the Sun (Berndt), xxi, 24

Department of Anthropology, Sydney University, xvi, xix, xxiii
djalga water goanna and emblem, symbolism of, 126–7, 132, 150, 158
Djambatpingu linguistic group, 32, 34, 35, 36, 37, 38, 42, 47, 48, 114, 155, 181, 204, 205, 207, 208, 221, 223, 237, 238, 239, 266, 267, 275, 276, 277, 286, 299
djanda goanna and emblem, symbolism of, 5, 6, 85, 99, 115, 136, 154, 178, 186, 253
Djanggawul, arrival on coast, 1, 2, 3, 5, 16, 17, 24, 27, 44, 46, 49, 53, 54, 80, 81, 86, 89, 90, 91, 93, 108, 116, 207, 209, 242, 265, 296, 303
—, as law-makers, 26, 45, 48, 51, 52, 279, 286, 287, 300, 307
—, as *rangga*, 5, 17, 114, 188, 194, 207
—, children of, 2, 4, 5, 6, 7, 10, 11, 16, 17, 18, 22, 30–1, 32, 33, 34, 36, 38, 39, 41, 42, 43, 44, 45, 47, 48, 49, 50, 51, 53, 56, 66, 78, 82, 83, 86, 87, 94, 111, 115, 116, 118, 124, 128, 131–2, 133, 136, 140, 151, 152, 154, 156, 157, 161, 162, 164, 166, 171, 174, 176, 177, 178, 179, 180, 181, 183, 185, 190, 193, 197, 198–9, 201, 202, 204, 206, 207, 208, 209, 210, 211, 212, 213, 214, 216, 221, 222, 224, 225, 233, 234, 236, 237, 238, 244, 245, 246, 247, 256, 257, 258, 259, 264, 265, 266, 268, 269, 270, 271, 272, 273, 274, 275, 276, 277, 278, 279, 280, 281, 285, 286, 287, 288, 289, 296, 298, 299, 300, 301, 302, 303, 304, 306, 307
—, dialects spoken by, 48, 180
—, footprints of, 102, 115
—, origin of, 1, 2, 3, 24, 81, 203, 296, 307
—, 'sons' of, 10, 136, 265, 290
—, superhuman abilities of, 54, 55, 56
Djanggawul cult, as relatively conservative, xvii, 308
— —, reasons for presentation of, xvii
— —, survival of in contact situation, 308
Djanggawul Sisters, as original custodians of sacred emblems and ritual, 15, 16–17, 19, 20, 39, 40, 49, 57, 58, 91, 110, 117, 157, 225, 232–3, 236, 237, 240, 241, 244, 245, 264, 265, 266, 289, 295, 296, 299, 300, 303, 306
— —, as 'ideal' women, 55–6
— —, as Mothers of *jiritja* moiety, 10, 47, 48, 286
— —, as novices, 22, 44, 52
— —, as original Mothers, 7, 10, 214, 277, 286, 296, 306
— —, bearing of children by, 2, 4, 6, 7, 10, 11, 12, 16, 17, 18, 22, 29, 30, 31, 32, 33, 34, 36, 37, 38, 41, 42, 43, 44, 47, 48, 49, 50, 51, 53, 82, 83, 86, 87,

111, 115, 116, 118, 124, 128, 131–2, 133, 136, 140, 141, 151, 152, 153, 154, 157, 161, 162, 164, 166, 171, 174, 175–6, 177, 178, 179, 180, 181, 183, 185, 190, 193, 197, 198–9, 201, 202, 204, 206, 207, 208, 209, 210, 211, 212, 213, 214, 216, 221, 222, 224, 225, 233, 234, 236, 237, 238, 244, 245, 246, 247, 256, 257, 258, 259, 264, 265, 266, 268, 269, 270, 271, 272, 273, 274, 275, 277, 278, 279, 280, 281, 285, 286, 287, 288, 289, 296, 298, 299, 300, 301, 302, 303, 304, 306, 307

Djanggawul Sisters, stressed at expense of Brother, 7, 10, 11, 20, 27, 37, 43, 49, 57, 58, 91, 110, 131, 136, 181, 236, 265, 296, 300, 306

Djapu linguistic group, 29, 32, 180, 203, 205

Djar(l)wak linguistic group, 29, 32, 38, 48, 203, 205, 209

djuda rangga and tree, identified with Djanggawul, 114, 188, 194

— — — —, symbolism of, 5, 6, 20, 27, 82, 90, 91, 95, 96, 98, 101, 103, 104, 109, 111, 112, 113, 114, 116, 117, 147, 148–9, 151, 152, 153, 154, 155, 157, 179, 189, 199, 207, 208, 209, 212, 213, 214, 222, 235, 238, 239, 257, 258, 259, 269, 272, 275, 276, 301, 302, 304, 305 (see also: *rangga*)

djunggawon rituals, 11, 14, 52, 58, 209, 247, 294

drawings, illustrating features of Djanggawul cult, xvi, 10, 11, 25, 91, 202, 203, 204, 205

—, left by Djanggawul, 26, 29, 44

Dreaming, eternal: see: Time, Aborigines' concept of

'dreamings' left by Djanggawul, 26, 27, 29, 30, 31, 32, 33, 34, 36, 41, 44, 48, 231, 240, 298

dreams, in relation to Djanggawul cult, xxi, xxii

dua moiety, xvii, xviii, xix, xxi, 2, 4, 14, 16, 18, 24, 25, 27, 28, 29, 34, 39, 41, 44, 46, 47, 48, 50, 51, 52, 54, 55, 60, 61, 81, 85, 89, 114, 135, 158, 175, 182, 221, 243, 294

duck, wild, as *rangga*, 112–3, 138, 151, 152

duju, significance of term, 209

duldjijuldji emblem, 1, 179 (see also: *rangga*)

Durkheim, Émile, xx, 13, 57

economic obligations in *nara* rituals, 15, 20

economy of Aborigines, correlated with ritual life, 5, 7, 13, 16–7, 22, 23, 40, 209, 243–4, 299, 305, 306, 307

Elementary Forms of the Religious Life, The (Durkheim), 57

Elkin, A. P., xviii, xx, xxiii, 5, 32, 54, 57, 276

emblems, sacred: see: *rangga*

Eternal Ones of the Dream, The (Róheim), 10

Evans-Pritchard, E. E., xxii

fertility, concept of, 3, 4, 5, 6, 10, 12, 13, 17, 18, 19, 21, 23, 50, 53, 55, 56, 57, 58, 82, 86, 90, 108, 109, 115, 116, 133, 154, 156, 176, 208, 214, 221, 222, 271, 272, 286, 302, 304–5, 306, 307, 308

fire, symbolized in ritual, 19

—, symbolism of, 17, 39, 162, 176

fish, as *rangga* emblems, 87, 125, 126, 132, 135, 144–7, 151, 152, 156, 157, 298, 302

—, symbolism of, 21, 87, 125, 135, 302

fish trap, symbolism of, 135, 144, 145, 146, 148, 152, 155, 156, 157, 161, 175, 302

foam, symbolism of, 21, 96–7, 108, 113, 115, 158, 206, 221–2, 223, 246, 274, 297, 304

foam marks, as *rangga* patterns, 17, 68, 87, 88, 91, 96, 97, 106, 109, 113

food, originally prepared by men, 17, 39, 40, 58, 243

—, provision of during *nara* rituals, 16–7, 22, 242–3

forked stick, in *nara* rituals, 19, 20

Frazer, Sir James, xxi

gadu (kinship term), 81

gagi, use of term, 209

galib(o)ingu, see: circumcision novices

Gandjawulgi linguistic group, 204, 205

ganinjari (*ganinjiri*) emblem, 5, 6, 20, 46, 85, 132 (see also: *rangga*)

Gillen, F. J., xx, 57

goanna, see: *djalga, djanda*

god, goddess: use of terms, 3, 10, 23, 55

goose, as *rangga*, 66, 86, 87, 124, 125, 131, 133, 135, 147–8, 152, 157, 164, 298

grading of rangga emblems, 4, 20, 21, 179–80

—, of sacred ritual, 12, 14, 15, 20, 21, 22, 210, 294

gudara (kinship term), 22, 44, 84

Gumaidj linguistic group, 90

Gunwinggu tribe, 19, 45

gurlga, use of term, 25, 113, 116, 212, 242, 246, 272, 274, 287

Guruguru linguistic group, 48

Gurwia clan, 86

Gwolamala linguistic group, 114, 156, 182, 207, 209, 238, 266, 276

Index

hair, pubic: symbolism associated with, 4, 18, 87, 133, 134, 156, 176, 177, 178, 206, 210, 211, 245, 287, 288, 289
Herskovits, Melville J., xxii, xxiii

incest, in Djanggawul mythology, 2, 26, 45, 48, 50, 51, 55
individual interpretation, 11, 52, 55, 201, 293, 294, 295
individual subordinated to social conscience, 293
informants, choosing of, xviii, xix, 294, 295
'inside' terms, use of, 1, 16, 18, 25, 27, 28, 33, 34, 61, 88, 155, 178, 179, 180, 209, 210, 221, 224, 237, 238, 246
invocations, sacred, 4, 15, 16, 18, 19, 21, 22, 25, 32, *et passim*

jiritja moiety, xvii, xviii, xix, 10, 14, 18, 25, 28, 34, 35, 36, 42, 44, 45, 46, 47, 48, 54, 55, 56, 85, 89, 90, 135, 175, 294, 295
— —, in relation to *dua nara* emblems and rituals, xvii, xviii, 14, 18, 22, 55, 175, 294
Journal of the Royal Anthropological Institute, 28
Julunggul snake, 41

Kaberry, P, 57
Kardiner, A., 307
Karlpu linguistic group, 29, 48, 133, 134, 135, 203, 205, 207, 266
Kunapipi (Berndt), xvii, xviii, 10, 11, 12, 16, 27, 41, 52, 54, 57, 58, 60, 62, 247, 261
Kunapipi cult and rituals, xvii, 10, 11, 14, 16, 27, 58, 294
Kupapingu (Gobabingu) linguistic group, 34, 36, 42

labour, division of between sexes, 56, 58, 233, 236, 242, 243, 244, 299, 306
Laintjung, xvii, xviii, 14, 28, 36, 44, 47, 51, 55
language, use of native, xix, xxii, 62, 201, 295
Lawrence, W. E., xviii
Lialaumiri linguistic group, 36
lindaritj parakeet, association with sun: see: sun
— —, symbolism of, 3, 4, 5, 17, 18, 19, 45, 46, 48, 50-1, 81, 82, 89, 90, 94, 97, 100, 104, 105, 109, 111, 112, 113, 117, 118, 133, 134-5, 139, 152, 170, 173, 181, 182, 199, 200, 208, 214, 220, 222, 224, 230, 234, 235, 239, 247, 255, 256, 268, 290, 297, 301, 302, 303

linguistic groups, xviii, xix, 14, 23, 29, 30, *et passim*
— —, origin of, 47, 48, 180
Love Songs of Arnhem Land (Berndt), 11, 60, 264, 267, 270, 271, 276
'L'Homme' (Paris), 57, 60

'Macassan' song cycle, 180, 298
Macassan traders on coast, 28, 29, 55, 89
Madarlpa linguistic group, 76, 90
Maidjara linguistic group, 43
Male and Female (Mead), 7, 57
mali, use of term, 207, 209
Man and his Works (Herskovits), xxii
mandiela ritual, 52
Marakulu linguistic group, 32, 135
Marangu linguistic group, 32
marei(j)in, 39, 54, 117, 156, 159, 179, 209, 270
mareiin cult, 19, 20
mari (kinship term), 2, 22, 84
marriage rules, xviii, 26, 51
Maung tribe, 222
mauwulan emblem, significance of, 1, 5, 6, 77, 82, 95, 154, 202, 221, 222, 237, 268-9, 301, 302, 304-5 (see also: *rangga*)
Mead, Margaret, 7, 57
men, likened to *rangga,* 18, 32, 285-6
menstruation, 58, 247, 268, 270-2, 296
Miralaidj, death and revival of, 35, 55, 56, 295
—, deferred to as leader, 93, 107, 121, 124, 125, 127, 128, 130, 140, 142, 143, 149, 150, 153, 162, 163, 165, 166, 167, 168, 169, 171, 172, 183, 185, 188, 190, 192, 196, 216, 226, 229, 238
Miwaitj linguistic group, xix
moieties, division in ritual, etc., xviii, xix, 14, 18, 22, 28, 44, 47, 51, 54, 55, 135, 175, 294
—, origin of, 10, 26, 47, 48, 51, 54 (see specifically: *dua; jiritja*)
mugul rumarang (kinship term, 84
Murdock, G. P., xviii
Murunggun linguistic group, 45
mythology, Djanggawul, expressed through ritual, xvii, xviii, xix, 4, 5, 6, 10, 12, 13, 14, 15, 16, 17, 18, 19, 20, 21, 22, 23, 51, 52, 53, 57, 60, 61, 293, 296, 307
— —, method of narrating, 52-3, 55, 61
— —, variations or discrepancies in, 1, 2, 3, 4, 5, 7, 12, 21, 24, 32, 39, 40, 41, 42, 45, 46, 47, 49, 50, 52, 53, 55, 58, 85-6, 292, 296

nara rituals, *dua,* background of, xvii, 12, 24, 40, 182, 221, 242, 259, 260, 261,

317

262, 265, 275, 276, 277, 286, 287, 290, 291, 293, 297, 298, 300, 304, 306, 307
nara rituals, factors governing participation in, 14, 15, 18, 20, 21-2, 179, 180, 210, 294
—— ——, first performances of, 20, 24, 26, 29, 39-41, 233, 236, 242, 243, 259, 260, 261, 262, 265, 275, 276, 277, 278, 284, 286, 290, 291, 299, 300, 306, 307
—— ——, men taking executive rôle in, 15, 18, 20, 40, 57, 233, 237, 242, 243, 265, 275, 290, 294, 299, 306
—— ——, purpose of, 23, 53, 61, 277, 307
—— ——, revelatory in nature, 14, 21, 52
—— ——, sequence of, xv, 16, 17, 18, 19, 20, 21, 22, 242
—— ——, sponsored by Djanggawul, 17, 24, 29, 277, 307
—— ——, symbolism of, 4, 14, 15, 16, 17, 18, 19, 20, 21, 22, 23, 85, 158, 177-8, 179, 207, 233, 242, 259, 260, 261, 262, 265, 268, 275, 276, 277, 287, 290, 291, 297, 300, 304, 307
nara rituals, *jiritja* xvii, 14, 294
nara shade or hut, allusions to in songs, 96, 109, 112, 113, 117, 118, 120, 297, 298, 299, 300, 301, 302, 304, 307, *et passim*
Native Tribes of Central Australia (Spencer and Gillen), 57
ngainmara mat, as female (uterus) symbol, 3, 4, 5, 6, 7, 11, 14, 16, 17, 31, 32, 33, 40, 50, 82, 83, 85, 86, 87, 90, 111, 113, 115, 117, 118, 133, 134, 135, 136, 140, 144, 151, 153, 154, 155, 156, 157, 158, 160, 161, 174, 175, 176, 177, 178, 180, 181, 182, 183, 185, 192, 193, 197, 198-9, 202, 204, 206, 208, 210, 211, 212, 213, 222, 223, 224, 226, 227, 229, 233, 234, 236, 238, 239, 244, 245, 246, 247, 256, 257, 258, 259, 265, 266, 268, 269, 270, 273, 274, 275, 278, 279, 280, 281, 285, 287, 288, 289, 298, 299, 300, 301, 302, 304, 306
—— —, ordinary uses of, 3, 6
—— —, placing of children in or on, 11, 31, 32, 33, 34, 47, 56, 87, 154, 156, 198-9, 210
—— —, sinking of, 66, 79, 80, 83, 86, 87, 91, 92, 297
—— —, symbolism of, 3, 4, 5, 6, 7, 11, 16, 17, 18, 19, 31, 32, 33, 40, 50, 66, 83, 86, 87, 90, 91, 92, 94, 99, 103, 110, 111, 113, 115, 116, 117, 118, 121, 129, 131, 132, 133, 135, 136, 139, 145, 146, 148, 149, 151, 152, 153, 154, 156, 157, 158, 160, 161, 163, 166, 170, 174, 175, 176, 177, 178, 180, 181, 182, 203, 206, 208, 210, 211, 212, 216, 218, 223, 224, 231, 233, 234, 239, 244, 246, 247, 252,

253, 254, 255, 256, 257, 258, 259, 266, 267, 268, 269, 270, 287, 288, 289, 290, 297, 298, 299, 300, 301, 302, 304, 306
ngandi (kinship term), 8
ngau(g) ngau(g), use of term, 209, 213, 270, 288
Ngeimil linguistic group, 29, 30, 31, 32, 33, 34, 48, 114, 133, 134, 135, 137, 152, 155, 156, 177, 178, 179, 181, 182, 203, 204, 205, 206, 207, 209, 221, 223, 238, 266, 276, 277
ngurlmak rituals, xvii, 11, 14, 58, 294

Oceania, xviii, xxi, 10, 54, 60, 62, 84
ochre, red, symbolic significance of, 17, 45, 78, 82, 303

paternity, physiological, 10, 18, 51, 57, 58, 154, 293, 303, 306
penis of Djanggawul brother, identified with *rangga*, 10-11, 26, 41, 48, 52, 110, 113-14, 134, 154, 156, 158, 234, 238, 244, 246, 257, 268-9, 270, 271, 276, 301, 302, 303
phonetics used in songs, xxi
polygyny, 7, 213
population of eastern Arnhem Land, xviii
pottery on Arnhem Land coast, 28
presentation of material in this study, xx, xxi, 201, 292
psychoanalysis, in relation to Djanggawul cult, 10, 307

Radcliffe Brown, A. R., xx
rangga emblems, as material symbols of cult, 3, 6, 22-3, 50, 53, 209, 297
—— —, as phallic symbols, 1, 5, 6, 20, 26, 32, 41, 48, 50, 87, 110, 113-14, 115, 116, 117, 133, 134, 135, 136, 154, 158, 177, 202, 234, 238, 245, 246, 257, 265, 268, 269, 270, 276, 300, 301, 302, 305, 306
—— —, attitude of neophytes towards, 14, 19, 20, 179-80, 209, 213
—— —, permanency of, 42, 52, 111, 223
—— —, preparation of, 15, 16, 17, 158, 298
—— —, symbolising people, 7, 16, 17, 18, 21, 22, 32, 82, 90, 94, 111, 115, 118, 124, 128, 131-2, 133, 136, 140, 144, 145, 147, 151, 152, 153, 154, 156, 161, 162, 164, 165, 166, 170, 171, 175, 176, 177, 178, 179, 180, 181, 185, 190, 192, 193, 195, 197, 198-9, 201, 202, 206, 207, 208, 209, 210, 211, 212, 213, 214, 215, 216, 221, 222, 225, 226, 233, 234, 237, 238, 244, 245, 246, 247, 249, 256, 257, 258, 259, 261, 264, 265, 266, 267, 269, 270, 271, 272, 273, 274,

Index

275, 276, 277, 278, 279, 280, 281, 287, 288, 289, 298, 299, 300

rangga emblems, symbolism of, 1, 5, 6, 7, 10, 16, 17, 18, 20, 21, 22, 23, 32, 42, 50, 52, 77, 78, 82, 86, 87, 89, 90, 91, 92, 95, 97, 98, 99, 101, 103, 104, 108–9, 110, 111, 115, 116, 117, 118, 124, 131–2, 133, 134, 135, 136, 138, 139, 141, 144, 145, 146, 147, 149, 150, 151, 152, 153, 154, 155, 156, 157, 158, 161, 162, 163, 165, 166, 170, 171, 175, 176, 177, 178, 179, 180, 181, 185, 190, 192, 193, 195, 197, 198–9, 201, 202, 206, 207, 208, 209, 210, 211, 212, 213, 214, 215, 216, 217, 221, 222, 223, 226, 233, 234, 235, 237, 238, 239, 244, 245, 246, 247, 249, 250, 255, 256, 257, 258, 259, 260, 261, 262, 264, 265, 266, 267, 268, 269, 270, 271, 272, 273, 274, 275, 276, 277, 279, 280, 281, 283, 284, 287, 288, 289, 290, 291, 297, 298, 299, 301, 302, 304, 305, 306

religion, comprehensiveness of, 55, 56, 57, 59, 180, 293

repetition, as feature of Djanggawul songs, 61, 92, 118, 137, 201, 266, 296

Research Committee, University of Sydney, xix

Riraidjingu linguistic group, 32, 38, 48, 89, 133, 134, 135, 155, 157, 179, 180, 203, 204, 205, 207, 266

Ritarngu linguistic group, 42

rituals, Djanggawul, in relation to myth and songs, xvii, xxi, 4, 6, 10, 12, 13, 14, 16, 17, 18, 19, 20, 21, 22, 23, 24, 39, 40, 41, 51, 52, 56, 57, 60, 61, 62, 85, 177–8, 179, 207, 237, 242, 243, 256, 258, 259, 260, 261, 264, 265, 268, 269, 272, 275, 276, 277, 290, 291, 293, 295, 297, 299, 300, 304, 307

Róheim, G., 10, 307

sacred aura, potentially harmful, 21

sea, importance of in *nara* rituals, 16, 17, 20, 85, 233, 242, 259, 260, 261, 262, 275, 276, 284, 304

seasons, in relation to Djanggawul cult, 5, 6, 18, 23, 108, 115, 131, 135, 155, 156, 242, 305

secrecy, associated with sacredness, 3, 4, 15, 16, 20, 27, 30, 34, 39, 40, 41, 57, 99, 102, 103, 115, 117, 124, 125, 126, 128, 129, 130, 131, 132, 136, 145, 146, 147, 148, 149, 150, 152, 156, 157, 158–9, 164, 167, 169, 178–9, 184, 186, 187, 188, 191, 192, 194, 195, 196, 198, 199, 206, 207, 209, 213, 216, 217, 218, 219, 220, 221, 227, 228, 231, 233, 234, 238, 240, 245, 250, 251, 252, 253, 254, 257, 260, 261, 262, 263, 266, 270, 277, 279, 280, 281, 282, 283, 284, 288, 290, 293, 300

sex, Aborigines' attitude towards, 6, 7, 11, 57, 302, 305

sexes, expected divergence in behaviour of, 56, 57, 58, 237, 245, 293, 299, 303, 306,

—, interdependence of, 7, 57, 58, 59, 303, 306

—, segregation of, 19, 31, 32, 40, 47, 56, 57, 58, 199, 211, 212–13, 214, 237, 256, 269, 278, 279, 280, 285, 287, 288, 299, 300, 306

Sexual Behaviour in Western Arnhem Land (Berndt), 6

shade, sacred, of circumcision novices, 45

— —, of Djanggawul, 20, 29, 30, 35, 38, 39, 40, 41, 42, 43, 45, 46, 47, 48, 94, 97, 98, 103, 106, 109, 111, 112, 113, 117, 118, 120, 121, 122, 123, 125, 126, 127, 128, 129, 131, 132, 136, 139, 142, 143, 145, 149, 150, 151, 152, 158, 162, 163, 164, 165, 166, 167, 168, 169, 170, 175, 176, 178, 179, 180, 181, 183, 184, 185, 188, 189, 190, 191, 195, 196, 197, 198, 201, 202, 203, 206, 208, 209, 210, 212, 214, 216, 217, 218, 219, 222, 225, 226, 228, 230, 231, 232, 233, 234, 236, 237, 241, 242, 243, 244, 247, 250, 252, 253, 254, 255, 256, 257, 259, 261, 262, 265, 267, 268, 269, 273, 275, 277, 283, 290, 298, 299, 300, 302

shaving, ceremonial, 18

shells, mangrove, symbolism of, 150, 158–9, 175–6, 240

social organization of eastern Arnhem Land, xviii, 51

songs, sacred, associated with *nara* rituals: see rituals, Djanggawul, in relation to myth and songs.

— —, introduced by Djanggawul, 29, 39, 44, 60, 61, 62

— —, power of, 40, 62, 243, 293

— —, variations or inconsistencies in, 55, 60, 239, 292, 293, 294–5, 296

sorcery, 35, 56, 272, 295

South Western Journal of Anthropology, xviii

Spencer, Sir Baldwin, xx, 57

'Stealing', of feathered strings, 15

—, of sacred emblems and songs, 15, 17, 19, 20, 38–9, 49, 57, 58, 225, 231–3, 236–7, 240–4, 264, 265, 266, 289, 295, 296, 299, 300, 303

'steaming', ritual, 19

Strehlow, C., xx

—, T., xxi

string, feathered, symbolism of, 3, 4, 5, 10, 18, 22, 42, 43, 48, 50–1, 52, 78, 82, 89, 90, 98, 100, 101, 104, 105, 108, 109, 110, 111, 112, 113, 115, 117, 118, 121, 131, 132, 150, 151, 152, 156, 161, 169,

Index

170, 171, 176, 178, 179, 182, 186, 201,
203, 211, 212, 220, 222, 227, 230, 234,
235, 238, 239, 247, 250, 255, 260, 261,
265, 266, 276, 277, 281, 283, 287, 289,
290, 291, 297, 298, 299, 301, 302, 303, 304
sun, association with Djanggawul, 2–3,
4, 5, 6, 17, 19, 41, 46, 50, 77, 78, 79, 81,
82, 83, 90, 92, 94, 98, 100, 108, 111,
113, 129, 130, 133, 139, 145, 146, 178,
186, 198, 202, 203, 211, 212, 214, 256,
268, 272, 274, 296–7, 300, 303, 304,
305
—, association with blood, 303
— — —, fire, 303
— — —, *lindaritj* parakeet, 3, 4, 5, 17,
26, 27, 45, 46, 50–1, 79, 81, 82, 89, 90,
94, 97, 104, 105, 108, 109, 110, 111,
113, 117, 139, 151, 169, 170, 172, 179,
181, 189, 192, 193, 199, 200, 212, 214,
219, 220, 223, 224, 229, 230, 235, 237,
239, 247, 255, 262, 263, 268, 277, 282,
289, 297, 299, 300, 303
—, rays, symbolism of, 3, 4, 17, 50, 82,
92, 111, 178, 202, 211, 212, 272, 274,
277, 290, 297, 303

Tax, Sol, xxiii
time, Aborigines' concept of, 20, 21, 23,
285, 293
totemism, association of Djanggawul
with, 5, 13, 14, 17, 18, 19, 20, 26, 29,
53–4, 88, 109, 111, 132, 133, 152, 156,
157, 158, 174, 240, 297, 298, 302, 304

umbilical cord, symbolism associated
with, 4, 10, 11, 17, 47, 201, 202, 204,
206, 210, 211, 212, 237, 238, 244, 247,
265, 273, 274, 276, 290, 299, 303, 307
University of Sydney, xix, xxiii

Viking Fund Series in Anthropology, 6

wagu (kinship term), 82, 90, 111, 113, 117,
222, 273–4
walg, use of term, 273–4
Waramiri linguistic group, 42

waridj (kinship term), 2, 64, 65, 67, 68,
69, 70, 71, 72, 73, 74, 75, 76, 77, 78,
79, 80, *et passim*
Warner, W. L., xvii, xviii, xxi, 1, 11, 12,
13, 16, 18, 21, 46, 49, 50
— —, discussion of Djanggawul cult,
12–13, 16, 21, 49–50
Wauwalak cult, in relation to Djanggawul,
xvii 11, 12, 13, 32, 54, 264, 271, 272
— Sisters, xvii, 11, 12, 32, 41, 54, 58, 247
Webb, T. T., xviii, 13
well, sacred, symbolism of, 5, 6, 17, 43,
99, 109, 110, 115, 116, 117, 135, 136,
154, 156, 157, 175, 177, 193, 206, 208,
209, 214, 224, 231, 238, 247, 265, 289,
299, 301, 302, 303, 304, 305
whale, symbolism of, 6, 83, 86, 87, 91,
92, 151, 160, 161, 174–5, 273, 297, 298,
302
women, attitude of, towards Djanggawul
cult, xix, xxii, 16, 59, 243, 293, 296
—, excluded from certain rituals, etc., 16,
30, 34, 39, 40, 57, 58, 242, 243, 293
—, in relation to concept of sacred, 4,
7, 12, 13, 14, 30, 31, 34, 39, 40, 41, 57,
58, 59, 199, 213, 214, 244, 257, 278,
279, 280, 281, 285–6, 287, 288, 289,
293, 294, 299, 300, 306
—, likened to *rangga* emblems, 4, 7, 31,
32, 213
—, original owners of *nara* ritual, emblems and songs, 7, 15, 16, 17, 19, 20,
39, 40, 41, 49, 57, 58, 237, 242, 243,
244, 245, 264, 265, 299, 300, 306
—, rôle of, during *nara* rituals, 16–17, 18,
19, 20, 21, 22, 57, 58, 237, 242–3, 244,
245, 276, 286, 293, 294
wonggar, 1, 5, 20, 27, 34, 35, 53–4, 240
worship, notion of, 3
Wulagi tribe, 48
Wulamba bloc, xix

yam, symbolism of, 98, 100, 101, 109,
115–16, 121, 131, 227, 228, 235, 238,
247, 250, 261, 276, 286, 298

For Product Safety Concerns and Information please contact our EU
representative GPSR@taylorandfrancis.com
Taylor & Francis Verlag GmbH, Kaufingerstraße 24, 80331 München, Germany

www.ingramcontent.com/pod-product-compliance
Lightning Source LLC
Chambersburg PA
CBHW060138280326
41932CB00012B/1561